THE CLINCHFIELD RAILROAD

SEE THE LAST PAGES OF THIS BOOK FOR A COMPLETE LIST OF THE UNIVERSITY OF
NORTH CAROLINA SOCIAL STUDY SERIES

The University of North Carolina Press, Chapel Hill, N. C.; Baker and Taylor Company, New York; Oxford University Press, London; Maruzen-Kabushiki-Kaisha, Tokyo; Edward Evans & Sons, Ltd., Shanghai.

Toe River at Mile-Post 161

THE CLINCHFIELD RAILROAD

*The Story of a Trade Route Across
the Blue Ridge Mountains*

BY

WILLIAM WAY, JR., A.M.

CHAPEL HILL
THE UNIVERSITY OF NORTH CAROLINA PRESS
1931

COPYRIGHT, 1931, BY
THE UNIVERSITY OF NORTH CAROLINA PRESS

TO MY MOTHER
MARIE WAGENER WAY
AND MY FATHER
REV. WILLIAM WAY, D.D.

A FOREWORD

To HAVE acted an humble unpretentious part in this drama of life seems to afford no certain safeguard against the scrutinous eyes of zealous biographers. Microscopic or impressionistic research can readily magnify a minor rôle to many times its true proportions. The biographical industry today reveals a tendency to work itself into a state of overproduction. However, one branch of the industry has been underworked. There have been far too few studies made of the lives of business undertakings. Such biographies should enrich enormously our present all too sterile fund of general economic history and thereby render invaluable assistance to serious students of social problems.

Furthermore, in the matter of usefulness, the history of a business enterprise has distinct advantages over the record of an individual's activities. It is wider in scope, and therefore less susceptible to personal bias. It is not on that account less human and colorful, but more so, because it reproduces the thoughts and actions of many people. It reflects a set of social relationships, and thus avoids the narrow individualism inherent in personal biographies. The life of an important undertaking usually covers a much longer period of time than the life of one man: thus continuity is maintained, and there is afforded a view of the operation of forces that require long periods in which to exert their full influence. An enterprise is created by the conjuncture of many forces, and it continues to be a focal point, in the complex interactions of these and other factors which entirely shape its life. A better understanding of the elements which contribute to the growth of economic organization does much to widen the theorist's critical perspective.

In the field of southern history, especially, there is urgent need for more of the suggested type of work. So much of our historical production has dealt with such traditional subjects as slavery, the Negro, the plantation, the War between the States, and the lives of prominent political leaders—all important factors in southern history, but the further study of which does not seem to promise sufficient explanation of those profound economic changes that have transformed the South in recent years. Regardless of how fondly he may cherish the past and ardently desire to turn men's minds back to the ideals of the fathers, the social theorist must deal with the problems of the present. For his purpose he needs to have a knowledge of those elements in the past which have been most influential in shaping present tendencies. Except in the field of agriculture, comparatively little investigation has been made of the growth of business organization in the South. There is great need for intensive historical research in commerce, industry, and finance.

A better knowledge of the development of commercial organization, in particular, should afford the student a useful approach to those intricate problems of production, exchange, distribution and taxation which grow out of our present economic organization. The character of economic organization is largely conditioned by transportation facilities. Hence the history of a transportation enterprise affords an unusual vantage point from which to view the economic evolution of a region.

The subject of this study is well chosen to reflect the dominant elements which have shaped, in a large measure, the economic history of an important section of the southeastern United States. Commercial ambition, agricultural domination, financial weakness, and industrial aspiration move through the story. It is the history of continuously renewed efforts in a great railroad venture which was designed to create a vast economic empire. The dream was never fully realized. The actual accomplishments were relatively meagre. The proposed railroad artery, which was to be the backbone of a gigantic commercial system, finally attained only the proportions of a short, highly specialized, local line. But this small achievement does not reflect today the strength and importance of all the forces which joined in its evolution. This study brings to us new light on a number of the major factors.

MILTON S. HEATH

Chapel Hill
April 29, 1931

PREFACE

ANY CONTRAPTION on wheels, particularly a train, has always had a fascination for boys. I was no exception. This fascination remained with me through high school and college and has grown upon me to such an extent that today I delight in watching a locomotive haul a string of cars, whether it be a snorting switch engine, a drag of heavy freight, a fast perishable freight train, or a passenger flyer. I now know a little concerning the forces brought to bear in the movement of these trains.

Through the passing years, railroads have been predominant in my mind. Upon entering the University of North Carolina, I selected my studies, in so far as one is able, in an attempt to become enlightened concerning the transportation problems of the country. Most of my elective courses dealt, either directly or indirectly, with transportation. Later, I registered for post-graduate work, and the necessity of writing a thesis loomed in the foreground. Upon what subject should I write? I knew, of course, that it would deal with railroads—it would have been folly to consider anything else. My friend, Dr. C. K. Brown, who at the time was teaching in the University, suggested the Clinchfield Railroad; the suggestion was promptly approved by Professor M. S. Heath, head of the transportation department, and by Dean D. D. Carroll, of the School of Commerce; and the matter was settled. Hence this volume.

I began the compilation of data with interest and enthusiasm, but the further I progressed, the more gigantic the task became. So far as I have been able to find, no comprehensive treatise has ever been written dealing with the history of the Clinchfield Railroad and its predecessors. Months were spent perusing old newspapers, magazines, reports, etc.; many books were read in the hope of finding even mere mention of the Clinchfield or discussion of some matter which referred, even though remotely, to the Clinchfield. Numerous letters were written and frequent trips were made in a determined effort to acquire knowledge of the subject. I am sure there are phases which are not covered in these pages. This I regret.

Two trips were made over the Clinchfield in order to familiarize myself with its properties. Undoubtedly, it represents a magnificent feat in civil engineering in its passage through the heart of the picturesque Blue Ridge mountains. I have attempted to describe portions of it in subsequent pages. While in the general offices of the company at Erwin, Tennessee, I talked with the different officials of the road, all of whom were most gracious and courteous. I spent several days in the territory. Again, I journeyed to Washington, D. C., where I studied numerous records in the libraries of the Bureau of Railway Economics and of the Interstate Commerce Commission. Months were spent in the Charleston Library and the library of the University of North Carolina. Several other trips of relatively minor importance were made.

In due course, the manuscript was submitted to the faculty of the University of North Carolina in partial fulfillment of the requirements for the degree of Master of Arts. Fortunately, it was accepted. Later, it was decided that the manuscript should be published. The present form represents many changes from the original, and an attempt has been made to bring the study up to date.

The entire work has proceeded under the personal direction and with the coöperation of my friend and former teacher, Professor Milton S. Heath, of the School of Commerce, University of North Carolina. Professor Heath has been untiring in his willingness to offer valuable criticisms, and I am also profoundly grateful to him for his Foreword.

During the course of investigation, so many people have rendered aid that specific acknowledgment to all is impossible. The officials of the Clinchfield have been magnanimous in their support, particularly Mr. L. H. Phetteplace, General Manager, and Mr. C. A. Smith, General Freight and Passenger Agent; while valuable information has also been furnished by Messrs. Charles Hewett, Auditor; W. S. Moseley, Mechanical Engineer; C. D. Moss, Trainmaster; E. M. Vogel, Chief Clerk to General Manager; P. C. Alford, of the traffic department; and the late W. C. Hattan, Chief Engineer.

Officials of the Atlantic Coast Line Railroad have likewise been considerate in offering suggestions and criticisms, especially Messrs. J. P. Walker, General Superintendent; O. T. Waring, Superintendent; J. C. Mixon, Chief Clerk to General Superintendent, and John L. Cobbs, Jr., Director of Public Relations,

PREFACE

who, effective February 15, severs his connection with the railroad to become affiliated with the Shell Oil Company. Mr. Mixon has read portions of the manuscript, and made various suggestions and criticisms too frequent to enumerate.

Dr. C. T. Murchison and Dr. J. B. Woosley, of the University of North Carolina faculty, have rendered valuable assistance and have maintained a genial interest in the preparation of the work. Dr. C. K. Brown, Professor of Economics, Davidson College, has offered many suggestions. To these gentlemen I gratefully acknowledge the aid which has been so cheerfully and unselfishly given.

Mr. O. K. Morgan, former office engineer of the Clinchfield, has been keenly interested in the manuscript and has given much first-hand information. Mr. Morgan even went so far as to compile a brief summary of events in the history of the Clinchfield as an aid in the preparation of this work. Frequent references are made thereto throughout the book. Colonel Fred A. Olds, of the North Carolina Historical Society, has likewise been helpful in the preparation of the manuscript, letting me have the use of an article written in 1908 covering his first trip over the completed line of the Clinchfield from Marion to Johnson City.

The arduous task of proof reading has been made easier by the generous coöperation of Messrs. J. E. Marshall and H. W. Jackson, of Savannah. These gentlemen have read every line of the galleys with me, and their aid is gratefully acknowledged. I likewise wish to thank Mrs. Alice T. Paine, of the University of North Carolina Press, for her numerous suggestions and untiring efforts in the preparation of the final form of the manuscript.

WILLIAM WAY, JR.

Savannah, Georgia
January 15, 1931

TABLE OF CONTENTS

Foreword by Professor Milton S. Heath		vii
Preface		ix
Introduction		xvii
I.	Special Problems in Southern Railroad Development	1
II.	The Estillville Convention	4
III.	Early Projects to Connect Charleston with the Ohio	13
IV.	Renewed Efforts to Reach the Ohio	33
V.	The Charleston, Cincinnati & Chicago Railroad	55
VI.	Further Development of the "Three C's"	76
VII.	The Period from 1895 to 1908	89
VIII.	The Carolina, Clinchfield & Ohio Railway	107
IX.	The Carolina, Clinchfield & Ohio Railway (Continued)	133
X.	The Construction of the Clinchfield	149
XI.	Crossing the Blue Ridge Mountains (By Col. Fred A. Olds)	172
XII.	The Clinchfield Lease	188
XIII.	The Clinchfield Railroad Today and Tomorrow	202
Appendix A. General Balance Sheet		221
Appendix B. Operating Statistics		223

CONTENTS

APPENDIX C. DETAILS OF OPERATING EXPENSES (1925-29) 226

APPENDIX D. EQUIPMENT PERFORMANCE 233

APPENDIX E. MISCELLANEOUS STATISTICS 237

APPENDIX F. FREIGHT CAR INTERCHANGE 238

APPENDIX G. METHODS OF OPERATION 253

APPENDIX H. GENERAL OPERATING INSTRUCTIONS...... 260

BIBLIOGRAPHY 279

INDEX 287

LIST OF ILLUSTRATIONS

Toe River at Mile-Post 161	*Frontispiece*
First Passenger Train to Reach Altapass, North Carolina	98
Mr. George L. Carter Driving the Last Spike of the Elkhorn Extension	116
C., C. & O. Locomotives	146
C., C. & O. Locomotives	148
Construction Scene on the South Slope of the Blue Ridge in North Carolina	152
Bridge over Toe River near Poplar, North Carolina	156
Cut near Mile-Post 234 in North Carolina	162
Flood Scene in the "Gorge"	182
Bridge over South Fork of Holston River and Holston Tunnel	218

LIST OF MAPS AND CHARTS

Map of Clinchfield Railroad	xvii
Map of Charleston, Cincinnati & Chicago Railroad	57
Profile of the Carolina, Clinchfield & Ohio	155
Profile of the South Slope of the Blue Ridge	158
Standard C., C. & O. Tunnel Sections	159
Three Sections of the Profile	167
Map of Louisville & Nashville Extension	212

INTRODUCTION

THE CLINCHFIELD Railroad is an amalgamated unit. No less than twenty corporations have contributed to the development of this trans-montane railway system. An analysis of the developments of these various consolidations may be accomplished by tracing the history of the following major components: The Charleston, Cincinnati, & Chicago Railroad; the Ohio River & Charleston Railway; the South & Western Railway; and the Carolina, Clinchfield, & Ohio Railway.

The main line of the Clinchfield extends from Elkhorn City, Kentucky, to Spartanburg, South Carolina, a distance of 277 miles. It traverses the rugged mountain region which divides the Ohio River valley from the southeastern piedmont and the seacoast belt of the Carolinas and Georgia. It is so situated strategically in its relation to the southeastern territory that it is an indispensable fuel line. It is also a short through route to the Ohio River crossings. It cuts through the mountain barrier between Kentucky and Virginia and again penetrates what is commonly called the Blue Ridge Mountains near the Tennessee-North Carolina line, probably the only location for a direct through line between the upper Ohio and the Carolinas. "Not only does it entirely penetrate this otherwise almost impassable country, but it does so with a high standard of construction and easy grades which fit it for the carriage of an immense tonnage."[1] Serving the rich coal fields of eastern Kentucky and western Virginia, the Clinchfield is of dominating importance in its relation to the coal supply of the Carolinas and Georgia.

At Elkhorn City, its northern terminus, the Clinchfield connects with the Big Sandy Division of the Chesapeake & Ohio Railroad, giving it direct connection with Cincinnati and Chicago, over which through trains are operated daily. A through route to the South is made possible by its connections at Spartanburg, either with the Southern Railway or the Charleston & Western Carolina Railroad, to Charleston, Savannah, and Florida points.

---

[1] 63 *I. C. C.*, p. 550.

xviii   INTRODUCTION

Although operated independently, the Clinchfield is under lease to the Atlantic Coast Line and the Louisville & Nashville railroads, jointly. The Charleston & Western Carolina is a subsidiary of the Atlantic Coast Line,[2] and it is probable that in the near future the former road will be entirely absorbed and operated by the latter. The Atlantic Coast Line controls the Louisville & Nashville through the ownership of a majority of the stock of the latter company.[3] Therefore, the completion of a proposed extension of the Louisville & Nashville from its Cumberland Division in eastern Kentucky to a point on the Clinchfield near St. Paul, Virginia, will establish a through system from the Ohio to the South Atlantic territory.

From Elkhorn City, the Clinchfield follows the "breaks" of the Big Sandy River, penetrates the Sandy ridge by a tunnel 7,854 feet in length, and cuts directly through the Cumberland Mountains to St. Paul, Virginia, where connections are made with its branch from Wilder, and with the Norfolk & Western Railway. Passing on southward, it intersects the Interstate Railroad at Miller Yard, Virginia. Crossing its 1,400-foot viaduct over Copper Creek, the Clinchfield connects with the old Virginia & Southwestern Railway, now a branch of the Southern Railway, at Speer's Ferry, Virginia. Immediately after leaving Speer's Ferry, it tunnels 4,135 feet through Clinch Mountain, passes through the thriving city of Kingsport, Tennessee, and reaches Johnson City, Tennessee, the "Metropolis of the Appalachian Summitland." Here it connects with the Memphis-Washington line of the Southern Railway, and with the East Tennessee & Western North Carolina Railroad.

South of Johnson City, the Clinchfield passes through Erwin, Tennessee, the division point of the line, and then follows the trail of Daniel Boone through the famous gorge of the Nolachucky and Toe rivers, which flow through a break in the Great Smoky Mountains. At Kona, North Carolina, connection is made with the Black Mountain Railway for Burnsville, North Carolina. South of Kona, the Clinchfield follows the north fork of the Toe River for a short distance, and then, boring its way through the mountains, comes out on the crest of the Blue Ridge at Altapass, North Carolina. Descending the southern slope of

[2] *Poor's Manual of Railroads*, 1915.
[3] Dozier, *A History of the Atlantic Coast Line Railroad*, p. 147.

the Blue Ridge with a maximum grade of only 1.2 per cent, compensated, it passes through eighteen tunnels, aggregating 16,391 feet in length, within a distance of fourteen miles. Following the North Fork of the Catawba, and later crossing the Catawba River, it meets the Asheville-Salisbury line of the Southern Railway at Marion, North Carolina; and, farther south, the Seaboard Air Line Railway at Bostic, North Carolina. Passing through the cotton fields of the Carolinas, and crossing the Broad and Pacolet rivers, the Clinchfield reaches its southern terminus at Spartanburg, where, in addition to the Southern Railway and the Charleston & Western Carolina Railroad mentioned above, it connects with the Piedmont & Northern Railway.[4]

The Clinchfield passes through a country rich in natural resources. The coal fields of southwest Virginia and southeastern Kentucky comprise an area of several hundred thousand acres. Large deposits of such basic raw materials as feldspar, kaolin, mica, glass sand, and quartz are found along the line. Rapid industrial development has taken place in the communities which this road serves, for example: Kingsport, Tennessee; Johnson City, Tennessee; Spruce Pine, North Carolina; and Spartanburg, South Carolina.

The Clinchfield cuts athwart the Appalachian Mountains and crosses seven important divides between watersheds. It passes through some of the most rugged and picturesque country east of the Mississippi. Its development of moderate curvature and light grades is a notable work among the railroads of America. In its construction were involved the moving of about twenty-five million cubic yards of earth and rock; the boring of fifty-five tunnels; and the building of bridges and viaducts of an aggregate length of almost five miles. Its construction is of the most permanent type and is outstanding for the great size of cuts and fills and the large quantities of grading. One-hundred-pound rail and limestone ballast are used along the entire line. The few bridges of wooden construction are being replaced by steel or concrete structures at the present time.[5]

---

[4] From blueprints furnished by the chief engineer, Clinchfield Railroad Company, Erwin, Tennessee, November, 1928.

[5] Data furnished by the chief engineer, Clinchfield Railroad Company, Erwin, Tennessee, November, 1928.

INTRODUCTION

The Clinchfield is the last of numerous attempts to cross the mountains and connect the Ohio with the South Atlantic. Numerous routes were surveyed and several companies were chartered to construct and operate the proposed roads. All of the projects were intended to serve practically the same territory, although different routes were decided upon to penetrate the mountains; but, in the main, they would have passed through the same sections of the country. In order to make clear the topographical conditions, as well as the historical significance of the earlier projects preceding the Clinchfield, the country traversed by the trans-montane roads will be described and a brief statement made concerning the important cities of the South during the ante-bellum period.

Charleston, South Carolina, gave the main impetus to all of the early projects. A history of the earlier roads shows the great interest manifested by that city in reaching the Northwest. From about 1830 to the beginning of the Civil War, Charleston seems to have been over-zealous on the projection of railroads. Vast sums of money were expended on any road which might prove beneficial to the declining trade of that city. In order, therefore, to make more clear the attitude of Charleston and its citizens toward the development of railroads, a brief summary of the more important projects to reach the Ohio River is given. The discussion is solely an attempt to familiarize the reader with the transportation conditions prevailing between the Southeastern coastal region and the territory beyond the mountains prior to the Civil War. From a physical standpoint, these projects were only remotely connected with the Clinchfield.

THE CLINCHFIELD RAILROAD

CHAPTER I

SPECIAL PROBLEMS IN SOUTHERN RAILROAD DEVELOPMENT

NATURE OF THE COUNTRY

DURING THE first half of the nineteenth century, and the period immediately preceding the Civil War, the South comprised seven well defined economic provinces. These provinces, as classified by Professor Ulrich B. Phillips, of Yale University, are the following:

1. Lowland and Piedmont Virginia.
2. The Charleston-Savannah coast district.
3. The Eastern Cotton Belt, extending from Virginia through Alabama and including the "Piedmont" district of the Carolinas.
4. The Western Cotton Belt, extending from western Alabama into Texas.
5. The fertile agricultural territory of Kentucky and middle Tennessee.
6. The Tennessee and Shenandoah valleys.
7. The Peninsula of Florida.[1]

Pronounced barriers separated these provinces, the most important of which were the belt of pine-barrens and the Blue Ridge and Cumberland mountains. The pine-barrens were a stretch of sandy, unfertile, non-productive, pine-grown country of very sparse population. The only need for transportation facilities was to furnish a means of connecting the sea coast with the inland cotton areas beyond. The most logical plan, and that which was followed by the early railroads, was to construct a single trunk line through the pine-barrens, and then branch out into the cotton producing territory.[2]

The Appalachian Mountains south of the Mason and Dixon line consist of a series of parallel ridges with low, intervening valleys. The eastern slope of the Blue Ridge is extremely steep and much more precipitous than the western. A glance at the

---
[1] *History of Transportation in the Eastern Cotton Belt*, pp. 1-3.
[2] *Ibid.*, p. 3.

2   THE CLINCHFIELD RAILROAD

profile of the Clinchfield on page 167 will well illustrate the point. These mountain walls have isolated the inhabitants of one area from adjoining areas and have prevented communication between the territories on opposite sides. "The mountain wall in the South confined the early inhabitants to the eastern side much more effectively than was the case in the North, where easy passes were to be found. It has had a profound influence in determining the direction of economic development and the channels of commerce in the Southeast. Artificial highways follow the natural passes across mountain ranges, and a lack of such passes results in a correspondingly small volume of trade between the sections on opposite sides of the barriers. On the other hand, where good passes exist, brisk trans-montane trade is certain to spring up. In the North passes are good, and there early developed a prevailing east and west trend of traffic; in North Carolina there are no passes, and many decades of the railroad era passed into history before the transportation system of the state possessed any characteristic which might be called distinctive."[3] What was needed was a direct route across the mountains to connect the grain and livestock areas and the Ohio Valley with the cotton belt and the seacoast.

The lay of the land determined the currents of transportation and commerce; the trade routes followed the lines of least resistance. There were four main classes of trade centers in the South during the ante-bellum period: (1) the seaports, which included Baltimore, Norfolk, Wilmington, Charleston, Savannah, Mobile, and New Orleans; (2) the cities located on the "fall line,"[4] of the larger rivers, where produce and supplies were exchanged, such as Alexandria, Fredericksburg, Richmond, Petersburg, Fayetteville, Columbia, Augusta, Milledgeville, Macon, Columbus, Montgomery, Shreveport, Nashville, and Knoxville; (3) the cities on large rivers, including Natchez, Vicksburg, Memphis, Louisville, and St. Louis; (4) the cities which owe their origin to the development of inland trade routes, mainly Atlanta and Chattanooga, and the cities whose trade was greatly increased thereby, such as Nashville, Knoxville, Louisville, and Cincinnati.[5]

---

[3] Brown, *A State Movement in Railroad Development*, p. 3.
[4] That is, the head of navigation.   [5] Phillips, *op. cit.*, pp. 6-8.

SOCIAL FACTORS

Railroad building was also influenced by social and economic factors, the more important of which were the following: (1) The fact that the population in the South was scattered would make passenger traffic light. (2) There was little interchange of products within each of the economic provinces, and hence there would be relatively no local freight. (3) There was a great demand for the outward movement of staples and the inward movement of supplies. (4) The great rush in the marketing season usually occurred from September to January. (5) Slavery caused a scarcity of labor, and consequently there was very little floating capital. (6) The plantation system dominated the country.[6]

FINANCING

Financing was the major problem. There were four main methods of procuring capital: (1) Some individuals were willing to invest their fortunes, or at least parts of them. (2) The states aided through the granting of liberal charters and subscriptions to stock. (3) Northern capitalists would purchase state bonds or subscribe to the stock. (4) The cities were keenly interested. "In the actual progress of road, canal, and railway building, these several resources were utilized in varying combinations."[7]

State construction and operation have not proved to be a great success, a condition which apparently was caused by the entrance of politics and the appointment of officials for political reasons. The Western & Atlantic Railroad is an excellent example. Built and for a time operated by the State of Georgia, corruption set in, which almost completely ruined the enterprise. Since 1870 it has been operated under lease by the Nashville, Chattanooga & St. Louis Railroad.[8] Another illustration is the North Carolina Railroad, now operated by the Southern Railway, and also the old Cape Fear & Yadkin Valley Railroad, now divided into two parts and operated by the Southern and the Atlantic Coast Line, respectively.

---

[6] *Ibid.*, p. 8.   [7] *Ibid.*, pp. 14–15.   [8] *Ibid.*, p. 333.

CHAPTER II

THE ESTILLVILLE CONVENTION

ONE OF the earliest movements to establish a trade route from the Ohio, across the mountains, to the South Atlantic territory was a convention held in Estillville, Virginia, September 10-13, 1831.[1] Very little information is available concerning this convention, and hence this discussion is unfortunately not as comprehensive as may be desired. Estillville was situated in southwestern Virginia, at a point believed to be the present site of Gate City.

The purpose of this convention was to determine a route for and to construct a wagon road to connect the "Ohio River, the great valley of the Tennessee River, and the Southern states."[2] The convention was attended by representatives from North Carolina, Tennessee, Virginia, and Kentucky.[3] It has been said that a delegation was also sent from Charleston, South Carolina, but it was lost in the mountains, and never reached its destination. The idea of the road was that it should "serve as a thoroughfare from North to South across the Alleghany Mountains, and affording the means of intercommunication between the fertile regions of the North and the commercial depots of the South."[4]

This movement is particularly interesting in connection with this study, because the proposed road would have followed, to a certain extent, the present route of the Clinchfield Railroad, and at least the same territory would have been traversed. It also shows the early desires of the people to connect the Ohio with the Atlantic, and at the same time provide an outlet for the mountain country.

---

[1] *Report of Col. Long to the Estillville Convention,* Sept. 10, 1831.

[2] *An Address Respecting the Charleston & Hamburg Rail-road and on the Rail-road System as Regards a Large Portion of the Southern and Western States of the North American Union, by Elias Horry, President of the South Carolina Canal and Railroad Company, Delivered in Charleston at the Medical College of the State of South Carolina on Wednesday, the 2nd of October, 1833, upon the Completion of the Road,* Charleston, 1833, p. 14. Hereafter referred to as *Elias Horry's Address.*

[3] *Report of Col. Long,* p. 8.   [4] *Ibid.,* p. 9.

THE ESTILLVILLE CONVENTION

As proposed, the road was to be constructed with a maximum grade of 7 per cent, except in a few instances where considerable savings in distance and cost would be obtained. The right of way was to be fifty-four feet wide, within which was included the twenty-one feet of surfaced roadway, four and a half feet for drains on each side, and a clearance of twelve feet on each side for fences, trees, etc.[5] The road was to begin at Pikeville, Kentucky. This town was situated on the navigable waters of the Big Sandy River, a tributary of the Ohio.[6] From Pikeville, it was to extend to a point near the southern base of Linville Mountain in North Carolina.[7] According to Horry, however, it was to run as far south as Camden or Columbia, South Carolina,[8] but this appears to have been an exaggeration.

In July, interested parties had requested the War Department to furnish army engineers to survey the route, and on July 16, 1831, Colonel Stephen H. Long was detailed by the United States Topographical Bureau to superintend the work.[9] In his report to the convention in September, Colonel Long said:[10]

Eligible routes for roads, leading through this country, can only be obtained in situations remote from the principal streams. The valley of the Big Sandy is rendered completely unfit for this purpose, by reason of the excessive freshets to which that stream is annually subjected, and the consequent liability of the bottoms to be inundated on such occasions. The increase of distance occasioned by the meandering of the streams may also be added as an objection. The river hills are too abrupt and precipitous in most places, and too much indented by deep ravines and other sinuosities, to admit the convenient passage of a road above the reach of high water. A far less expensive, and more direct route, than that afforded by pursuing the valley of this stream, may be found commencing at Portsmouth, on the Ohio, and pursuing the following localities, viz.: ascending in the valley of Tygart's creek, and proceeding thence to the valley of Little Sandy, or ascending the valleys of the Ohio and Little Sandy, to a point suitable for a divergence from the valley last mentioned, towards that of Big Sandy—thence crossing Blane's and Tom's creeks, and descending in the best direction for Paint creek—thence crossing Abbot's hill, and following the valley

---

[5] *Ibid.*, p. 10.
[7] *Report of Col. Long*, p. 9.
[9] *Report of Col. Long*, p. 9.
[6] *Elias Horry's Address*, p. 15.
[8] *Elias Horry's Address*, p. 15.
[10] *Ibid.*, pp. 14-16.

of Big Sandy to the mouth of Mud creek—thence ascending the creek last mentioned, crossing a ridge at its head, and proceeding down a branch to Robinson's creek, and thence by a route hereafter to be described, to the Sounding gap of Cumberland mountains, &c. Instead of passing by the mouth of Mud creek, it may be advisable to cross from Paint to Beaver, and thence to Mud creek, and by the route before mentioned. The distance from Portsmouth to the Sounding gap, by either of these routes, will not probably exceed 120, or 125 miles.

The timber growth of this region, adapted to the purposes of building, consists of white oak, poplar, chestnut, walnut, white ash, hemlock, pitch pine, and some white pine, together with various other trees of inferior quality. The three varieties last mentioned are found only in particular localities, except the pitch pine, which is found on most of the mountains. The other varieties are to be met with, in almost every part of the country.

With respect to the natural passes, leading across these mountain ranges, very few that are eligible, as sites for the contemplated road are to be met with, and none are to be found having a general coincidence with a straight line joining the points assumed as extremities of the road. The most prominent ridge of each range, however, affords a pass, or depression, far more favorable than any others presented by the same ridge. The passes and ridges alluded to, are as follows, viz.: A depression in Cumberland mountain, called Sounding gap, at which the road must ascend to the height of 600 feet, above the immediate base of the mountain; Two water gaps, leading past this mountain, viz.: one made by the Russell, and the other by the Pound, forks of Sandy river, and presented at the distance of 14 to 20 miles North Eastwardly of Sounding gap; both of which are represented as utterly impracticable, on account of the ruggedness of the country, at their sources, and the frequency and abruptness of the cliffs, by which the chasms through which they flow are walled in their passage through the mountains. No other depression, so far as we could judge from observation and inquiry, can be regarded as coming into competition with the Sounding gap. A road crossing at this point, however, must unavoidably be located on a mountain slope, very steep in many places, and on the North side, for a distance of about half a mile, having a slope or inclination of five degrees.

The only pass, afforded by Clinch mountain of the middle range, is a very remarkable water gap, called Big Moccasin gap, at which the passage is almost a dead level, at a depression quite as low, as the water table of the vicinity. The residue of this mountain is a continued series of nobs with slight depressions between them, none of which are readily accessible for a road, within a distance of about 30 miles from this gap.

The passage of the Blue-Ridge, may be regarded as presenting the greatest difficulty to be encountered by a road crossing the South range of mountains. Three passes across this mountain have been examined, viz.: one leading through a depression called M'Kinney's gap, another through Turkey Cove gap, and a third through Buck Creek gap; the last of which is deemed utterly impracticable, by any ordinary means, for a road at an inclination less than five, and for the distance of half a mile, less than six degrees. The altitudes of these depressions above the Catawba river, at their lowest points, may be estimated as follows, viz.: height of Buck Creek gap, 2,000 feet; height of Turkey Cove gap, 1,800 feet; height of M'Kinney's gap, 1,600 feet. Their height respectively above the water table on the North side of the mountain, may be estimated at 800 feet for Buck Creek gap, 300 feet for Turkey Cove gap, and 150 feet for M'Kinney's gap.

Other mountain ranges and spurs, too numerous for particular description, at this time, present themselves on the several routes that have been examined, opposing obstacles in the way of a road more or less difficult to be surmounted, the nature and extent of which may be inferred from the tables hereto annexed. An enumeration of the several gaps and passes across and between them, and the routes leading through them, is rendered unnecessary, inasmuch as the positions of the former and the localities of the latter, as well as the courses &c. will be clearly exhibited on the chart, intended to accompany this paper.[11]

A few remarks with reference to the present road, leading Northwardly and Southwardly, through this section of the country, will suffice under this view of our subject.

With the exception of a road commencing at Kingsport on Holston river, and leading in a Southwesterly direction, through Jonesborough, and across the Walnut mountain, to Asheville, North Carolina; and another, in a Northwesterly direction, from Morganton, North Carolina, through M'Kinney's gap of the Blue-Ridge, Elizabethton and Blountville, to Estillville, Virginia, and thence in a Westerly direction towards Cumberland gap; there are no roads leading in a direction in any degree co-incident with that of the contemplated road, that can be regarded as passable for loaded carriages, wagons or carts, except for short distances merely, and utterly impracticable for such carriages across the mountain ridges.

---

[11] This chart is not available.

8 THE CLINCHFIELD RAILROAD

Indeed, most of the ridges intended to be traversed by this road, seem hitherto, to have been regarded as altogether impassable for a road likely to subserve the purpose of an active trade and intercourse between the countries north and south of the Alleghanies. The district through which it is now proposed to open a thoroughfare, although situated near the centre of the United States, and surrounded on all sides by countries abounding in wealth and population, is even less accessible, at the present time for want of tolerable roads, than many districts, situated on our most remote frontiers. A portion of the district situated between the Ohio and Clinch rivers, and embracing an extent, from North to South, of more than 150 miles, is utterly impassable for carriages of burden, or indeed, for vehicles of any kind, upon the roads now travelled, which are of a character in many places, almost to preclude travelling on horseback.

Leaving Pikeville, the route, as located by Colonel Long, would go up the valley of Elkhorn Creek to the base of the Cumberland Mountains, and thence to Sounding Gap. "This route is very favorable for a road, except at a few points where side cutting will be required for short distances."[12]

The road would go downward from Sounding Gap to Pound Fork, up the valley of Indian Creek to Indian Creek Gap, and down the West Fork. It would follow a small stream up to Little Stone Gap, then down Wild Cat Valley to Flat Lick, cross the Clinch River and Copper Creek, and on through Estillville to Big Moccasin Gap. From this point, several routes were surveyed and presented to the convention for its consideration.

First, the line would go via Elizabethton, up the valley of the Doe River and Cranberry Creek, through McKinney's Gap on the summit of the Blue Ridge, and down the valley of Pepper's Creek and the North Fork of the Catawba River to the foot of Linville Mountain, a distance of ninety-three miles.

Secondly, it would cross the Holston River, go down Reedy Creek to the Watauga River, and up a valley to the Doe River, and thence to Linville Mountain as in the first outline, eighty-five and a half miles.

The third route would pass by Pactolus and Jonesboro, "across a tract of fine rolling country," up the valley of the Nolachucky River near the base of Unaka Mountain, through the Gorge to the mouth of Pigeon Roost Creek, up the valleys of

---

[12] *Report of Col. Long*, p. 23.

THE ESTILLVILLE CONVENTION 9

the Toe River and Grassy Creek to Turkey Cove Gap, and thence down the Blue Ridge in the valley of Turkey Cove Creek to the foot of Linville Mountain, eighty-four miles.

The fourth line branched off from the third at Turkey Cove Creek, crossed the Toe River and a spur of Green Mountain to Crabtree Creek, and joined the third route at Grassy Creek, ninety miles.

The fifth was the same as the third to Pactolus, from which point it followed the valleys of Kendrick's Creek and of another small stream to the east end of Buffalo Mountain; thence, it followed Buffalo Creek to its source, crossing a ridge to Unaka Cove, up Indian Creek, through the gap of Iron Mountain, and down Bean's Creek, near Garland, to the base of Linville Mountain, eighty-one miles.[13]

It was estimated that the cost of the entire road would be $801,592.[14] Such a low figure seems almost inconceivable, and particularly so when compared with the enormous sums expended upon the construction of the Clinchfield.

It is interesting to note that the second route suggested by Colonel Long, southward from Moccasin Gap, is in a general way similar to one of the lines proposed by the Western North Carolina Railroad in 1855. Although the North Carolina road would have ascended the south slope of the Blue Ridge by way of Linville River, it was to have followed the Doe River into Tennessee.[15]

According to the original plans of the Estillville project, the road would connect with another road at Linville Mountain leading to Morganton, North Carolina, sixteen miles distant, and there branch out to different sections of the country. A table of distances from the southern terminus at the foot of Linville Mountain, as presented by Colonel Long, is as follows:[16]

TABLE I

Greenville, South Carolina	60 miles
Camden	145 miles
Columbia	149 miles
Charleston	240 miles

---

[13] *Ibid.*, pp. 23-26. [14] *Ibid.*, p. 34.
[15] Brown, *A State Movement in Railroad Development,* p. 101.
[16] *Report of Col. Long,* p. 20.

10 THE CLINCHFIELD RAILROAD

    Augusta, Georgia .... 200 miles
    Savannah .... 280 miles
    Fayetteville, North Carolina .... 185 miles
    Raleigh .... 200 miles
    Wilmington .... 250 miles
    New Bern .... 275 miles
    Washington, D. C. .... 350 miles

No further information is available concerning subsequent developments of the Estillville plan. However, in 1836, the route was considered as a possible line for the Louisville, Cincinnati & Charleston Railroad;[17] but Mr. James G. Holmes, who conducted the survey, reported unfavorably on it. So far as available records show, no further efforts were made to construct a road through this territory until the organization of the Charleston, Cincinnati & Chicago Railroad in 1886.[18] That portion of the report of the South Carolina commissioners concerning the route surveyed by Mr. Holmes is as follows:

    From the Paint rock on the French Broad river, where Col. Gadsden and Mr. Holmes separated, Mr. James G. Holmes pursued the course to Estillville, in Virginia, passing up the valley of Paint creek, and by the Turnpike, across the lofty summit of Paint mountain, thence down in the valley of the Nolachucky, across that stream to Greenville, in Tennessee, and thence by the most direct route, and the valley of Horse creek to Kingsport (the Boat Yard), on the north side of the South fork of the Holston, one mile above its confluence with the North fork. Estillville is known as the place where a convention of citizens from Kentucky, Virginia, Tennessee, North Carolina and South Carolina, was held in 1831, for the purpose of establishing a turnpike road from the navigable waters of the Big Sandy river in Kentucky, to the end of the Linville mountain, in North Carolina. This being the most direct route for connecting the eastern part of Kentucky and Tennessee, and the western part of Virginia and North Carolina with the Atlantic, a line on the map direct from Charleston to Cincinnati, will pass at or near Estillville, in the general direction of this route; many intelligent citizens of the several interested States became well informed of the true character of the country, and a survey was made by Col. Long, of the United States Topographical Engineers, under the orders of the government. The report of which, to the Estillville convention,

---

[17] See Chapter III below.   [18] See Chapter V below.

THE ESTILLVILLE CONVENTION 11

has been kindly furnished and is herewith presented. Availing himself of the information readily furnished from these sources, confirmed from personal observations in part, as far as the limit of time would permit, Mr. Holmes presents the following views of this route:

From Portsmouth, on the Ohio River, to the foot of the Cumberland Mountains near Sounding Gap, is regarded by Col. Long as an ascending plane 100 miles long, presenting an irregular broken surface, intersected by rivers and streams flowing from hills and knobs varying in elevation from 100 to 200 feet, near the river, to 800 feet near the foot of the mountains, and presenting obstacles to the construction even of a turnpike road, deemed quite as numerous and as difficult as those presented by the Alleghany Mountains. In this direction are encountered the obstacles presented by the Big Sandy, the Licking and Kentucky rivers, with their various tributaries. In general characteristics these streams resemble each other. The valley of the Big Sandy and its principal fork, vary in width from 3/4 of a mile to 300 or 400 yards, subjected to annual freshets, varying in places from 50 to 60 feet, above extreme low water, and walled in by high precipitous banks, deeply indented with ravines and water courses, thus presenting innumerable obstacles to the construction of a turnpike road, the only practicable route for which, must be sought at a distance from the water courses, and then can only be obtained by inclined planes of great elevation, varying from 2 to 5 degrees, or from 184.2 to 460.5 feet per mile. From the foot of Cumberland Mountain to the summit of Sounding Gap, which is decidedly the best gap in this direction, is an elevation of 600 feet to be surmounted only by steep mountain slopes of great angle, in one place at least 5 degrees. The water gaps, formed by the head waters of the Russel and Pound forks of Sandy River, lying 15 or 20 miles northeast of Sounding gap, are deemed impracticable from their rugged, steep and winding character. The rest of the route will be best appreciated by a knowledge of the general character of the country. The Alleghany Mountains are here divided into 3 general ranges. The north comprehending the Cumberland, Powell's and Guest's mountains, with their numerous spurs. The middle, comprehending Clinch Mountain and several ridges, such as Copper, Moccasin, Chestnut, Baffal's, are situated between the principal branches of the Tennessee, and the southern range comprehending the Blue Ridge or main Alleghany, dividing the Atlantic from western waters. The Iron Mountains, of which the Yellow Unaka, Green, Roan, Stone, Buffalo, are constituent parts or spurs, is a distinct ridge. The Black, Linnville, Grand Father Table,

THE CLINCHFIELD RAILROAD

and most of the other noted mountains are only spurs of the Blue Ridge. The South mountain separated by an extensive tract of rolling country, is of moderate height. The subordinate spurs or ridges connected with these mountains lie in all directions. The elevation of these mountains and ridges above the principal stream in their immediate vicinity, may be estimated at 600 to 3,000 feet, and at 1,600 to 4,000 feet above tide-water. The natural passes of these mountains have no general coincidence with a straight line, joining the assumed extreme points. The most favorable are Sounding Gap, in the Cumberland Mountains, already spoken of. Big Moccasin Gap, in the Clinch Mountains, at which the passage is almost a dead level, quite as low as the Water Table of the vicinity. The Blue Ridge is regarded as presenting on this route the greatest difficulty. Three passes were examined by Col. Long, McKinney's Gap, Turkey Cove Gap, and Birch Creek Gap. The last impracticable at an inclination of less than 5 degrees and for half a mile 6 degrees or 552.6 feet per mile. Buck Head Gap is 2,000 above Catawba River. Turkey Cove Gap is 1,800 feet, and McKinney's Gap 1,600 feet above the Water Table, on the north side their heights are estimated at 800 feet for Buck Creek Gap, 300 feet for Turkey Cove Gap, and 130 for McKinney's Gap. Other mountain ranges and spurs in this route present numerous obstacles in the way of a road. No one acquainted with these obstacles can conceive a more difficult route, and all the testimony, as well as the opinion we have from those best informed concur in so regarding it. The most intelligent citizens of Virginia, Tennessee and North Carolina with whom Mr. Holmes conversed, expressed a decided preference for a route by the French Broad river, to a more direct one across these several ranges of mountains. Without, therefore, pursuing the entire route, but judging from the evidence before him, as well as his own observations in part, Mr. Holmes has no doubt that a reconnoissance of the country, and the future surveys of it, should be directed to the waters of the Tennessee below this line.[19]

---

[19] *Report of the South Carolina Commissioners to the Knoxville Convention on the Subject of the Proposed Railroad from Charleston to Cincinnati and Louisville,* Knoxville, July 5, 1836.

CHAPTER III

EARLY PROJECTS TO CONNECT CHARLESTON WITH THE OHIO

THE IDEA of establishing a trade route across the Blue Ridge Mountains was an early one. As early as 1800, a private turnpike was opened to traffic between eastern Tennessee and Spartanburg, South Carolina. This route followed the valley of the French Broad River through North Carolina to what is now the city of Asheville, and thence across the summit of the Blue Ridge through Saluda Gap. The road, extending to Columbia and Charleston, became commonly known as the "State road."[1] The highway bears the same name today.

The great South Carolina statesman, John C. Calhoun, foresaw the need of adequate transportation facilities throughout the country. He believed that a system of roads and canals would make the wealth of the country more uniform, and would hold the people together in closer bonds of union. In December, 1816, he introduced a bill in the United States Congress whereby the government profits in the national bank would be set aside for such a purpose. The bill passed the House and Senate, but was vetoed by President Madison on the grounds that it was unconstitutional.[2]

Charleston, at that time, was a thriving metropolis of the South Atlantic, and the fifth largest city in the United States.[3] Its coastwise and foreign trade consisted chiefly of cotton and rice for export, while grain, flour, and provisions were imported.[4] It also engaged in a brisk slave trade, and from 1804 to 1807, two hundred and two cargoes of negro slaves disembarked at Charleston.[5] It was the center of social activities of the South, to which people came from all parts of the country.[6]

Following the panic of 1819, the commerce of Charleston began rapidly to decline, and decadence set in. Its people believed

---
[1] *Elias Horry's Address*, p. 14.   [2] Hunt, *John C. Calhoun*, p. 30.
[3] Jennings, *History of Economic Progress in the United States*, p. 115.
[4] *Ibid.*, p. 342.
[5] Bogart, *Economic History of the United States*, p. 134.
[6] Beard, *The Rise of American Civilization*, I, 142.

that railroads were their only salvation to revive the diminishing commerce; that railroads would tend to restore the depreciated value of property. Northern and eastern cities were flourishing while real estate in Charleston had declined to half its former value, and industry, apparently, had little or no encouragement. Everything considered, it seemed that railroads would be "eminently beneficial to the State."[7]

Any such project would necessarily have to cross the entire state. There are seven well defined physical divisions within South Carolina, through which any road would have to pass. These regions, named in the order in which they occur from the seacoast westward, are described in a pamphlet entitled *South Carolina*, issued by the United States Railroad Administration, from which the following is quoted, with slight variations and omissions: (1) The Coast Region, a narrow border fringing the coast and extending inward about ten miles. It includes the sea islands and the extensive salt marshes. In the early days, rice was grown on an immense scale along the coast. (2) The Lower Pine Belt, or Savannah Region, lying inland and parallel with the Coast Region. This region has an average width of about fifty miles, and an average elevation of about 150 feet. It includes the tidal estuaries of rivers and considerable country lying above tidal influences. In this region there are extensive swamps and undrained lowlands. (3) The Upper Pine Belt lies still further inland. Here there is an elevation from 125 to 250 feet. Its surface is comparatively level, but gently rolling, and comprises some of the most productive land in the state. (4) The Red Hill Region is irregular in outline and consists of a series of hills on the northeastern border of the Upper Pine Belt and among the sand hills. (5) The Sand Hill area, stretching across the state from the Savannah River, opposite Augusta, Georgia, to the North Carolina state line near Hamlet. This area is intersected by a number of rivers, the valleys of which are very fertile. The sand hills themselves are not naturally rich. They have a sandy soil, upon which there was an original growth of pine and scrub oaks. (6) The Piedmont Region includes the whole of ten and parts of eight other western counties and is the largest region in the state. The elevation ranges from 350 to 1,000

---

[7] *Elias Horry's Address*, p. 3.

CHARLESTON'S EARLY PROJECTS 15

feet. In the ante-bellum period, this was the great inland cotton producing area. (7) The Alpine Region of South Carolina gives way to the Blue Ridge Mountains of western North Carolina, penetration of which by railroads is difficult and expensive. The western slope of the Blue Ridge tapers off into the fertile valleys of the Tennessee River, but beyond this is another mountain barrier formed by the Cumberland Range. Any line, therefore, must pass through not only a relatively desolate territory, but also an extremely rugged country which naturally appeared to resist all attempts of conquest by civil engineers.

In an attempt to get back the former trade of Charleston, the Charleston & Hamburg Railroad was organized. In 1821 Robert Y. Hayne, a man of national prominence, had suggested the idea of a steam railroad as a means of solving the transportation problem of South Carolina. He suggested the building of a road from Charleston to Augusta, Georgia, with a branch to Columbia.[8] The South Carolina legislature passed an act authorizing the formation of the company on December 10, 1827,[9] and on January 30, 1828, the South Carolina Canal & Railroad Company was chartered to build a line from Charleston to Hamburg, with branches to Columbia and Camden.[10] Hamburg is situated on the South Carolina bank of the Savannah River directly opposite Augusta. The primary motive for the construction of the road was to take away the trade of the Savannah River between Augusta and the city of Savannah. The State of South Carolina subscribed $250,000, without interest, to the project.[11] Stock subscription books were opened to the public in Charleston, Columbia, Camden, and Hamburg; but the people of Charleston were the only ones to subscribe. However, the Charleston subscription of 3,501 shares was sufficient to form the company.[12]

The road, opened to traffic in 1833, covered a distance of 126 miles—the longest steam railroad in the world—at a cost of $5,625.92 a mile.[13] This road, including the "branches" which were later constructed to Columbia and Camden, respectively,

[8] Jervey, *Robert Y. Hayne and His Times*, p. 383.
[9] *Elias Horry's Address*, p. 6.
[10] *Niles' Register*, Vol. XXXVIII (March 27, 1830).
[11] *Ibid.*, Vol. XXXVII (Jan. 2, 1830).   [12] *Elias Horry's Address*, p. 8.
[13] Phillips, *History of Transportation in the Eastern Cotton Belt*, p. 153.

16 THE CLINCHFIELD RAILROAD

is now operated by the Southern Railway. It seems that the original idea was to extend the road in later years to the West.[14]

An interesting incident concerning the road was published in the *American Railroad Journal* of December 13, 1834, as reprinted from the *Charleston Courier*, which is as follows: "A most unprecedented and pleasing circumstance was witnessed on Sunday last at the Railroad Depository, being the arrival of three locomotives at one time, having at their train sixty freight cars laden with 986 bales of cotton."[15]

The Columbia branch was begun in 1835. It was to leave the main line at Branchville and pass through the towns of Orangeburg and Kingville, a distance of sixty-eight miles. The Camden branch was to extend from Kingville, a distance of thirty-seven miles. They were completed in 1842 and 1848, respectively.[16]

Before the completion of the Charleston & Hamburg road, the people of Charleston began planning and promoting a great railway to the far distant Northwest, and here the great agitation for railroads on the part of Charleston began in earnest. Delegates were sent to railroad conventions all over the South, and large appropriations and enormous sums of money were recklessly subscribed to many projects. The people wanted the lines immediately established to Camden and Columbia, and they eventually hoped to cross the mountains to the Ohio. Meanwhile, the Georgia Railroad had begun construction of its line from Augusta to Athens, with the ultimate intention of reaching Tennessee and Kentucky, and connecting with the road from Paris, Kentucky, to Cincinnati.[17] James A. Meriwether, of Eatonton, Georgia, in a letter to Elias Horry, president of the Charleston & Hamburg road, dated June 8, 1831, inquired as to the possibility of influencing the people of Charleston to subscribe to a railroad to the West. This line was to begin at Augusta, extend through the entire state of Georgia, and pass near Muscle Shoals, to Florence on the Tennessee River.[18]

---

[14] *Proceedings of the Citizens of Charleston Embracing the Report of the Committee, and the Address and Resolutions Adopted at a General Meeting in reference to the Proposed Rail-road from Cincinnati to Charleston,* 1835, p. 7.

[15] Quoted by Phillips, *op. cit.*, p. 161.

[16] *Ibid.*, p. 174.

[17] *Ibid.*, p. 170.

[18] *Elias Horry's Address*, p. 30.

CHARLESTON'S EARLY PROJECTS 17

The earliest idea of the establishment of a railroad from the Ohio to the South Atlantic came in 1827. E. S. Thomas, a resident of Cincinnati and a native of Charleston, suggested the idea of a railroad to connect those two cities, but no definite action was taken at the time.[19] From available information, this appears to be the first suggestion.

On September 3 and 4, 1832, a convention was held in Asheville, North Carolina, the ultimate aim of which was "to connect the navigable waters of the West with the Atlantic." Mitchell King, of Charleston, was elected chairman. The proposed route was to begin at Knoxville, follow the French Broad River through the Paint Rock cut to Asheville, and thence to Columbia, where it would connect with the South Carolina Railroad. The president of the United States was requested to detail army engineers to survey the route.[20] A bill was forthwith introduced in the United States Senate by Senator Arnold in regard to the "expediency of making an appropriation" for surveying a route to connect the navigable waters of the French Broad with the South Carolina Railroad, by way of Hickory Nut Gap in the northwest corner of Rutherford County, North Carolina.[21]

The South Carolina legislature immediately voted $1,000 as a part of the necessary $3,000 to cover the costs, upon the condition that North Carolina and Tennessee would do likewise. These states, believing that this was a scheme to attract trade to Charleston and that no advantage would be realized elsewhere, were somewhat suspicious of the entire proposition. Hence, the project failed;[22] but with it the dreams of Charleston to be directly connected with the Ohio most assuredly did not die, although they may possibly have suffered a relapse for a few weeks.

The very next year, a big celebration was held in Charleston to commemorate the completion of the road to Augusta. For that period, it was indeed a "noble undertaking."[23] At this celebration of 1833, Elias Horry, president of the road, delivered

---

[19] *Address of Colonel A. Blanding to the Citizens of Charleston on the Louisville, Cincinnati, and Charleston Rail-Road*, 1836, p. 10. Hereafter referred to as *Blanding's Address*.

[20] *Elias Horry's Address*, p. 20.

[21] *Niles' Register*, Vol. XLII (March 10, 1832).

[22] Phillips, *op. cit.*, p. 171.

[23] *Niles' Register*, Vol. XLII (August 18, 1832).

a fiery address, urging an extension of a railroad from his line to the Northwest. The city of Charleston, of course, was to be the main beneficiary of such a system, and loud was he in his praise of the city. "No other city between New York and New Orleans is better situated for commerce than Charleston, and particularly since the establishment of our road to Hamburg. . . . As a city, none other in the United States, or elsewhere, surpasses Charleston for health. Her inhabitants . . . have become habituated to her air or climate, enjoy uniform health, and many have lived to great ages. Strangers, and those of them who are men in business, visit and remain in Charleston, without risk, three-fourths of the year, and in cases of emergency, Sullivan's island is an immediate resource." Its advantages as a seaport are most pronounced, for its safe spacious harbor, with excellent shipping facilities, makes it the equal of any along the Atlantic coast. The very absence of ice during the winter gives it an advantageous position over the northern ports ![24]

With such resources, Horry believed, Charleston was the most logical eastern terminus of any trans-montane project. The Charlestonians, of course, had always believed this; but Horry's address stimulated them to even greater zeal. He said that a railroad must be built across the mountains, and "the West looks toward us with anxiety."[25] He even went so far as to suggest the best locations for a route. One, approaching Charleston, was up the French Broad River to the Chatigua, thence along the South Carolina side of the Tugaloo and Saw rivers to Vienna, and on to Edgefield, at which point it would connect with the Hamburg road. Another, which appears to be a more practical route, passed through Saluda Gap to Greenville, South Carolina, and thence through Laurens, Newberry, and Columbia, to his road at Branchville.[26] The former suggestion would have been much more advantageous to the Charleston & Hamburg road, as it would have afforded a considerably longer haul than the latter. Whether or not Horry had this in mind is, of course, problematical.

Although undeveloped for many years, today a railroad follows the route south of Greenville. The Charleston & Western

---

[24] *Elias Horry's Address*, p. 18.   [25] *Ibid.*, p. 20.   [26] *Ibid.*, p. 30.

CHARLESTON'S EARLY PROJECTS

Carolina operates a branch from that city to Laurens, where direct connections are maintained with the Columbia, Newberry & Laurens Railroad to Columbia. Both of these roads are controlled by the Atlantic Coast Line, joint lessors of the Clinchfield, and the Atlantic Coast Line operates its own line from Columbia to Charleston. South of Columbia, the Southern Railway operates the line through Branchville to Charleston.

Horry's address stimulated interest, and in 1835, a meeting of the citizens was held in regard to the proposed road to Cincinnati. The Hon. Edward W. North, addressing the assembled citizens, stated that "South Carolina will not be found wanting, but on the contrary will be prepared to do her part in the prosecution of so noble an enterprise." South Carolina, and particularly Charleston, not only did her part, but even to the extent that millions of dollars were sunk in the enterprise. Charlestonians continued to contribute, even after subscriptions from other sources had ceased, in the vain hope of reaching the Ohio. "As the oldest member of the original thirteen, South Carolina should set an example to the other states by leading the way in this national enterprise," continued North.[27]

At this time, from Virginia to Texas there were no direct means of communication with the valley of the Ohio, "not even by a good post-road."[28] It was argued that these two regions should be connected, and a railroad terminating "at Charleston will furnish the very latest means of effecting this most desirable object."[29] A road to Cincinnati would "lay open to our citizens the entire trade of the great West, and furnish to the inhabitants of those vast regions, the rich productions of the South."[30]

North, like the great majority of his contemporaries, was too optimistic over the accomplishments such a line would realize. He believed that unbounded wealth and prosperity would certainly come to Charleston, and rapidly lift it out of its decadence into a period of continued prosperity. He thought Charleston would be destined to become "the Commercial Emporium of the South." The road would strengthen the bonds of union

---

[27] *Proceedings of the Citizens of Charleston Embracing the Report of the Committee, and the Address and Resolutions Adopted at a General Meeting in Reference to the Proposed Rail-Road from Cincinnati to Charleston,* 1835, p. 8.
[28] *Ibid.*   [29] *Ibid.*, p. 11.   [30] *Ibid.*, p. 13.

between the two sections, and bind the people together with a greater understanding and sympathy.[31]

The proposed route was the shortest existing one to the Atlantic, which of course meant cheaper rates. The accessibility to the ocean and excellent shipping facilities placed Charleston in a very favorable position. The following table of distances from Cincinnati was submitted before the meeting:[32]

TABLE II

To Charleston, via the proposed road	607 miles
New York, via the Great Lakes	950 miles
Philadelphia, via Pittsburgh	850 miles
Baltimore, via Wheeling	650 miles
Mobile, via the Valley of the Tennessee River	780 miles

The common means of communication from Cincinnati was long and dangerous. In order to reach the Atlantic, one would have to travel down the Ohio and Mississippi rivers, thence across the Gulf of Mexico, and through the treacherous Florida Keys. This route was naturally expensive, and the hazard great. "A safe and direct commerce is anxiously desired."[33]

Enthusiasm was high in Charleston, and definite plans were immediately set up to form a company. The legislature of South Carolina passed an act in 1835 chartering the project under the name of the Louisville, Cincinnati & Charleston Railroad Company. The charter was most liberal. Some of its features were that for a period of thirty-six years no other company could build a line parallel to it within a distance of twenty miles; that subscriptions of $5 could be paid upon the stock, of which the par value was $100, and the company might assess every sixty days for the balance if it so desired; that there was no limit to the capitalization; that all properties, both tangible and intangible, would be forever exempt from taxation, unless the rate of dividends should exceed the legal rate of interest; and in 1836, banking privileges were added, resulting in the establishment of the Southwestern Railroad Bank.[34]

The original plan was for the road to extend directly to Cincinnati; but the Kentucky legislature held that this was discrimi-

---

[31] *Ibid.*, p. 15.   [32] *Ibid.*, p. 18.
[33] *Elias Horry's Address*, p. 17.

CHARLESTON'S EARLY PROJECTS

nating against Louisville, and refused to grant the charter. In order to overcome any such possible difficulties, it was decided to build the line to Lexington, Kentucky, and there branch out to Cincinnati, Louisville, and Mayesville.[35]

The road would have passed through a cultivated and fertile country, which was believed to be sufficiently active to support the road of itself. It would share in the trade of the Ohio and compete with the water route to New Orleans, all of which would be to the advantage of Charleston. At Louisville, it would connect with a road projected to Indianapolis and Lafayette, with the ultimate aim of reaching Lake Michigan.[36] "The two great lakes and the extensive regions around them, although 1,000 miles from the Atlantic, will thus be connected with it at Charleston." It was believed a trade would also be developed with Missouri and Illinois.[37]

Another meeting of the citizens of Charleston was held in 1836, at which Colonel A. Blanding made an eloquent speech. He discussed the route of the proposed road and pointed out its advantages. "The Cumberland and Kentucky coal is bituminous, of great purity, and for domestic uses superior to any found in the United States.... It is in every respect equal and generally superior to the English." The coal fields are located in the hills and mountains above the general surface of the country adjacent to them, he continued, and so the coal does not have to be raised from deep pits.[38] Similar conditions exist in the coal area served by the Clinchfield.

Blanding was indeed most optimistic about the industrial development of the territory. Because of the presence of considerable high grade iron ore, which "is not excelled by any in the United States," he believed that there would be great capital investments along the line. He thought manufacturers of railroad equipment would locate there, and, everything considered, there would be an enormous profit to the road.[39] He likewise believed the salt deposits found in the Cumberland Mountains would be exploited to the advantage of the road and of Charleston.

---

[34] Phillips, *op. cit.*, p. 181.
[36] *Ibid.*, p. 6.
[38] *Ibid.*, p. 14.
[35] *Blanding's Address*, p. 2.
[37] *Ibid.*, p. 20.
[39] *Ibid.*, p. 17.

"The striking peculiarity of our road, unlike all those which unite the East and West," he continued, was the fact that it would embrace every variety of climate and production, with the sole exception of sugar, "which blesses our wide extended territory. It is, therefore, capable of sustaining a vast internal trade in agricultural exchanges, and in time of war would be more productive than in time of peace. It would then also possess this additional advantage, that when the Northwest has become an extensively manufacturing country, to which it is fast advancing, our road would be the channel of exclusive supply to the South of these articles, when a hostile fleet might prevent their importation from the North and East."[40]

The road "when opened" would carry from the West such products as beef, pork, flour, tobacco, hemp, bagging, bale-rope, cordage, manufactures of cotton, and wool; and carry from the South, cotton, rice, indigo, and foreign imports, "which are purchased by the proceeds of southern agricultural productions." These commodities would be hauled over a direct line by a single operation, which would eliminate the charges of transfer and the great risks incident thereto. The existing water route by way of the Mississippi consumed several weeks, while the new road would move goods "in the short period of 10 or 15 days."[41] Today, freight is handled between Cincinnati and Charleston by the Clinchfield and its connections in five days.

Blanding called attention to the fact that the South was devoted to agriculture, and so the Northwest would naturally turn to the South to market and exchange its products. In time of need, the South would look to the Northwest, and "she may look with confidence.[42] Our road is wanted. Make it, and you have taken a further bond from fate; you have bound the Northwest still stronger to you, and you may rest assured, that your institutions are secure, your property safe, and that your repose will not be disturbed. The road will pass through South Carolina, cutting our state into two equal parts . . . and will mean the perpetuation of our institutions."[43] Mr. B. Drake, of Cincinnati, in a letter to Colonel Blanding on January 1, 1836, stated that "the great Rail Way, between Cincinnati and

---

[40] *Ibid.*, p. 22.
[42] *Ibid.*, p. 30.
[41] *Ibid.*, p. 23.
[43] *Ibid.*, p. 27.

CHARLESTON'S EARLY PROJECTS

Charleston, is the most magnificent and important public work that has yet been projected in our country."[44]

During this period, South Carolina had become a great cotton producing state. "Everything has given place to this valuable staple," and its citizens were yearly becoming "more dependent upon their neighbors beyond the mountains for the many necessities of life."[45] The people in the upper portions of the state were essentially cotton planters, while rice and sea-island cotton were produced in large quantities along the coast. Staples were brought from the West to Charleston by way of the water route through New Orleans, "a route so long, circuitous, and attended with so many disadvantages, and dangers, that the profit to the producer, and the value to the consumer, are incalculably impaired."[46]

Robert Y. Hayne, of Charleston, was elected president of the road. General Hayne, although a very young man, had attained a high place in the public eye, and his prominence was probably more definitely reached upon his memorable debate with Daniel Webster in the United States Senate. Hayne was prominent in public affairs, and he particularly had at heart the interests and development of his native state. Besides being a member of the United States Senate, he was, at different times, governor of South Carolina, speaker of the House, attorney general, and the first mayor of Charleston.[47]

Soon after the Charleston meeting, the South Carolina legislature appropriated $10,000 for a survey of the country "for the purpose of ascertaining the best practicable route for a Rail-Road" between the Ohio River and that city.[48] The city council of Charleston likewise appropriated $5,000 to aid in the execution of this work. Colonel James Gadsden, Colonel A. H. Brisbane, and Mr. James B. Holmes were appointed as commissioners to conduct the survey.[49]

In making its appropriation, the South Carolina legislature had anticipated similar action by the legislatures of North

---

[44] *Ibid.*, p. 38. [45] *Niles' Weekly Register*, Vol. LI (Sept. 17, 1836).
[46] *Ibid.* [47] Jervey, *op. cit.*
[48] *Report of the South Carolina Commissioners to the Knoxville Convention on the Subject of the Proposed Railroad from Charleston to Cincinnati and Louisville*, Knoxville, July 5, 1836, p. 4. Hereafter referred to as *Report of the South Carolina Commissioners*. [49] *Ibid.*

Carolina, Tennessee, and Kentucky. The South Carolina commissioners were, therefore, instructed to unite their efforts with representatives of the other states. Since those states failed to pass such acts, the South Carolina delegation decided to limit their work solely to surveys across the mountains, in which they were aided by United States army engineers detailed by the secretary of war.[50]

Surveys of the several routes were made, one of which was conducted by James B. Holmes and follows almost identically the present line of the Clinchfield,[51] but was declared "to be inadmissible."[52] Col. Brisbane conducted a survey through the Pickens district of South Carolina, Rabun Gap, and down the Little Tennessee River to Knoxville, but this was likewise held to be unfavorable.[53] This later became the route of the ill-fated Blue Ridge Railroad.[54]

As a result of its investigations, the commission reported that "it cannot be doubted that there is no route within the limits of the existing charter, by which a Rail Road can be carried across the Blue Ridge, that must not pass along the valley of the Frenchbroad river; and the commissioners are under a full conviction that this valley affords, *by far*, the best channel of communication, between the Ohio River and the Atlantic Ocean. This opinion is founded upon some personal observation, extensive inquiries, and explorations and surveys of the general routes which have been suggested."[55] The commissioners were of the opinion that this route would follow a straight line from Charleston to Lexington, Kentucky, where the road would branch out to Cincinnati and Louisville.[56]

Then came the great railroad convention in Knoxville on the fourth of July, 1836, at which there were over four hundred representatives from nine states. Robert Y. Hayne was elected permanent chairman,[57] and again was Charleston in the foreground of a railroad movement.

---

[50] *Ibid.*
[51] See Chapter II above.
[52] *Report of the South Carolina Commissioners*, p. 5.
[53] *Ibid.*
[54] See Chapter IV below.
[55] *Report of the South Carolina Commissioners*, p. 5.
[56] *Niles' Weekly Register*, Vol. LI (Oct. 15, 1836).
[57] Phillips, *op. cit.*, p. 183.

CHARLESTON'S EARLY PROJECTS

The report of the South Carolina commissioners was submitted to the convention,[58] and the proposed route as recommended was agreed upon.[59] The estimated cost of constructing a double track road was as follows:[60]

TABLE III

Charleston to Branchville, a second track, 62 miles @ $4,500	$ 279,000
Branchville to Columbia, 62 miles @ $11,483	711,946
Thence to the junction of the Thicketty and Broad rivers, 65 miles @ $12,000	780,000
Thence to the junction of the Green and Broad rivers, 52 miles @ $14,300	743,600
Thence to Asheville, 40 miles; first 10 miles through Blue Ridge @ $40,000; next 30 @ $12,000	760,000
Thence down the French Broad to the mouth of the Nolachucky, 60 miles @ $30,000	1,800,000
Thence into eastern Tennessee to the junction of the Elk with the Clear Fork, 90 miles @ $30,000	2,700,000
Thence to Cincinnati, 190 miles @ $12,162	2,310,780
Branch to Louisville, at the cost of the road from Charleston to Columbia	990,000
Branch to Maysville, 60 miles @ $12,162	729,720
Total	$11,805,046

Besides the main line to Cincinnati, and the Louisville and Maysville branches, other branches were authorized to connect with the roads into Virginia, North Carolina, and Georgia.[61]

The Georgia delegation objected to this route, because, of course, Charleston and South Carolina would realize the benefits of the resultant trade at the expense of Georgia and Savannah. The Georgians were, therefore, permitted to build a "branch" from Knoxville, but at their own expense. Although they did not further attack the Louisville, Cincinnati & Charleston, they built a line of their own, the Western & Atlantic Railroad, which proved to be a success, while the Louisville, Cincinnati & Charleston failed.

---

[58] *Report of the South Carolina Commissioners*, p. 3.
[59] Phillips, *op. cit.*, p. 183.
[60] *Niles' Weekly Register*, Vol. LI (Oct. 15, 1836).
[61] *Ibid.*

The four million dollars necessary to secure the charter was raised without difficulty. Charleston was praising herself and optimistically looking forward to the trade which was certain to be hers.

It seems to have been the current opinion of this period that railroads could not compete with canal travel in the highlands, because it was believed that locomotives were unable to pull a train of loaded cars up the grades. However, Niles, in attacking this belief, stated that an eight-wheel steam locomotive on the Lehigh, which obtained its power from anthracite coal, pulled fifty-two cars weighing about sixty tons over an average grade of 2.46 per cent for 250 miles. "By this experiment, the doctrine heretofore pretty currently established, that railroads cannot compete with canals for heavy transportation, has been exploded."[62]

Discussing the railroad development throughout the United States, an editorial states that "in South Carolina we behold a company fully organized, just undertaking the most magnificent work of the age—a road of nearly 600 miles in length, reaching from a point on the Charleston and Augusta road to the Ohio River. How visionary was this project deemed, only 18 months since, and yet it will be fully realized in less than seven years. The steps taken by the company indicate an intention of prosecuting the work with the greatest energy. Wherever railroads have been commenced in the South, there have been displayed a zeal and activity truly surprising."[63]

John C. Calhoun had never favored the proposed route via the French Broad River. In fact, it seems that he was not particularly anxious to strike the Ohio at all. In 1835, he favored the extension of the South Carolina Railroad from Augusta to Memphis and the Mississippi Valley, as was originally planned. He claimed that South Carolina should center its interests in the Southwest and the country "far to the west of Cincinnati," instead of the Northwest.[64] He undoubtedly wanted such a route, and he says "if it succeeds, South Carolina will be prosperous beyond all former calculations, and the Union of the States will be as lasting as the rocks and moun-

---

[62] *Ibid.*, Vol. LII (Aug. 19, 1837).
[63] *Niles' National Register*, Vol. LIII (Nov. 25, 1837).
[64] Meigs. *The Life of Calhoun*, p. 359.

CHARLESTON'S EARLY PROJECTS

tains which will be passed and overcome by the contemplated road."[65] However, local jealousies among the various towns along the line prevented such a plan.[66]

Still Calhoun was not satisfied. During the summer of 1836, he heard of a "pass" through the mountains in the northwestern corner of South Carolina. He personally surveyed the territory, and located the gap, which he named Carolina Gap to distinguish it from Rabun Gap, thirty-five to forty miles southwest of it. In commenting on the advantages of this route, he said "it is difficult to imagine a pass through a mountain region finer than this section" along the Tuckasiege River, and it is also "remarkably straight."[67] Extending a straight line from Charleston through the gap, one would strike the Mississippi nearly at the mouth of the Missouri, and cross the Ohio somewhat below the Wabash.

The route as proposed by Calhoun would pass through the Carolina Gap, the pinnacle of the line, which he claimed to be accessible from both sides. Leaving the gap, it would pass through the town of Cashiers, in Jackson County, North Carolina, and down the Tuckasiege River to the head of navigation on the Little Tennessee, a distance of 340 miles from Charleston.[68] Although this route was demonstrated to be impractical the following year,[69] Calhoun charged the South Carolina legislature with discrimination and favoritism toward the French Broad route.[70]

The directors of the road met at Flat Rock, North Carolina, during the fall of 1837 to determine the salaries of officials and to make a change in the engineering department. The salary of the president was fixed at $6,000, but, according to the minutes of the meeting, "General Hayne has generously declined to receive more than $4,000 and his traveling expenses during the ensuing year, in consideration of the moneyed embarrassment of the times." The engineering department was reorganized into four "brigades" under the general supervision of the chief engineer, whose salary was to be $8,000 per year, plus an allowance of $2,000 for traveling expenses.[71]

---

[65] *Charleston Courier*, Nov. 26, 1835.
[66] Meigs, *op. cit.*, p. 360.
[67] *Niles' Weekly Register*, Vol. LI (Oct. 8, 1836).
[68] *Ibid.*
[69] Meigs, *op. cit.*, p. 360.
[70] Jervey, *op. cit.*, p. 405.
[71] *Niles' National Register*, Vol. LIII (Nov. 25, 1837).

Calhoun had been elected a director of the Louisville, Cincinnati & Charleston Railroad in 1837;[72] but he resigned in 1838 because of the difference in opinion as to the route. Upon resigning, he wrote to President Hayne that "to go beyond Columbia, unless with a full understanding that the other states will do their share, will but add to our embarrassment," and that if the road was finished, it would be superseded by the one through Georgia.[73] Calhoun's warning was ignored at the time, much to the distress of supporters of the road two years later.

The South Carolina Railroad agreed to begin the construction of its branch to Columbia as soon as the Louisville, Cincinnati & Charleston had built and put into operation one hundred miles of its road. This branch was to tap the main line between Charleston and Hamburg at Branchville, and extend through Orangeburg and Kingville to Columbia. One author intimates that this could easily have been accomplished if the discussion instituted by Calhoun had not arisen against the proposed route through Saluda Gap and along the French Broad River.[74] The Columbia branch was not completed until 1842.[75]

The Southwestern Railroad Bank was chartered by the South Carolina legislature on December 21, 1836, on the condition that two of the three states through which the road passed would concur in granting the charter.[76] This was accomplished in 1838, and by the end of the following year, it had a capital of $1,500,000, and was reported as yielding a profit of eight per cent.[77] The authorized capital was $12,000,000. The bank had the privilege of issuing notes to an amount up to twice the capital and it could contract debts to three times the capital. It was chartered for a period of thirty-one years, and the central bank was located at Charleston, but with the power of establishing branches.[78]

Both Hayne and Blanding died in 1839,[79] and with their passing, interest in the project began to wane. Hayne had been

---

[72] Meigs, *op. cit.*, p. 359. [73] *Ibid.*, p. 363.
[74] Jervey, *op. cit.*, p. 420.
[75] *Niles' National Register*, Vol. LXII (July 2, 1842).
[76] Phillips, *op. cit.*, p. 189.
[77] *Niles' National Register*, Vol. LVII (July 20, 1839).
[78] Phillips, *op. cit.*, p. 189.
[79] *Niles' National Register*, Vol LVII (Oct. 12, 1839).

CHARLESTON'S EARLY PROJECTS

the guiding spirit of the road from its inception, and his death was indeed a blow to the success of the road. Vardry McBee was elected to succeed Hayne as president.[80]

The panic of 1837 and the so-called "Cotton panic" of 1839 terminated all ideas of crossing the mountains to Tennessee and the Ohio.[81] The one great staple crop of the South was cotton, and upon this single crop the wealth and good fortune of the region depended; yet, all the time the people were plunging deeper and deeper into debt, and, at the same time, they were courageously entering upon internal improvements. South Carolina was no exception. Although the railroad bank escaped disaster, it, like other credit institutions throughout the country, was in an exceedingly strained financial condition.[82]

At a meeting of the directors in September, 1839, the road was found to be in a bad financial condition. Its indebtedness amounted to over two millions of dollars, while, to add to its embarrassment, over a million was due its creditors by the first of the year. Other imperative demands were also very near at hand, and the resources available for all of these purposes were insufficient. The directors dared not call on the stockholders for further advancements, and even if they had done so, it is doubtful whether the people could have raised the money.[83]

Tennessee and North Carolina both wanted to abandon the project, and in 1840, Tennessee definitely withdrew. This seems to bear out Calhoun's warning to Hayne in regard to the necessity of knowing that these states would do their share in the work. In a letter to Andrew Pickens Calhoun, he said, "Thus ends the humbug."[84]

The stockholders in North Carolina and Tennessee demanded the return of their investments, less the survey charges. The South Carolinians, therefore, decided to reorganize the company, and the citizens of the two states were reimbursed for their investments, less $2.50 per share to cover the costs of the surveys. On December 20, 1842, the Louisville, Cincinnati & Charleston was amalgamated with the South Carolina Canal & Railroad Company, and became the South Carolina Railroad

---

[80] Meigs, *op. cit.*, p. 364.   [81] Phillips, *op. cit.*, p. 197.
[82] McGrane, *The Panic of 1837*, pp. 18, 112-15.
[83] Jervey, *op. cit.*, p. 509.
[84] Meigs, *op. cit.*, p. 364.

Company.[85] And thus temporarily ended the idea of building a railroad from Charleston and Columbia to the Ohio.

The physical condition of the main line to Hamburg had been permitted to depreciate to such an extent that something had to be done at once. This, together with the howl from the stockholders for dividends on their investment, resulted, in 1852, in the complete renovation of the entire system. Heavy seventy-pound T-rail was laid, the road bed was improved, the equipment was augmented, the Charleston terminal was enlarged, a bridge was erected across the Savannah River at Augusta, and a physical connection was established with the Georgia Railroad. This was financed by calling for the remaining $25 due on each share.[86]

Hayne and Calhoun were undoubtedly sincere, both in their desires to connect Charleston with the country beyond the mountains, and in their beliefs as to the route the road should follow. Hayne seemed to foresee the inevitable clash between the North and the South on the "Abolition" question, and he believed the only means to prevent it was to draw the country together by "a bond of interest so strong as to stand the tugs of differing views."[87] In 1836, the Indiana legislature adopted a resolution exactly following Hayne's view.[88] Hayne, therefore, wished to bind the South and West together by the indissoluble tie of common business interests.

Calhoun's idea, however, was somewhat different. He wanted to strike through the Southwest, and thereby connect the South—the slave-holding states. He apparently desired to unite the various states of the South with each other. He thought Hayne's plan had been "merely a wild dream," and one author even goes so far as to say that "the complete failure and long abandonment of the Hayne plan certainly seems to justify Calhoun's views, and such has been the accepted opinion since."[89]

Such a statement can hardly be held as entirely justifiable, for within ten years after the failure of the Louisville, Cincinnati & Charleston, considerable attention was again directed toward uniting Charleston with the great Northwest by means

---

[85] Phillips, *op. cit.*, p. 197.
[86] *Ibid.*, p. 215.
[87] Jervey, *op. cit.*, p. 394.
[88] *Charleston Courier*, April 8, 1836.
[89] Meigs, *op. cit.*, p. 365.

CHARLESTON'S EARLY PROJECTS

of a through railroad system. This latter project was to follow still another route. At the beginning of the Civil War, a railroad was projected from Spartanburg through Saluda Gap and down the French Broad River to Morristown and Knoxville.[90] This road has been built, and today it represents an important link of the Southern Railway system. Again in 1887, a road was projected from Charleston to tap the Ohio, and this road, as it exists today, forms the Clinchfield Railroad. However, current opinion around 1840 did follow Calhoun's views, and after the abandonment of the Louisville, Cincinnati & Charleston Railroad, Charleston turned its eyes to the route originally advocated by Calhoun through Georgia.

If Charleston had set upon one definite project, instead of trying to build a network of railroads radiating out of that city, the Louisville, Cincinnati & Charleston would probably have been completed by 1850. Such concentrated action is exemplified by the Baltimore & Ohio Railroad in Maryland. Local interests were too prevalent in South Carolina, while enough money was spent on relatively minor projects to complete the road to Cincinnati.

When the independent roads were completed by way of Asheville, it was too late to create the anticipated traffic. The channels of trade had been pretty definitely fixed by such roads as the New York Central, the Pennsylvania System, and the Baltimore & Ohio. It seems that the southern roads were continually working against each other. If the Louisville, Cincinnati & Charleston had been completed by the early fifties, the new route would undoubtedly have set up new industries, and the channels would have been established. Kentucky and Tennessee would probably have used it as an outlet for their products instead of the Georgia built road—the Western & Atlantic—in connection with the Central of Georgia and the other Georgia roads.

At the outset, Kentucky and Ohio were not particularly interested, for they really wanted a road of their own, the culmination of which desire is the Louisville & Nashville Railroad. Indiana, on the other hand, was very favorable to the project, perhaps because of its isolation from markets.

---

[90] *DeBow's Review*, Vol. XXIX (Oct., 1860).

Possibly the greatest difficulty toward the success of the project was the attitude of the cotton planters. During a year of depression, they became greatly interested but had no money to invest; then, as soon as the crops began to yield a profit, the railroad could take care of itself, so far as they were concerned. Interest, therefore, centered in the cities.

Another probable reason for its failure was the general distrust of corporations on the part of the public.[91] Corporations were created by special acts of the various state legislatures, and it was not until after the Civil War that the practice of incorporation became sufficiently common to justify general laws. Up to 1853, eighty per cent of the corporations which were chartered turned out to be frauds.[92] Quite naturally, it was practically impossible to sell stock away from the immediate locality or the territory served by the road. Stock holding was something new. Besides, it was not known whether railroads would realize a sufficient return on the enormous capital investment to justify an individual in purchasing shares.

At any rate, the Louisville, Cincinnati & Charleston Railroad undoubtedly failed. For the time it killed Charleston's wonderful dream of the great benefits it would derive from the golden trade of the Northwest. As J. D. B. DeBow said, "The noble Hayne died in the service of the enterprise; but it all failed, and the grass continued to grow in the streets of Charleston."[93]

---

[91] Ripley, *Main Street and Wall Street*, p. 21.
[92] *Ibid.*, p. 23.
[93] *DeBow's Review*, Vol. I (Jan., 1846).

CHAPTER IV

RENEWED EFFORTS TO REACH THE OHIO

WHEN THE failure of the Louisville, Cincinnati & Charleston Railroad became apparent, Charleston centered its attention upon the Georgia road as a means of reaching the Ohio. A railroad was projected from Augusta in 1834, the ultimate destination of which was to have been the navigable waters of the Tennessee River. During the early days of construction the idea was sponsored by Athens, Georgia, through which city the road was to pass.[1] The main line of this road, the Georgia Railroad, was completed to Atlanta, and was opened to traffic on October 13, 1843, a distance of 175 miles from Augusta, at a cost of $3,100,000.[2] However, Athens was only connected with the line by a poorly equipped branch.[3]

The Western & Atlantic, the road built by the State of Georgia as a result of its disapproval of the Louisville, Cincinnati & Charleston, was completed and placed in operation from Atlanta on November 19, 1850.[4] This road was originally intended to reach Knoxville and connect with the project of the Louisville, Cincinnati & Charleston to Kentucky and Ohio; but opposition arose in Tennessee, and as a result the road was to terminate at Ross' Landing, or Rossville, a point on the Tennessee River approximately on the state line.[5] However, as actually built, the road reached Dalton, Georgia, according to the original plan, and was later extended to Chattanooga by special permission of the Tennessee legislature. This road is still owned by the State of Georgia but is operated under lease by the Nashville, Chattanooga & St. Louis Railroad.[6]

In 1836, the Hiawassee Railroad was projected from Knoxville to connect with the Western & Atlantic, and was to follow the branch of the Tennessee River bearing that name. The

---
[1] Phillips, *History of Transportation in the Eastern Cotton Belt*, p. 229.
[2] *Hunt's Merchants' Magazine*, Vol. XXVIII (Jan., 1853).
[3] Phillips, *op. cit.*, p. 223.
[4] *Hunt's Merchants' Magazine*, Vol. XXVIII (Jan., 1853).
[5] *Niles' National Register*, Vol. LXIII (Dec. 24, 1842).
[6] See Chap. I above.

project failed, but it was revived as the East Tennessee & Georgia Railroad and was completed to Dalton in 1855. By 1858, connections had been established with Nashville, Memphis, and with points in Virginia. The road realized "unprecedented prosperity, and made a fair profit in spite of competition from any and all quarters."[7] This line, which was later extended to Atlanta, is now a part of the Southern Railway system.

This system of independent roads gave Charleston an outlet to the valley of the Tennessee, but the benefit derived therefrom did not approximate the expectations of that city. The completion of the Central of Georgia from Atlanta placed Savannah in direct communication with Knoxville, and that city received most of the trade which had been anticipated by Charleston.

When the projected systems through Georgia actually began construction and seemed likely to be completed, Editor Niles, in forecasting the abandonment of the Louisville, Cincinnati & Charleston, wrote: "Any editor who pretends to think that there are actually to be built two railroads between Charleston and Knoxville, must either be a fool himself, or feel anxious to make fools of his readers."[8]

An interesting fact about the Georgia road is that one of the first sleeping cars in the South was operated between Charleston and Atlanta in 1858 over the South Carolina and the Georgia Railroads, respectively.[9]

Charleston next turned its attention to reaching the Mississippi. During the summer of 1845, a meeting was called in Nashville "to consider the practicability and expediency of connecting that city with Charleston" by means of a railroad which would connect with the Western & Atlantic at Chattanooga. It was decided to be advisable, especially since 446 of the 576 miles had either been completed or were under construction. The existing water route was 2,460 miles. It was believed that coal would furnish the bulk of the traffic.[10]

In October, 1845, the citizens of Charleston assembled in a meeting with great enthusiasm and excitement. Eloquent

---

[7] Phillips, *op. cit.*, pp. 373-75.
[8] *Niles' National Register*, Vol. LVII (Oct. 12, 1839).
[9] Phillips, *op. cit.*, p. 251.
[10] *Niles' National Register*, Vol. LXIX (Sept. 20, 1845).

RENEWED EFFORTS TO REACH THE OHIO 35

speeches were heard, and, as one spokesman said, "The connection of the waters of the Mississippi with the Atlantic shore" would be realized "as the dawn of a great and glorious day for Charleston." Nine men, headed by John C. Calhoun, were named as delegates to represent its interests at the Memphis convention, and thus did Charleston embark upon another railroad enterprise.[11]

The great Memphis convention during the early winter of 1845-46, was "not second to any which has assembled since the adoption of the Federal Constitution."[12] Plans were made to establish a southern route to the far West, and to build branches to Memphis and Nashville, via Atlanta. The Memphis convention represented pretty definitely the change of mind of South Carolina and Charleston by their desire to strike the Mississippi and the country beyond instead of reaching up to the Ohio. At any rate, the Memphis & Charleston Railroad was organized in 1850, to extend from Memphis to Chattanooga[13] and was opened to traffic in 1857, at which time imposing ceremonies were held in both cities to celebrate "the marriage of the waters of the Atlantic and the Mississippi."[14]

A great delegation from Memphis and the West brought a hogshead of water of the Mississippi River to Charleston, "and it was pumped, with great parade, by a fire engine over the High Battery into Charleston harbor, while in the evening visitors and natives celebrated 'this marriage' by a ball given in its honor."[15] The parade through the city to the High Battery "was on a scale of splendor and amplitude rarely ever witnessed in our city and presented a most brilliant appearance."[16]

"An interesting souvenir of the occasion is a timeworn copy of the menu of the dinner at the Military Hall," writes William G. Mazyck in *The Sunday News*, of Charleston, in June, 1924. "It is printed in exceedingly small type upon dainty lace-edged paper, reminding one of the Valentines of that day, and is as follows:[17]

---

[11] *Ibid.*, Vol. LXIX (Oct. 18, 1845).
[12] *DeBow's Review*, Vol. I (Jan. 1846).
[13] *Ibid.*, Vol. IX (Aug., 1850).   [14] *Ibid.*, Vol. XXIII (July, 1857).
[15] Smith and Smith, *The Dwelling Houses of Charleston, South Carolina*, p. 88.
[16] *Charleston Mercury*, April 1, 1857.   [17] *The Sunday News*, June 1, 1924.

THE CLINCHFIELD RAILROAD

Citizens' Dinner
In honor of the
Guests of the City of Charleston
from the West.

BILL OF FARE

SOUP

Couter with eggs. Green Turtle.

COLD DISHES

Westphalia Ham. Smoked Tongue.
Chicken Salad. Lobster Salad.
Boned Turkey in Jelly. Pate de
foie gras in Jelly.
New York Corned Beef.

RELISHES

Anchovy.   Olive Farcie.

FISH

Boiled Fresh Salmon. Boiled Fresh
Cod. Boiled Bass. Fried Halibut.
Fried Whiting. Fresh Mackerel.

SAUCES FOR FISH

Worcestershire Sauce.   Anchovy
Sauce.   Walnut Catsup.   Mushroom
Catsup.
Madeira Sauce.
Turtle Steaks.   Turtle Fins.
Boiled Lamb, Caper Sauce. Turkey,
Oyster Sauce. N. Y. Capons Mushroom.
Chicken Pie. Macaroni Pie. Sauce.
Sweet Bread with Truffles. Fricas-
sed Chickens with Truffles.
A la mode Beef. Pigs Feet stewed
with Tomatoes. Fricandeau of
Veal.
Capons, stewed with Truffles.
Chickens, Tomato Sauce. Ducks,
Olive Sauce.
New York Beef. New York Goose.
Boned Turkey. Lamb. Veal.
Pork. Pig.

GAME
Venison, Currant Jelly. Wild Turkey. Wild Duck.

VEGETABLES
Philadelphia Asparagus. Rice. Carrots. Potatoes. Salad. Green Peas. Spinach. Turnips. Cauliflowers. Beets. Sweet Potatoes.

PASTRY
Plum Pudding. Orange Pudding. Apple Pudding. Cocoanut Pudding. Tarts. Macaroons.

DESSERT
Ornament consisting of a train of Cars, crossing the bridge from Memphis to Charleston.
Ship of Nougat. Pyramid of Barrels of Rice and Bales of Cotton. Nougat Cornucopia, filled. Nougat Urns, filled. Baskets filled with Glace Fruit.
Meringue Pyramid. Cocoanut Drops. Pyramid of Almond Rings. Pyramid of Macaroons. Charlotte Russe. Jelly. Blanc Mange. Gateau glace au Rhum. Foam Cake. Fruits glaces. Pound Cake.

ICE CREAM
Pine Apple. Vanilla. Lemon. Almond. Soe. Chocolate. Coffee.

FRUIT
Apples. Oranges. Bananas. Almonds. Raisins. Figs. Nuts. Brandy Green Gages. Brandy Apricots. Brandy Peaches.

An interesting article in this connection appeared in a recent issue of a Charleston paper. "Today at Memphis, Tennessee, will be celebrated the seventy-second anniversary of the

Mississippi-Atlantic wedding, performed in 1857, when the Memphis and Charleston Railroad was first opened. Mayor Thomas P. Stoney, of Charleston, as a feature of the ceremony, will pour a barrel of water from the Atlantic into the Mississippi River, reënacting the similar ceremony of 1857."[18]

Again, Charleston was disappointed, for "today the Memphis and Charleston pours its trade into another port, leaving to Charleston only a memory and the huge debt incurred in its construction."[19]

However, early in 1851, explorations were made from Anderson, South Carolina, for another railroad to connect South Carolina with the Northwest.[20] By the end of the next year, charters were obtained from the various states through which the road would pass, and it became known as the Blue Ridge Railroad. As outlined in its charter, the road was to begin at Edgefield, a point on the Charleston & Hamburg line near Aiken, and extend via Abbeville and Anderson through Clayton and the Rabun Gap, in the northeastern corner of Georgia; thence down the Little Tennessee River and across the "pan-handle" of North Carolina to Knoxville, a distance of 195 miles. The South Carolina legislature voted to guarantee its bonds up to $1,250,000.[21] At Knoxville, it would connect with the road to Chattanooga. These two cities had by this time become important commercial centers. The route would cross some exceedingly rough country, and the original surveys called for thirteen tunnels. Charleston, of course, was greatly interested and optimistic over its development, and almost immediately subscribed over a million dollars.[22] The road was believed to be "the most magnificent railroad project of the day," and, apparently, it was not difficult to estimate "the immense commerce that it must one day pour forth in the direction of Charleston."[23]

The Blue Ridge Railroad would have the advantage of important connection at Knoxville, the terminus of the East Tennessee & Georgia, and the East Tennessee & Virginia, while the roads into Kentucky would place it in direct contact with Louisville and Cincinnati, all of which would mean the realization of

---

[18] *News and Courier*, July 9, 1929.   [19] Smith and Smith, *op. cit.*, p. 88.
[20] *DeBow's Review*, Vol. XIII (July, 1852).
[21] *Ibid.*, Vol. XVI (April, 1854).   [22] Phillips, *op. cit.*, pp. 376-77.
[23] *DeBow's Review*, Vol. XIV (Feb., 1853).

RENEWED EFFORTS TO REACH THE OHIO 39

Charleston's early dream of tapping the Northwest. In regard to the division of the road according to states, 52 miles would be located in South Carolina, 16 in Georgia, 73 in North Carolina, and 53 in Tennessee.[24]

In an article entitled "Will Charleston Command the Trade of the West," DeBow writes that the object of the road "is to put Charleston in direct communication with the Ohio River, to draw the vast trade by the way-side, now diverted to points less congenial, and to enable her, by a line possessing superior advantages, not only to grasp the rich stores south of the Ohio, but to compete for the trade north of the Ohio to the lakes, and west of the Mississippi and Missouri. That she will be able to do this successfully, I entertain no doubt, and the trade ... may be looked to with confidence, both as a profit to the road, and an increase of the trade of the city."[25]

Construction of the road began in the fall of 1853. The contract was awarded to Anson Bangs & Company of New York, but this firm soon disposed of its properties to A. Birdsall & Company. As the result of an investigation, which revealed that the new company had neglected all the heavy work, the contract was cancelled on April 1, 1856. Rails had been laid only from Anderson to a point a short distance beyond Pendleton, in Pickens County, South Carolina. At Anderson, it connected with a branch of the Greenville and Columbia road.[26]

President Frost, in his annual report, brought out the fact that Savannah was benefiting by the trade from eastern Tennessee over the network of Georgia railroads, and Virginia was getting a considerable portion over the East Tennessee & Virginia road, via Bristol and Roanoke. North Carolina was projecting a road to tap the East Tennessee & Virginia at Morristown, Tennessee, by way of Asheville and the French Broad route. "The tendency and effort of these roads to drain the commercial resources of Charleston must be manifest," he continued. "When they work their efforts, the trade of Charleston must be limited to the products and wants of South Carolina." President Frost urged the continuance of the project. Over his road, the distance from Knoxville to Charleston would be 103

---

[24] *Ibid., Vol.* XXII (April, 1857).   [25] *Ibid.*
[26] Phillips, *op. cit.*, p. 378.

miles nearer than to Savannah, and 46 miles nearer than Richmond. Since trade would naturally follow the shortest route to the Atlantic and hence benefit from the saving of both time and cheaper rates, it was expected that the completion of the road would result in all the commerce of eastern Tennessee coming to Charleston. "The economical and political importance of its construction outweighs even its commercial benefits." South Carolina forthwith subscribed a million dollars.[27]

"The road will realize the early dream of South Carolina to unite herself with Louisville and Cincinnati, by a direct and expeditious route, as it was exhibited in the convention held 25 years ago in Knoxville," writes DeBow on the advantages of the Blue Ridge Railroad. This road would have placed Knoxville only 410 miles from Charleston, and therefore much nearer than the rival ports of Richmond, Norfolk, or Savannah. "Without the Blue Ridge Railroad, Charleston and South Carolina have little opportunity of sharing in the advantage of a commercial connection with the navigable waters of the west."[28]

It is quite probable that the panic of 1857 had its effects on the road. The usual agitation was prevalent to push the work of construction as rapidly as possible. However, funds were apparently not available, and by the time of the outbreak of the Civil War, work had ceased.

By 1861, twenty-five miles of the road were in operation as far as Walhalla, South Carolina, while over two and a half million dollars had been expended.[29] Over two-thirds of the 5,800-foot tunnel through Stump House Mountain had been completed.[30] Within the limits of South Carolina, construction work had been completed as follows: three-fourths of the grading, one-third of the tunnel excavation, three-fourths of the drain masonry, one-fourth of the bridge masonry, and more than one-fourth of the track had been laid; in Georgia: almost one-half of the grading, two-thirds of the drain and bridge masonry, and one-seventh of the tunnel work had been accomplished.[31]

Although the length of the road in South Carolina and Georgia comprised only about 30 per cent of the total mileage,

---

[27] *DeBow's Review*, Vol. XXIV (Jan., 1858).
[28] *Ibid.*, Vol. XXIX (Sept., 1860).
[29] *Ibid.* [30] Phillips, *op. cit.*, p. 379.
[31] *DeBow's Review*, Vol. XXIX (Sept., 1860).

RENEWED EFFORTS TO REACH THE OHIO 41

it involved approximately 58 per cent of the cost of the entire project. The estimated cost of the road was seven million dollars. Colonel Gwynn reported the following estimates for its completion from Walhalla to Knoxville:[32]

TABLE IV

Walhalla to Clayton	31 miles	$1,320,165
Clayton to Franklin	22 miles	589,636
Franklin to Nantahala	28 miles	899,958
Nantahala to Tennessee line	38 miles	859,132
Tennessee line to Maysville	37 miles	879,706
Maysville to Knoxville	17 miles	307,915
Total		$4,856,512

The Civil War seems definitely to have prevented further work, or at least there is no available information of activities during that period.

After the war, the South rallied to return to its former position and immediately set about to rebuild its transportation system. DeBow writes that "we cannot fail to pay a tribute to that fore-sightedness and energy in the South which, in the calm following war, is taking hold of railroads with an unprecedented vigor, and restoring them and increasing them without a parallel anywhere. . . . It means the rehabilitation of the South." The Union armies had worked havoc, for at the close of the war, there was not one efficient railroad in the South.[33]

The Blue Ridge project was revived in the summer of 1866, and a big meeting was held in Charleston, which resulted in the sending of a deputation to Cincinnati. "Though the people of South Carolina are not in a position to do much just now, they realize fully the advantages such a connection with the Ohio will give them, and they will coöperate heartily with any enterprise calculated to consummate so desirable an end."[34]

G. A. Trenholm, chairman of the commission which went to Cincinnati, reported that the completion of the road from Louisville and the Ohio to Knoxville was assured, and he ad-

---
[32] *Ibid.*, Vol. XXIX (Dec., 1860).
[33] *Ibid.* ("After the War Series"), Vol. 1 (April, 1866).
[34] *Ibid.*, Vol. II (July, 1866).

vocated the early completion of the Blue Ridge. "To leave it in its present condition . . . will be to bridge the stream, and stop short of the shore; to win the race, and neglect to take the prize."[35] Mr. Trenholm reported that thirty-four miles were actually in operation and only 164 miles remained to be built. The heaviest and most costly work had been completed. South of Knoxville, a stretch of twenty miles was ready for the rails, and also the stone abutments and piers had been erected for the bridge across the Holston River. Another company had begun construction of a road from Knoxville to Louisville and Cincinnati. About three million dollars had already been spent, and if $4,500,000 could be raised, the work could be easily completed. Mr. Trenholm also pointed out that the route via Asheville and the French Broad River was not only much longer, but it would also necessitate the construction of 320 miles of new road at a cost of about twelve million dollars. Quite naturally, therefore, the Blue Ridge road was more advantageous.[36] Although Mr. Trenholm urged the early completion of the road, he said "it must, nevertheless, be admitted that the source from whence the capital for its completion is to be drawn, remains still unrevealed."[37]

During the latter part of 1867, the road received permission from the South Carolina legislature and the city council of Charleston to issue preferred stock. The stock was placed on sale, but with very little success. Northern capital was apparently not interested in investing in the South "owing to the political conditions of the country."[38] Local consumption of the stock was probably limited by the general financial embarrassment of the country at that time.

In 1871, the chief engineer advocated a narrow-gauge road of three feet instead of the five feet originally planned. According to his report, such a change would mean the saving of $4,495 per mile of track, or 42 per cent; grading and bridging

---

[35] *Report of the Several Committees of the City Council of Charleston, the Blue Ridge Railroad of South Carolina, the Chamber of Commerce, and the Board of Trade of Charleston, South Carolina, on the Subject of the Blue Ridge Railroad*, 1866, p. 6. Hereafter referred to as *Report of the Several Committees*.

[36] *DeBow's Review* ("After the War Series"), Vol. II (Sept., 1866).

[37] *Report of the Several Committees*, p. 11.

[38] *DeBow's Review* ("After the War Series"), Vol. V (Jan., 1868).

RENEWED EFFORTS TO REACH THE OHIO

costs would be lessened 20 per cent; and the length of the road would be reduced. Rolling stock costs would be reduced to about one-half, and operation 25 per cent.[39] However, it seems that no action was taken, and, from available information, the idea of further extending the road from Walhalla lay dormant for a number of years.

Early in 1880, an interesting letter was written to the editor of the Charleston *News and Courier* complaining about the "ruinous railroad rates," which is quoted herewith:[40]

INDIANTOWN, S. C.

TO THE EDITOR OF THE NEWS AND COURIER:

I bought a heifer from Mr. Stribling, of Pendleton, Anderson County, South Carolina, for which I paid $50, and she was shipped to Kingstree, S. C. The freight charged was $30.50, as follows:

Blue Ridge Railroad	$9.00
Greenville & Columbia Railroad	6.00
Wilmington, Columbia & Augusta R. R.	8.50
Northeastern Railroad	7.00

Is there no protection for the public, or are we left to the mercy of unscrupulous corporations?

(Signed) W. H. KENNEDY

It costs $8.60 to ship a cow today over the same route used by Mr. Kennedy, i.e., via the Blue Ridge and Southern to Columbia, and the Atlantic Coast Line to Kingstree, by way of Florence.[41]

Soon after the chief engineer's report, an article appeared in the *News and Courier* attempting to revive interest in the project. It seems that keen competition existed between the Western & Atlantic and the Louisville & Great Southern roads in an effort to reach the Atlantic Ocean. The latter company was about to enter upon an agreement with the Central of Georgia Railroad to handle its traffic out of Atlanta, upon the completion of its line to that point, when the Western & Atlantic immediately leased the Georgia Central. This gave the Western and Atlantic direct communication with tidewater at Savan-

---

[39] *Report of the Chief Engineer of the Blue Ridge Railroad*, July 24, 1871, p. 19.
[40] *News and Courier*, Jan. 9, 1880.
[41] From information received at the office of the assistant general freight agent of the Atlantic Coast Line at Charleston.

nah. The Louisville & Great Southern contemplated the construction of a link between its road at Livingston, Kentucky, and Caryville, Tennessee, the western terminus of the Knoxville & Ohio Railroad. The Great Southern would then "turn its eyes" in the direction of Charleston.[42]

Eighteen miles from Knoxville to Maryville, on the old Blue Ridge route, had been completed. This left only 156 miles to Walhalla, a considerable portion of the heavy work having been completed before the war. The completion of the proposed southern extension to Aiken, on the South Carolina Railroad, would not only bring Charleston nearer Knoxville than by way of the Asheville route, but it would also remove its dependence upon the East Tennessee, Virginia & Georgia Railroad, through Morristown, for the Knoxville traffic. The article in the *News and Courier* reported that:

> The Louisville and Great Southern Railroad has just acquired control of a road running from Louisville to Michigan City on Lake Michigan, at which point it has both rail and water connections with Chicago. We see no reason therefore why the Louisville and Great Southern should remain any considerable time without an outlet to the ocean practically under its own control, and certainly free from any dictation by its great competitor; or why it should not be able to offer to Chicago, Cincinnati and Louisville better facilities for ocean transportation, both in point of distance, time and cost than Col. Cole[43] will be able to offer St. Louis by his direct line or the other cities through his connection with them. There is less actual railroad to be built to establish a line to Charleston, via Knoxville, than would have to be constructed to complete any other route; and the results when built will be much more favorable. . . . There is no reason for a panic, and there is no reason for rash confidence. Charleston has a magnificent opportunity because for the first time this port is necessary to the freedom and success of extensive railroad systems. The Western lines will seek Charleston as a means of avoiding the pen into which Col. Cole seeks to drive them. But Charleston must do her part. Commercial fortune never comes to cities which do nothing to deserve it. Natural advantages are often a bane, by reason of the indolence they encourage. The West looks to Charleston, but Charleston must be ready to meet the West halfway. Such a chance as Charleston now has will not

---

[42] *News and Courier*, Jan. 16, 1880.
[43] That is, the Georgia combination.

soon return. It will never return, if the Western lines which oppose Col. Cole are allowed to forget that Charleston exists and make permanent arrangements with other ports.[44]

It appears, from available information, that practically nothing of any importance was done to revive the Blue Ridge road until the summer of 1887, when it was rumored in Anderson, South Carolina, that the road had been purchased by a group of northern capitalists. According to a news article from that city, the new owners "are now having the route surveyed with a view to extending it across the mountains, which has caused some of our moneyed men to prick up their ears and feel around about their old pantaloons for the extra loose nickels; they think that move means good luck to Anderson."[45]

An interesting editorial appeared a few weeks later which stated that "little confidence can be safely reposed in the rumor now current that a northeast syndicate has undertaken the work" of reviving the Blue Ridge Railroad. Continuing, the editorial states that "it is almost too good to be true. Yet it seems strange that a line which offers so many advantages should not be exploited, especially as those who now take hold of the project will derive considerable benefit from the millions of money which were spent upon the road before the war. Although no work of consequence has been done since 1861, the old grading and tunnelling can in a large measure be utilized. This was shown when the route was carefully examined some years ago. When, then, we say that we can put but little faith in the fresh statements on the subject, we have no intention of discouraging anybody, and merely want to avoid another disappointment."[46]

Soon afterwards, the project was definitely abandoned. Although it is controlled today by the Southern Railway, the Blue Ridge Railroad is operated as such from Belton, a point on the line of the Southern between Greenville and Columbia, through Anderson to Walhalla, all of which points are in South Carolina.

As was the case of the ill-fated Louisville, Cincinnati & Charleston Railroad, it seems that if Charleston had centered its interests solely in the Blue Ridge Railroad it would un-

---
[44] *News and Courier*, Jan. 16, 1880.
[45] *Ibid.*, Sept. 6, 1887.
[46] *Ibid.*, Sept. 21, 1887.

doubtedly have been completed. The city invested much more in other projects, designed primarily to bring it more trade, than would have been necessary to complete the Blue Ridge.

Charleston was still desirous of establishing itself as an entrepôt for the surrounding country. Besides its investments in the Georgia Railroad, the Western & Atlantic, and the Memphis & Charleston, as mentioned above, it subscribed liberally to the following roads: the Charlotte & South Carolina, extending from that city to Columbia, via Chester, completed in 1852; the Greenville & Columbia, completed in 1853; the Northeastern, between Charleston and Florence, which was distinctly the result of Charleston's efforts and to which Charleston contributed almost half a million dollars, completed in 1854; the Wilmington & Manchester, connecting with the Northeastern at Florence; the Cheraw & Darlington, likewise tapped by the Northeastern at Florence, and completed in 1851; the Charleston & Savannah, completed in 1860.[47]

By 1860, it was realized that few, if any, of the railroads produced the trade which had been expected. They injured some cities, such as Charleston, and benefited others—Atlanta, for example. The effect was that attention was diverted from the seaboard to the Piedmont and the eastern and western trade centers.

The Blue Ridge Railroad was undoubtedly the work of Charleston interests, and state aid was secured as a result of Charleston's influence in the legislature. At any rate, the disappointment over its failure was shared by the merchants and shippers of Charleston, the planters of the upper Piedmont, and the farmers of eastern Tennessee; "and Charleston still longs in vain for the trade of the golden West."[48]

THE COMMERCE OF SOUTH CAROLINA[49]

By the time of the final abandonment of the Blue Ridge Railroad, the importance of Charleston as a port had appreciably declined in favor of New York, Boston, and other eastern cities. In a paper prepared by Elwood Fisher in 1848, the following statement occurs:

---

[47] Phillips, *op. cit.*, pp. 338-55.
[48] *Ibid.*, p. 380.   [49] From the *News and Courier*, Jan. 1, 1887.

RENEWED EFFORTS TO REACH THE OHIO

For the first quarter of a century of the present Government up to 1816 the South took the lead of the North in commerce, as at the end of that period the exports of the Southern States amounted to about thirty millions of dollars, which was five more than the northern. In 1816, South Carolina and New York were the greatest exporting States of the Union, South Carolina exporting more than $10,000,000, and New York $14,000,000.

The same writer showed that even in manufactures, the South, at that period, excelled the North in proportion to population. However, at the date on which he wrote (1848), he said: "Since that period (1816) a great change has occurred; the harbors of Norfolk, of Richmond, of Charleston and Savannah have been deserted for those of Philadelphia, New York and Boston; and New Orleans is the only Southern city that pretends to rival its northern competitors. The grass is growing in the streets of the cities of the South which originally monopolized our colonial commerce, and maintained their ascendancy in the earlier days of the Union."

Fisher accounted for the decline in the foreign trade of the Southern cities by saying: "It was at this period that the system of direct taxation was finally abandoned, and the whole interest of the public debt, as well as the increased expenditure of the Government, was made chargeable on the foreign commerce of the country."

Whether or not the reason given for the decline in the foreign trade of the South was correct, there is no doubt about the fact that the decline was great. The foreign trade of the Carolina ports was reviving at the outburst of the Civil War. The value of exports from Charleston and Beaufort for 1860 amounted to $21,193,723, but in 1870 the exports had declined to $10,818,669. In 1880, the value of exports had reached and slightly exceeded those of 1860, amounting to $21,559,763; but in 1885, dropped to $19,734,779.

The value of exports for Charleston alone has been as follows:[50]

TABLE V

1860	$21,179,350
1870	10,772,071

[50] *Ibid.*

48 THE CLINCHFIELD RAILROAD

1880 .... $19,590,627
1885 17,882,560

The value of the merchandise imported into South Carolina in 1860 was $1,569,570. This declined in 1870 to $505,394, and in 1880 to $231,435, but in 1885 reached $524,171. While the imports in 1885 amounted to only about one-third of the value of those of 1860, it had more than doubled since 1880. It is important to note the extent of the foreign trade of South Carolina and the countries with which such relations were maintained. It will be noticed in the following table that there was an increase of more than twenty per cent in the foreign tonnage transported in 1885 over the tonnage of 1880.

The following statement shows the tonnage of vessels entered and cleared at the ports of Charleston and Beaufort during the years 1880 and 1885:[51]

TABLE VI

ENTERED	1880		1885	
	VESSELS	TONNAGE	VESSELS	TONNAGE
Charleston	255	116,283	231	124,785
Beaufort	59	29,554	60	48,918
	314	145,837	291	173,703
CLEARED				
Charleston	282	142,318	270	148,754
Beaufort	74	38,525	92	78,420
	356	180,843	362	227,174

Of the vessels which entered in 1880, there were 36 American, with a tonnage of 11,985 tons; and 278 foreign, with a tonnage of 133,852 tons. In 1885, there were 18 American ships of 3,057 tonnage, and 273 foreign ships of 169,746 tonnage. Of the vessels cleared in 1880, there were 37 American of 14,640 tonnage, and 319 foreign of 172,103 tonnage; in 1885, 31 American of 7,880 tonnage, and 331 foreign of 219,294.

---

[51] *Ibid.*

RENEWED EFFORTS TO REACH THE OHIO 49

The following table is submitted to show the total tonnage transported by the railroads of South Carolina for the fiscal year ending June 30, 1886:[52]

TABLE VII
1885-86

Articles	Total	Brought Into State (estimated)	Shipped Through or Out of State (estimated)
Bacon, lbs.	69,873,499	38,430,425	31,443,074
Live Stock, h'd	38,432	21,138	17,294
Domestics, lbs.	27,166,282	....	27,166,282
Fertilizers, tons	292,621	136,000	156,621
Flour, bbls.	607,502	334,126	273,376
Hay, bales	183,171	100,744	82,427
Lard, lbs.	2,242,031	1,233,117	1,008,914
Liquor, bbls.	17,783	9,775	7,998
Lumber, ft.	73,003,638	....	73,003,638
Melons, cars	581	....	581
Oranges & lemons, pkges.	235,620	235,620	....
Rice, clean, lbs.	12,359,746	....	12,359,746
Rice, rough, bu.	78,317	....	78,317
Naval Stores, bbls.	175,534	....	175,534
Ros. & Turp., tons	46	....	46
Salt, sacks	50,555	50,555	....
Syrup & molasses, bbls.	5,459	5,459	....
Tobacco, lbs.	7,262,511	4,049,381	3,213,130
Vegetables, pkges.	266,580	146,619	119,961
Grist, bbls.	63,164	34,740	28,424
Cotton, bales	637,766	100,000	537,766
Grain, bu.	3,437,553	1,890,654	1,546,899
Meal, lbs.	1,849,823	1,017,202	832,621
Feed & Mill Stuff, lbs.	796,351	437,663	358,688
Peas, lbs.	500,105	275,056	225,049
Cotton Seed, tons	13,791	....	13,791

[52] *Ibid.*

TABLE VII—1885-86—*Continued*

Articles	Total	Brought Into State (estimated)	Shipped Through or Out of State (estimated)
Misc. Farm Prod. tons	36,865	....	36,865
Wood, cords	16,922	9,307	7,615
Cotton Seed Oil, bbls.	19,037	....	19,037
Cotton Seed Oil Cans	72	....	72
Paper Stock, lbs.	794,967	425,081	369,886
Ditto, pkges.	11,868	6,500	5,368
Ice, cars	26	26	....
Brick, cars	400	400	....
Furniture, lbs.	299,826	299,826	....
Clay, lime, cement, bbls.	33,174	18,245	14,929
Shingles & Staves, bbls.	7,509,960	5,624,970	1,874,990
Misc. Forest Products, tons	4,188	....	4,188
Granite & limestone, tons	34,959	....	34,959
Cotton Ties & Bagging, tons	1,626	1,626	....
Coal, lbs.	5,912,080	3,251,680	2,660,400
R. R. Iron, lbs.	16,342,000	8,988,100	7,353,900
Iron, lead & Min. prod., tons	10,071	10,071	....
Manufactures, tons	3,481	1,914	1,567
Miscellaneous, tons	16,534	9,093	7,441
Merchandise, lbs.	443,470,115	243,908,612	199,561,503
Merchandise, pkges.	88,433	48,643	39,790

Revival of the Blue Ridge Project

During the nineties, the route of the Blue Ridge Railroad was again called to the attention of the people of Charleston. Although it does not fit in chronologically at this point, it may be well to devote a few pages to the attempt to revive the project.

RENEWED EFFORTS TO REACH THE OHIO 51

With the failure of the Charleston, Cincinnati & Chicago Railroad in 1894,[53] an agitation was started in Charleston to complete the Blue Ridge road. It will be recalled that the road was already in operation from Belton to Walhalla, and from Maryville to Knoxville. Considerable construction had also been completed when the original company failed in 1861. Concerning the possibility of completing the road, the Charleston *News and Courier* says in an article entitled "Here Is an Opportunity":[54]

While Charleston business men are looking for western railway connections, the business men on the other side of the mountains are looking for an outlet to the sea, and if the two can get together there seems to be an excellent chance of giving this city a system of railroads which will place the splendid advantages of this port at the disposal of the producers of the West. It will be remembered that Mayor Ficken a short time since took occasion to say that the great need of Charleston was a through line railroad, and that Mr. George A. Wagener took occasion to endorse his words and to express his willingness to participate in any enterprise looking in this direction.

While this was going on in Charleston, a syndicate of capitalists in Knoxville were mapping out a plan for building a road through the Blue Ridge Mountains. Rumors to this effect have been heard for some time, and now the *Knoxville Tribune* gives the matter a more dignified shape than it has yet assumed. That paper says that the proposed line will follow the survey of the Rabun Gap Railroad from a point on the Little Tennessee River, thirty miles southwest of Knoxville, to Anderson, S. C. The famous Rabun Gap tunnel,[55] which is nearly half completed, will be utilized, and the road will be built on comparatively easy grades.

A fiery news dispatch from Anderson says that

the people of Anderson would like to know what Charleston is going to do about the railroad question recently presented by Mr. George A. Wagener and Mayor Ficken. Mayor Ficken and Mr. Wagener are favorably known to our business men and our people have confidence in their judgment, and Anderson should be gratified if their suggestions should take definite shape. Indeed, the time has come for prompt and vigorous action. Anderson will willingly join Charleston in crossing the mountains. Our people have the pluck and energy to build a road from here to Knoxville, and we are willing to spend and

---

[53] See Chapter V below.   [54] *News and Courier*, Oct. 1, 1894.
[55] That is, the Stump House tunnel.

be spent, if necessary to complete the work. Then let us away with the old idea that "all things come to him who waits," for in this age of activity, "all things come to him who judiciously works." Other points are awake and on the alert in the matter.

Anderson desires to know whether Charleston means business or shall we put down your editorial and Mr. Ficken's and Mr. Wagener's remarks as the last spasmodic effort of a few patriotic citizens to save the business of Charleston? Anderson invites you to go in with us. Then, why not get up a real business committee to join with a like committee from Anderson and other points along the proposed route and with Knoxville push this road to an early completion? Unless you do, the opportunity may pass, never to return, for we must have the road, and now is the time to go to work in earnest.[56]

From all appearances, the idea apparently had been dormant for several months, when in April, 1895, the question arose as to the possibility of organizing a construction company to build the proposed road. However, it seems that the plans had been in the making, but the parties concerned had requested that no publicity be given the enterprise. "Matters have now reached the point," says the *News and Courier*, that "the paper is authorized to state what has been done, and what is being contemplated."

The plan called for two lines. The southern branch would extend to Macon, Georgia, whereby it was hoped traffic would be obtained from the Birmingham district. The northern branch would pass through Greenwood and Anderson to Knoxville. This latter route would follow almost the identical line of the old Blue Ridge road. It was believed that the line could be established by means of the organization of a construction company with a capital stock of $500,000.[57]

"Railroads operated in the interest of other ports and cities have built a Chinese wall around Charleston," said the paper. This was truly the case, for Charleston had been hemmed in by the Georgia and North Carolina roads, and also by the trunk lines further north and the "Queen and Crescent" and the Louisville & Nashville systems to the south. The outposts of the territory which acknowledged Charleston's prestige were such towns as Yemassee, Branchville, and Lanes, all of which were within a radius of about fifty miles of the city. "With these facts

---

[56] *News and Courier*, Oct. 5, 1894.   [57] *Ibid.*, April 10, 1895.

RENEWED EFFORTS TO REACH THE OHIO

staring them in the face, it would seem that the people of Charleston would rise as a man and form the construction company which has been proposed," continued the *News and Courier*.[58]

"For two generations it has been the dream of Charleston to establish direct communication with the great West," said an editorial a few days later. "For over thirty years we have been waiting for someone else to build roads for us, and have gradually allowed every railroad in the State to pass from our possession, until today we do not control a single line."[59]

Such an article would appear almost daily in an attempt to stir up the people to action. As a news dispatch from Yorkville stated, "The *News and Courier* is certainly doing its part towards pointing out to the business men of Charleston the wonderful advantages to be derived from building and equipping a railroad from the West to that city, and although many people have very little faith in the *News and Courier's* ability to induce Charleston to take her money out of her stocking and build the much needed railroad, still the paper is to be commended for the intelligent and faithful work that it is doing. . . . People sympathize with Charleston on account of the many hardships and disasters through which she has passed, but their sympathy does not go far enough to cause them to bestow their patronage when they are in the market, if some other town offers them greater inducements."[60]

The Security Construction Company was organized early in June to build the road from Walhalla to Maryville. At its first meeting on the fifteenth of the month, George A. Wagener was elected president, and Morris Israel vice-president. The following were appointed members of a "working committee": George A. Wagener, Morris Israel, R. Goodwyn Rhett, Waring P. Carrington, and T. R. McGahan. The board of directors was composed of George A. Wagener, Morris Israel, John F. Ficken, Thomas R. McGahan, John G. Simonds, J. Adger Smyth, Carston Wulbern, Waring P. Carrington, William M. Bird, Charles H. Drayton, and R. Goodwyn Rhett.[61]

Commenting upon the meeting, the paper says that "much satisfaction was expressed by the stockholders over the selection of Messrs. Wagener and Israel as officers of the company. The

---

[58] *Ibid.*, April 11, 1895.
[60] *Ibid.*, April 24, 1895.
[59] *Ibid.*, April 18, 1895.
[61] *Ibid.*, June 16, 1895.

financial and executive ability of both gentlemen are known to every one in Charleston, and everybody feels that in their hands the company is not only perfectly safe, but has the best chance of successfully accomplishing its ends."[62]

Although a few subscriptions were raised to the stock of the construction company, available information would indicate that the project was finally abandoned within the next year, never to be revived again.

[62] *Ibid.*, June 23, 1895.

CHAPTER V

THE CHARLESTON, CINCINNATI &
CHICAGO RAILROAD

GENERAL JOHN H. WILDER, an iron capitalist of Chattanooga, had, as a Union officer during and after the Civil War, traversed Georgia, South Carolina, western North Carolina, eastern Tennessee, and southwestern Virginia. He had been attracted by the mineral possibilities and the many natural advantages for industrial development of the territory, and he realized the necessity of a railroad to develop the region. During the early months of 1886, he interested capitalists in a project to connect the rich coal fields of southwestern Virginia and eastern Kentucky with the North and South, by means of a railroad across the mountains from some point on the Ohio River to the Atlantic.[1]

On September 30, 1886, a company was forthwith organized, which was named the Charleston, Cincinnati & Chicago Railroad Company.[2] The road soon became commonly known as simply the "Three C's." It was incorporated under a special act of the Tennessee legislature on March 29, 1887, and under the general laws of that state on August 5, 1889.[3] The general offices of the company were established at 45 Broadway, New York City.[4]

The route decided upon was indeed an ambitious one. Beginning at Charleston, it would cross the pine barrens, the swamps of the Santee River, and pass through the cotton lands of Clarendon, Sumter, Kershaw, Lancaster, and York counties, South Carolina. Entering the Piedmont section south of Rock Hill, it would pass through Blacksburg (then called Black's), later cross over into North Carolina, and serve the towns of Shelby, Rutherfordton, and Marion. Soon after leaving Marion,

---

[1] From an unpublished manuscript by O. K. Morgan, "The Story of the Clinchfield," p. 1. Written as an aid in the preparation of this study.
[2] *News and Courier*, Aug. 25, 1888.
[3] Interstate Commerce Commission, Valuation Docket No. 364, I. C. C., p. 27.
[4] "Investors' Supplement," *Commercial and Financial Chronicle*, Vol. XLVI (March, 1888).

it would begin its laborious climb across the Blue Ridge Mountains to Johnson City, Tennessee; thence to Estillville (now Gate City), Virginia, and on across the Cumberland Mountains to Ashland, on the Kentucky side of the Ohio River—a total distance of 621 miles. Three branches were later added to the proposed road: one from Lancaster to Charlotte, a distance of 40 miles; another from Blacksburg to Augusta, by way of Newberry, 130 miles; and the third from Rutherfordton to Spartanburg, 45 miles.[5]

Valuable connections would be realized along the line. In addition to the ocean shipping anticipated at Charleston, the "Three C's" would also tap the Charleston & Savannah Railroad at that point. At Sumter, it would intersect the Wilmington, Columbia & Augusta road;[6] and at Camden, the South Carolina Railroad.[7] At Lancaster, its line to Charlotte would branch out. The Charlotte, Columbia & Augusta[8] would be crossed at Rock Hill, and branches of the same road at Lancaster[9] and at York.[10] At Blacksburg, the northern terminus of its branch to Augusta, the "Three C's" would intersect the Richmond & Danville.[11] At Shelby, it would connect with the Carolina Central from Charlotte and Wilmington.[12] Its branch to Spartanburg would join the main line at Rutherfordton. Connection would be made with the Western North Carolina Railroad at Marion. It would cross the Eastern Tennessee, Virginia & Georgia at Johnson City, and the Norfolk & Western at St. Paul (Minneapolis), Virginia. Finally, at Ashland, it would connect with six roads leading to such cities as Cincinnati, Chicago, Toledo, Cleveland, and Pittsburgh.[13]

At a distance of about thirty miles southward from Ashland, the projected road entered the vast coal deposits, then known as the "Peach Orchard mines." Twenty miles further south,

---

[5] *Commercial and Financial Chronicle*, Vol XLVI (March 31, 1888).
[6] Now the Atlantic Coast Line.   [7] Now the Southern Railway.
[8] Formerly the Charlotte & South Carolina.
[9] Projected between Cheraw and Chester.
[10] Between Chester and Lenoir.
[11] Formerly the Charlotte-Atlanta Air Line, now the main line of the Southern Railway.
[12] Now the Seaboard Air Line.
[13] Map, "Investor's Supplement," *Commercial and Financial Chronicle*, March, 1892, p. 26.

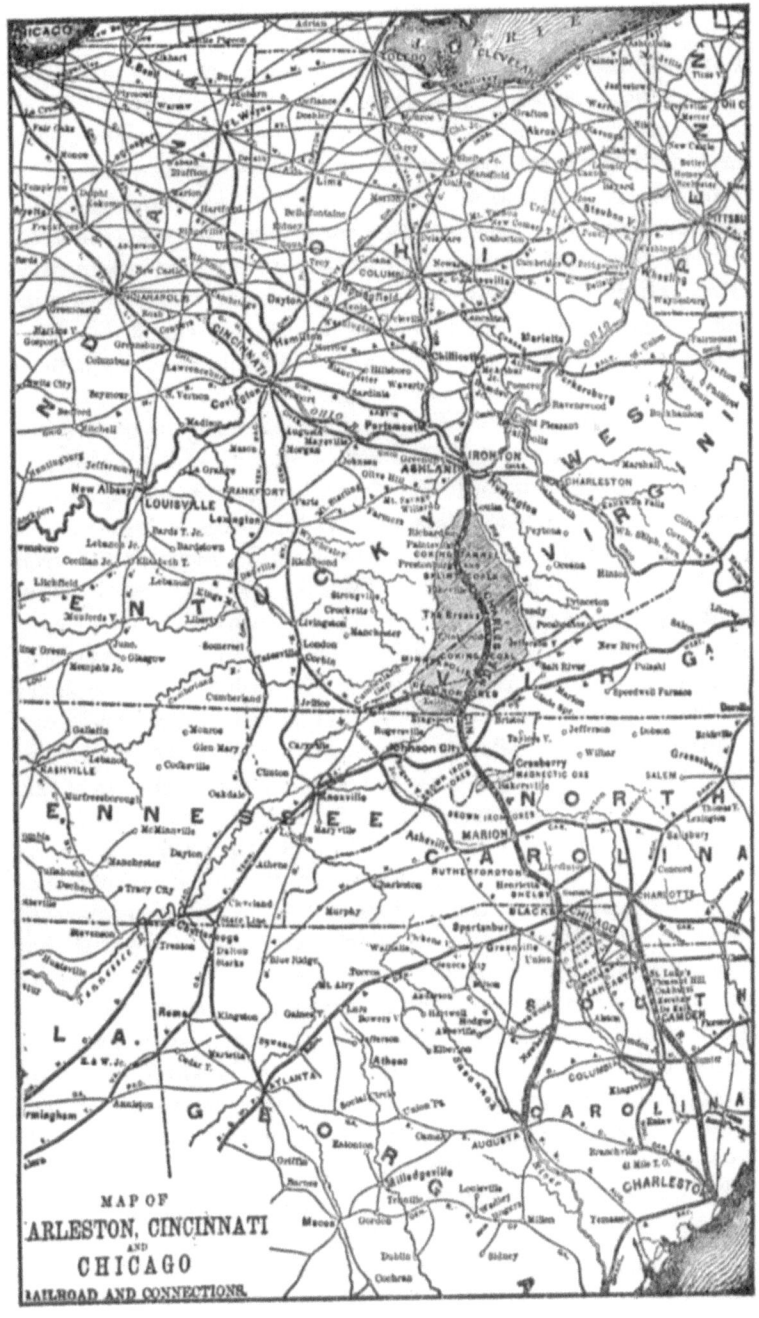

CHARLESTON, CINCINNATI & CHICAGO RAILROAD
From Commercial and Financial Chronicle, March, 1892.

it passed through a territory containing one of the largest deposits of splint coal to be found in the United States, a territory where, in addition to other varieties of bituminous coal, large beds of cannel coal were located. This region was reputed to be "the richest field of mineral wealth in the country." Near the boundary line between Kentucky and Virginia, the road traversed beds of specular hematite iron ore and other fields of coal, both of which were reported to be of excellent quality and in quantities declared to be practically inexhaustible. Further south, the road would serve the valuable iron deposits of the Cranberry bed in North Carolina.[14]

"The importance of these several deposits may be understood without going into details, from the following statement of the relative convenience and therefore the relative cheapness of handling the ores, as compared with like ores in other parts of the United States," says an editorial in the *News and Courier* of Charleston, South Carolina. "Mr. Swank, a special Government expert, says in the United States Census for 1880: 'From the ore mines of Lake Superior and Missouri to the coal of Pennsylvania is one thousand miles. Connellsville coal is taken six hundred miles to the blast furnaces of Chicago, and seven hundred and fifty miles to the blast furnaces of St. Louis.' The 'Three C's' will bring the coking coal and iron ores within one hundred miles of each other and new furnaces already in operation in the Ohio valley . . . will tax the freight capacity of the road." At the outset, it was anticipated that the demands would be heavy from the factories, towns, and cities located along the southern end of the line, and it was estimated that these demands would increase every year. "The conditions all indicate that the new road will have nearly as much business as it can manage in handling ores alone, and no class of freight is perhaps more desirable." Large forests of hardwood were located along the line, the revenue freight from which, it was estimated, would be sufficient to pay the interest on the bonds for years after the completion of the road.[15]

In addition to the relative local development predicted by General Wilder, it was believed that the new road would open up a new outlet from the Northwest, and make use of Charleston

---

[14] *News and Courier*, July 1, 1887.   [15] *Ibid.*

as its export point. In discussing the advantages of such a plan, the *New York Maritime Register* says:

There is no good reason why Charleston should not in time become a great seaport. With the proper facilities in hand, it ought to become the outlet for the products of a large extent of country in the interior, in fact, one of the most important on the Atlantic Seaboard. A scheme looking in this direction has already come to light. The plan is to connect Charleston with certain parts of the West directly by railroad, and in connection therewith to establish a line of steamers to Glasgow to complete this new transportation route. The scheme is certainly good, and there is no doubt that it might be accomplished.... The port of Charleston will undoubtedly continue to grow in commercial importance.... As that port avails itself of the opportunities of securing better communication with the rich agricultural and mining country at its back, it will soon see the beginning of that prosperity so much desired. It is the exercise of business energy and enterprise that will give to Charleston its future importance, and no artificial means can supply the place of these qualities.[16]

A meeting was held in Camden on January 14, 1887, to promote the interests of the "Three C's." Among those present were Senator M. C. Butler, General Wilder, and Colonel R. A. Johnson, of Boston, general manager of the road. In his speech, Colonel Johnson promised that if the township would subscribe for at least $40,000 of stock, in addition to $125,000 already taken by the county, work would begin at Camden within ten days. He explained that the reason they wanted to begin at Camden was that an arrangement had been made with the South Carolina Railroad to haul iron from Charleston. It was cheaper to ship by water to Charleston, and thence by rail to Camden, than over the Richmond & Danville road.[17]

General Wilder was then introduced. He drew a beautiful picture of the road from the phosphate beds and deep harbor of Charleston, through the winter resort of Camden and the summer resorts of western North Carolina, along the entire road to Ashland. He claimed that the completion of the road was certain, for if it were a poor investment capitalists would not have placed their money in it. "Coal will be brought to

---

[16] *Ibid.*, Feb. 14, 1887.   [17] *Ibid.*, Jan. 15, 1887.

THE CLINCHFIELD RAILROAD

Charleston for about $3 a ton," and Charleston would be made the best coaling port in the South. "There will be no bad grades," and "it will be a straight and through road, with through cars from Charleston to Ashland and Chicago." According to a newspaper report, "General Wilder used strong and good argument, and changed more than one capitalist of Camden in favor of the road."[18]

Senator Butler, a director of the road, spoke mainly about the necessity for Charleston to have an outlet to the West in order to compete with Savannah—the same old story! He added, however, that "the road would relieve the present isolated condition of Camden, and would greatly increase the business of South Carolina's chief city, Charleston."[19]

Prior to his visit to Camden, General Wilder had spent considerable time along the line with the view of establishing blast furnaces and rolling mills at suitable points. "General Wilder is enthusiastic over the outlook, in the territory through which the new road is to run, for iron manufactures," says the *New York Tribune.* "He found there a seemingly unlimited vein of iron ore, of the kind best adapted for making Bessemer steel; and five extensive seams of coal of three different varieties, all in such positions that they can be reached by adits run into the sides of the mountains, in place of shafts such as are largely required in the coal fields of Pennsylvania. There are, also contiguous to the line of the road in Tennessee and Virginia, veins of fine marble, and great areas of hardwood timber."[20]

During the first of March, one hundred and fifty tons of steel rail was received in Charleston for the "Three C's." On March 14, ground was broken at Camden for the construction of the road. The Massachusetts & Southern Construction Company, of Boston, was awarded the contract to build the road at an estimated cost of $21,000,000.[21] Meanwhile, work had been steadily progressing on the forty-five miles between Blacksburg and Rutherfordton. This line was completed early in March and was placed in operation on April 18, 1887.[22]

Sumter soon became alarmed that the road would not pass through it as originally planned. Some of its citizens feared

---
[18] *Ibid.*   [19] *Ibid.*   [20] *Ibid.,* Jan. 28, 1887.
[21] *Commercial and Financial Chronicle,* Vol. XLVI (March 31, 1888).
[22] *Ibid.*

that the "Three C's" would utilize the South Carolina Railroad from Camden to Charleston, and others believed a line would be built through Bishopville to Florence, and thence to Charleston via the Northeastern. An agitation was started by a few citizens, whereby it was felt that if the township would appropriate $40,000 in bonds, the road would be virtually assured. Sumter should offer the directors "some inducement to bring the road here," says a press dispatch. "The people of Sumter for the past year seem to have gone to sleep about this important matter, while the towns about us are wide awake on the subject, and are straining every nerve to secure this route. There is scarcely any doubt that the people of this township would vote almost solidly for the issuing of the bonds, as they finally realize that Sumter's future prosperity depends solely on the new railroads that she can secure."[23]

Sumter's fears, however, were soon eased by a statement from Colonel Johnson, general manager of the road, while in Camden locating a site for the depot and machine shops. Colonel Johnson is reported to have said that "as soon as the road is finished from Camden to Blacks [burg], the work will be immediately pushed in the direction of Sumter."[24]

According to a letter dated July 20, 1929, from the Honorable J. A. Raffield, mayor of Sumter, there are no records of the bonds having been issued.[25] At any rate, the question again arose. It was reported in the *Wateree Messenger* of Camden that a reply to the query from officials of the road was to the effect that the company was waiting for Sumter to offer some inducement in the way of a large county subscription. If such a subscription were not raised, the road would pass five or six miles from the township. In this event it seemed that the general verdict of the Sumter people was, "Let her pass!," continued the *Messenger*. A dispatch from Sumter says: "The citizens here have long since concluded that there is nothing so damaging to the interest and prosperity of a town as a large bonded indebtedness, and they do not propose to incur a cent of it. The Three C's would undoubtedly be a fine thing for Sumter, but the people would prefer to forego the advantages it would yield,

---

[23] *News and Courier*, May 9, 1887.   [24] *Ibid.*, June 30, 1887.
[25] From a personal letter from the Hon. J. A. Raffield, mayor of Sumter, July 20, 1929.

rather than incur a debt which would hang over them for years to come. There is, however, a gentleman in Sumter who has been in some way connected for some time with the Atlantic Coast Line, and who is probably in a position to know, who says positively that the Three C's has already signed a contract with the Coast Line authorities for the use of the Central Railroad from Sumter to Charleston. If this be true, there can no longer be any doubt as to the intention of the Three C's Company."[26]

The very next month (November), the question was again raised as to the route south of Camden. When asked his views by a newspaper representative, Colonel Johnson was reported to have said: "We have settled down to two plans, one of which we shall decide upon very soon. One of these plans is to go by Sumter; in each plan there are certain objections or difficulties to overcome. If Sumter County desires the road, it must make it known in a tangible way. There are reasons why we should like to go by Sumter, and I have about made up my mind to let Sumter County decide it for itself. If the people there are ready to help us over some of the difficulties of that line, I should say we would build to Charleston via Sumter. But it is very hard to get the mass of the voting people to appreciate the value of this line of railroad to them. They seem to act as though they are doing a great favor to the road by making a subscription to its capital stock, but it is what the road will do for them that they should consider. With coal landed at from $2.75 to $3.25 per ton in a healthful location, a town larger than Sumter would grow up in less than two years, and it is a much greater benefit to a town already started like Sumter. If those people value this connection with the Ohio Valley and the West, and will show it, I believe I can promise them the road."[27]

A fiery editorial appeared in the Charleston *News and Courier* of March 21 stressing the importance of the "Three C's" to Charleston, and lamenting the lack of interest displayed by its citizens. It seems that a meeting was held in that city for the purpose of enlisting the active support of Charleston capitalists in promoting the success of the road, but only "one or two of our enterprising moneyed men took the trouble even to attend the meeting." The editorial emphasized the natural advantages

---

[26] *News and Courier,* Oct 3, 1887.   [27] *Ibid.,* Nov. 25, 1887.

THE "THREE C'S" 63

which the ocean offered Charleston, "but we are doing nothing to help ourselves, while other places are up with the lark, and hard at work. . . . If Atlanta had contented itself with the fact that it was situated on Peachtree Creek, and with the idea that trade was compelled to come to it, Atlanta would have been Marthaville unto this day and to the end of time. But the mountain did not go to Mahomet, and so Mahomet very sensibly went to the mountain. . . . The capitalists of Charleston should at least hold a meeting and pass resolutions that they have heard with satisfaction that the road is going to be built, and that they will welcome to Charleston any results of that new spirit of enterprise which they themselves do not possess, but which they are pleased to recognize in others. The most of us are poor, but we can at least pass resolutions."[28]

It is probably difficult to understand this apparent change in the attitude of Charlestonians toward reaching the Ohio. Prior to the Civil War, as has been pointed out in preceding chapters, they became wildly excited and over-optimistic whenever any railroad company was organized, and particularly so when such a road would strike the Northwest. Charleston had been the leader of every such project. It is doubtful if there was any real opposition to the "Three C's" on the part of Charleston, but there was certainly less interest shown therefor than had been manifested for earlier projects. Possibly the foremost cause of this change of mind was the lack of funds, for the South, as a whole, had not yet recovered from the war; and in addition, Charleston was just beginning to get back on its feet following the disastrous earthquake of 1886. But there are other possible explanations. The city may have become antagonized at the internal improvements engendered by the Reconstruction. When the war ended, a great many southern people apparently felt that the world was about to come to an end, and they did not seem to care what happened. They believed there was absolutely no future, and so there was no use to try to succeed, as was the case with Louis Harvey, war president of the Richmond & Danville, who disposed of all of his business interests soon after President Davis evacuated Richmond.

---
[28] *Ibid.*, May 21, 1887.

64 THE CLINCHFIELD RAILROAD

Since Charleston had been the prime mover in a lost cause, the collapse of the Confederacy may have tended to cause its citizens to isolate themselves from the rest of the country. The fact that the road was being financed by northern interests and promoted by northern capitalists may have been sufficient reason for Charleston to remain relatively unconcerned about it, and particularly so since it would run into "Yankeedom." It must be borne in mind that southern people, and especially those in Charleston, were still prejudiced against the North, or anything whatsoever sponsored by the North. The very name of the road itself was enough to intensify this feeling. The newspapers, however, had always hoped for the creation of the port, and, naturally, they looked to a through route to the West as the chief means of accomplishing it. At this time (1887), the papers of Charleston took advantage of every opportunity to revive a road to the Ohio but the public interest had undoubtedly waned. As someone has said, "Charleston seemed to enjoy its poverty as its only heritage," and such appears to have been the case. Hence, interest in the "Three C's" centered in the upper part of the state.

About this time, a rumor was circulated that the "Three C's" would take over the Georgia & Carolina Midland Railroad. "Plenty of money is said to be behind the combination, and it is reported here [in Augusta] that the wealthy owners of the South Carolina Railway are the money power."[29]

At a meeting of the stockholders and officials of the Midland company in Columbia on the first of June, a resolution was adopted "that it is for the best interest of every stockholder of this company that this enterprise merge and consolidate with the Charleston, Cincinnati & Chicago Railroad."[30] This meant the establishment of the branch from Blacksburg to Augusta.

It was expected by Charleston that that city would realize great advantages by the consolidation. "As the 'Three C's' will work in harmony with the South Carolina Railroad, there will be no interruptions and hindrances in the shape of broken connections and strangulating schedules," states an editorial in the *News and Courier.* "There will be competition between

[29] *Ibid.,* May 26, 1887.   [30] *Ibid.,* June 2, 1887.

THE "THREE C'S"

Charleston and Savannah for the business of the 'Three C's,' but Charleston can easily secure the first place, particularly when the Union Depot shall be built, and when the expense of handling freight be brought to the lowest notch. For Western business and for the business of the whole line down to Black's,[31] and from Black's via Camden, Charleston has the advantage of position. The whole State will be open to our merchants, and the vast trade of the West, inward and outward, will find here its natural and proper port. The possibilities opened to the view by the 'Three C's' are well nigh incalculable. There is in that line the breath of new life and hope for Charleston, and not at the expense of any other community, or to its injury."[32]

York, South Carolina, favored the general plan of consolidation, but opposed the establishment of Blacksburg as the point of intersection with the main line. It was believed, of course, that York should be the junction. It seemed that the original plan of the line from Union to Blacksburg, about twenty-eight miles, would be over undesirable country, necessitating bridges over both the Pacolet and Broad rivers. It was argued that the road would pass through only two townships which could subscribe only $75,000 at the most. From Union to York, on the other hand, is only fifteen miles, and the line would cross the Broad River at Pinckney's Ferry, a point just below the intersection of the Pacolet and Broad rivers. Bullock's Creek Township, through which this line would pass, had already subscribed $32,000. In addition, such a route, it was claimed, would serve to bring forth a large subscription from York County. It seemed possible that a line could be built from York to Charlotte.

A news dispatch from York, dated June 6, states: "A county subscription cannot be carried without enlisting the sections through which this new link would be run, but with it, county subscriptions would be well nigh assured, and York County would have more than one hundred and fifty miles of railroad in her borders. Then again, Charlotte, N. C., would probably give a liberal subscription for the road. The city is free of debt and might give enough to build the twenty mile gap and not hurt herself. It looks as if Charlotte would be a most desirable terminus for all parties, from Augusta up." The dispatch also

---

[31] That is, Blacksburg. [32] *News and Courier*, June 3, 1887.

stated that about 500 "hands"[33] were at work on the "Three C's" within the county.[34]

Two "large new engines" were delivered to the "Three C's" at Blacksburg the first of July, the weight of which was forty-five tons each. They were named the "Rutherford" and the "Cleveland." In addition, there were also fifteen new freight cars of twenty tons capacity.[35] Today, the Clinchfield owns and operates locomotives weighing 531,000 pounds, and freight cars of a capacity as high as fifty-five tons.[36]

On July 21, the engineers began work on the old Georgia & Carolina Midland between Augusta and Newberry, 68 miles of which had previously been graded for a narrow gauge road.[37] Early in August, surveys were run over the entire line between Augusta and Union, by which, where practicable, the alignment was changed and some grades reduced.[38] Blacksburg was reached on October 4.[39]

A special meeting of the stockholders of the "Three C's" was held in Columbia on the second of August, at which 16,000 shares of a par value of $100 were represented. Resolutions were passed accepting the acts of the legislatures of South Carolina, North Carolina, Virginia, Tennessee, and Kentucky favorable to the road.

The consolidation of the Georgia & Carolina Midland with the "Three C's" was completed. It was decided that this branch should be called the Augusta Division of the road, and all the indebtedness of the Midland would be liquidated at once. "This should convince any who may have been skeptical, that the Charleston, Cincinnati, and Chicago Railroad Company is in earnest; and the people in this section of the country through which the Augusta Division will run are to be congratulated upon having the 'Three C's' take hold of their road."[40]

The company voted to take up and cancel the bonds which had been issued under a mortgage dated October 1, 1886, and new bonds were authorized to be issued to cover the entire line from Charleston to Ashland. It was reported that the counties

---

[33] That is, laborers.   [34] *News and Courier*, June 9, 1887.
[35] *Ibid.*, July 2, 1887.
[36] From data furnished by the mechanical engineer, Clinchfield Railroad Company, Erwin, Tennessee, Nov., 1928.
[37] *News and Courier*, July 22, 1887.   [38] *Ibid.*, Aug. 3, 1887.
[39] *Ibid.*, Oct. 7, 1887.   [40] *Ibid.*, Aug. 3, 1887.

and towns through which the road ran had voted aid to the amount of about one and a half million dollars. This was payable in their six and seven per cent bonds in exchange for an equal amount of stock.[41]

During the middle of August, laying of the rails began at Camden. It was expected to open the road as far as Lancaster by October, and, according to the *Edgefield Examiner*, "from that time on heavy freight trains will arrive in Charleston every day from the line of the 'Three C's'."[42] It would indeed be an interesting problem for some one to ascertain from whence the tonnage would be derived for these "heavy freight trains." Regardless of where these trains would be made up, the roadbed and trestles had been completed through to Lancaster. A representative of the *News and Courier* made a trip over the line, presumably by horseback, and in his report he stated that the bridges "look like they will last forever. The timbers are very massive and finely put together."[43]

"Quite a heated meeting" of about seventy business men was held in Camden on September 16 to confer about the action of the county commissioners in regard to the bonds subscribed to the road. The people of Camden were not willing to put the bonds on deposit with the Boston Safe & Deposit Company, trustee, until construction had been completed.

According to the contract, $25,000 of the bonds would be issued and delivered when the roadbed was completed and ready for the rails from the Sumter County line to Camden; $50,000 more of the bonds were to be issued and delivered when the roadbed was completed and ready for the rails from Camden northward ten miles, and the remaining bonds in similar installments. Hence, the people thought they were to issue the bonds in installments as portions of the road were finished. It was claimed that the main object of the subscription was concerning the line from Sumter, no work on which had been done, for then Camden would benefit from the competition between the "Three C's" and the South Carolina Railroad.

This called for an explanatory speech from Mr. P. H. Nelson in behalf of the railroad company. He said that it was difficult to impress upon the people that the "Three C's" company did

---

[41] *Commercial and Financial Chronicle,* Vol. XLVI (March 31, 1888).
[42] *News and Courier,* Aug. 22, 1887.   [43] *Ibid.,* Aug. 26, 1887.

not want the bonds, but wanted them deposited subject to the order of the commissioners of Kershaw County, and to be delivered when the contract was complied with, so that better loans could be effected by using these bonds as collateral. He further showed the absurdity of insisting on the road's being built to the Sumter County line, for the company could not be forced to go further. If they stopped there, and even if trains were occasionally run to the county line, this would be of no benefit to Camden in any way.

After considerable discussion and further explanation, a motion was passed to issue the bonds and place them on deposit with the Boston Safe & Deposit Company. Another resolution was passed that Camden was not opposed to the road, and the township appreciated the benefit it would realize from the road.[44]

"Track laying has commenced in earnest on the Charleston, Cincinnati, and Chicago Railroad," says an interesting dispatch from Camden entitled "From the Sea to the Lakes." "A machine is used which is a great help in track laying. The ties and iron are carried out in advance of the cars loaded with the track laying material, and it is there met by hands, who lay the ties in proper position at the measured distances apart, and the iron is spiked down and jointed by another crowd. The ties are carried out on rollers that are kept in motion by a stationary engine on the forward flat car. The rollers suspended by wire ropes reach out several yards ahead of the car, and can receive the ties placed on the rollers by hand, seven or eight car-lengths in the rear, or as far as there are sections to reach."[45]

At a meeting of the stockholders in Charleston on October 13, the following gentlemen were chosen directors: Frank Coxe, of Philadelphia, Pennsylvania; Henry K. Baker, and William F. Calender, of Springfield, Massachusetts; J. T. Wilder, of Chattanooga, Tennessee; P. P. Dickinson and D. N. Coats of New York, New York; E. S. Brewer, of Hartford, Connecticut; Peter J. Sinclair, of Marion, and H. D. Lee, of Shelby, North Carolina; and Richard Dozier, of Georgetown, M. C. Butler, of Edgefield, and James D. Blanding, of Sumter, South Carolina. Colonel Frank Coxe was reëlected president.

[44] *Ibid.,* Sept. 19, 1887.
[45] *Ibid.,* Oct. 7, 1887.

THE "THREE C'S" 69

The general manager of the road, Colonel Johnson, reported that an agreement had been entered into with the Western North Carolina Railroad for trackage rights between Marion and Asheville. The line from Camden to Marion was expected to be opened by June, 1888. This meant that the "Three C's" would compete with the road via Spartanburg for the trade of western North Carolina. Colonel Johnson stated that through trains would be operated from Charleston to Asheville as soon as his road was opened for traffic. He also reported that the company wished to reach Charleston "on its own merits," and not be dependent upon either the South Carolina Railroad from Camden or the Atlantic Coast Line from Sumter for its connections with the city.[46]

According to a report in the *Rock Hill Herald*, Colonel T. E. Mattson, chief engineer of the road, returned to Rock Hill during the first part of December from an inspection trip in Kentucky. He was reported to have accepted sixty miles of newly constructed road southward from Ashland to White House, Kentucky.[47] However, only eight miles were placed in operation, extending from Richardson to White House.[48]

Colonel Mattson went over the line from White House to the "breaks" of the Big Sandy River in the Cumberland Mountains, about sixty miles, which is approximately the present route of the Chesapeake & Ohio Railway from Ashland to Elkhorn City. Here he met Captain W. J. Johnston's corps of engineers who were locating the final line to Johnson City.[49]

By the end of March, all the preliminary surveys had been completed northward to Marion. Seven corps of engineers were placed at work making a location for the line across the Blue Ridge to Johnson City.[50] Funds with which to construct this important link were raised in England by General Wilder through the London banking firm of Baring Brothers.[51]

The road was completed northward from Camden to Rock Hill during the middle of August, 1888, and the first regular

---

[46] *Ibid.*, Oct. 14, 1887.   [47] *Ibid.*, Dec. 12, 1887.
[48] "Investors' Supplement," *Commercial and Financial Chronicle*, Vol. XLIX (July, 1889).
[49] *News and Courier*, Dec. 12, 1887.
[50] *Commercial and Financial Chronicle*, Vol. XLVI (March 31, 1888).
[51] From an unpublished manuscript by O. K. Morgan, "The Story of the Clinchfield," p. 2.

passenger train was operated the twentieth of the month. Plans were immediately made for an excursion from Charleston.[52]

THE OPENING OF THE ROAD TO ROCK HILL

The newspaper stories of the excursion to Rock Hill are indeed interesting and enlightening. The account of the excursion published in the columns of the *News and Courier* of August 23, 1888, is cited herewith:

The all-important excursion of the business men and merchants of Charleston to Rock Hill will leave here at 7 o'clock this morning (August 23) from the Line Street Depot, South Carolina Railway. The excursion will mark the opening of the Charleston, Cincinnati and Chicago Railroad to Rock Hill and is one of the most interesting and important affairs of the kind ever gotten up in the railroad history of the State, being intended to bring the business men of Charleston into closer relations commercially and socially with the people of the hills of York.

The following is a partial list of the excursionists who will go from Charleston:

Cotton Exchange—A. W. Taft, E. C. Williams, Jr., J. M. Seignious, W. J. McCormack; Merchants' Exchange—J. A. Enslow, C. G. Matthews, Geo. Bell, J. P. O'Neill; Chamber of Commerce—T. R. McGahan, Wm. S. Hastie, T. Pinckney Lowndes; Builders' and Dealers' Exchange—Geo. Egan, D. A. J. Sullivan, J. D. Murphy; East Bay Merchants—W. M. Bird, Henry Bayer, H. F. Bremer, Wm. Johnson, A. McCobb, Jr., C. Wulbern; Meeting and Hayne St. Merchants—H. R. Simons, T. A. Wilbur, J. J. Westcoat, C. M. Drake, T. R. McGahan, R. C. Barkeley, F. Panknin, N. A. Hunt; Bankers, Insurance Agts., Publishers, Merchants, Lawyers—H. A. M. Smith, W. S. Hastie, W. A. Courtenay, C. L. Walter, T. P. Mood, O. E. Johnson, M. Israel, R. M. Sims, Joseph Bock; S. B. Pickens, general freight agent and passenger agent South Carolina Railway, and the Hon. George D. Bryan, Mayor of Charleston, E. I. Waring, general claim agent South Carolina Railway, S. E. Welch, A. F. C. Cramer, Frank E. Taylor. Delegations of five merchants each will be taken on at Camden and Lancaster.

As the Three C's Road when completed will constitute the shortest route from the Ohio River to the South Atlantic Seaboard, connecting the various railroad systems of the west with the railroad systems of the South, it will be seen at once that it is destined to be the

---

[52] *News and Courier*, Aug. 21, 1888.

great highway of passenger and merchandise traffic to and from the west, for which Charleston has so long been working and waiting. The route to Rock Hill is an interesting and for the most part new one and the trip, apart from its pleasant social features will embody much of practical interest and value to every true business man, having the future prosperity of Charleston at heart.

Col J. H. Averill, Superintendent of the South Carolina Railway, will personally supervise the excursion, and Capt. W. A. Bradley will act as conductor of the train, which will be a "special," composed of the monarch palace cars of the Charleston, Cincinnati & Chicago Railroad. The excursion train will leave at 7 o'clock on the first section of Train 53, better known as the "Greenville Express." The first stop will be made at Summerville to take on the invited guests who are living there. A short run will then bring the excursionists to Pregnall's, the junction of the Eutawville Railroad, which is fast stretching out towards Sumter to reclaim for Charleston the valuable business of that section. No stop will be made at Branchville, soon after passing which place the train will go through the great cotton belt of Orangeburg County, presenting for the inspection of the excursionists, the finest cotton crop that this section has known in years.

At the Congaree River will be seen the work on the new draw span, which the South Carolina Railway is now engaged in building, in order to open the upper waters of the river to navigation by the boats of the Charleston Steamboat Company. After passing the Wateree Swamps the train will enter the great cotton belt of Sumter and Kershaw counties, affording, as it passes, a picturesque view of the Santee Hills in the distance.

At Camden a stop of five minutes will be made to take on the delegation of merchants from that city, and the train will then enter upon the beginning of the Three C's Railroad, which is fast piercing the way from Charleston to the great West.

From Camden to DeKalb, a distance of ten miles, the road passes through pine forests and sand hills. Westville, fifteen and a half miles distant from Camden, is the first station of any importance reached. While showing up very small at present, the town has been regularly laid off, lots have been sold and contracts are now out for over twenty houses and stores soon to be built there.

At Kershaw, six and a half miles distant, the Lancaster line is reached. This station has been named in honor of Judge Kershaw, and it is expected will be the largest business center on the line from Camden to Lancaster. This town has also been regularly laid off.

Many lots have been sold and before the year is out it will show up from twenty-five to thirty buildings. It lies in the center of one of the finest lumber districts in the State.

Three and one half miles from it are the Haile Gold Mines and the rich lands of Lynch's Creek. These lands which heretofore have given much of their cotton and produce to Cheraw and other points, whence it was carried to Wilmington and the north, have all been made tributary to Charleston by the Three C's Road. Stick a pin in this, business men of Charleston, and representatives of the Cotton Exchange, and see to it that your buyers are there this season.

Oakhurst, four miles and a half distant, lies at the entrance to one of the greatest cotton growing districts in the State. From this point to Rock Hill, the excursionist will scarcely lose sight of a cotton field, and as acre after acre of the staple plant is unfolded to his view will realize the truth of the old saying that "Cotton is King." A building boom has also been started at Oakhurst and it is expected that a fine town will soon stand there.

A run of two miles and a half takes the party past Salem Church and the Mineral Spring. The latter has considerable reputation among the people of the neighboring county and is quite a resort for picnic parties. Its owner, Mr. Heath, resides at Munro, N. C., and talks of improving the property and laying out a town at this place. If his ideas are carried out, the place will be brought into repute and will doubtless in time become a very popular resort. Pleasant Hill marks the location of another town and station three-quarters of a mile further along the line. It now exists in name only, but is destined to become a town of considerable importance, as it will draw business largely from the section of the country lying around it and Munro, N. C. At a distance of six miles is St. Luke's. It is at present only a flag station, but its business is developing so fast that it is expected that a side track and depot will have to be placed there.

A run of four miles carries the train into the town of Lancaster. It is said that the hospitable people of Lancaster feel somewhat slighted at not having been given an opportunity to entertain a delegation from Charleston. It is therefore hoped that the management can see their way clear to allow the excursionists a chance to stop over at Lancaster on their return from Rock Hill. Lancaster is well worthy the attention of Charleston's business men. It is a distributing point for from 12,000 to 15,000 bales of cotton each year and the centre of a large trade with the surrounding country as far up as Munro. It is besides the terminus of the Cheraw & Chester narrow gauge road, running from Chester to Lancaster. The grading has been carried some distance beyond Lancaster and at the last meeting of the stockholders a resolution was passed urging the Richmond & Danville people to complete the line.

Leaving Lancaster the train soon enters what is known as the Waxhaws. This is the section of country lying in proximity to the Catawba River up among the high lands, and reputed to be the most productive cotton lands in the State. There will be two railroad stations between Lancaster and the Catawba River, one at Riverside, six miles from Lancaster, and the other at Springdell, a mile and a half from Catawba River. Springdell is situated about two miles from the Georgia, Carolina and Northern Railway now under construction from Munro to Chester. The latter point will be reached about the 15th of September, when Springdell will be a competing point for the cotton lying between the two roads. Charleston's cotton merchants are advised also to make special note of Springdell, as it will be the competing point for about two thousand bales of cotton, which should properly come to Charleston.

Crossing the Catawba River at an elevation of seventy-five feet above low water, the excursionists are afforded a fine view of the iron bridge of the Georgia, Carolina and Northern Railroad, two miles above. Three miles from the river the Three C's road crosses the line of the Georgia, Carolina and Northern Railroad. A junction will be built at this point, and it is authoritatively stated here that the management of both roads will offer every facility for Charleston to secure her full share of the business from this point to Munro. This will also open a new route from Charleston to Charlotte, N. C., with a difference of only five miles as compared with the present route. It is understood that the management of the Georgia, Carolina and Northern Railroad are working in harmony and in connection with the Three C's road.

Rock Hill, which is the destination of the excursion party, lies eight miles beyond the junction and the road to it is made through another magnificent stretch of cotton fields. No attempt is made here to describe this thriving little city, as the excursionists will have ample opportunity to see and judge of it for themselves. Such of the excursionists as are visiting the city for the first time will be struck with its size and importance, while those who are returning after an absence of some little time will be surprised at the rapid march of improvement and the many handsome buildings now to be seen there.

The excursionists will arrive at Rock Hill at 1:45 this afternoon, when they will be taken in charge by a committee of the citizens and entertained at a dinner to be given in their honor. Speech making will follow and such an exchange of convivialities as will indissolubly unite the two cities with the golden links of friendship and commerce. The excursionists will remain in Rock Hill until 11 o'clock tomorrow morning, when they will leave for Charleston.[53]

Commenting upon the success of the excursion, the *News and Courier* says:

The Charleston excursionists returned from Rock Hill at half-past two o'clock yesterday afternoon (August 24), deeply impressed by all that they had seen on their trip over the "Three C's" Road and enthusiastic at the matter of their reception and entertainment by the good citizens of Rock Hill.

Nothing could have been more complete than the arrangements for the entertainment of the visitors. Shortly after one o'clock the committee repaired to the depot with carriages to meet the excursionists, who, upon their arrival, were welcomed to the city by Mayor A. E. Smith with a few pertinent remarks delivered in the presence of the assembled citizens. The visitors were then escorted to the Carolina Hotel, where they were entertained at the expense of the committee. The freedom of the city was extended to the visitors, vehicles being stationed at the hotel under the direction of the committee and at the pleasure of the visitors during the afternoon.

In the evening, the excursionists were tendered a grand reception at Roddey's Hall. The interior of this beautiful building had been appropriately decorated beforehand with tri-colored bunting and all other evidences of the artistic touch of Rock Hill's many fair ladies. The entertainment was a fitting sequel to the unbounded hospitality of the day, and in all respects worthy of the free-hearted and patriotic people of this beautiful and progressive little city.

On Thursday night after the reception at Roddey's Hall, the enthusiasm amounted to an ovation. The crowd gathered in front of the Carolina Hotel, and would not be satisfied until two of the party, Messrs. W. J. McCormack and A. E. Gonzales, both of whom were known to have fine voices, had been heard in song. The latter was also called upon for a repetition of the sermon of "Rebbren Kinlaw," of Gullah dialect fame. Another Charlestonian well known for his humor and ready wit so carried the town by storm that it is said he was tendered the presidency of the fire department as an inducement to reside permanently in Rock Hill.

Yesterday morning the excursionists were escorted to the depot in carriages, and at eight o'clock started for home. The representatives from Lancaster and Camden accompanied the party down as far as

---

[53] *News and Courier*, Aug. 23, 1888.

their respective destinations, where they disembarked amid the cheers of those on board the train. When in the neighborhood of Fort Motte, a tempting lunch was served by Colonel Averill, at the conclusion of which the party organized themselves into a meeting, with Mr. T. A. Wilbur as chairman and Mr. W. S. Hastie as secretary. The following resolutions of thanks and appreciation were then proposed by Mr. T. P. Lowndes, and were unanimously adopted and ordered to be published:

"*Be it resolved,* That the delegates from the several commercial associations and the representatives of other business interests of Charleston tender their sincere thanks to Superintendent Averill and to the officers of the South Carolina Railroad and the Charleston, Cincinnati, and Chicago Railroad for the kindness and courtesy extended to them on the occasion of the opening of the latter road to Rock Hill, S. C., connecting that thriving and important town with the City of Charleston.

"And be it further resolved, That the representatives from Charleston hereby express their warm appreciation of the whole-souled hospitalities extended by the citizens of Rock Hill, and above and beyond all other considerations for their kindly words and the assurances of their desire for closer and more intimate business relations with the people of their metropolis."

It was believed that the opening of the road would bring a great deal of business to Charleston, and also develop the territory through which it passed. In speaking of the service which the road would render to the public, Superintendent Averill said:[54]

For Rock Hill, I can promise that the train schedules will always be so arranged that the people on the Lancaster line from Lancaster to Yorkville can have the option of trading at Lancaster, Rock Hill, or Yorkville; they can go into either of these places from eight to ten o'clock A.M., do their trading and return to their homes from two to six o'clock P.M.; that you can leave your homes at a reasonable hour in the morning, go direct to Columbia, spend four to six hours, and return the same evening, reaching home by or before ten o'clock P.M.; that when you want to visit Charleston, you can leave here at 2:15 P.M., you are swiftly carried the 207 miles, and at 9:10 P.M. are in the City by the Sea. You spend the next day with your Charleston friends, purchasing your goods. They are shipped to the depot that evening. The fast freight starts with them at 8 P.M. Camden and Lancaster are passed; their freight is left on sidings to be unloaded when

---

[54] *Ibid.,* Aug. 25, 1888.

day comes, and at 9 A.M., when you, having left Charleston at 7 A.M., are two hours out on your return trip, your freight is at your doors awaiting delivery, thirteen hours from Charleston. You give us your cotton today for the east or export via Charleston. We load it this afternoon; the through train leaves here at 6 P.M.; and at 7 A.M. it is in our Charleston yard, and your cotton is soon at the water front ready for shipment. Can our friends of the Richmond and Danville (Railroad) do better than this? I think not, and all we ask is a fair trial, and we think we can guarantee satisfaction."

And in such a manner was the Southern division of the Charleston, Cincinnati & Chicago Railroad opened to traffic.

CHAPTER VI

FURTHER DEVELOPMENT OF THE "THREE C'S"

THE INTERVENING link of the "Three C's" between Rock Hill and Blacksburg, via York, was completed during the early part of December, 1888,[1] and was placed in operation early in January, 1889.[2] This meant a completed line of 147 miles from Rutherfordton, North Carolina, to Camden, South Carolina; and in connection with the South Carolina Railroad at the latter point, 290 miles of railroad to Charleston.[3] No through trains were operated over the entire line. However, connections were maintained whereby the traveler could leave Rutherfordton at 9:30 A.M., and arrive in Charleston at 9:10 P.M.; returning, he would leave Charleston at 7 A.M., and reach Rutherfordton at 7:30 P.M.[4]

During the latter part of the year (1888), the "very handsome and substantial" passenger station was completed at Shelby. "In architectural design and in all its apportionments, it is equal to anything in the South. It is a marvel of neatness and beauty."[5]

A new locomotive was delivered to the company at Camden on January 12. "The new monster engine of the 'Three C's' is worth looking at," says a news dispatch from that town. "The boiler is placed high on six drivers, four and one half feet in diameter, each one being controlled by a steam brake. The cylinders are 24 by 19 inches. The weight of the enormous machine is sixty tons. The fuel used is *coal*, the fire boxes being eight feet long and about five feet in height and width."[6] Although the present day rolling stock of the Clinchfield is discussed in a subsequent chapter, it is interesting to make a comparison of this "monster" with one used at the present time. In all probability, this engine was intended for freight service. The smallest freight locomotive on the Clinchfield is the "Con-

---

[1] *News and Courier*, Jan. 1, 1889.   [2] *Ibid.*, Jan. 8, 1889.
[3] "Investors' Supplement," *Commercial and Financial Chronicle*, Vol. XLIX (July, 1889).
[4] *News and Courier*, Jan. 8, 1889.   [5] *Ibid.*, Jan. 3, 1889.
[6] *Ibid.*, Jan. 15, 1889.

solidation" type of eight drive wheels of 51 inches diameter, with a total weight of 175,000 pounds. Two such engines are now in service.[7]

An editorial in the *Rutherford Banner* stated that Rutherfordton was anticipating commercial relations with Charleston, and pointed out that in ante-bellum days, Charleston was the market, "in fact the only market of this up-country. It is within the recollection of many that nine-tenths of the goods sold here were bought in Charleston and hauled from there in wagons. There is no reason why this intercourse should not be re-established, and we believe the City by the Sea[8] will realize the importance of the matter and do its duty. . . . The importance to our people of the completion of the 'Three C's' did not fully dawn upon us until the *News and Courier* of Monday morning was laid upon our table, bright and fresh, at eight o'clock the same evening," continued the editorial. "Then we began fully to appreciate the opening of this great line."[9]

Rutherfordton, at this time, was not only the northern terminus of the "Three C's," but also the western terminus of the Carolina Central, the latter having been completed in 1886. Located at the foot of the mountains, it had, since early in the nineteenth century, established itself as the distributing point for a large section of country. Wagon trains moved to and from the mountain fastnesses of the Blue Ridge. The immediate environment of the town was rich in agricultural products, timber, and, to a less extent, mineral resources. The agricultural products were varied and abundant. The sorghum industry was an extensive and profitable one, several varieties of cane being cultivated in the county. "Rutherford County Syrup" became famous as far west as Louisville and Cincinnati, while thousands of gallons were shipped annually into eastern North and South Carolina.

Like most of the earlier settlements in the Carolinas prior to the Civil War, Rutherfordton was an aristocratic town, the center of wealth and refinement. Most of her people were farmers and slave owners, and, of course, suffered greatly from the war.

---

[7] From data furnished by the mechanical engineer, Clinchfield Railroad Company, Erwin, Tennessee, Nov., 1928.

[8] That is, Charleston.

[9] As reprinted in the *News and Courier*, Jan. 8, 1889.

FURTHER DEVELOPMENT 79

By 1870 the county was virtually bankrupt. Unused to toil and lacking in transportation facilities, except the cross-country wagon caravans, the people hailed as the beginning of a new era the completion of the Carolina Central from Wilmington, and shortly afterwards, the "Three C's." The town boomed. Wagons from the rich back country brought produce for distribution to various railroad points. The lumber industry grew by leaps and bounds, and vast quantities of high-grade timber were manufactured by the local saw mills for shipment over the railroads.[10]

An excursion was arranged by the "Three C's" from Rutherfordton and Shelby to Charleston. Although Charleston had been in direct rail communication with these towns since the first of the year, there had been no formal meeting of the people residing at the two ends of the road. The party reached Charleston on the evening of February 27, 1889, and were "hospitably entertained" by the several "Commercial Exchanges" of the city. At a dinner given in honor of the visitors, Captain Frederick W. Wagener, chairman of the committee on trade and transportation, delivered the address of welcome. His speech was reported as being "eloquent and suggestive, and was greeted by a great deal of applause."[11]

The question arose regarding the validity of the township bonds issued at various points in South Carolina as an aid in the construction of the road. In a test case brought before the supreme court of South Carolina in April, it was held that these bonds were valid and were entitled to the same legal status as county bonds.[12]

Meanwhile, plans to push the "Three C's" westward continued. Kierman's News Agency reported in the *Commercial and Financial Chronicle* that a contract had been signed by the railroad company for the construction of 250 miles of line from Rutherfordton to "the new town of Minneapolis, in southwest Virginia, at the crossing of the Clinch River." Here, the road would connect with the Norfolk & Western Railway, and "probably with a proposed eastern extension of the Louisville & Nashville, which is to come through Big Stone Gap."[13] The contract,

---
[10] *Ibid.*, Feb. 6, 1889.   [11] *Ibid.*, March 1, 1889.
[12] *Commercial and Financial Chronicle*, Vol. XLVIII (April 20, 1889).
[13] *Ibid.*, XLVIII (Feb. 16, 1889).

involving about two and a half million dollars, was awarded on February 13, 1889, through the Massachusetts & Southern Construction Company, to McDonald, Shea & Company,[14] "the well known railroad builders of Knoxville, Tennessee."[15]

General Thomas L. Rosser was reported to have said in New York City that he had seen signatures affixed "to a construction contract which means a new trunk line across the American Continent, and a new trans-Atlantic route for freight and passengers. It means also the development by civilization of the birthright of the Cherokee Nation, the last and richest corner of this great land of ours, to yield its treasures to the locomotive and the forge.

"Have you ever noticed that the great American trunk lines run from northeast to southwest through the richest portion of the country?" continued General Rosser.

To the north, the country is crossed more evenly by the New York Central and Pennsylvania systems, but their general trend is from the northeast to the southwest. The Baltimore and Ohio, the Chesapeake and Ohio, the Norfolk and Western, and the Richmond and Danville systems take their course southwest from the Atlantic coast. Hence, parallelism and competition. But why not have a trunk line cutting across all these and running from the southeast Atlantic Coast across the new mineral regions of the south, which is the mineral depot of the world, to the great northwest, the grain depot of the world? This has become a practically accomplished fact by the award yesterday of the two and a half million dollar construction contract by the Charleston, Cincinnati and Chicago Railroad.

Take a map and see how uniformly the great railroads run to the Southwest from the Atlantic Seaboard. Now look at Charleston, S. C., and take a bird's-eye view of the new railroad route from that southeastern port straight up to the Northwest, through Western North Carolina, Eastern Tennessee, Southwestern Virginia, and Eastern Kentucky to the great grain regions of the Northwest. The Charleston, Cincinnati and Chicago Road proposes to run from Ashland, Ky., to Charleston, and the Massachusetts and Southern Construction Company are to build it through so far. From Camden to Charleston it uses the lines of the South Carolina Railway, which it will eventually buy.

---

[14] *News and Courier*, Feb. 15, 1889.
[15] *Commercial and Financial Chronicle*, Vol. XLVIII (Feb. 16. 1889).

FURTHER DEVELOPMENT

The connections with New York are made indirectly by cutting the great trunk line systems with which traffic arrangements are and are to be made, and directly by the Old Dominion and Bay lines of Steamers and the Seaboard Railroad system, which connects directly with the Charleston, Cincinnati and Chicago Railroad at Catawba Junction. The Bay Line also gives direct connection with Baltimore and Philadelphia.

There is a romantic interest attaching to the wonderful mineral country which will be tapped now for the first time. It is the heritage of the Cherokee Nation and the story is that unprincipled white men bought it from the Cherokees for a consideration of pots, pans and kettles. So ignorant were the Cherokees of what they were selling, and so artful were the whites, that the latter took from the side of one hill enough iron to make all the pots, pans and kettles mentioned in the deed, and of such purity that the ore itself was beaten into the required utensils without putting fire to it. I know it to be a fact that at Wilder's forge, in that country, Gen. Wilder takes out ore so pure that it requires no treatment. The Indians undoubtedly used to make their horse shoes out of the ore. The hard woods now found in that country are walnut, cherry, ash, white oak, black walnut, red oak, white pine and poplar. Some of the poplar logs are from four to six feet in diameter.[16]

During the latter part of August, ninety-two of the three-thousand-dollar bonds of the Massachusetts & Southern Construction Company were purchased by the Boston Safe & Deposit Company for redemption at 103 and interest, or $3,119 per bond.[17]

In September the railroad company issued $6,000,000 fifty-year five per cent bonds to provide for the construction of the line to Minneapolis. These were sold to a New York and Philadelphia syndicate, headed by Wharton Barker, of Barker Brothers & Company, of Philadelphia.[18]

In June, 1890, the Massachusetts & Southern Construction Company brought suit against various townships in York and Lancaster counties, in the United States Circuit Court at Charleston, for failure to deliver the bonds which were issued to the road. By the terms of the contract between the "Three

---

[16] *News and Courier*, Feb 15, 1889.
[17] *Commercial and Financial Chronicle*, Vol. XLIX (Aug. 31, 1889).
[18] *Ibid.*, Vol. XLIX (Sept. 28, 1889).

C's" and the construction company, the latter was to build the railroad and take the bonds issued by the townships as part payment. When the road was completed, the townships in York and Lancaster counties refused to deliver the bonds, amounting to about $277,000. The company brought the case before the supreme court of South Carolina, the decree of which was in favor of the company. The townships still refusing to deliver the bonds, suit was brought in Federal court. This court held that the bonds were a valid obligation against the townships, and the Boston Trust Company, who held the bonds as trustee, was ordered to make immediate delivery to the construction company.[19]

The grading of the line between Johnson City and Minneapolis was completed during the summer of 1890. However, it appeared that no ties were available, and hence the rails could not be laid. About the same time, the *Railroad Gazette* reported that a contract had been let for the construction of the branch from Blacksburg to Newberry, South Carolina. About a thousand men were at work, and it was expected to be completed by July, 1891. Final locations of the line had also been made through to Ashland.[20] The road between Rutherfordton and Marion was opened to traffic in November. By April of the following year, it was expected that the 125 miles across the mountains to Johnson City would be completed, "and less than $500,000 remains to be expended to finish it."[21]

At the close of the year 1890, the series of financial reverses began to set in which finally resulted in a foreclosure sale in 1893. Early in December, 1890, Barker Brothers & Company failed. Since this firm had been furnishing funds for the construction of the line to Minneapolis, work necessarily had to be stopped. On December 8, Samuel Tate, of Memphis, Tennessee, was said to have been appointed receiver; but the Massachusetts & Southern Construction Company claimed that this report was without foundation. It was reported at the offices of the road in New York City that there was little owing outside of the bonded indebtedness.[22]

A few days later, the United States Circuit court at Charleston granted an injunction restraining all suits against the road,

---

[19] *Ibid.*, Vol. L (June 28, 1890).   [20] *Ibid.*, Vol. LI (July 26, 1890).
[21] *Ibid.*, Vol. LI (Nov. 15, 1890).   [22] *Ibid.*, Vol. LI (Dec. 13, 1890).

and appointed Samuel Lord, of Charleston, temporary receiver. The petition and complaint was filed by Barker Brothers & Company. The contractors had begun proceedings in the state courts of Tennessee to sell the graded roadbed in that state, "thereby dismembering the road and greatly impairing its value as security to its bondholders." It was reported that efforts were being made by the railroad company to complete the road and place it in operation, and thereby avoid the appointment of a permanent receiver.[23] By the end of February, however, receivers had been appointed, as follows: A. B. Harris, for the portions of the road in Kentucky and Virginia; Samuel Tate, for the Tennessee portion; and D. H. Chamberlain for the North and South Carolina portions.[24]

The bondholders agreed upon a plan of reorganization under which they relinquished their first lien on the property for $8,300,000, and admitted a new mortgage for $4,500,000 to be placed ahead of their bonds. The proceeds of this loan were to be used in completing gaps in the line in North Carolina and Tennessee, for new equipment, and for discharging contractors' liens.[25]

The reorganization, as agreed upon, authorized two series of bonds. The first series of ten-year bonds were to be issued at the rate of $12,000 per mile, but not to exceed $4,500,000, at six per cent. These bonds were redeemable in five years, at the option of the company, at 103 and accrued interest. Only $2,500,000 would be issued immediately. These would be used as follows: $780,000 for completing the road; $561,000 for paying for old and purchasing new equipment; $95,000 for the floating debt; and the balance of $1,064,000 for interest during construction and other contingencies.

The second series bonds would be consolidated 5s, issued at the rate of $35,000 per mile, and aggregating about $13,000,000. Of these, $7,345,000 would be used to exchange for the $6,000,000 in bonds which were then outstanding, bond for bond, and with sufficient reserve to retire the first series, upon the cancellation of which the consolidated 5s would become the first lien.

---

[23] *News and Courier*, Dec. 13, 1890.
[24] *Commercial and Financial Chronicle*, Vol. LII (Feb. 28, 1891).
[25] *Ibid.*, Vol. LII (May 23, 1891).

The remaining $2,000,000 of the first series could be issued only with the consent of a majority of the holders of the second series, and for the purpose of completing 71 miles of new road. These first series bonds would be a first and prior lien on the whole property. Under this plan, arrangements were made for funds with which to complete the road at once, and put it in operation.[26] John Goldthwait, of Boston, was elected chairman of the reorganization committee on July 28. A. B. Harris, of New York City, was named secretary.[27]

On June 4, Judge Bond, of the United States Circuit court at Charleston, signed a decree authorizing D. H. Chamberlain, receiver for the road, to purchase all of its equipment—consisting of 13 locomotives, 15 coaches, and 286 freight cars—for $221,514, the amount due the Massachusetts & Southern Construction Company on the original purchase. "The claims for this amount are held by certain banks and other parties, payment to be made in receivers' certificates at six per cent, maturing in two years."[28] Chamberlain was ordered by Judge Simonton, of the United States Court in Greenville, South Carolina, to issue these certificates to the amount of $230,897.[29]

In February, 1892, McDonald, Shea & Company, and William Kenefick, railroad contractors, brought suit against the "Three C's" in Jonesboro, Tennessee, for the amount due for construction work, with the result that a sale of the road within Tennessee was ordered.[30] The seventy-five miles within the state were sold at Johnson City on May 12 to Samuel Hunt, for the reorganization committee, for $200,000. McDonald, Shea & Company had a debt against the road amounting to $450,000; and Kenefick, $140,000.[31] The sale was confirmed by the Tennessee courts, thereby giving the bondholders control of the property. "There are no obstacles now to the reorganization of the company," says the *Commercial and Financial Chronicle*, "and the pushing forward to completion of the links of the road necessary to complete the line."[32]

Upon the death of A. B. Harris in March, Judge Jackson, of the United States District court in Nashville, appointed H. N. Taylor, of Knoxville, receiver to succeed Harris.[33]

---

[26] *Ibid.*, Vol. LII (June 27, 1891).
[28] *Ibid.*, Vol. LII (June 6, 1891).
[30] *Ibid.*, Vol. LIV (Feb. 18, 1892).
[32] *Ibid.*, Vol. LV (July 2, 1892).
[27] *Ibid.*, Vol. LIII (Aug. 1, 1891).
[29] *Ibid.*, Vol. LIII (Aug. 8, 1891).
[31] *Ibid.*, Vol LIV (May 14, 1892).
[33] *Ibid.*, Vol. LIV (March 19, 1892).

FURTHER DEVELOPMENT 85

Receiver Chamberlain reported to the United States Circuit Court at Charleston that the gross earnings of the road from March 15, 1891, to March 31, 1892, had been $170,245, an increase of $20,058 over the preceding year. Operating expenses were $185,342, or a deficit of $15,096; while during the preceding year, operating expenses had been $183,216, or a deficit of $33,028.[34]

At a meeting of the bondholders during the middle of July, a new reorganization plan was adopted. The $7,345,000 first mortgage bonds which were then outstanding would be retired, and new first mortgage five per cent bonds amounting to $8,925,000 would be issued. The new bonds would cover the entire line from Sumter, South Carolina, to Ashland, Kentucky, at the rate of $17,500 per mile. The proceeds of the new bonds would be used in the following manner: $6,000,000 to complete the line; $500,000 for rolling stock; $600,000 for interest during construction; $300,000 to take up receivers' certificates; and the balance to settle claims.

Second mortgage bonds would be issued at the rate of $10,000 a mile to take up the outstanding $7,345,000 first mortgage bonds and back coupons for two years. New preferred and common stock would be issued. For each $1,000 of the outstanding bonds, the holder would be given $550 in the new second mortgage bonds, $500 in the new common stock, and $450 in the new preferred stock. Coupons would be treated in the same manner. The outstanding stock, amounting to $25,000 a mile, would be surrendered for the new, four to one.[35]

This plan was later amended to extend the road to Richardson, Kentucky, and to acquire, if possible, by lease or otherwise, the Big Sandy Division of the Chesapeake & Ohio Railway from Richardson to Ashland; and make a traffic agreement with the Atlantic Coast Line or the South Carolina Railroad from Sumter to Charleston.[36] The five per cent first mortgage bonds were changed to six per cent forty-year first mortgage gold bonds. To retire the old bonds with interest, it was authorized to issue $4,462,000 of second mortgage bonds, series "A," on the whole line, and $4,462,500 of series "B." No interest was payable on series "A" for the first two years, at which time it would be

---

[34] *Ibid.*, Vol. LIV (June 11, 1892).   [35] *Ibid.*, Vol. LV (July 23, 1892).

[36] The South Carolina Railroad had built a branch into Sumter from a point on its Camden line near Kingsville.

scaled up annually from one to five per cent, one per cent each year. There would be five per cent interest on series "B" only if earned above all prior charges during the first ten years, and thereafter it became obligatory. The old bondholders would exchange each $1000 bond for $500 of series "A," $500 series "B," and $700 in new stock.[37]

A "panic" was created in the railroad company when the English banking firm of Baring Brothers became insolvent. It will be remembered that this firm had become interested in the road in 1888, at which time it underwrote funds for the construction of the line across the Blue Ridge as a result of General Wilder's visit to London. Hence, when it failed, all construction ceased. "The project fell, and carried to financial ruin many of those interested. General Wilder told the writer it cost him personally $750,000," writes O. K. Morgan.[38]

In March, 1893, a decree ordering the sale of the "Three C's" was filed in the United States Circuit court in Charleston. The minimum price was fixed at $550,000.[39] It was sold at auction on May 2 for that amount to Charles E. Hellier, of Boston, representing the bondholders. This placed the entire line in control of the bondholders' committee. The receiver reported a deficit of $25,602 for the year. Four series of receivers' certificates had been issued, aggregating $276,897.[40] The funds with which the property was purchased were raised chiefly in Boston and Philadelphia, two-thirds, it was reported, coming from the latter city.[41]

The reorganization plan approved by the bondholders called for $8,032,500 to pay the debts of the company and to complete the road. It was proposed to issue first mortgage bonds on the 510 miles of projected road at $17,500 per mile, or a total of $8,925,000. The purchaser of each $1,000 bond was to receive four shares of stock issued at the rate of $25,000 per mile, the par value of which was fixed at $100. Including a proposed issue of second mortgage bonds, the road would have a bonded indebtedness of $17,850,000. The capital stock of $12,750,000

---

[37] *Commercial and Financial Chronicle,* Vol. LV (Sept. 17, 1892).
[38] "The Story of the Clinchfield," p. 2.
[39] *Commercial and Financial Chronicle,* Vol. LVI (March 11, 1893).
[40] *Ibid.,* Vol. LVI (May 6, 1893).
[41] *Ibid.,* Vol. LIX (Dec. 15, 1894).

FURTHER DEVELOPMENT

would have brought the total to $60,000 per mile.[42] The new company of the reorganization plan was named the Ohio River & Charleston Railway Company.[43]

Within a few months, the general plan of reorganization had evidently been well received by the public. Concluding a long editorial upon the approval of the plan, the *News and Courier* states:

> Financially, therefore, the road is again on its feet. It is in strong, competent hands. It remains for Charleston to give it and its new owners the most cordial welcome. Governor Chamberlain stated truly the only wise or tolerable policy for the City and the State—that is, the policy of hearty support and coöperation on our part in promoting the success of the new company. It is our plain interest, our plain duty as citizens and friends of Charleston. The new company announces a policy in one respect liberal and conservative at once—the policy of relying on building up the business of Charleston and employing her citizens in the service of the railroad. Great possibilities in business lines now lie before us. The dream of Hayne, Aiken, Calhoun, Gourdin, Trenholm and their associates may yet be realized by us. The great West may yet find her ports for her vast exports along this coast. Such a movement seems possible. We believe it awaits only the determined effort of the business interests and forces of these seaboard States and cities. Deep water in our harbor . . . beckons this traffic hither as never before. It stirs the blood of the dullest Charlestonian to picture her in all her straits. We shall love her no more in her prosperity, but we shall be happier when she shall have taken her place again among the commercial centers of the country. The dawn of all this we hope is signified by the advent of the new "Old Reliable."[44]

In addition to the line from Camden to Marion, and the eight miles near White House, discussed in preceding pages, the "Three C's" had constructed several miles in Tennessee. Twenty miles had been completed and placed in operation from Johnson City southward to Chestoa, near Unaka Springs.[45] This section is a part of the Clinchfield. Sixteen miles northward from John-

---

[42] *Ibid.*, Vol. LVII (Oct. 14, 1893).
[43] "Investors' Supplement," *Commercial and Financial Chronicle*, Vol. LVII (Nov. 11, 1893).
[44] May 21, 1894.
[45] "Investors' Supplement," *Commercial and Financial Chronicle*, Vol. LV (Nov. 9, 1892).

son City, to a point nine miles beyond the Devault ford on the Watauga River, had been completed and rails partially laid, but no trains were regularly operated. This portion was not utilized by the Clinchfield, and is now "merely a scar on the surface of the earth." From this point, nine miles beyond the Devault ford, to Dante, Virginia, about eighty miles of the grading was approximately ninety per cent completed when the "Three C's" collapsed. Only two short sections of this form a part of the Clinchfield. One, six and a half miles long, became the Lick Creek & Lake Erie Railroad, extending from Fink to Dante, Virginia, which later became a part of the Clinchfield. The other section is about eight miles southward from St. Paul.[46]

---
[46] Morgan, "The Story of the Clinchfield," p. 2.

CHAPTER VII

THE PERIOD FROM 1895 TO 1908

THE OHIO RIVER & CHARLESTON RAILWAY

IN NOVEMBER, 1894, the Ohio River & Charleston Railway Company was organized as the successor of the Charleston, Cincinnati & Chicago Railroad Company. Samuel Hunt, of Cincinnati, was elected president of the new company.[1]

As pointed out in the preceding chapter, all of the property of the "Three C's" had been sold to Charles E. Hellier, who represented the bondholders. The road remained in the hands of the bondholders until the organization of the new company. Four corporations were formed to take over the line according to the states in which it was located.

The Ohio River & Charleston Railway Company of Virginia, chartered under a special act of the general assembly of that state on February 12, 1894, bought the portion of the road in Virginia on November 10. Charles E. Hellier sold the remaining sections on the thirteenth of the month, as follows: the portion in South Carolina, to the Ohio River & Charleston Railway Company of South Carolina, chartered under the general laws of that state on June 29; in North Carolina, to the Ohio River & Charleston Railway Company of North Carolina, chartered under the general laws of that state on July 7; and in Tennessee, to the Ohio River & Charleston Railway Company of Tennessee, the date of its charter not being available. These four companies consolidated on November 13, 1894, and formed the Ohio River & Charleston Railway Company, incorporated under articles of consolidation filed in South Carolina on December 3, 1894, and in Virginia on March 18, 1895. The dates of filing similar articles in North Carolina and Tennessee are not available. The new company was an Ohio corporation.[2]

---

[1] *Commercial and Financial Chronicle*, Vol. LIX (Nov. 17, 1894).

[2] Valuation Docket No. 354, I. C. C., "Tentative Valuation Report of the Properties of the Carolina, Clinchfield and Ohio Railway Company," 1917, pp. 26-27.

The agreement of consolidation stated an authorized capital of 60,000 shares of non-cumulative preferred, and 90,000 shares of common stock with a par value of $100 per share.[3] By the end of the first year's operations, 24,742 shares of preferred, and 37,113 shares of common stock had been issued.[4] It was reported that this new company was controlled, respectively, by the Finance Company of Pennsylvania, and by the Investment Company of Pennsylvania, both of which were located in Philadelphia.[5]

An agitation was again started in Sumter in an attempt to have the line extended southward from Camden as had been originally planned. The people of the county apparently had undergone a great change of mind in regard to the road, for it will be remembered that when the "Three C's," in 1887, attempted to interest the citizens of Sumter in the project, the officials of the road were received with cold indifference. Now, Sumter County seemed enthusiastic and anxious to complete the line, but still the people did not wish to subscribe to stock or make any monetary contributions whatsoever. According to the *Sumter News,*

A large and enthusiastic body of representative citizens from Sumter, Rafting Creek, Providence and Spring Hill townships were present at a meeting at Gaillard's Cross Roads yesterday which was called in the interest of the proposed Sumter and Camden branch of the Three C's Road. The meeting was very encouraging and every one present manifested considerable interest in the road, and said that they were willing to do everything in their power to assist in the building of the Sumter and Camden branch. There were representatives from all the townships through which the proposed line would pass. All present regretted the absence of Messrs. Hunt and Collier, president and treasurer, respectively, of the Three C's Railroad Company. The meeting was presided over by Dr. J. E. Rembert, of Rafting Creek Township, and Major E. F. Burrows, of Providence, acted as secretary. Col. J. D. Blanding spoke at length, as also did Mr. W. Y. L. Marshall.

A resolution was introduced and unanimously adopted whereby all present pledged themselves to give the right of way and to do

---

[3] *Ibid.,* p. 68.

[4] "Investors' Supplement," *Commercial and Financial Chronicle,* Vol. LXI (Oct., 1895).

[5] *Commercial and Financial Chronicle,* Vol. LXIV (Jan. 23, 1897).

OHIO RIVER & CHARLESTON RAILWAY

all in their power to assist in the building of the Sumter and Camden Railroad, and to make efforts to induce those not present, of the different townships, to also give the right of way and to assist in the building of the road. Several prominent gentlemen present, in addition to subscribing land for the right of way, said they would also give, free of charge, all of the timber necessary to the building of the road through their land.

Working committees from each township were appointed to see about having the rights of way signed and to induce others not present, to give lands for the right of way and to induce the people generally to show interest in the road.

The people of the different townships through which the Sumter and Camden branch would pass are certainly greatly interested in the road, and will do all they can to assist in its construction, except pay out money. Money is out of the question with them. Sumter is perhaps interested more than any township on the road, and our citizens should make some move towards showing the Three C's Rail Road Company that Sumter is really interested in the building of the branch. Not that Sumter has not already shown her interest, but Sumter must keep moving until it is decided, one way or the other, whether the Sumter and Camden Road will come to Sumter.[6]

When questioned regarding the possibility of building the extension to Sumter, President Hunt was reported to have said that "he could not see much hope of inducing the syndicate to invest any more money in South Carolina." This attitude, it seems, was caused by the legislature of the state refusing to make a rebate of about $30,000 for taxes overpaid by the road, while rebates had been granted to other railroad companies.[7]

Commenting upon the matter, the *Sumter Item* says that "when a General Assembly legislates against capitalists, it cannot be expected that moneyed men will place their money and interests in a State that would not protect them. The Sumter and Camden branch was a certainty before the General Assembly treated them as it did, and Mr. Hunt has said that this was the whole cause of the building of the branch being so doubtful at present."[8]

Several days later, John J. Collier, secretary of the railroad company, wrote: "There is very little to say about the Camden branch at present. Our people have turned their attention in

---

[6] *Sumter News*, Jan. 22, 1895. [7] *News and Courier*, Feb. 6, 1895.
[8] *Sumter Item*, Feb. 4, 1895.

other directions. Whether or not we shall be able to revive interest in the extension, depends somewhat, I think, on the interest the people of Sumter take in the enterprise. I have seen in the South Carolina papers several references to a movement in Charleston to get another railroad connection.[9] As Charleston has already a through connection to Knoxville, and about as short a line as it is practicable to make, it would seem to me that an independent line from the southwest Virginia coal fields to Camden, thence to Charleston, would be of more value to the city, especially as it would give a much shorter connection to Louisville, and Cincinnati and the west than the present line, besides opening up about two hundred miles of new territory, which would seek an outlet at the port of Charleston in competition with the ports on the middle Atlantic coast."[10]

As indicated in this letter, the railroad company expected aid from both Sumter and Charleston. However, no aid was forthcoming, and the line from Camden to Sumter was never constructed by the Ohio River & Charleston Railroad. However, this line was built by the Northwestern Railroad of South Carolina in 1901. The Northwestern later acquired a line between Sumter and St. Paul, in Clarendon County near the Santee River, from the Charleston, Sumter & Northern Railway, which was the approximate route planned by the "Three C's."[11] At the present time the Northwestern is operated under lease by the Atlantic Coast Line.[12]

In July, 1895, the security holders of the road voted to issue new first mortgage bonds, both on the completed line and also on a proposed extension. These bonds were to be issued at a rate not exceeding $15,000 a mile. It was decided to extend the line to the "Breaks" of the Big Sandy River in Kentucky, which is the present terminus of the Clinchfield. This extension "will traverse a rich coal, iron, and timber territory, and extend in South Carolina to a general cotton manufacturing and agricultural district."[13]

---

[9] That is, revival of the Blue Ridge project. See Chapter IV above.

[10] *News and Courier*, April 24, 1895.

[11] From a letter from the Hon. J. A. Raffield, Mayor of Sumter, Sumter, S. C., July 20, 1929.

[12] From a letter from Mr. John Wilson, president of the Northwestern Railroad Company of South Carolina, Sumter, S. C., July 17, 1929.

[13] *Commercial and Financial Chronicle*, Vol. LXI (July 6, 1895).

OHIO RIVER & CHARLESTON RAILWAY 93

In January, 1897, it was decided to extend the line from Blacksburg to Gaffney, South Carolina. To finance this, a bond issue of $600,000 was authorized, of which $100,000 would be reserved for old claims.[14] The Mortage Trustee & Finance Company, of Philadelphia, was appointed trustee.[15]

The annual report of the Finance Company of Pennsylvania says that "preliminary papers have been signed for the sale of a portion of the Ohio River & Charleston Railroad for bonds amounting to $1,092,000." This section to be sold included the main line from Camden to Marion, 171 miles, and the branch from Blacksburg to Gaffney of about eleven miles, completed in September, 1897. It was reported in Philadelphia that the South Carolina & Georgia would be the purchaser.[16] This company was the result of a reorganization of the old South Carolina Railroad in May, 1894. It was proposed to extend the Gaffney branch to Spartanburg, a distance of twenty-nine miles.[17]

During the latter part of May, 1898, the sale of the Southern division of the road[18] was ordered by Judge Simonton, of the United States Circuit court at Charlotte, under foreclosure of the mortgage of 1897. The Finance Company of Pennsylvania was trustee for the bonds.[19] President Hunt, the only bidder, purchased the road in behalf of the bondholders for $98,010. It was believed that the South Carolina & Georgia Railroad would take over the ownership and control of the property at an early date.[20]

This prediction was correct, for the South Carolina road signed a contract to operate the road in North and South Carolina, and took possession on the first of September.[21] The Southern Carolina & Georgia company was incorporated in North Carolina on September 14, with a capital stock of

---

[14] *Ibid.*, Vol. LXIV (Jan. 23, 1897).
[15] "Investors Supplement," *Commercial and Financial Chronicle,* Vol. LXV (July, 1897).
[16] *Commercial and Financial Chronicle,* Vol. LXVI (May 7, 1898).
[17] "Investors' Supplement," *Commercial and Financial Chronicle,* Vol. LXVII (July, 1898).
[18] That is, between Marion and Camden.
[19] *Commercial and Financial Chronicle,* Vol. LXVII (July 2, 1898).
[20] *Ibid.*, Vol. LXVII (Aug. 6, 1898).
[21] *Ibid.*, Vol. LXVII (Sept. 10, 1898).

$500,000, as the successor of the Ohio River & Charleston Railway within the limits of the two Carolinas. Samuel Hunt remained president of the newly formed corporation.[22] The new system was named the South Carolina & Georgia Extension Railroad, and functioned under an operating contract and not a lease.[23]

The entire system of the South Carolina & Georgia Railroad was leased to the Southern Railway on April 29, 1899. It was also proposed to include the entire line of the Ohio River & Charleston Railroad in the lease, thereby guaranteeing the bonds of the latter company; but the Southern abandoned the proposal. All the stocks and bonds of the Extension road were sold to a syndicate, and, in accordance with the terms of the lease, the line was operated independently by the Southern Railway. Samuel Hunt continued as president.[24] The mortgage bonds of $1,800,000 on the Ohio River & Charleston, held by the Boston Safe Deposit & Trust Company, were redeemed by the issuance of new bonds to a similar amount.[25]

Commenting on the importance of this consolidation to South Carolina, an editorial in the *Commercial and Financial Chronicle* says: "The lease of the South Carolina and Georgia Railroad (the old South Carolina Railroad) to the Southern Railway, entered into last week, is an event of importance. . . . The people of Charleston seem to be gratified, and well they may be, for they get what they have so long desired—namely, connections with the Ohio and Mississippi rivers through the rich coal and iron fields of the South. With its affiliated lines, the Southern controls about eight thousand miles of road, much of which, in a measure will be a tributary to Charleston. There does not seem to be the slightest inclination to think that the consolidation will be harmful, which is rather significant, as showing, that the people of South Carolina appreciate the benefits in store for them."[26]

At this time, the Southern Railway, in addition to its main line between Atlanta and Washington and numerous branches,

---

[22] *Ibid.*, Vol. LXVII (Sept. 24, 1898).

[23] "Investors' Supplement," *Commercial and Financial Chronicle*, Vol. LXVII (Oct., 1898).

[24] *Commercial and Financial Chronicle*, Vol. LXVIII (May 6, 1899).

[25] *Ibid.*, Vol. LXVIII (May 20, 1899).

[26] *Ibid.*, Vol. LXVIII (May 6, 1899).

THE SOUTH & WESTERN RAILWAY

had previously acquired control of the line following the route of the old Louisville, Cincinnati & Charleston Railroad from Columbia to Knoxville, via Spartanburg and Asheville. Connections were made at Harriman Junction, Tennessee, with the Cincinnati, New Orleans & Texas Pacific Railroad, an "auxiliary line," to Cincinnati and Louisville.[27]

After three years of independent operation, the South Carolina & Georgia Extension Railroad was merged into the Southern Railway system in 1902.[28] This road from Marion to Charleston is today one of the lines embracing the Charleston Division of the Southern. In such a manner, therefore, did the vast majority of the road constructed by the old "Three C's" pass into the hands of the Southern, a competitor of the present Clinchfield.

Meanwhile, construction had slowly progressed on the northern end of the Ohio River & Charleston Railway in Tennessee and Virginia. During 1899 and 1900, its road had been completed and placed in operation southward from Johnson City to Caney, near Huntsdale, North Carolina. This gave a total line of about 38 miles. Northward from Johnson City, grading had been completed as far as Gate City (formerly Estillville), 40 miles, and between Clinchport and Minneapolis, about 40 miles.[29] This property, and the franchises of the company, were sold to the South & Western Railway in June, 1902, and were turned over to the new owners on the first of July.[30]

THE SOUTH & WESTERN RAILWAY

The organization and development of the property of the present Clinchfield Railroad presents a complicated problem in corporate operations extending over the six-year period from 1902 to 1908, in which thirteen railway companies were involved. Nine of these companies were all called the South & Western Railway, and George L. Carter was the guiding hand through the development of the new enterprise. Blair & Company, of New York, were the principal bankers for these various

---

[27] "Investors' Supplement," *Commercial and Financial Chronicle,* Vol. LXVIII (April, 1899).
[28] *Ibid.,* Vol. LXXVII (April, 1903).
[29] *Ibid.,* Vol. LXXII (April, 1901).
[30] Valuation Docket No. 364, I. C. C., p. 26.

railway companies. The road itself was controlled by the Cumberland Corporation and by the Clinchfield Coal Corporation, which, in turn, were controlled by Blair & Company. The Clinchfield Coal Corporation was a subsidiary of the Cumberland Corporation. The properties of the South & Western were consolidated in 1908 to form the Carolina, Clinchfield & Ohio Railway.

The Cumberland Corporation was a holding company which held as assets the stock and non-negotiable debt of the South & Western Railway, the stock of the Clinchfield Coal Corporation, and a block of Seaboard Air Line Railway stock.[31]

The Clinchfield Coal Corporation owned some 300,000 acres of coal lands in southwestern Virginia and also stock and non-negotiable debt of the South & Western Railway. The capitalization of the corporation consisted of $15,000,000 six per cent preferred stock, all of which was paid in, and $25,000,000 common stock.[32]

Early in January, 1905, a group of New York capitalists, through the Union Trust Company, of New York, entered a bid to purchase the Clinchfield Coal Corporation, of which the South & Western Railway was a subsidiary, for $2,600,000, subject to a mortgage of $1,150,000 on its coal property.[33] The directors of the coal company, however, later authorized a plan providing for the sale to be made to George L. Carter, who was also a director, for $2,448,333. According to the terms of the sale, Carter paid $10,000 in cash, and agreed to expend $500,000 on the railroad for betterments and improvements by March 1, 1906. In the event that he did not carry out his contract, the property would revert back to the sellers. Upon the completion of the betterments and improvements, Carter had the right to pay the remainder of the purchase money in fifty-year 4 per cent bonds to the amount of $3,250,000.[34]

This plan, however, was disapproved by the stockholders of the coal corporation at a meeting in Bristol, Virginia, on January 23, who voted to set aside the sale to Carter as had been authorized by the directors. All of the directors, except Carter,

---

[31] *Commercial and Financial Chronicle*, Vol. LXXXIII (July 2, 1906).
[32] *Ibid.*
[33] *Ibid.*, Vol. LXXX (Jan. 7, 1905).
[34] *Ibid.*, Vol. LXXX (Jan. 21, 1905).

THE SOUTH & WESTERN RAILWAY

were removed, and Charles M. Allaire, of New York City, was elected to succeed James Clark as president.[35]

A second bid was entered for the purchase of the Clinchfield Coal Corporation, and it was sold in May to a syndicate composed of Thomas F. Ryan, James A. Blair, J. B. Dennis, N. B. Ream, and T. J. Coolidge, all of whom were directors of the Seaboard Air Line Railway Company. Blair & Company had previously purchased a block of Seaboard stock in 1904, which, "with other friendly interests," was said to give Blair & Company control of the Seaboard. Commenting on the purchase of the Clinchfield Corporation, President J. M. Barr, of the Seaboard, presumably attempting to cover the inter-railroad relations, said that his road had no connection with it, and "no conclusions have yet been reached by the Seaboard in this connection."[36] However, it is quite obvious that the Seaboard planned either to obtain control of the coal corporation and the South & Western Railway, or at least to establish close relations with them.

Soon after its sale, the properties of the Clinchfield Coal Corporation were further expanded by the purchase of the coal lands of the Inter-State Coal & Iron Company, aggregating about 75,000 acres in Russell, Dickinson, Buchanan, and Wise counties, Virginia. The purchase price was "something over" $1,500,000.[37]

In 1906, $15,000,000 six year five per cent bonds, with the New York Trust Company as trustee, were issued by the coal corporation and sold largely to Blair & Company. These bonds were issued to raise funds for the completion of the South & Western from the coal fields to a connection with the Seaboard Air Line at Bostic, near Rutherfordton, North Carolina, thereby creating a new outlet for Clinchfield coal.[38] Thus, the credit of the parent coal company was used to finance the expansion of the road.

The above discussion shows that the control of the South & Western Railway was centered mainly in Blair & Company, New York bankers. The subsequent development of the road it-

---

[35] *Ibid.*, Vol. LXXX (Jan. 28, 1905).
[36] *Ibid.*, Vol. LXXX (May 27, 1905).
[37] *Ibid.*, Vol. LXXX (June 3, 1905).
[38] *Ibid.*, Vol. LXXXIII (July 2, 1906).

self will be analyzed according to the states through which it passed.

North Carolina: A South & Western Railway was incorporated under a special act of the legislature of North Carolina on March 4, 1901.[39] According to the terms of its charter, it was empowered to build a road from either Southport or Wilmington, North Carolina, to any point on the state lines of South Carolina, Virginia, or Tennessee. Terminal properties were acquired in Southport under the name of the Southport Harbor Company. The railroad properties of the company consisted of about thirty miles of completed road from the point where the Ohio River & Charleston Railway had constructed near Huntsdale, southward to Altapass. Twenty-six miles of the road, from the point near Huntsdale to Spruce Pine, had been built by the Carolina Construction Company for the railroad during 1901 and 1902. The remaining four miles to Altapass were constructed by the railroad company itself in 1905. Considerable grading was completed southward towards Marion.

One thousand shares of stock were authorized, of which 995 were held by William E. Worth.[40] In October, 1904, the road, northward from Spruce Pine to the Tennessee state line, was sold to the South & Western Railway, incorporated in Kentucky and Virginia in September, 1902.[41]

In December, 1905, the South & Western Railroad Company was chartered under the general laws of North Carolina for the purpose of absorbing the properties of the South & Western Railway Company, organized in 1901.[42] It is well to note the terminology of the names of these two companies: the first was called a rail*way*, the second, a rail*road*. The new company was organized to construct and to operate the road from the Tennessee state line, through North Carolina, to the South Carolina state line, a distance of about one hundred and twenty miles. The partly constructed railroad and all the rights of way from Spruce Pine to Marion were purchased from the preceding North Carolina company on September 20, 1906; and on September 24, it purchased the completed road between Spruce Pine and the Tennessee state line from the Kentucky and Vir-

---

[39] Valuation Docket No. 364, I. C. C., p. 26. [40] *Ibid.,* pp. 64-65.
[41] *Ibid.,* p. 61. [42] *Ibid.,* p. 27.

First Passenger Train to Reach Altapass, North Carolina

THE SOUTH & WESTERN RAILWAY 99

ginia company, mentioned above.[43] In other words, the second South & Western Rail*road* simply absorbed all the properties originally held by its immediate predecessor, the South & Western Rail*way*, incorporated in North Carolina in 1901.

On February 4, 1908, the second North Carolina company entered into a contract with the Meadows Company, a construction company, to complete the road from Altapass to the South Carolina state line. In payment for this work, it deposited with the Meadows Company $594,000 in its stock, and $1,200,000 in first mortgage ten-year five per cent gold bonds. The total authorized capital was $600,000. The non-negotiable debt of the railroad company consisted of a credit to the Cumberland Corporation of $168,750. Of this, $150,000 represented the portion of the amount agreed to be paid for the cancellation of $371,000 thirty-year five per cent gold bonds issued by the South & Western of Kentucky and Virginia on the line between Spruce Pine and the North Carolina-Tennessee state line. The remaining $18,750 represented the accrued interest on the bonds.[44]

The South & Western Rail*road* Company, of North Carolina, constructed no new road. Its properties, as will be shown later, were conveyed to the Carolina, Clinchfield & Ohio Railway in 1908.[45]

Tennessee: The first company which was organized, from a chronological standpoint, bearing the name of the South & Western Railway was incorporated under the general laws of the state of Tennessee on December 30, 1901.[46] This company was authorized to construct a road from the North Carolina-Tennessee state line in the valley of the Nolachucky River, to the Virginia-Tennessee state line in Sullivan County. However, no road was constructed. One thousand shares of stock, of a par value of $100, were authorized, of which 996 were subscribed to by George L. Carter. This company existed for only four months, for in April, 1902, it was merged into another South & Western Railway.[47]

The second South & Western Railway to be incorporated in Tennessee was a consolidation of the company described above, and of another railway which had been organized in Virginia.[48]

---

[43] *Ibid.*, p. 80. [44] *Ibid.*, pp. 80-81. [45] *Ibid.*, p. 27.
[46] *Ibid.* [47] *Ibid.*, p. 73. [48] See below.

100   THE CLINCHFIELD RAILROAD

The new railway company was incorporated in Tennessee on April 29, 1902, and in Virginia on April 19, 1902. It constructed no road. Seven thousand shares of capital stock were authorized, exchangeable one for two of the stock of the preceding companies. The properties of the Ohio River & Charleston Railway within Tennessee and Virginia were purchased by the new company in June, 1902, and it acquired control of this property on the first of July.[49] To finance this, in June the stockholders voted to issue $600,000 first mortgage three per cent bonds on the line of the Ohio River & Charleston, due January 1, 1952. The rates of interest were to be three per cent through the year 1904, and three and one-half per cent thereafter.[50] All the properties of this new organization were conveyed in September, 1902,[51] to still another company, the South & Western Railway of Virginia and Kentucky.[52]

The Kingsport Southern Railway was incorporated under the general laws of Tennessee on July 30, 1906,[53] for the purpose of building a line from a point about five miles below the mouth of Sinking Creek in Washington County, Tennessee, to the Virginia state line. It also acquired the right of way of the South & Western Railway, discussed in the preceding paragraph, between these two points, for which it assumed the fifty-year gold bonds issued in 1902. Its entire capital stock of $10,000 was sold at par. No road was constructed by this company,[54] and its properties were acquired by the South & Western Railroad Company, incorporated in Tennessee in December, 1906.[55]

The third South & Western Railway to be formed in Tennessee was chartered under the general laws of that state on July 30, 1906. This company was to have built and operated the road from the southern terminus of the Kingsport Southern Railway to Erwin. On November 24, 1906, it purchased the line between Johnson City and the North Carolina state line, formerly owned by the preceding South & Western Railway organized in 1902. In payment for this, it assumed the $371,000 thirty-year gold bonds and $662,602 of the non-negotiable debt

---

[49] Valuation Docket No. 364, I. C. C., p. 66.
[50] *Commercial and Financial Chronicle*, Vol. LXXIV (June 12, 1902).
[51] See below.   [52] Valuation Docket No. 364, I. C. C., p. 26.
[53] *Ibid.*, p. 27.   [54] *Ibid.*, p. 79.   [55] *Ibid.*, p. 27.

THE SOUTH & WESTERN RAILWAY 101

of the latter company. One hundred shares of stock were issued, but there was no additional construction.[56] This plan was ratified by the stockholders on October 10.[57]

This third organization, called the South & Western and the Kingsport Southern railways, was consolidated into the South & Western Railroad Company, incorporated under articles of consolidation filed in Tennessee on December 8, 1906.[58] An agreement was signed by the officials of the two predecessor companies on November 20, by which all of their respective properties were turned over to the new organization. It leased the North Carolina road on January 1, 1908, and thereafter operated the line from Johnson City to Altapass, about 67 miles.

The authorized capital of the new company was $10,000,000, but only about one-half was issued. Two hundred shares were exchanged for the stock of its predecessors, share for share. The first mortgage fifty-year 5s, of a par value of $600,000, which had been issued in 1902 by the second company of the South & Western in Tennessee on the properties of the Ohio River & Charleston within that state, were assumed in the consolidation. There were retired $300,000 by a cash payment, for which the railway company gave short term notes of a like amount. The remaining $300,000, held by the Cumberland Corporation, were cancelled by an exchange of a like amount of non-negotiable debt to affiliated companies. The $371,000 five per cent thirty-year gold notes, assumed from the preceding company, were retired in 1908 by a cash payment.

An agreement was entered into with the Meadows Company, a construction company, in February, 1908, to complete the road from Johnson City to the Virginia state line. The railway issued a block of its stock, aggregating $2,250,000, to the construction company to apply on the contract for the building of the projected road. Likewise, $650,000 first mortgage ten-year 5s, due February 1, 1918, were issued to the Meadows Company. However, no new road was constructed.[59]

---

[56] *Ibid.*, pp. 77-78.
[57] *Commercial and Financial Chronicle*, Vol. LXXXIII (Nov. 3, 1906).
[58] Valuation Docket No. 364, I. C. C., p. 27.
[59] *Ibid.*, pp. 73-77.

102 THE CLINCHFIELD RAILROAD

The properties of this company were conveyed to the Carolina, Clinchfield & Ohio Railway in 1908.[60]

Virginia: A South & Western Railway was chartered under a special act of the Virginia general assembly on April 2, 1902,[61] for the purpose of building a line from the point where the original South & Western Railway of Tennessee terminated on the Virginia-Tennessee state line, to "any point on the Kentucky-Virginia state line in the vicinity of the Breaks of the Sandy." George L. Carter held 992 of the authorized 1,000 shares. No road was constructed,[62] and within a period of three weeks after its formation, this company was merged into the South & Western Railway, incorporated in Virginia on April 19, and in Tennessee on April 29, 1902, as discussed above.

Under articles of consolidation filed in Virginia on September 15, 1902, and in Kentucky on September 15, 1902, a South & Western Railway was chartered with George L. Carter as its president.[63] This company acquired the properties brought about in the merger of the South & Western in Virginia on April 19, and in Tennessee on April 29, 1902, as noted in the preceding paragraph; and also of a Kentucky company which had been organized to build the road from the "Breaks" of the Big Sandy River to Pikeville. On October 14, 1904, the line to Spruce Pine was purchased from the North Carolina company, but it was resold to the newer North Carolina company in December, 1906.[64]

This new railway company had an authorized capital stock of $10,000,000, par $100, of which $110,000 were issued.[65] Non-negotiable debt to affiliated companies was incurred in the receipt of $737,662 from the Clinchfield Coal Company and the Cumberland Corporation.[66] The $600,000 bonds of the Tennessee company, issued in 1902, were assumed by the new company as part payment for that property. $371,000 five per cent thirty-year gold notes were issued in 1904 upon the acquisition of the North Carolina property.[67] All of these bonds were underwritten by a syndicate headed by the Union Trust Com-

[60] *Ibid.*, p. 27.   [61] *Ibid.*   [62] *Ibid.*, p. 72.   [63] *Ibid.*, p. 26.
[64] *Ibid.*, pp. 61-62
[65] "Investors' Supplement," *Commercial and Financial Chronicle*, Vol. LXXIX (July, 1904).
[66] Valuation Docket No. 364, I. C. C., p. 62.   [67] *Ibid.*

THE SOUTH & WESTERN RAILWAY 103

pany of Baltimore. In addition to the railroad, this syndicate controlled the Cranes' Nest Coal Company, which owned extensive tracts of coal and mineral lands in Wise County and other parts of southwestern Virginia.[68]

In August, 1902, this railway company was reported to be planning to extend its line westward to a connection with the Detroit Southern Railroad at Ironton, Ohio.[69] It was rumored that this extension was in the interest of the Seaboard Air Line Railway as a connecting link between that company and the Ohio River.[70] However, nothing seems to have come of it. It will be remembered that the Seaboard Air Line was well represented on the directorate of the Clinchfield Coal Corporation, which controlled the South & Western Railway jointly with the Cumberland Corporation, while the latter corporation in turn controlled the coal company. Blair & Company, the New York bankers, controlled all of them, together with the Seaboard Air Line.[71]

During 1905, plans were made by this South & Western Railway, which, as the *Commercial and Financial Chronicle* said, "is controlled by the Seaboard interests," to establish a through line from the coal fields near Elkhorn City, Kentucky, to Spartanburg, South Carolina.[72] While the general plan of the old "Three C's" was followed in so far as the country traversed was concerned, new surveys were made on the entire line, with the result that easier curves and lower grades were adopted. This company became the main basis upon which the Carolina, Clinchfield & Ohio Railway was formed in 1908.

Kentucky: The South & Western Railway of Kentucky was chartered on April 2, 1902, under the general laws of that state, to build a road from the terminus of the Virginia company, in the "Breaks" of the Big Sandy River, to Pikeville. No road, however, was constructed, and it was merged with the Virginia company in September, as discussed above.[73]

---

[68] *Commercial and Financial Chronicle,* Vol. LXXIX (July, 1904).
[69] *Ibid.,* Vol. LXXV (Aug. 9, 1902).
[70] *Ibid.,* Vol. LXXV (Oct. 25, 1902).
[71] See above.
[72] Vol. LXXXI (Nov. 18, 1905).
[73] Valuation Docket No. 364, I. C. C., p. 65.

THE LICK CREEK & LAKE ERIE RAILROAD

The Lick Creek & Lake Erie Railroad was incorporated under a special act of the general assembly of Virginia on March 25, 1902.[74] The purpose of the organization was to construct a line "from a point on the line of the Norfolk & Western Railway Company, near the mouth of Lick Creek in Wise or Russell County, Virginia, in a northerly direction up the valley of Lick Creek into Dickinson County, not to exceed 20 miles." About seven miles were constructed from Fink to Dante.

All the authorized capital stock of $100,000 was issued, the par value of which was $100. Of this, 495 shares were issued to Stilson Hutchins in December, 1902, "for the considerations of the payment and assumption by him of all debts and liabilities of this company incurred prior to November 1, 1902." First mortgage thirty-year five per cent gold bonds of $200,000 par value were likewise issued and delivered to Hutchins. This action was taken under the authority of a resolution of the stockholders dated December 22, 1902.[75]

The properties of the Lick Creek & Lake Erie Railroad were conveyed to the Carolina, Clinchfield & Ohio Railway in 1908.[76]

THE ELKHORN SOUTHERN RAILWAY

The Elkhorn Southern Railway was chartered in Virginia on October 4, 1906,[77] to build a road "through the coal and timber fields of Dickinson and Buchanan counties, Virginia."[78] As built, the road extended from Kiser, a point on the Norfolk & Western, to Wilder, about eight miles.[79] This line is a part of the present "Dumps Creek" branch of the Clinchfield.

Short-term five per cent notes were authorized to the extent of $800,000. These notes, with a face value of $797,556.75, were issued to the Meadows Company for construction of the road. Fifty shares of stock were issued.[80]

THE CLINCHFIELD NORTHERN RAILWAY

Although the Clinchfield Northern Railway was not organized until a few years after the period included within the limits

---
[74] *Ibid.*, p. 27.   [75] *Ibid.*, p. 83.   [76] *Ibid.*, p. 27.   [77] *Ibid.*, p. 28.
[78] *Commercial and Financial Chronicle*, Vol. LXXXIII (Nov. 3, 1906).
[79] Valuation Docket No. 364, I. C. C., p. 85.   [80] *Ibid.*, p. 86.

CLINCHFIELD NORTHERN RAILWAY

as set forth in the title of this chapter, possibly it is germane to discuss the road at this time, because within a few months after its formation, it was turned over to the Carolina, Clinchfield & Ohio Railway.

The Clinchfield Northern Railway was incorporated under the general laws of Virginia on September 30, 1911,[81] for the purpose of acquiring by purchase or lease a right of way for a railroad from a point in the Road fork of Dumps Creek in Russell County, Virginia, to a point on the Kentucky line near the "Breaks" of the Big Sandy River, a distance of about thirty miles. On October 3, the company acquired from the Elkhorn Southern its franchises, but no constructed road, in Russell, Dickinson, Buchanan, and Wise counties. This was conveyed to the Clinchfield on May 27, 1912.[82]

SUMMARY OF EVENTS

Of the eighteen railroad companies discussed in this chapter, fourteen did not construct any road. The other four companies built and operated about eighty miles of road, as follows:[83]

TABLE VIII

Ohio River & Charleston Railway (Ohio):
  Johnson City to Chestoa (acquired from the
    "Three C's") .... 20.000 miles
  Chestoa, Tennessee, to the vicinity of Huntsdale,
    North Carolina .... 18.600 miles
South & Western Railway (North Carolina):
  From the vicinity of Huntsdale to Altapass, North
    Carolina .... 25.655 miles
Lick Creek & Lake Erie Railroad:
  From Fink to Dante, Virginia.............. 6.770 miles
Elkhorn Southern Railway:
  Kiser to Wilder, Virginia................. 8.206 miles

All these properties were conveyed to the Carolina, Clinchfield & Ohio Railway, and they form a part of the present Clinchfield Railroad system.

---

[81] *Ibid.*, p. 281.   [82] *Ibid.*, p. 85.   [83] *Ibid.*, p. 29.

THE CLINCHFIELD RAILROAD

George L. Carter was at the head of all these projects. He was "the father of the revised plan of a modern railroad of low grades and easy curvature to connect the Ohio Valley with the Atlantic Coastal Plain," writes O. K. Morgan. "During this period, Mr. John B. Dennis, for Blair & Company, was the financial manager, and to him great credit is due for the skilled manner in which the very important work of financing was handled."[84]

---
[84] "The Story of the Clinchfield," p. 3.

CHAPTER VIII

THE CAROLINA, CLINCHFIELD & OHIO RAILWAY

EARLY IN 1908, the stockholders of the several companies owning and operating the different sections of roadway between Elkhorn City and Spartanburg voted to consolidate all of their respective properties into one system.[1] A new South & Western Railroad Company had been incorporated for this purpose under the general laws of Virginia on January 26, 1905.[2] On March 9, 1908, papers were filed in Nashville, Tennessee, changing the name to the Carolina, Clinchfield & Ohio Railway Company, with general offices in Johnson City,[3] thus defining its location in a more comprehensive manner.[4] The name Clinchfield was derived from the Clinch River, which skirts the southern edge of the coal fields.[5]

The properties of the various roads were acquired as follows: the property of the South & Western Railway, of Virginia, December 24, 1906; of Tennessee, on March 31, 1908; of North Carolina, on April 16, 1908; the Lick Creek & Lake Erie Railroad, on June 1, 1908; the completed road of the Elkhorn Southern Railway in Virginia, on September 30, 1911; and the Clinchfield Northern Railway, on May 27, 1912.[6]

The principal bankers of the Carolina, Clinchfield & Ohio Railway were Blair & Company, of New York City, and the Cumberland Corporation, of Virginia. The railway company had issued certain of its securities to the two companies to raise funds for the construction and reconstruction of its property, and for the retirement of other obligations. The Meadows Company, under contract with the Clinchfield and its predecessors,[7] constructed 154 miles of road from Dante, Virginia, to a point on the North Carolina-South Carolina state line. It also built

---

[1] *Commercial and Financial Chronicle,* Vol. LXXXVI (Jan. 25, 1908).
[2] Valuation Docket No. 364, I. C. C., p. 26.
[3] *Commercial and Financial Chronicle,* Vol. LXXXVI (March 14, 1908).
[4] The general offices were later transferred to Erwin, Tennessee.
[5] Morgan, "The Story of the Clinchfield," p. 3.
[6] Valuation Docket No. 364, I. C. C., pp. 26-28.
[7] See Chapter VII above.

108 THE CLINCHFIELD RAILROAD

the line from this latter point to Spartanburg, South Carolina, which was incorporated as the Carolina, Clinchfield & Ohio Railway Company of South Carolina. In payment for this work, the Clinchfield issued securities to the Meadows Company, and in return, received other securities held by the latter. Blair & Company, and the Cumberland Corporation likewise had been the principal bankers of the construction company.[8]

The par value of the securities issued was as follows:[9]

TABLE IX

Capital Stock, common	$14,964,000
Capital Stock, preferred	15,000,000
First Mortgage Five Per Cent Bonds	10,000,000
Ten-Year Five Per Cent Gold Notes	2,000,000
Total	$41,964,000

The following were the securities and current assets received:[10]

TABLE X

First Mortgage Five Per Cent Bonds of the Carolina, Clinchfield & Ohio Railway of South Carolina	$3,000,000.00
First Mortgage Three Per Cent Bonds of the South & Western Railway of Tennessee	300,000.00
Accrued interest on the bonds of the predecessor companies	82,083.33
Total	$3,382,083.33

The Cumberland Corporation subsequently disposed of the mortgage bonds and the ten-year notes for cash proceeds of $8,750,000 and $1,750,000, respectively. The stock was held by the corporation until its dissolution in 1916. Prior to that time, it had acquired $10,036,000 of additional common stock of the Clinchfield Railway through the exchange of $5,000,000 preferred stock and $5,036,000 in other securities.[11]

On March 9, 1908, the railway company increased its authorized capital stock from $7,600,000 to $27,000,000, of

---

[8] Valuation Docket No. 364, I. C. C., pp. 30-32.
[9] Ibid., p. 32.   [10] Ibid.   [11] Ibid.

CAROLINA, CLINCHFIELD & OHIO RAILWAY 109

which $15,000,000 were six per cent preferred and $12,000,000 were common.[12] In December of the same year, this was increased to $30,000,000 divided into shares of $100 par value, half of which were common and half preferred.[13] In June, 1912, the capitalization was increased to $40,000,000, of which $25,000,000 were common and $15,000,000 preferred.[14]

At a meeting of the directors of the Clinchfield Railway in Bristol, Tennessee, on March 23, 1908, it was decided to issue $15,000,000 thirty-year five per cent first mortgage bonds, dated June 1, on the entire road from Dante to Spartanburg. These bonds were also secured by the road's equipment and by $3,000,000 first mortgage bonds of the Carolina, Clinchfield & Ohio Railway Company of South Carolina. The Farmers' Loan & Trust Company, of New York, was named trustee. The purpose of the issue was to retire the bonds of three constituent companies, amounting to $3,000,000. These had been deposited as collateral to secure an issue, dated February 1, 1908, of $3,000,000 one-year six per cent notes by the Cumberland Corporation. An additional $3,000,000 would be reserved for equipment, and the remaining $9,000,000 would be issued for construction purposes.[15] The stockholders voted on May 25 authorizing the issue.[16] Blair & Company purchased $10,000,000 of the bonds, the other $5,000,000 being reserved for future improvements and betterments.[17] In April, 1909, Blair & Company offered a portion of these bonds for sale at 96, and interest yielding over $5\frac{1}{4}$ per cent, due June 1, 1938, but subject to prior redemption at the company's option at 110.[18]

Soon after the sale of the total bond issue to Blair & Company, an article appeared in the *Commercial and Financial Chronicle* suggesting that close relations would be maintained between the Seaboard Air Line and the Clinchfield. The article says that "James A. Blair, of Blair & Company, is a director of the Seaboard Air Line Railway, and this fact, in conjunction with the fact that the Cumberland Corporation owns a block

---

[12] *Commercial and Financial Chronicle*, Vol. LXXXVI (May 14, 1908).
[13] *Ibid.*, Vol. LXXXVII (Dec. 19, 1908).
[14] *Ibid.*, Vol. XCIV (June 15, 1912).
[15] *Ibid.*, Vol. LXXXVI (April 4, 1908).
[16] *Ibid.*, Vol. LXXXVI (May 30, 1908).
[17] *Ibid.*, Vol. LXXXVII (Aug. 22, 1908).
[18] *Ibid.*, Vol. LXXXVIII (April 10, 1909).

of Seaboard stock and the further circumstance that the Seaboard is making elaborate preparations for the handling of the tidewater coal traffic of the new line, indicate that very close relations are to be maintained between the Seaboard and the new road."[19]

Regular train service was inaugurated between Johnson City and Marion on September 8, 1908, a distance of 98 miles. The lines northward from Johnson City to Dante, and southward from Marion to Bostic, were expected to be opened to traffic by February, 1909, and to Spartanburg, by September of the same year.[20] Bostic is the point of connection with the Seaboard Air Line. The road was completed to that station in January, 1909,[21] and placed in operation to Spartanburg on October 28, 1909, making a total of 244 miles of main line.[22] The "Dumps Creek" branch from St. Paul to Hurricane, twelve miles, was opened in May, 1910,[23] and was extended four miles further in 1912.[24]

A rolling stock equipment trust agreement was executed early in February, 1909, to provide new equipment at a cost of $3,236,238. Of this amount, $636,238 were paid in cash, and the remaining $2,600,000 were represented by $1,600,000 series "A," and $1,000,000 series "B" five per cent equipment gold notes. The second series were not issued until the next year. The series "A" notes, in denominations of $1,000.00 and dated December 1, 1908, were payable in semi-annual installments of $130,000 each, beginning June 1, 1909, and ending December 1, 1918. The Bankers Trust Company, of New York, was named trustee. Interest was payable in June and December at the office of Blair & Company, "the venders of the equipment." The equipment purchased was as follows:[25]

1. Cars to be delivered by the Pressed Steel Car Company, December, 1908, to July, 1909:

---

[19] *Ibid.*, Vol. LXXXVII (Sept. 12, 1908).
[20] *Ibid.*, Vol. LXXXVII (Dec. 19, 1908).
[21] *Ibid.*, Vol. LXXXVIII (Jan. 23, 1909).
[22] *Ibid.*, Vol. LXXXIX (Nov. 6, 1909).
[23] "Investors' Supplement," *Commercial and Financial Chronicle*, Vol. XCI (Oct., 1910).
[24] "Supplement, Railway Stocks and Bonds," *Commercial and Financial Chronicle*, Vol. XCV (Oct., 1912).
[25] *Commercial and Financial Chronicle*, Vol. LXXXVIII (Feb. 13, 1909).

CAROLINA, CLINCHFIELD & OHIO RAILWAY 111

1,600 all steel fifty-ton hopper cars.
500 all steel fifty-ton gondola cars.
6 all steel baggage and mail cars.
100 all steel fifty-ton composite flat cars.
250 thirty-ton steel underframe box cars.
100 thirty-ton wooden flat cars.

2. Cars to be delivered by other manufacturers, January to April, 1909:

   1 steel wrecker (car and crane).
   2 steel underframe baggage and mail cars.
   15 steel underframe caboose cars.
   12 sixty-foot steel underframe vestibule passenger cars.

3. Locomotives to be delivered by the Baldwin Locomotive Works:

   15 consolidation freight locomotives (2-8-0).
   4 ten-wheel passenger locomotives (2-6-0).
   1 Mallet articulated compound freight locomotive (2-6-6-2).

A mortgage was made to the Equitable Trust Company, of New York, as trustee for $5,000,000 ten-year five per cent gold notes of $1,000 each, dated July 1, 1909. The entire issue was sold. These notes followed and were subject to the authorized $15,000,000 bond issue of 1908, of which $5,000,000 had been held by the railroad.[26] Of this last amount, $3,000,000 were retired in July, 1912, in a readjustment of the finances of the Cumberland Corporation. In September, holders of the remaining $2,000,000 were given the privilege of conversion into preferred stock of the railway at par.[27]

On January 15, 1910, the Clinchfield issued the $1,000,000 equipment trust notes, series "B," for equipment costing $1,375,285, of which $375,285 was paid in cash. The Union Trust Company, of New York City, was trustee. These notes were payable in semi-annual installments of $50,000, maturing January 15, 1920. The following equipment was purchased:[28]

750 fifty-ton all steel hopper cars.
250 fifty-ton all steel gondola cars.
4 Mogul Mallet locomotives (2-6-6-2).

---

[26] *Ibid.*, Vol. LXXXIX (July 31, 1909).
[27] *Ibid.*, Vol. XCV (Oct. 1, 1912).
[28] *First Annual Report*, Carolina, Clinchfield & Ohio Railway, for the year ended June 30, 1911, p. 23.

20 sixteen-yard dump cars.
12 steel-underframe passenger cars.

Early in 1910, arrangements were made with the Southern Railway to handle the Clinchfield's coal from Spartanburg to Charleston. The Southern planned to erect terminals at the latter city to handle coal for export at the same rate as Norfolk.[29]

At a meeting of the stockholders on February 2, 1911, the following were elected directors of the Carolina, Clinchfield & Ohio Railway Company: Thomas F. Ryan, Frank A. Vanderlip, George B. Dennis, C. L. Blair, E. D. Adams, W. K. Whigham, Robert C. Ream, N. B. Ream, George L. Carter, I. T. Mann, William M. Ritter, W. B. Donham, W. T. Rosen, E. T. Watson, and M. W. Potter. Of this number, Vanderlip, Whigham, N. B. Ream, and Rosen were directors of the Seaboard. Mark W. Potter, chairman of the board, was elected president to succeed George L. Carter, resigned.[30]

In June, 1911, it was "widely reported" that a joint lease of the Clinchfield was being considered by the Seaboard Air Line and the Chesapeake & Ohio railroads.[31] The combined roads would give a through route from Chicago to the Atlantic seaboard. However, it appears that no final action was ever taken on the proposition.

The properties of the Elkhorn Southern Railway in Virginia were conveyed to the Clinchfield on September 30, 1911.[32] Prior to this time, the Clinchfield had operated the 5.6 miles under lease.[33]

First mortgage five per cent gold notes of $5,500,000, dated May 1, 1912, were issued for construction work on the Elkhorn extension. These notes were secured by the mortgage on the line from Dante, Virginia, to the Kentucky state line, thirty-two miles, and by the $500,000 first mortgage five per cent gold notes, issued by the Clinchfield Northern Railway of Kentucky to the Carolina, Clinchfield & Ohio, on the property from the

---

[29] *Commercial and Financial Chronicle*, Vol. XC (Feb. 26, 1910).
[30] *Ibid.*, Vol. XCII (Feb. 4, 1911).
[31] *Ibid.*, Vol. XCII (June 24, 1911).
[32] Valuation Docket No. 364, I. C. C., p. 28.
[33] *Second Annual Report*, Carolina, Clinchfield & Ohio Railway Company, for the year ended June 30, 1912, p 7.

CAROLINA, CLINCHFIELD & OHIO RAILWAY

Virginia-Kentucky state line to Elkhorn City. The Bankers Trust Company was named trustee.[34]

On February 2, 1914, President Potter wrote that the "Elkhorn extension, which is of the same high standard as the line now in operation, is expected to be opened for traffic in the summer of 1914, and upon its completion the railway will become an important link in a new route for passenger and freight business between the Ohio Valley and territory north, and the great agricultural and manufacturing districts of the southeastern coastal states. A traffic arrangement with the Chesapeake & Ohio Railway insures the coöperation of that line in developing business via the Clinchfield route."[35]

The Cumberland Corporation sold its holdings of Seaboard Air Line stock in May, 1912, the proceeds from which were utilized in retiring its $15,000,000 collateral trust notes, due June 12. The corporation also issued $5,500,000 first mortgage three-year 5s, dated May 1, 1912, secured by the proposed forty mile extension of the Clinchfield from Dante to Elkhorn City, eight miles of which had already been completed. It was estimated that the new line would cost about $5,000,000. These bonds were sold by Blair & Company at 98½, and interest yielding 5½ per cent.[36] At this time, the Cumberland Corporation owned $30,000,000 common and $10,000,000 preferred stock of the railway company. It also owned all of the outstanding stock of the Holston Corporation, which owned "valuable lands along the railway and at Charleston, representing an investment of over $600,000 and believed to be worth considerably more."[37]

The bonds issued by the Cumberland Corporation in 1912 were retired on June 1, 1915, by the issuance of $5,000,000 one-year five per cent collateral trust notes. The new notes were secured by $25,000,000 common and $5,000,000 preferred stock of the railway company, and were redeemable at 101 on December 1, 1915. The New York Trust Company was trustee.[38]

It was reported by President James H. Allport in August, 1912, that the Clinchfield Coal Corporation was capable of

---

[34] *Ibid.*, p. 19.
[35] *Commercial and Financial Chronicle*, Vol. XCVIII (Feb. 28, 1914).
[36] *Ibid.*, Vol. XCIV (May 25, 1912).
[37] *Ibid.*, Vol. XCV (Aug. 17, 1912).   [38] *Ibid.*, Vol. C (June 5, 1915).

producing annually about two million tons of coal. The Clinchfield Syndicate had been organized in December, 1910, to purchase from the Cumberland Corporation the stocks and obligations of the Clinchfield Coal Corporation, and subsidiary companies, for $10,000,000. This had been carried out and the properties of the coal company were turned over to the syndicate the next year. According to the agreement, the syndicate acquired obligations as follows:[39]

TABLE XI

Clinchfield Coal Corporation	$3,950,000
Cumberland Corporation	1,365,000
Carolina, Clinchfield & Ohio Railway	3,323,750

"The financial position of the Carolina, Clinchfield, and Ohio Railway is strong," reported the syndicate managers on July 1, 1912. "The readjustment of outstanding securities[40] is designed to put the company in an excellent position to meet its obligations and care for any additional capital expenditures required by growth of its business. In view of the large cash investment represented by the common stock and the present and prospective earning power of the railway ... the syndicate managers believe its capital investment is conservative. Its common stock now has great value, which should steadily increase, and show the members of the Cumberland Syndicate an attractive return on their investment." The managers were N. B. Ream, T. F. Ryan, J. A. Blair, W. B. Donham, W. T. Rosen, and I. T. Mann.[41]

On August 1, 1912, $1,000,000 equipment trust certificates, series "C," were issued to cover equipment costing $1,385,761.59, of which $385,761.59 had previously been paid in cash. These certificates matured in semi-annual payments of $50,000 each, with the final payment on August 1, 1922. The New York Trust Company was trustee. The notes covered the following equipment:[42]

---

[39] *Ibid.*, Vol. XCV (Aug. 17, 1912).

[40] That is, $5,000,000 additional common stock issued to the Cumberland Corporation.

[41] *Commercial and Financial Chronicle*, Vol. XCV (Aug. 17, 1912).

[42] *Second Annual Report*, Carolina, Clinchfield & Ohio Railway Company, for the year ended June 30, 1912, p. 20.

CAROLINA, CLINCHFIELD & OHIO RAILWAY 115

1,000 fifty-ton all steel hopper cars.
6 Mogul Mallet type freight locomotives (2-6-6-2).
3 Pacific type passenger locomotives (4-6-2).

The railway company issued $350,000 five per cent equipment trust gold notes, series "D," dated July 1, 1913, and due in fourteen semi-annual installments of $25,000 each from January 1, 1914, to January 1, 1920. The New York Trust Company was trustee. William M. Read & Company offered these notes for sale.[43] The cost of the equipment was $431,000, of which a cash payment of $81,000 was made by the company. The following equipment was purchased:[44]

475 thirty-ton steel underframe box cars.
25 thirty-ton steel underframe stock cars.

In the fourth annual report to the stockholders, President Potter writes: "There is now under construction at Charleston, South Carolina, a pier and modern coal handling facilities for the loading of coal to vessels. These facilities will be an important assurance of increased earnings to our company, as they will afford an opportunity for the coals of Southwest Virginia and Eastern Kentucky to reach tidewater and the markets beyond, via the Clinchfield Railway."[45] This pier, built by the Southern Railway, was completed in 1915.[46]

The Sandy Ridge tunnel, near Dante, was completed on May 21, 1914, work on which had started June 1, 1912. This tunnel is over a mile and a half long.[47] The last spike in the Elkhorn extension was driven on February 9, 1915,[48] and the road was opened to traffic on July 1 of the same year.[49]

During 1914, the Clinchfield Coal Corporation had mined and sold about 1,500,000 tons of coal. With the completion of the docks at Charleston "for the handling of Clinchfield coal," writes President C. E. Backus of the coal company, "the cor-

---

[43] *Commercial and Financial Chronicle*, Vol. XCVII (July 5, 1913).
[44] *Seventh Annual Report*, Carolina, Clinchfield & Ohio Railway Company, for the year ended December 31, 1917, p. 20.
[45] *Fourth Annual Report*, Carolina, Clinchfield & Ohio Railway Company, for the year ended June 30, 1914, p. 11.
[46] *Commercial and Financial Chronicle*, Vol. CI (Oct. 30, 1915).
[47] *Ibid.*, Vol. XCVIII (May 30, 1914).
[48] *Ibid.*, Vol. C (Feb. 20, 1915). [49] *Ibid.*, Vol. CI (July 3, 1915).

poration is in a strong position to develop an important trade with Cuba, Mexico, South America, and other foreign markets."[50]

The coal corporation forthwith organized the Clinchfield Navigating Company, Incorporated, and bought a 5,500-ton ship during 1915. Contracts were signed for three 4,000-ton ships to be delivered in the fall of 1916. These vessels were to be used principally to take care of the Clinchfield's export and coastwise trade handled through the Southern Railway's coal terminals at Charleston. These terminals were modern in every respect, embracing a 375-foot pier with electric coal-handling facilities capable of loading ships at the rate of one thousand tons per hour.[51] This meant an average of one fifty-ton car every three minutes.

An interesting feature of these terminals is that no switch engine is necessary to spot the cars. The loaded cars are originally shunted on a track with a slight grade, the brakes are set, and the engine leaves. The brakes on each car are released as that car is needed, and it rolls down into the conveyor which lifts it over the hold of the ship, empties it, and returns it to the trestle. It rolls back in the direction from whence it had come, but on a lower level from the loaded cars.

On October 1, 1914, the railway purchased 300 steel underframe stock cars, two Pacific (4-6-2) type passenger locomotives, and one switch engine at a cost of $309,604, of which $49,604 was paid in cash. There were issued $260,000 of five per cent equipment trust certificates, series "E," payable in twenty semi-annual installments of $13,000 each from April 1, 1915, to October 1, 1924. The New York Trust Company was trustee.[52]

Knauth, Nachod & Kuhne, in recommending the railway company's first mortgage 5s of 1908, of which $14,500,000 were outstanding, said: "This road was originally constructed to furnish an outlet for coal traffic from the extensive coal fields of southwestern Virginia, especially for the Clinchfield Coal Corporation, which is closely affiliated with the railroad, guaranteeing it the handling of the corporation's traffic. As the

---

[50] *Ibid.*, Vol. C (March 13, 1915).   [51] *Ibid.*, Vol. CI (Dec. 18, 1915).
[52] *Fifth Annual Report,* Carolina, Clinchfield & Ohio Railway Company, for the year ended June 30, 1915, p. 10.

Mr. George L. Carter Driving the Last Spike of the Elkhorn Extension

CAROLINA, CLINCHFIELD & OHIO RAILWAY 117

country contributary to the railroad is rich in timber and minerals, many new industries have located along the line. In consequence, the merchandise freight traffic of the railway has increased greatly."[53] In November, 1915, $250,000 first mortgage bonds were issued for betterments and improvements.[54]

In April, 1916, the directors of the Cumberland Corporation proposed the dissolution of the corporation. The assets at that time consisted of $10,000,000 preferred and $25,000,000 common stock, at par, of the Clinchfield Railway. The indebtedness, including estimated expenses of dissolution, was approximately $5,937,500. In order to meet this debt, the directors planned to offer the 250,000 common shares of the Carolina, Clinchfield & Ohio Railway to the common stockholders of the corporation at $25 a share. To insure the sale of the stock, an agreement was entered into with an underwriting syndicate, of which Blair & Company was syndicate manager. Upon the completion of this sale, the corporation would have available for distribution $10,000,000 of six per cent preferred and $25,000,000 common stock of the corporation. Each preferred shareholder would receive two shares of Clinchfield Railway preferred stock for each three shares of preferred stock of the corporation. Common stock subscriptions would be payable in full on May 15, 1916, or, at the election of the subscriber, $8.33 per share could be paid on that date, and the balance on or before May 1, 1917, with six per cent interest from May 15, 1916.

Under this plan, the debts of the corporation which were ahead of the preferred stock would be paid, and Carolina, Clinchfield & Ohio preferred stock distributed without imposing on the preferred stockholders any burden of raising the necessary cash. Common stockholders, who were willing to share in the burden of paying the debts, might also share in the future growth of the railway.[55] This plan was approved by the stockholders on May 8, and application was made to list both the common and the preferred stock of the railway on the New York Stock Exchange.[56]

---

[53] *Commercial and Financial Chronicle,* Vol. CI (Dec. 18, 1915).
[54] *Sixth Annual Report,* Carolina, Clinchfield & Ohio Railway Company, for the year ended June 30, 1916, p. 10.
[55] *Commercial and Financial Chronicle,* Vol. CII (April 15, 1916).
[56] *Ibid.,* Vol. CII (May 13, 1916).

Upon the dissolution of the Cumberland Corporation, the railway acquired the entire capital stock of the Holston Corporation, aggregating $750,000. Indebtedness of $758,848 of the Clinchfield Railway to the Cumberland Corporation was also cancelled. The railroad issued $1,500,000 of its preferred stock to the corporation for the transactions.[57] In addition, the railway company guaranteed the payment of principal and interest of the Holston Corporation's realty and collateral trust convertible five per cent ten-year gold notes, amounting to $1,500,000.[58]

The Holston Corporation owned valuable real estate along the line of the road at Kingsport, Johnson City, Erwin, and Altapass, and extensive terminal property at Charleston, upon which large expenditures had been made. It owned $1,500,000 of Carolina, Clinchfield & Ohio preferred stock, which it acquired from the Cumberland Corporation.[59] "In addition," President Potter wrote, it "owned considerable real estate at various points along the line of the railway, some of which will become important as sites for additional industries."[60]

On April 1, 1916, $300,000 five per cent notes were issued, payable in monthly installments of $12,500 for two years, for the purchase of ten Mallet (2-8-8-2) freight locomotives.[61] On the same date, the Clinchfield acquired the Black Mountain Railway by lease, whereby payment was guaranteed of principal and interest of the latter's first mortgage five per cent gold bonds. These bonds amounted to $500,000, and matured in annual installments of $25,000, commencing April 1, 1917. It was believed that the earnings of the Black Mountain Railway would be sufficient to care for these payments.[62] The Black Mountain Railway extended from Kona, a point on the Clinchfield in North Carolina, through Burnsville to Eskota. The rails were recently removed from the right of way between Burnsville and Eskota.[63]

---

[57] *Ibid.*, Vol. CIII (Oct. 28, 1916).

[58] *Sixth Annual Report*, Carolina, Clinchfield & Ohio Railway Company, for the year ended June 30, 1916, p. 10.

[59] *Commercial and Financial Chronicle*, Vol. CIII (Oct. 28, 1914).

[60] *Sixth Annual Report*, Carolina, Clinchfield & Ohio Railway Company, for the year ended June 30, 1916, p. 10.

[61] *Ibid.*, p. 10.   [62] *Ibid.*

[63] From data furnished by the chief engineer, Clinchfield Railroad Company, Erwin, Tennessee, November, 1928.

CAROLINA, CLINCHFIELD & OHIO RAILWAY 119

John B. Dennis was elected chairman of the board to succeed Mark W. Potter, who had previously been appointed president of the road upon the resignation of George L. Carter.[64]

The New York Stock Exchange had listed $9,503,000 six per cent preferred, and $24,990,000 common stock of the railway. In November, authority was given to increase the preferred to $13,500,000, and the common to $25,000,000. First mortgage bonds of $200,000 were issued by the company on November 23.[65]

On January 1, 1917, 500 fifty-ton all steel hopper cars, and five steel underframe caboose cars were purchased at a cost of $903,113.75, of which $143,113.75 was paid in cash. For the balance, $760,000 five per cent equipment trust certificates, series "F," were issued, payable in twenty semi-annual installments of $38,000, beginning July 1. The New York Trust Company was trustee.[66]

A new bond issue, dated February 1, 1917, and due February 1, 1920, of $6,000,000 first mortgage five per cent gold notes was made to retire the $5,500,000 issue of May 1, 1912, due May 1, 1917, for the Elkhorn extension. The extra $500,000 was to be used "for other purposes." The bonds were secured by a first mortgage on the line between Dante and the Virginia-Kentucky state line, 32 miles, and by $500,000 of first mortgage five per cent gold notes of the Clinchfield Northern Railway of Kentucky.[67] No additional mortgage was permitted while these notes were outstanding. Members of an underwriting syndicate offered the bonds for sale at 97½, and interest yielding six per cent. Blair & Company was fiscal agent.[68]

Additional equipment was purchased on the second of April, which included seven Mallet (2-8-8-2) type and nine Mikado (2-8-2) type freight locomotives. The Commercial Trust Company, of Philadelphia, trustee, issued equipment trust certifi-

---

[64] *Sixth Annual Report,* Carolina, Clinchfield & Ohio Railway Company, for the year ended June 30, 1916, p. 11.
[65] *Commercial and Financial Chronicle,* Vol. CIII (Nov. 26, 1916).
[66] *Seventh Annual Report,* Carolina, Clinchfield & Ohio Railway Company, for the year ended December 31, 1917, p. 20.
[67] *Ibid.,* p. 11.
[68] *Commercial and Financial Chronicle,* Vol. CIV (March 17, 1917).

cates, series "G," of a total amount of $840,000, bearing five per cent interest, for rent of the engines for a period of ten years. A cash payment of $252,950 was made by the railway company. The certificates were payable in semi-annual installments of $42,000 until April 1, 1927. Upon the final payment, the equipment reverted to the railway.[69]

On May 18, $475,000 first mortgage five per cent gold bonds, $50,000 six per cent convertible first income debentures, and $250,000 six per cent second income debentures of the Black Mountain Railway were purchased. The consideration was $475,000, payable in promissory notes at six per cent interest, due January 1, 1920.[70]

Of the principal sum of $7,362,950 equipment trust obligations issued by the end of the fiscal year 1917, the Clinchfield had paid $4,261,000, leaving $3,101,950 outstanding.[71]

By a proclamation dated December 26, 1917, Woodrow Wilson, President of the United States, took possession of the major railroad systems of the country at twelve o'clock noon, December 28, 1917. However, for the purpose of accounting, control did not become effective until January 1, 1918. This power was conferred upon the president by Acts of Congress dated August 29, 1916, April 6, and December 7, 1917. William G. McAdoo was appointed director general of railroads.[72]

According to the contract entered into between the various railroads and the director general, acting in behalf of the government, the roads were to receive annually an amount equivalent to their respective average net operating incomes for the three years ended June 30, 1917. Out of this compensation, plus other corporate incomes, the companies paid their corporate expenses, and the costs of additions and betterments. If the latter were approved or ordered by the director general, the companies received interest on the cost of the work upon its completion; but if such constructions were for war purposes and of no permanent value to the railroad, the company could claim from the government the amount expended. The properties

---

[69] *Seventh Annual Report,* Carolina, Clinchfield & Ohio Railway Company, for the year ended December 31, 1917, p. 10.

[70] *Ibid.,* p. 11.

[71] *Ibid.*

[72] Cunningham, *American Railroads: Government Control and Reconstruction Policies,* pp. 329-30.

CAROLINA, CLINCHFIELD & OHIO RAILWAY 121

of the companies were supposed to have been kept in good condition by the government, and returned to the roads in approximately the same condition as of January 1, 1918.[73]

The Clinchfield, in connection with the Southern Railway, was placed under the direction of Federal Manager E. H. Coapman.[74]

Concerning federal control, President Potter stated in the annual report of the Clinchfield: "It is believed that the line of this company, serving as a connecting link between the gathering and distributing lines in the Central West and the Southeast and affording the shortest and most efficient route between important sections, will, under government control as a part of a national transportation system, perform its national transportation function and handle tonnage which should, upon consideration of economy and efficiency, flow to and over it. By being able, in connection with relatively light burdened lines at the north and south, to efficiently transport traffic between producing and consuming points in the North and South, it should render important service to the shippers, while it relieves circuitous overburdened main lines. It is expected that in determining the compensation for the use of the railway under federal control, consideration will be given to the fact that the properties have been passing through a development period, and that the rental will be determined by recent earnings and the value of the line as a part of the national system."[75]

The policies of unification incorporated under federal control applied principally to the following features of operation:[76]

Joint use of passenger and freight terminals.
Joint use of yards and engine houses.
Consolidation of car inspection forces.
Joint use of running tracks.
Joint use of motive power and cars.
Short routing of freight.
Diversion of export traffic to southern ports.
Consolidation of city ticket offices.

---

[73] *Ibid.*, pp. 56-58
[74] *Commercial and Financial Chronicle,* Vol. CVII (July 20, 1918).
[75] *Seventh Annual Report,* Carolina, Clinchfield & Ohio Railway Company, for the year ended December 31, 1917, p. 12.
[76] Cunningham, *op. cit.,* p. 68.

122 THE CLINCHFIELD RAILROAD

Abolition of off-line offices.
Elimination of competitive activities.
Standardization of new locomotives and cars.
Simplification of inter-road accounting.
Standardization of operating statistics.

In May, 1918, the United States Railroad Administration sanctioned outlays to the Clinchfield for equipment aggregating $4,492,750; and for improvements, $398,475.[77]

The annual compensation for the Carolina, Clinchfield & Ohio Railway during the period of federal control was fixed at $1,804,970.46.[78] However, if the system of accounting in use by the railroad administration had credited the railroads with car hire throughout the entire period, the total income of the Clinchfield for 1917 would have been about $2,177,000.[79]

On January 1, 1920, Director General Walker D. Hines, who had succeeded McAdoo, approved an extension of two years of the $6,000,000 five per cent Elkhorn extension first mortgage gold notes, maturing January 1, 1920. The extended notes retained all their mortgage rights, and were to bear six per cent interest per annum, the holders being paid $20 for each $1,000 extended. The railway company accordingly requested Blair & Company to arrange the extension, and the holders were requested to present their notes at the New York Trust Company for extension, at which time they received the interest of the coupon due January 1, 1920, and the extension payment of $20.[80]

An equipment trust agreement was executed by Director General Hines, with the Guaranty Trust Company of New York as trustee, by which "some seventy leading railroad companies" received approximately $360,000,000 in new rolling stock. The Clinchfield's allocation was $6,792,625, the eighteenth largest of the seventy-four roads concerned. Those roads which received over $5,000,000 were as follows:[81]

---

[77] "Supplement, Railway Stocks and Bonds," *Commercial and Financial Chronicle*, Vol. CVII (Nov., 1918).
[78] *Eighth Annual Report*, Carolina, Clinchfield & Ohio Railway Company, for the year ended December 31, 1918, p. 7.
[79] *Commercial and Financial Chronicle*, Vol. CX (Jan. 3, 1920).
[80] *Ibid.*
[81] *Ibid.*, Vol. CX (March 6, 1920).

TABLE XII

Pennsylvania	$61,921,394
Baltimore & Ohio	19,135,498
Chicago, Milwaukee & St. Paul	18,142,700
Frisco Lines	15,028,111
New York Central	14,848,010
Chesapeake & Ohio	12,348,800
Wabash	12,111,160
Louisville & Nashville	11,149,399
Southern Railway	10,977,193
Chicago & Northwestern	10,744,675
Pere Marquette	10,739,920
Missouri Pacific	10,705,992
Illinois Central	10,103,597
Atlantic Coast Line	8,807,868
Chicago & Rock Island	8,762,610
Santa Fe	7,917,480
Norfolk & Western	7,673.680
Boston & Maine	6,948,715
Carolina, Clincheld & Ohio	6,792,625
Chicago, Burlington & Quincy	6,561,925
Central Railroad of New Jersey	6,294,114
Big Four	5,654,805
Michigan Central	5,495,775

Federal control of railroads terminated at 12:01 A.M., March 1, 1920, and the roads were returned to private management under the terms of the Transportation Act of that year. The four outstanding features of this act were as follows: (1) the transition from federal to private control; (2) the new rate making rule; (3) the provisions for railroad consolidation; and (4) the creation of the railroad labor board.[82]

"During the 26 months of Federal control," writes Professor William J. Cunningham of Harvard University, "there were serious dislocations in the normal flow of traffic and much disturbance in operating and financial features from the viewpoint of the individual companies. Serious doubts were entertained whether many carriers could successfully stand the shock of the change, and there were fears that general financial embarrassment might follow the cessation of payment of the Govern-

---

[82] Cunningham, *op. cit.*, pp. 219-21.

ment rentals which the companies had received during federal control. To avoid disaster of that kind the act provided for a six months' transition period (commonly referred to as the guarantee period) in which the properties would be operated by the companies under their individual organizations under a guarantee that the Government would make up the difference between what the railroads individually earned during the six months, and one-half of the average annual net railway operating income earned by the individual railroads during the three years ended June 30, 1917. In other words, the railroads were assured of net railway operating income equal to the rentals paid by the Government during the period of Federal control."[83]

The Clinchfield was one of the few railroads which refused to accept the six months' period of federal guaranty. Some of the other roads which acted in a similar manner were the Southern Railway, the Pere Marquette, the Richmond, Fredericksburg & Potomac, and the Atlanta & West Point.[84] By this action, the Clinchfield's net railway operating income for the six months exceeded the guarantee by $417,086.35, after making allowances for the increases in wages fixed by the newly organized United States Railroad Labor Board. The increase in freight and passenger rates allowed by the Interstate Commerce Commission did not become effective until August 26, 1920.[85]

In May, 1920, Mark W. Potter resigned from the presidency of the Clinchfield Railway to become a member of the Interstate Commerce Commission.[86] He was succeeded by Norman S. Meldrum on June 24. The following resolution was adopted by the board of directors upon the resignation of President Potter, dated June 17:[87]

WHEREAS, Mr. Mark W. Potter has for many years as Counsel, Director, and President rendered invaluable services to this Company and to the communities which it serves, being always a keen student of the varied and intricate problems of railroading, a staunch advocate of the highest standards of construction, operating, and conduct

---

[83] *Ibid.*, pp. 221-22.
[84] *Commercial and Financial Chronicle,* Vol. CX (May 22, 1920).
[85] *Tenth Annual Report,* Carolina, Clinchfield & Ohio Railway Company, for the year ended December 31, 1920, p. 7.
[86] *Commercial and Financial Chronicle,* Vol. CX (May 25, 1920).
[87] *Tenth Annual Report,* Carolina, Clinchfield & Ohio Railway Company, for the year ended December 31, 1920, p. 12.

CAROLINA, CLINCHFIELD & OHIO RAILWAY 125

of business, a firm but just and patient executive, and a public servant of rare foresight, ability, and lofty ideals; and

WHEREAS, the President of the United States, in recognition of the preëminent qualifications of Mr. Potter for that office, has appointed him an Interstate Commerce Commissioner; and

WHEREAS, it is desired in behalf of the stockholders, directors, officers, and employees of this Company to express their deep appreciation of Mr. Potter's services to this Company and of the sense of public duty which has impelled him to accept the aforesaid office;

Now, therefore, be it resolved, That the resignation of Mr. Mark W. Potter as a Director and President of this Company be, and the same hereby is accepted with greatest possible regret.

On June 24, 1920, the board of directors of the Clinchfield authorized an issue of six per cent cumulative income debentures not to exceed $6,000,000, dated July 1, 1920, and payable July 1, 1935. The bonds were to be issued to the government in return for a loan of the same amount, obtained under section 210 of the Transportation Act of 1920.[88] The proceeds were to assist in financing "immediately pressing maturities." The Interstate Commerce Commission approved a loan of $2,000,000 from its revolving fund of $300,000,000,[89] secured by the deposit of $5,000,000 ten-year notes of 1909.[90] The Commission later increased the loan to $5,000,000.[91]

Of the $5,000,000 authorized, $4,324,000 were sold on December 31, the proceeds of which were used to redeem $4,124,000 loans and bills payable of the railway company, and $200,000 loans and bills payable of the Holston Corporation, as guaranteed by the railway.[92]

Equipment trust agreement Number 11, dated January 15, 1920, and amended September 1, 1920, covered the following equipment:

1,750 fifty-five-ton all steel hopper cars.
300 fifty-ton steel underframe box cars.
10 Mallet (2-8-8-2) type locomotives.

---

[88] *Ibid.,* p. 11.
[89] *Commercial and Financial Chronicle,* Vol CXI (July 17, 1920).
[90] *Tenth Annual Report,* Carolina, Clinchfield & Ohio Railway Company, for the year ended December 31, 1920, p. 22.
[91] *Commercial and Financial Chronicle,* Vol. CXI (July 31, 1920).
[92] *Tenth Annual Report,* Carolina, Clinchfield & Ohio Railway Company, for the year ended December 31, 1920, p. 11.

The agreement was executed by Walker D. Hines, director general of railroads, and the Clinchfield, with the Guaranty Trust Company of New York as trustee. The total cost of the equipment was $6,211,779.48, of which a cash payment of $1,779.48 was made. Equipment trust notes were issued totaling $6,210,000 at six per cent interest, and payable in fifteen annual installments of $414,000 each, beginning January 15, 1920.[93]

In April, 1922, $3,588,000 of these notes were offered by Ladenburg, Thalman & Company, and the National City Bank at prices to yield from 5.30 per cent to 5.75 per cent, according to maturity.[94] In February, 1924, Hornblower & Weeks, of New York City, offered $1,518,000 of these notes at prices to yield a similar amount.[95]

A contract was signed by the railway company and the American Railway Express Company covering express operations for a period of five years, beginning September 1, 1920.[96]

The year 1920 contained many unusual railroad features. Within it were embraced the concluding two months of federal control, the six months' "guarantee period" for the majority of the roads in the country, and four months of private operation. The year ushered in a new rule of rate making under the Transportation Act; and a new era in labor relations, with the railroad labor board dominating in wage fixing and the formulation of working rules.[97] The year was one of superlatives. It had the greatest traffic, greatest operating revenues, and greatest operating expenses, and the smallest net railway operating income since the Interstate Commerce Commission began to keep such records in 1888.[98]

At the end of that year, the board of directors of the Carolina, Clinchfield & Ohio Railway was composed of John B. Dennis, chairman; C. L. Blair, M. N. Buckner, N. S. Meldrum, W. W. Miller, W. T. Rosen, T. F. Ryan, and Elisha Walker, all of New York City; D. B. Wentz, of Philadelphia; W. M. Ritter, of Washington, D. C.; and J. W. Pless, of Marion, North Caro-

---

[93] *Ibid.*, p. 12.
[94] *Commercial and Financial Chronicle,* Vol. CXIV (April 15, 1920).
[95] *Ibid.*, Vol. CXVIII (Feb. 9, 1924).
[96] *Tenth Annual Report,* Carolina, Clinchfield & Ohio Railway Company, for the year ended December 31, 1920, p. 13.
[97] Wolf, *The Railroad Labor Board,* pp. 88-94.
[98] Cunningham, *op. cit.,* pp. 236-37.

CAROLINA, CLINCHFIELD & OHIO RAILWAY 127

lina. The officers of the company were N. S. Meldrum, president; C. L. Blair, J. J. Campion, and I. McQuilkin, vice presidents; L. H. Phetteplace, general manager; E. C. Bailly, secretary; J. W. Sanders, treasurer; and H. G. Morison, general solicitor. The general offices were located in Johnson City, Tennessee.[99]

The mileage, not including sidings and yard tracks, operated by the Clinchfield was as follows:[100]

TABLE XIII

Main line: MILES
Kentucky-Virginia state line to North Carolina-South Carolina state line.................255.97
Clinchfield Northern Railway of Kentucky, Elkhorn City to Kentucky-Virginia state line..... 2.79
Carolina, Clinchfield & Ohio Railway of South Carolina, North Carolina-South Carolina state line to Spartanburg....................... 18.09

                                                          276.85
Branch line:
Carbo to Laurel Junction, Virginia............ 5.71   5.71

Trackage rights:
Norfolk & Western Railway, Carbo to St. Paul, Virginia.................................. 8.45   8.45

Total mileage operated...................   291.01

On December 1, 1921, there were issued $676,000 additional fifteen-year six per cent cumulative income debentures of the authorized $6,000,000, dated July 1, 1920.[101] On May 6, 1921, $550,000 was accepted as full settlement of all accounts between the company and the United States Railroad Administration.[102]

A mortgage and deed of trust dated December 15, 1922, of all the properties of the Carolina, Clinchfield & Ohio Railway was made to the Equitable Trust Company of New York as

[99] *Tenth Annual Report,* Carolina, Clinchfield & Ohio Railway Company, for the year ended December 31, 1920, p. 3.
[100] *Ibid.,* p. 7.
[101] *Eleventh Annual Report,* Carolina, Clinchfield & Ohio Railway Company, for the year ended December 31, 1921, p. 10.   [102] *Ibid.*

128 THE CLINCHFIELD RAILROAD

trustee, providing for an authorized issue of first and consolidated mortgage gold bonds to an aggregate amount of $50,000,000. "These bonds are issuable from time to time in series, and may have such dates and maturities (not later than December 15, 2072), bear such rate or rates of interest, and contain such provisions as to redemption, convertibility, exchangeability and otherwise, as the Board of Directors or Executive Committee of the Company, subject to the provisions and conditions of the mortgage and deed of trust, may from time to time determine." Of these bonds, the following amounts were set aside for specified purposes:[103]

$9,500,000 series "A" bonds, dated December 15, 1922, and payable December 15, 1952, bearing six per cent interest annually, redeemable in whole or in part up to December 15, 1937, at 102½ and at 0.5 per cent less during each twelve months' period thereafter.

$200,000 for refunding an equal principal amount of first mortgage thirty-year 5s of Lick Creek & Lake Erie Railroad, maturing April 1, 1926.

$4,923,200 for refunding eighty per cent of the face amount of various equipment trust obligations aggregating $6,154,000.

$15,000,000 for refunding an equal principal amount of five per cent realty and collateral trust convertible notes of the Holston Corporation, maturing April 1, 1926.

$1,500,000 for refunding an equal principal amount of five per cent realty and collateral trust convertible notes of the Holston Corporation, maturing April 1, 1926.

The balance for reimbursing the company for capital expenditures subsequent to December 15, 1922.

Bonds are also required to be set aside and reserved from time to time for the refunding of prior liens on properties purchased with the proceeds of these bonds.

This mortgage was secured by the entire line of railroad and all the properties of the company, as follows: by the main line of the Carolina, Clinchfield & Ohio Railway from the Kentucky-Virginia state line to the North Carolina-South Carolina state line, 255.36 miles, and the "Dumps Creek" line, 5.71 miles; by equipment; by the entire capital stock and $3,000,000 first mortgage gold bonds, dated December 1, 1909, of the Caro-

---

[103] *Twelfth Annual Report,* Carolina, Clinchfield & Ohio Railway Company, for the year ended December 31, 1922, p. 10.

CAROLINA, CLINCHFIELD & OHIO RAILWAY

lina, Clinchfield & Ohio Railway of South Carolina; by the entire capital stock and $500,000 of first mortgage five per cent gold notes, dated May 1, 1912, of the Clinchfield Northern Railway of Kentucky; and the entire capital stock of the Holston Corporation. The issue was subject to the mortgage for $15,000,000 on the line of railway from Dante, Virginia, to the North Carolina-South Carolina state line, 233.47 miles, and on stocks and bonds of the Carolina, Clinchfield & Ohio Railway of South Carolina; and the mortgage for $200,000 on the entire line from Fink Yard to Dante, Virginia, 7.5 miles.[104]

Early in December, application was made to the Interstate Commerce Commission for authority to issue the $9,500,000 series "A" bonds, which were to sell at not less than 91½.[105] Such authority was granted on December 28.[106] The proceeds of $8,000,000 of the total issue of $9,500,000, together with other funds in the treasury of the company, were used to repay the United States Government one-year six per cent secured loans for $1,000,000 and $5,000,000, respectively, due December 31, 1922; and the United States Government ten-year six per cent secured loan for $2,000,000, due July 9, 1930. Upon the repayment of these bonds, there were surrendered to the railway company the securities deposited as collateral, consisting of $1,000,000 first mortgage thirty-year 5s, issued under mortgage to the Farmers' Loan & Trust Company as trustee, dated June 1, 1908; $6,000,000 five per cent Elkhorn first mortgage gold notes, extended, issued under mortgage to the New York Trust Company as trustee, and dated February 1, 1917; and $5,000,000 ten-year five per cent mortgage gold notes, extended, issued under mortgage to the Equitable Trust Company as Trustee, dated July 1, 1909.

The proceeds of the remaining $1,500,000 were utilized for the purpose of reimbursing the company's treasury for installments of equipment trust obligations paid during the period from January 1, 1921, to October 1, 1922; and for disbursements for road and equipment during the same period.[107]

---
[104] *Ibid.*, p. 19.
[105] *Commercial and Financial Chronicle*, Vol. CXV (Dec. 16, 1922).
[106] *Ibid.*, Vol. CXV (Dec. 23, 1922).
[107] *Twelfth Annual Report*, Carolina, Clinchfield & Ohio Railway Company, for the year ended December 31, 1922, pp. 10-11.

130 THE CLINCHFIELD RAILROAD

An agreement was entered into with the Southern Railway, lessee of the old Virginia & Southwestern, whereby the Clinchfield was granted trackage rights over the line from Frisco, Tennessee, to Albert Yard, Virginia, a distance of 13.60 miles.[108]

Early in 1922, ten Mallet type (2-6-6-2) locomotives were sold for $185,000. This equipment was to be rebuilt and modernized, and subsequently repurchased by the railway company.[109] On March 15, 1923, $500,000 five per cent equipment trust certificates, series "H," were issued for the repurchase of the ten rebuilt locomotives. Payments were due in semi-annual installments of $25,000, maturing on March 15, 1933. The issue was redeemable as a whole upon thirty days' notice at 102½ and accrued interest. The trustee was the Metropolitan Trust Company of the City of New York. The cost of the equipment was $700,000, of which $200,500 was paid in cash, $185,000 being derived from the sale of the locomotives the previous year.[110]

On July 31, 1923, the line of the Interstate Railroad was placed in operation from Norton, Virginia, to a connection with the Clinchfield at Miller Yard, Virginia.[111]

Equipment trust certificates, series "I," were issued June 1, 1924, for $1,000,000, with the Chase National Bank of the City of New York as trustee. The cost of the equipment was $1,441,320, of which $441,320 was paid in cash. The notes bore the usual five per cent interest for ten years, and payments were due in semi-annual installments of $50,000. The following equipment was purchased:[112]

10 Mallet (2-8-8-2) type articulated compound freight locomotives.
10 Mikado (2-8-2) type freight locomotives.

These certificates were sold by Blair & Company at prices to yield from 4.0 per cent to 5.3 per cent, according to maturity.[113]

In accordance with a resolution adopted by the board of directors on October 9, 1924, the capital of the railway was

---

[108] *Ibid.*, p. 11.   [109] *Ibid.*, p. 39.

[110] *Thirteenth Annual Report,* Carolina, Clinchfield & Ohio Railway Company, for the year ended December 31, 1923, p. 10.

[111] *Ibid.*

[112] *Fourteenth Annual Report,* Carolina, Clinchfield & Ohio Railway Company for the year ended December 31, 1924, p. 21.

[113] *Commercial and Financial Chronicle,* Vol. CXVIII (June 14, 1924).

CAROLINA, CLINCHFIELD & OHIO RAILWAY 131

decreased to $25,000,000 common stock by the retirement of $13,500,000 of preferred stock. This action was approved by the stockholders at a special meeting held at Bristol, Virginia, on October 20.[114] The entire stock of the company was stricken from the lists of the New York Stock Exchange.[115]

On October 16, 1924, the $5,000,000 six per cent cumulative income debentures of July 1, 1920, were retired and cancelled. These bonds were due in 1935.[116]

The present lease of the Carolina, Clinchfield & Ohio Railway to the Atlantic Coast Line and the Louisville & Nashville railroads, jointly, became effective in 1925, further discussion of which is given in Chapter XII.

THE CLINCHFIELD NORTHERN RAILWAY OF KENTUCKY

The Clinchfield Northern Railway of Kentucky was incorporated under the general laws of that state on October 2, 1911, for the purpose of building a railroad from Elkhorn City, Pike County, to the Virginia state line near the "Breaks" of the Big Sandy River, about three miles. When the line was completed, the road was placed in operation by the Carolina, Clinchfield & Ohio Railway under a lease agreement for ninety-nine years, dated July 1, 1915, and has since been controlled by the Clinchfield through the ownership of its outstanding capital stock. Construction was financed by the Clinchfield, for which the latter company was reimbursed by the issuance to it of the funded debt of the Kentucky company.

The entire authorized capital stock of $5,000 was issued, the proceeds of which were used to purchase the property and franchises of the Elkhorn Southern Railway. This consisted of a right of way and surveys in Pike County, and were conveyed to the Kentucky company on October 11, 1911.

Early in 1912, the company issued $500,000 first mortgage five per cent gold notes to the Clinchfield in payment for original construction work. The Clinchfield had expended $479,663.49,

---

[114] *Fourteenth Annual Report,* Carolina, Clinchfield & Ohio Railway Company, for the year ended December 31, 1924, p. 10.

[115] *Commercial and Financial Chronicle,* Vol. CXIX (Nov. 1, 1924).

[116] *Fourteenth Annual Report,* Carolina, Clinchfield & Ohio Railway Company, for the year ended December 31, 1924, p. 10.

and held the balance for subsequent additions and improvements.[117]

Under the terms of the lease agreement, the Clinchfield paid the Kentucky company an annual rental of $25,000—the interest on its funded debt. The Clinchfield maintains, manages, and operates the property, and pays all taxes and other charges. However, the Kentucky company is obligated to reimburse the lessee for all improvements made upon the property.[118]

The Clinchfield Northern Railway of Kentucky owned no rolling stock.

The Carolina, Clinchfield & Ohio Railway of South Carolina

The charter incorporating the Carolina, Clinchfield & Ohio Railway Company of South Carolina was accepted by the secretary of state on December 4, 1909, "thus ending the long outstanding dispute with the authorities of the state as to the right to incorporate under the laws thereof." On November 27, the judiciary of South Carolina, including the supreme court justices and the circuit court judges, had declared by a divided vote "the Act of 1909, under which the company had previously sought to incorporate, as unconstitutional," and refused a mandamus directed to the secretary of state.[119]

The South Carolina company constructed the road northward from Spartanburg to a point on the North Carolina state line in connection with the line of the parent company, about 18 miles, thus forming the main line of the Clinchfield from Spartanburg to Dante; and, upon the completion of the Elkhorn extension in 1915, to Elkhorn City.

This company authorized and issued $12,000 capital stock, and $300,000 first mortgage bonds on its property, all of which were acquired by the Clinchfield. Like the Clinchfield Northern Railway of Kentucky, the South Carolina company was constructed and was operated under lease by the Carolina, Clinchfield & Ohio Railway. It owned no equipment.[120]

---

[117] *Valuation Docket No. 364 I. C. C.*, pp. 55-57.
[118] *Ibid.*, p. 59
[119] *Commercial and Financial Chronicle*, Vol. LXXXIX (Dec. 11, 1909).
[120] *First Annual Report*, Carolina, Clinchfield & Ohio Railway Company, for the year ended June 30, 1911, p. 7.

CHAPTER IX

THE CAROLINA, CLINCHFIELD & OHIO RAILWAY
(Continued)

RESULTS OF OPERATION

WHEN THE Atlantic Coast Line and the Louisville & Nashville railroads acquired control of the Carolina, Clinchfield & Ohio Railway on January 1, 1925, the latter company operated the following lines of railroad:[1]

TABLE XIV

Main line: MILES

Kentucky-Virginia state line to North Carolina-South Carolina state line................... 255.97

Clinchfield Northern Railway Company of Kentucky, Elkhorn City to Kentucky-Virginia state line 2.79

Carolina, Clinchfield & Ohio Railway of South Carolina, North Carolina-South Carolina state line to Spartanburg...................... 18.09

276.85

Branch lines:

Carbo to Wilder, Virginia.................... 8.40
Hurricane Junction to Shaft, Virginia.......... 1.20
Bostic Yard, North Carolina, to junction with Seaboard Air Line Railway.................... 0.79

10.39   287.24

Trackage rights:

Norfolk & Western Railway, Carbo to St. Paul Virginia 8.45
Southern Railway, Frisco, Tennessee, to Albert Yard, Virginia 13.60

22.05   309.29

---

[1] *First Annual Report*, Clinchfield Railroad Company, for the year ended December 31, 1925, p. 18.

134 THE CLINCHFIELD RAILROAD

Sidings:

Leased	153.13
Operated by railway, but owned by industries	22.53
Trackage rights	4.10
	179.76
Total mileage operated	489.05

The development of traffic is an expensive and slow process, and particularly so for a new railroad; but without it, the entire enterprise would result in a dismal failure. Practically every railroad has undergone this large development cost at some stage in its history. The officials of the Clinchfield decided upon three general policies to secure business for the road, which, as pointed out by O. K. Morgan, were as follows: (1) development of the coal fields; (2) development of local industries; and (3) participation in through traffic.[2]

In 1905, there had been coal mining operations carried on at Dante for some ten or more years, the products being delivered to the Norfolk & Western Railway, six and one-half miles away. The capacity of these mines was enlarged and continuously increased, and upon the opening of the Clinchfield in 1909, it amounted to about sixty cars a day. During 1916-18, new mines were opened at Trammel, Moss, and Haysi, Virginia, and at Elkhorn City. The coal was shipped to either Marion, Bostic, or Spartanburg, and there distributed over the South Atlantic states. Previous to this time, the South Atlantic territory had been supplied by the Pocahontas, the Tennessee, and the Alabama fields. Clinchfield coal literally had to force its way into this market by its own merits, and by the partial displacement of those sources of supply. This was no simple matter, and to this day it is not any easier. It requires skilled salesmanship, hard solicitation, and heavy expense.

The coals of southwestern Virginia and southeastern Kentucky are celebrated for their high heat values. They represent the highest types of gas, steam, and coking coals, and are uniformly high in carbon and volatile matter. The following are typical analyses of Clinchfield coals:[3]

---

[2] "The Story of the Clinchfield," pp. 5-9.

[3] *The Mineral Resources of the Clinchfield Territory*, p. 7. Issued by the Industrial department of the Clinchfield Railroad Company, 1928.

CAROLINA, CLINCHFIELD & OHIO RAILWAY

TABLE XV

Moisture	.50	1.00	.95
Volatile matter	32.70	35.30	36.95
Fixed carbon	60.80	57.80	55.95
Sulphur	.60	.80	.60
Ash	6.50	6.90	7.10
B. T. U.	14580	14740	14510

These coals have been subjected to coking tests, and the results have shown them to be the equal of the Connellsville product. In physical properties, the coke from this coal is of a silvery color, has a metallic ring, and breaks in large, strong pieces, with small cells. The following is an analysis of coke from Clinchfield coal:[4]

TABLE XVI

Volatile matter	1.85%
Fixed carbon	87.24%
Ash	10.91%

"Things do not 'just happen'," writes O. K. Morgan, in regard to the development of local industries. "No territory ordinarily grows of its own right in these days when all communities are striving for growth. A vast amount of effort must be made. Great expenditures must be entailed. To build up a local industry a start is usually made from the zero line. Early the resources of the Clinchfield were virtually card indexed by engineers, geologists, chemists and experts of all lines, working at the behest and under the direction of the industrial department of the railroad. With sound data in hand, then began the dissemination of this information and quests for prospects that might be interested and available. Some were interested in mining coal, cres, kaolin, and feldspar; others in the manufacture of timber, brick, cement, tile, etc."[5]

Kingsport renders an excellent illustration of this local development. Here were found materials suitable for the manufacture of cement. Operators were interested, and a cement factory was established—the first industry of any consequence at Kingsport. To do this, railroad rates had to be fixed and

---

[4] *Ibid.*, p. 8.
[5] Morgan, *op. cit.*, p. 8.

approved by the Interstate Commerce Commission which would be suitable and advantageous to all interests. The plant had to be located at a point available to coal, limestone, shale, and gypsum; and a market had to be established. All conditions were fulfilled, and the industry was established. The railroad realized a revenue from raw materials flowing to the plant, and from the finished product going to the markets.

Johnson City, Erwin, and Spruce Pine are other outstanding examples of local growth brought about directly and indirectly by the Clinchfield.

Concerning the participation in through traffic between the North and the South, Mr. Morgan writes:

Here is a volume of existing traffic, the sum total of which is only slightly augmented by the construction or operation of a railroad such as the Clinchfield. It is a free field for all legitimate competitors. Examination of a map shows conclusively that in so far as the Clinchfield is concerned, the tributary territory in the North is bounded by Chicago on the west, and Pittsburgh and Buffalo on the east; in the South it is limited by the meridian passing through Atlanta on the west and the Atlantic ocean on the east. Within this area old established lines—such as the L. & N., Southern, N. & W., Chesapeake & Ohio—easily handled the volume of traffic, and the Clinchfield entered as a competitor at an advantage as to certain zones, and at a disadvantage as to the remaining other zones.

The Clinchfield entered this competitive field upon the completion of its line to Elkhorn City in 1915. This traffic had not been awaiting the Clinchfield, in fact it apparently did not know of the Clinchfield's existence, and worse yet seemed not to care at all about it. Much might be said in praise of the president of the railroad, Mr. Mark W. Potter, and of Mr. J. J. Campion, its vice president and traffic manager, and of the twenty-odd wide awake and alive young men who courageously faced the necessary expenditures and tackled the job of compelling the business world of the North and South to listen to the facts of the existence of the Clinchfield, and its advantages to the business world as a shipping medium. They wrought mightily and have had splendid success.[6]

The following tables show the annual operating revenues and expenditures from 1910 through 1924. It is interesting to note the through merchandise business which was built up during

---

[6] *Ibid.*, p. 7.

CAROLINA, CLINCHFIELD & OHIO RAILWAY 137

this period. In 1910, it amounted to only about 23 per cent of the total traffic, while on January 1, 1925, it was approximately 44 per cent, and almost the same as coal. The main source of income, of course, has been derived from the handling of coal, but this has decreased almost 15 per cent as compared with the total volume of traffic on the road in 1924. This decline was caused, to a large extent, by the increase in merchandise freight, from $260,000 in 1910 to over $3,800,000 in 1924; however, the revenue from coal had increased from $700,000 in 1910 to over $4,250,000 in 1924.

The year 1921, following the return of the railroads to private management, was indeed one of widespread business depression. Manufacturing and merchandising declined throughout the country, which, of course, had its effect upon the carriers. The decline in the volume of traffic began in December, 1920, and continued through 1921. The average net ton-miles of freight handled by the roads comprising the Southern region showed a decrease of 20.6 per cent for 1921 as compared with the preceding year. The Clinchfield fared better, for its freight had declined only 9.7 per cent. The operating revenues for this group of roads were 10.7 per cent less than in 1920, while those of the Clinchfield declined only 1.28 per cent. Freight cars per train on the Clinchfield averaged 51.4, which, according to President Meldrum, was the heaviest movement in the Southern region.[7] The tables follow:

---

[7] *Eleventh Annual Report,* Carolina, Clinchfield & Ohio Railway Company, for year ended December 31, 1921, p. 10.

TABLE XVII
SUMMARY OF OPERATING REVENUES
(From *Annual Report*, Carolina, Clinchfield & Ohio Railway Company, 1910-1924.)

YEARS ENDED JUNE 30	COAL	MERCHANDISE	PASSENGER	MAIL AND EXPRESS	MISCELLANEOUS	TOTAL
1910	$ 709,579.03	$ 263,777.70	$141,956.03	$ 17,213.76	$ 18,864.36	$1,151,390.88
1911	1,140,606.32	448,893.77	171,504.18	20,170.92	30,580.13	1,811,755.32
1912	1,537,257.71	566,732.35	167,333.61	22,337.84	28,141.79	2,321,803.30
1913	1,582,886.00	794,584.12	202,102.83	24,555.66	30,555.93	2,634,634.54
1914	1,583,207.11	817,042.73	224,579.58	26,317.04	27,961.96	2,679,208.42
1915	1,322,795.41	699,983.25	185,484.31	26,139.90	26,372.97	2,260,775.84
1916	1,797,029.67	1,002,622.43	234,188.51	30,292.37	37,311.04	3,101,444.02
Dec. '31						
1915	1,483,576.22	784,469.98	194,156.77	27,015.53	25,852.97	2,515,071.47
1916	1,783,739.31	1,147,916.54	253,984.64	37,721.13	53,125.18	3,276,486.80
1917	2,217,197.91	1,639,311.56	322,119.07	46,554.38	60,207.19	4,285,390.11
1918	2,972,224.65	1,508,955.39	441,727.22	36,587.96	62,890.04	5,022,385.26
1919	3,906,669.10	1,815,700.02	440,683.95	45,021.50	69,751.57	6,277,826.14
1920	4,478,865.43	2,371,383.96	546,480.38	97,692.15	66,458.27	7,560,880.19
1921	4,024,728.43	2,765,418.97	522,692.77	83,000.41	68,271.64	7,646,112.22
1922	4,414,682.97	2,558,359.66	482,369.19	100,745.73	52,444.61	7,608,602.16
1923	4,934,252.58	3,595,294.33	551,330.64	95,788.78	80,653.06	9,257,319.39
1924	4,256,448.97	3,818,026.76	446,594.37	97,734.75	73,719.45	8,692,524.30

TABLE XVIII

Ratio of Each Class of Operating Revenues to Total Operating Revenues

Years Ended June 30	Coal	Merchandise	Passenger	Mail and Express	Miscellaneous
1910	61.63	22.91	12.33	1.50	1.63
1911	62.95	24.78	9.47	1.11	1.69
1912	66.21	24.41	7.21	0.97	1.20
1913	60.08	30.16	7.67	0.93	1.16
1914	59.09	30.50	8.38	0.98	1.05
1915	58.51	30.96	8.21	1.16	1.16
1916	57.94	32.33	7.55	0.98	1.20
Dec. 31					
1915	58.99	31.19	7.72	1.07	1.03
1916	54.44	35.04	7.75	1.15	1.62
1917	51.74	38.25	7.52	1.09	1.40
1918	59.18	30.04	8.80	0.73	1.25
1919	59.04	32.11	7.02	0.72	1.11
1920	59.24	31.36	7.23	1.29	0.88
1921	53.92	37.05	7.01	1.11	0.91
1922	58.03	33.62	6.34	1.32	0.69
1923	53.30	38.84	5.96	1.03	0.87
1924	48.97	43.92	5.14	1.12	0.85

TABLE XIX
Summary of Operating Expenses
(From *Annual Reports*, Carolina, Clinchfield & Ohio Railway Company, 1911-1924.)

Years Ended June 30	Maintenance of Way and Structures	Maintenance of Equipment	Traffic	Transportation	General	Total
1910	$ 135,748.15	$ 190,589.41	$ 66,318.09	$ 270,867.65	$112,711.14	$ 776,234.44
1911	165,200.50	238,335.53	81,304.65	406,676.47	106,340.54	997,857.69
1912	167,768.36	256,517.78	82,938.48	456,925.94	96,575.36	1,060,725.92
1913	181,825.10	260,711.05	96,763.26	466,973.45	112,356.97	1,118,629.83
1914	190,866.50	330,396.46	102,917.21	506,224.94	124,882.20	1,255,287.31
1915	250,577.63	278,773.16	101,441.46	449,415.61	125,538.24	1,192,309.24
1916	305,885.71	390,069.57	164,600.89	558,972.22	133,858.71	1,540,807.64
Dec. 30						
1915	286,889.88	303,089.63	113,005.25	467,422.55	126,668.51	1,284,731.30
1916	289,720.14	447,317.87	221,016.76	647,025.38	147,772.64	1,742,278.48
1917	426,170.00	635,479.74	227,980.01	986,370.26	179,023.15	2,450,309.64
1918	684,515.12	1,171,404.91	110,363.13	1,621,288.19	163,390.46	3,748,029.87
1919	966,414.25	1,524,824.43	70,044.83	1,966,366.11	176,506.85	4,702,570.71
1920	1,050,184.94	1,915,917.60	221,020.17	2,546,885.82	259,761.95	5,991,271.09
1921	979,799.06	1,740,747.17	269,116.40	2,084,818.32	250,225.27	5,320,170.72
1922	890,358.58	1,621,631.94	263,707.11	2,011,720.04	231,822.72	5,015,786.66
1923	942,975.04	2,631,854.89	302,807.95	2,536,396.00	242,856.05	6,653,392.20
1924	1,045,063.91	2,163,352.09	309,045.08	2,122,075.36	269,737.90	5,904,984.05

TABLE XX

Ratio of Each Class of Operating Expenses to Total Operating Expenses

Years ended June 30	Maintenance of Way and Structures	Maintenance of Equipment	Traffic	Transportation	General
1910	11.79	16.55	5.76	23.53	9.79
1911	9.12	13.15	4.49	22.45	5.87
1912	7.23	11.05	3.57	19.68	4.16
1913	6.90	9.89	3.67	17.72	4.27
1914	7.12	12.33	3.84	18.90	4.66
1915	11.08	12.33	4.49	19.88	5.55
1916	9.86	12.58	5.31	18.02	4.32
Dec. 31					
1915	11.41	12.05	4.49	18.58	5.04
1916	8.84	13.65	6.75	19.75	4.51
1917	9.95	14.83	5.32	23.01	4.18
1918	13.63	23.32	2.20	32.28	3.25
1919	15.39	24.28	1.11	31.32	2.81
1920	13.89	25.34	2.92	33.68	3.44
1921	13.13	23.32	3.61	27.93	3.35
1922	11.70	21.31	3.47	26.44	3.05
1923	10.19	28.43	3.27	27.40	2.62
1924	12.02	24.89	3.55	24.41	3.10

TABLE XXI

Summary of Income Accounts

(From *Annual Reports*, Carolina, Clinchfield & Ohio Railway Company, 1911-1924.)

Years ended June 30	Net Operating Revenues	Non-Operating Revenues	Gross Income	Taxes	Fixed Charges	Surplus Carried to Profit and Loss
1910	$ 375,156.44	$ 125,964.12	$ 501,120.56	$ 47,795.39	$ 838,516.74	*$ 385,191.57
1911	813,397.63	145,396.32	959,293.95	66,508.28	1,030,866.36	*138,080.69
1912	1,261,077.38	29,509.74	1,290,587.12	86,637.28	1,021,821.22	182,128.62
1913	1,516,004.71	247,861.65	1,763,866.36	106,978.42	914,573.87	742,314.07
1914	1,423,921.11	348,918.17	1,772,839.28	131,322.25	941,402.80	700,114.23
1915	1,068,466.60	171,276.74	1,239,743.34	164,266.95	927,670.84	147,805.55
1916	1,560,636.38	346,836.02	1,907,472.40	155,280.39	1,191,953.47	560,238.54
Dec. 31						
1915	1,230,340.17	222,166.46	1,452,506.63	164,266.95	1,058,002.77	209,885.52
1916	1,534,208.32	398,684.06	1,932,892.38	155,280.39	1,189,893.39	587,718.60
1917	1,835,080.47	567,436.38	2,402,516.85	226,877.05	1,275,845.52	899,794.28
1918	1,274,355.39	229,648.11	1,503,695.64	208,457.89		
1919	1,575,255.43	132,297.75	1,707,553.18	226,523.14		
1920	1,569,609.10	1,167,933.45	2,737,542.55	370,749.60	1,618,274.48	748,518.47
1921	2,143,941.50	877,206.46	3,021,147.96	440,000.00	1,594,720.08	896,427.88
1922	2,592,815.50	963,121.71	3,555,937.21	565,000.00	1,553,570.23	1,437,366.98
1923	2,603,927.19	837,571.94	3,441,499.13	600,000.00	1,531,621.24	1,309,877.89
1924	2,787,540.25	752,188.37	3,539,728.62	690,000.00	1,532,846.52	1,316,882.10

* Deficit

CAROLINA, CLINCHFIELD & OHIO RAILWAY

Securities Owned

It will be recalled that there were mentioned in the preceding chapter some of the securities held by the Clinchfield, the aggregate value of which on December 31, 1924, was over $7,000,000. From an operating point of view, the more important were those issued by the Carolina, Clinchfield & Ohio Railway of South Carolina, the Clinchfield Northern Railway of Kentucky, and the Lick Creek & Lake Erie Railroad. The Clinchfield owned all of the outstanding securities of these three companies.

TABLE XXII

Securities Owned by the Carolina, Clinchfield & Ohio Railway Company as of December 31, 1924

(From *Fourteenth Annual Report,* Carolina, Clinchfield & Ohio Railway Company, p. 22.)

Company	Shares	Each	Par Value	
Stock				
Southport Harbor Company	20,000	$100	$2,000,000	
Holston Corporation	7,500	100	750,000	
Spartanburg Land Company	7,500	100	750,000	
Lick Creek & Lake Erie R. R. Co.	1,000	100	100,000	
C. C. & O. Ry. of South Car.	120	100	12,000	
Clinchfield Northern Ry. of Ky.	50	100	5,000	
Total stock				$3,617,000.00
Bonds				
C. C. & O. Ry of South Car.	3,000	1,000	$3,000,000	
Clinchfield Northern Ry. of Ky.	500	1,000	500,000	
Black Mountain Railway Co.	300	1,000	300,000	
Black Mountain Ry. First Income Debentures	50	1,000	50,000	
Black Mountain Ry. Second Income Debentures	250	1,000	250,000	
Total bonds				4,100,000.00
Total par value				$7,717,000.00
Book value				$7,301,055.11

TABLE XXIII

BALANCE SHEET OF COMPANIES CONTROLLED BY THE CAROLINA, CLINCHFIELD & OHIO RAILWAY COMPANY AS OF DECEMBER 31, 1924

(From *Fourteenth Annual Report,* Carolina, Clinchfield & Ohio Railway Company, pp. 44-45.)

Assets

Clinchfield Northern Railway of Kentucky:
    Investment in road..................... $ 519,461.69

Holston Corporation:
Investment in real estate	$ 296,319.81	
Real estate improvements	247,274.55	
Investment in stocks and bonds	73,100.00	
Construction of Charleston terminal	362,980.57	
Other investments	170,222.68	
Cash	17,728.81	
Other current assets	87,270.77	
Profit and loss	1,078,375.54	
		2,333,272.73

Lick Creek & Lake Erie Railroad Company:
    Franchise 100,000.00

Southport Harbor Company:
Real estate	1,999,000.00	
Profit and loss	20,608.71	
		2,019,608.71

Spartanburg Land Company:
Real estate	747,602.00	
C. C. & O. Ry. deposit account	7,606.10	
		755,208.10

Liabilities

Clinchfield Northern Railway of Kentucky:
Capital stock	$ 5,000.00
Funded debt matured unpaid	500,000.00*
Non-negotiable debt to affiliated companies	12,605.45
Additions to property through income and surplus	1,871.30
Profit and loss—balance............Dr.	15.06
	$ 519,461.69

* Owned by the Carolina, Clinchfield & Ohio Railway Company.

CAROLINA, CLINCHFIELD & OHIO RAILWAY 145

Holston Corporation:
Capital stock	750,000.00	
Realty and collateral trust convertible notes 5s	1,500,000.00	
Current liabilities	83,138.06	
Deferred credit items	134.67	
		2,333,272.73

Lick Creek & Lake Erie Railroad Company:
Capital stock	100,000.00

Southport Harbor Company:
Capital stock	2,000,000.00	
C. C. & O. Ry. advances	19,608.71	
		2,019,608.71

Spartanburg Land Company:
Capital stock	750,000.00	
Profit and loss	5,208.10	
		755,208.10

Equipment

It will be seen from the tables below that the Mallet type locomotive is used more extensively than others. As the name implies, this type has four sets of drivers and four cylinders, while the general types of engines in common use have only two. These locomotives are capable of handling an immense tonnage, and it is not at all uncommon to see one of the Clinchfield's "700's" hauling ninety to one hundred loaded coal cars en route from the mines in southwestern Virginia to the Piedmont section of North Carolina. Over 1,700 large hopper cars, with a capacity of fifty-five tons, are used exclusively for the coal traffic passing over the road.

The character of the Clinchfield line, with its long, easy grades, makes an ideal condition for the operation of Mallet locomotives. The first Mallet was purchased from the Baldwin Locomotive Works in 1909 as an experiment.[8] As the figures below indicate, its performance proved most satisfactory, for in 1924, there were forty-eight of these high powered engines in regular train service. The original Mallets, twenty-one in number, were of the 2-6-6-2 type—that is, simply, two wheels

---

[8] *Railway Age Gazette*, Vol. XLVIII (Sept. 9, 1910).

146   THE CLINCHFIELD RAILROAD

under the pilot, or "cow-catcher," one on each side; six drivers to the first two cylinders, and six drivers to the second two cylinders, or three on each side for each cylinder; and two trailer wheels under the cab, one on each side. In 1919, the Clinchfield received its first order of the 2-8-8-2 type, which, as the table on page 147 shows, has a greater tractive power than the 2-6-6-2 type. In 1924, there were twenty-seven of this newer type in service.

On account of the generous clearance provided along the line, it was possible to build these locomotives to large dimensions. The width of the newer Mallets is 11½ feet, and they have a maximum height of 16 feet 8 inches. This width allowed ample room for the use of crank pins of good proportions, and avoided any cramping of the design. This equipment was built to the Clinchfield's specifications, and not according to the United States' standard designs.[9] The Mikado type and the larger Mallet type locomotives are fired by automatic stokers.[10]

The Pacific (4-6-2) type locomotives are used exclusively for passenger service. Built according to the specifications of the company, they are well adapted for hauling relatively heavy trains on long grades. Five of these engines are in use, and their operating results have been entirely satisfactory.

The tables below show the equipment owned by the Carolina, Clinchfield & Ohio Railway on December 31, 1924, as compared with June 30, 1910, and upon the formation of the company in 1908:[11]

TABLE XXIV
LOCOMOTIVES

TYPE	1908	1910	1924	AVERAGE WEIGHT	TRACTIVE POWER
Mogul (freight), (2-6-0)	1	1	0	126,000	21,400
Ten-wheel (passenger), (4-6-0)	1	5	5	158,420	27,480
Consolidation (freight), (2-8-0)	2	2	0	146,500	33,580
Consolidation (freight), (2-8-0)	0	0	2	175,000	41,160

[9] *Railway Review*, Vol. LXV (July 26, 1919).

[10] From information furnished by the mechanical engineer, Clinchfield Railroad Company.

[11] *Commercial and Financial Chronicle*, Vol. LXXXVIII (Feb. 13, 1909), and *Annual Reports*, Carolina, Clinchfield & Ohio Railway Company, 1910-1924.

C. C. & O. Locomotive 740. Class L 3

C. C. & O. Locomotive 411. Class K 1

CAROLINA, CLINCHFIELD & OHIO RAILWAY 147

TABLE XXIV—Continued

Type	1908	1910	1924	Average Weight	Tractive Power
Consolidation (freight), (2-8-0)....	2	17	15	199,150	43,882
Mallet (freight), (2-6-6-2).........	0	1	0	375,373	76,786
Mallet (freight), (2-6-6-2).........	0	0	21	368,626	73,859
Mallet (freight), (2-8-8-2).........	0	0	27	532,785	102,080
Mikado (freight), (2-8-2)..........	0	0	21	307,986	54,929
Pacific (passenger), (4-6-2)........	0	0	5	253,120	40,764
Total freight and passenger....	6	26	96		
In work train.................	0	0	3		
Leased (to Black Mt. Ry.)....	0	0	1		
Total	6	26	100		

TABLE XXV

Passenger Cars

Type and Construction	1908	1910	1924
Mail, baggage and express, wood......................	1	1	0
Combination baggage and mail, wood...................	3	3	0
Combination baggage and mail, steel underframe........	0	2	0
Combination baggage and mail, all steel...............	0	6	6
Express, wood	1	1	0
Express, steel underframe.............................	0	0	6
Coaches, wood	1	1	0
Coaches, vestibule, steel underframe...................	0	12	23
Coaches, gas-electric, all steel.........................	0	0	1
Official, wood	1	1	0
Official, steel underframe.............................	0	1	2
Total	7	28	38

TABLE XXVI

Freight Cars

Type and Construction	Capacity in Tons	1908	1910	1924
Stock, steel underframe...................	30	0	0	286
Box, wood	30	235	235	114
Box, steel underframe.....................	30	0	250	685
Box, steel underframe.....................	50	0	0	299
Flat, wood	20	6	6	0
Flat, wood	25	16	16	0
Flat, wood	30	11	111	31

TABLE XXVI—Continued

Type and Construction	Capacity in tons	1908	1910	1924
Flat, all steel	50	0	100	100
Gondola, all steel	50	0	750	736
Hopper, all steel	50	0	2,350	3,716
Hopper, all steel	55	0	0	1,747
Caboose, steel underframe	..	1	16	40
Total	..	269	3,834	7,754

TABLE XXVII

Work Equipment

Type and Construction	1908	1910	1924
Wrecker, all steel	0	1	1
Camp, wood	20	20	58
Dump, all steel	0	20	28
Pile driver, steel underframe	1	1	1
Derrick, all steel	1	1	2
Steam shovel, steel underframe	2	2	2
Scoop, wood	2	2	1
Spreader, wood	3	3	4
Scale test, all steel	0	0	1
Cabin car, wood	0	0	1
Total	29	50	99

C. C. & O. Locomotive 150. Class P 1

C. C. & O. Locomotive 511. Class M 2

CHAPTER X

THE CONSTRUCTION OF THE CLINCHFIELD

The Carolina, Clinchfield & Ohio Railway was designed for and built with the primary purpose of handling at a minimum cost heavy train loads of coal, southbound from southwestern Virginia; and of handling the resulting movement of northbound empties as economically as possible. All of this coal traffic has to be hauled over the Blue Ridge Mountains. The natural obstacles presented to the builders were great.

The common practice in the building of American railroads has been to lay a line as cheaply and as expeditiously as possible which should create a good part of the traffic it was to carry. With the growth of that traffic, the line has been improved, rebuilt piece by piece, and, if successful, has kept abreast of the requirements made on it. The result has been an uneven development. Often one division has received improvements and additional facilities, not because its need was greater than that of some other division, but because one superintendent could present his argument for his needs in a more convincing manner than could another. Furthermore, in an endeavor to spend an appropriation in such a way as to get the very best facilities at some particular point, this weak link in the chain has often been so strengthened as to be disproportionately better than any other link.

The Clinchfield builders had ample money to build a road, all at one time, without going through what is in the long run the expensive and unscientific process of building "piece-meal." The result was that the road was designed and constructed in a scientific manner to do a particular piece of work at the lowest possible cost of operation. The road was planned by an operating man with an engineer's training—M. J. Caples. No expense was spared in the preliminary surveys, and a great amount of time, patience and study was put into the planning of the road. Throughout these preliminary plans, the consistent object was adhered to: of making a homogeneous, evenly de-

150   THE CLINCHFIELD RAILROAD

veloped transportation system which was to be built with the very best standards without extravagance.[1]

In the first annual report to the stockholders, for the fiscal year ended June 30, 1911, President Potter wrote that the road was built to provide an outlet for coal and furnish a new and short route across the mountains from the Northwest to the Southeast,

over which the cost of operation would be materially lower than upon competing lines and over which improved service would be rendered. The construction of this line not only facilitates the development of a large coal business in the South but also provides a line of less resistance than any heretofore existing between the territory north of the Ohio River and the South Atlantic States and ports thereof.

Low grades, especially against southbound movements, were adopted to reduce train mileage and lower transportation cost. The roadbed was in the first instance built in the most substantial manner, with a view of keeping the cost of maintenance of way down to a minimum. The grades are such that southbound freight trains may be loaded for a grade of three-tenths of one per cent by using helper engines to assist these trains over short sections of heavier grade . . .

The road was constructed in accordance with the best prevailing practice. The cuts and embankments are wide, so that the track may be kept clear, drainage maintained in cuts, and the inevitable settlement which always takes place on a newly constructed road may be overcome at a minimum of expense. All important bridges are built with concrete abutments and the piers with steel superstructures, designed under Cooper's E-60 specifications. This standard, though in advance of the general practice of other roads when the bridges were constructed, has since been adopted by many of the leading railroads of the country. The general adoption of the Mallet type locomotive . . . is a justification of the heavy bridge construction.

Passing sidings with a capacity of from 100 to 120 cars are provided, generally 8 miles apart, and at certain places, 4 miles apart. The locations for these sidings were selected to favor loaded movements and to facilitate the starting of long, heavy freight trains. Water tanks are of substantial construction, and were built at the ends of passing sidings so as to favor the heavy traffic and to reduce

---

[1] *Railway Age Gazette,* Vol. LVI (April 24, 1914).

CONSTRUCTION OF THE CLINCHFIELD 151

the number of stops to a minimum. Nearly one-half of the tanks are supplied by gravity.[2]

When the Carolina, Clinchfield & Ohio Railway was organized as the successor to the South & Western in 1908, the lines of railroad in operation consisted of about seventy-seven miles. This embraced the sixty-seven miles of main line between Johnson City and Altapass, the six miles from Fink to Dante, and the "Dumps Creek" branch.[3] It is interesting to know some of the details involved in the completion of the entire line from Elkhorn City to Spartanburg.

As was pointed out in Chapter VIII, the line between Altapass and Marion was opened to traffic on September 8, 1908;[4] and the first regular train from Dante to Spartanburg was operated on October 28, 1909.[5] The road northward from Dante to Elkhorn City, commonly called the Elkhorn Extension, was placed in operation in October, 1914.[6] This latter section will be discussed separately at the end of this chapter.

The promoter and builder of "this magnificent road" was George L. Carter, and today "it stands as a monument to his genius—one of the greatest pieces of railroad construction east of the Rocky Mountains."[7] Concerning Mr. Carter, William H. Stone writes that "to his never-failing faith, his unbounded confidence and persistent determination is due more than to any other cause the success of the project. He never ceased in his efforts to impress capitalists with the true value of the undertaking, and was finally rewarded by securing the backing of some of the leading financial interests of the country. Moreover, he convinced them that in order to be a real success and serve its real purpose, the road must be constructed along the broad lines he had planned for it, which meant the outlay of many millions of dollars."[8]

---

[2] *First Annual Report,* Carolina, Clinchfield & Ohio Railway Company, for the year ended June 30, 1911, pp. 7-8.
[3] See Chapter VII above.
[4] *Commercial and Financial Chronicle,* Vol. LXXXVII (Dec. 19, 1908).
[5] *Ibid.,* Vol. LXXXIX (Nov. 6, 1909).
[6] "Supplement," *Commercial and Financial Chronicle,* Vol. XCIX (Oct., 1914).
[7] *Scientific American,* Supplement, Vol. LXI (July 31, 1909).
[8] *Manufacturers' Record,* Vol. LV (Feb. 11, 1909).

The *Scientific American*, in an article by J. O. Lewis entitled "The Costliest Railroad in America," says that the Clinchfield is the only railroad which crosses the entire Alleghany Mountains at right angles. Rising from 790 feet above sea level at Spartanburg, it climbs by exceptionally low grades to an altitude of 2,629 feet where it crosses the Blue Ridge. The elevation of Elkhorn City is 795 feet. "Instructions were given the engineers that surveys be made which would give the road the lowest possible grade and yet the shortest route to the coast. To do this was the riddle which has just been solved in the finishing of the line from Dante to Bostic." In celebration of its completion, the Commercial Club of Johnson City, Tennessee, gave a large banquet to the officials, which was attended by many prominent men of the country, including W. M. Finley, president of the Southern Railway; F. P. Howe, Philadelphia, president of the East Tennessee & Western North Carolina Railroad; and presided over by Congressman W. P. Brownlow, of the First Congressional District of Tennessee, as toastmaster.[9]

In order to handle as economically as possible the heavy freight trains which would pass over the line, it was necessary to build a road of low grades and easy curves. Once the plans were determined upon, every effort was made to build at the outset a road on which future maintenance charges would be at a minimum, and to cross the mountain ranges with the lowest possible grade. On account of the rugged character of the territory traversed, numerous lines were surveyed before the final location was determined. In some cases, as many as six and seven alternate lines were surveyed, thereby covering all possible gaps through the mountains. The result is the present location. Surveys were also conducted from Spartanburg to Columbia, with Charleston as the ultimate destination; but it was decided unwise to build a road parallel to the existing lines.[10]

The line was located, plans prepared, and construction work was carried on toward completion. Many intricate engineering and construction problems were confronted and overcome,

---

[9] *Scientific American*, Supplement, Vol. LXI (July 31, 1909).

[10] Except where references are stated, further information in this chapter was obtained, either by personal observation or from the chief engineer, Clinchfield Railroad Company, Erwin, Tennessee, 1928.

Construction Scene on the South Slope of the Blue Ridge in North Carolina

CONSTRUCTION OF THE CLINCHFIELD

apparently regardless of the expense entailed. Mountains were laid low and valleys filled in, tunnels followed one another in rapid succession, and in numerous places large steel viaducts were constructed. "In fact, the predominating determination in the minds of all was to maintain the grade. No matter what engineering difficulties presented themselves, no matter what the cost would be, the grade must be maintained."[11] To do this, and not depart from the plans, extraordinarily heavy construction was necessarily involved. As a result, the maximum grade against southbound traffic is 1.5 per cent. However, this grade is located between Elkhorn City and the "Breaks" of the Big Sandy River, a distance of about seven miles, and, therefore, does not affect the heavy coal trains, which, for the most part, are made up at Dante. The grade up the west slope of the Blue Ridge is 0.8 per cent, except for a short distance between Unaka Springs and a point about eight miles north of Huntsdale, where it is 1.49 per cent. Against northbound traffic, the maximum grade of the entire line is 1.7 per cent, located on the six miles between Fink and Dante, while up the east slope of the Blue Ridge it is only 1.2 per cent. All grades are compensated 0.035 per cent per degree of curvature. For example: a 1 per cent grade on a straight line would require the same tractive effort from a locomotive as a 0.65 per cent grade on a 10 degree curve.[12]

Southward from Dante, the Clinchfield leaves the old roadbed of the "Three C's" near Starnes Bend, about eight miles north of Clinchport, Virginia, where it passes from the west bank of the Clinch River to the east bank, and rises gradually to avoid the heavier grades of the location adopted by its predecessor. This section of the work between Starnes Bend and Clinchport involved unusually heavy excavation in solid cliff, the slopes extending in many cases far up the mountain sides. The broken nature of the country on this section rendered necessary numerous fills of extraordinary size, these ranging in length up to 1,000 feet, and in depth from 75 to 135 feet. This latter height is found at the crossing of Gate Creek, opposite Clinchport, the highest on the line, where 250,000 cubic yards of

---

[11] *Manufacturers' Record*, Vol. LV (Feb. 11, 1909).
[12] From information received from the mechanical engineer, Clinchfield Railroad Company, Erwin, Tennessee (Nov., 1928).

material were required in its construction. "Under usual circumstances of railroad construction, openings of such magnitude would be invariably crossed on trestles, or at best steel bridges."[13] The Clinchfield, however, has adhered constantly to its policy of constructing a roadbed such as to require minimum maintenance in the future, and has, therefore, filled such ravines with solid embankments.

At Copper Creek, immediately south of Clinchport, a deep ravine is crossed by a heavy steel viaduct 1,360 feet in length. From the base of the rails to the stream below is a distance of 168 feet. Only about one hundred yards to the west, and parallel to the Clinchfield, is the line of the old Virginia & Southwestern, now the Southern Railway, following the east bank of the Clinch River and about 150 feet below the level of the Clinchfield. In this vicinity, the roadway is virtually cut into the sides of the mountain, almost perpendicularly above the tracks of the Southern. A little over a mile south of Copper Creek is the station at Speer's Ferry, built on a high trestle above the Southern Railway, at the end of which is the entrance of the 4,135-foot tunnel through Clinch Mountain. After crossing the North and South Forks of the Holston River, and passing through Kingsport, the line of the railroad breaks across the various ridges and valleys which slope in a northeasterly direction to the Watauga River, and finally reaches Johnson City. Just north of Johnson City, the road passes through its longest cut, called Soldiers' Home cut. It is 3,000 feet long, and has a maximum depth of 85 feet. In its excavation, there was involved the removal of about 500,000 cubic yards of earth. The material was hauled several miles to Knob Creek fill, 2,700 feet long.

At Erwin, sixteen miles south of Johnson City, are located the operating headquarters of the company. Extensive terminal facilities, shops, and a modern building for the general offices of the company have been erected. The large railway yard stretches out for some distance beyond the ends of the town along a flat valley almost completely surrounded by high mountains. One must necessarily climb a grade to go in any direction from Erwin.

---

[13] *Engineering News*, Vol. LXI (Jan. 21, 1909).

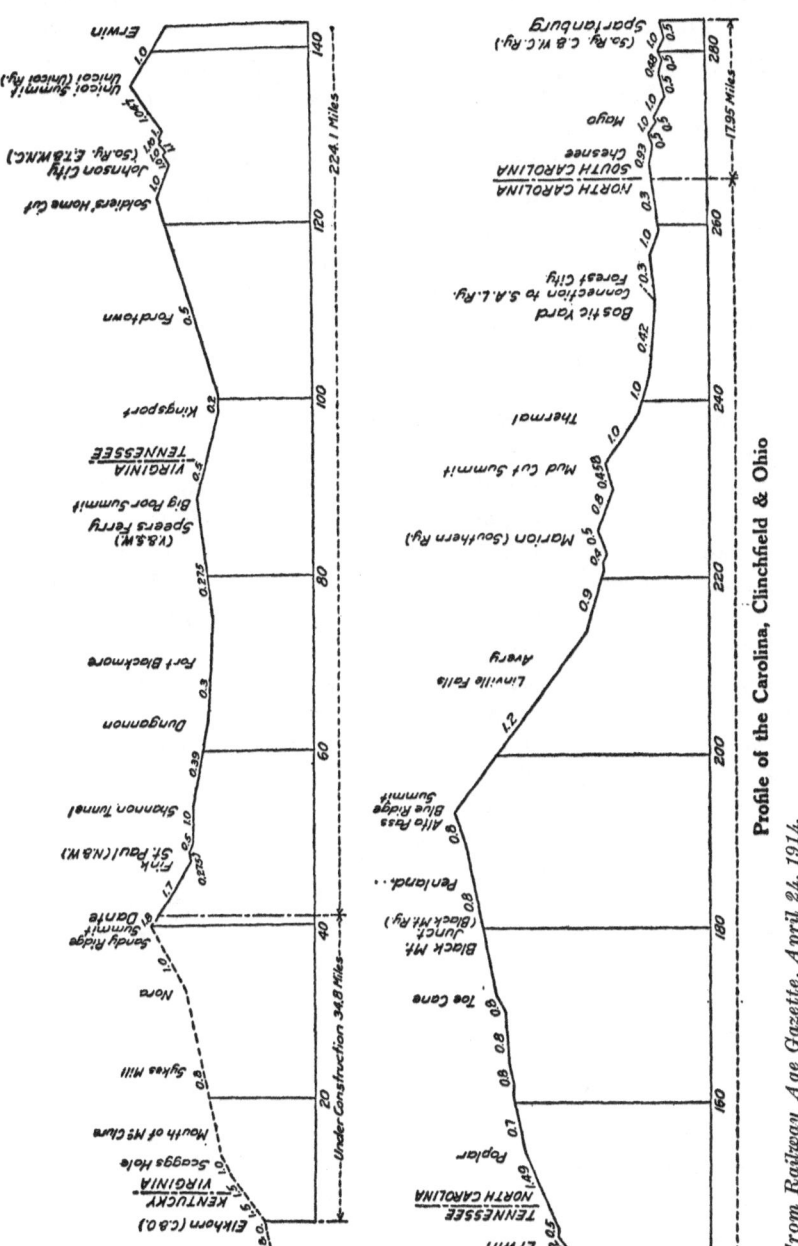

Profile of the Carolina, Clinchfield & Ohio

From *Railway Age Gazette, April 24, 1914.*

156   THE CLINCHFIELD RAILROAD

About four miles south of Erwin, the line enters the wonderful scenic gorge of the Nolachucky River, and follows it for about eight miles. Here, the mountains rise almost precipitously to a height of 1,200 feet. The roadbed is hewn from the solid ledge and follows the tortuous course of the river, which in places reverses itself in direction. For several miles in this section, concrete abutments drop perpendicularly from the surface of the right of way to the river's edge. On one side, the roadway represents a long concrete bridge; on the other, a huge cut in solid rock.

While gathering data on the Clinchfield at the general offices of the company in Erwin, the author was told an interesting story in regard to a piece of construction work near Poplar, at the south end of the Gorge. The story is as follows: In about 1905, the Southern Railway, "considering the C. C. & O. a menace to the integrity of its property," began surveys for a competitive line, presumably to forestall the construction of the Clinchfield, then the South & Western. The Southern was planning to extend its line from Embreeville through the Gorge, and on across the mountains. The two lines crossed and recrossed, and practically coincided at numerous places. At one point near Poplar, the rights of way of the two companies crossed at grade in a tunnel. Litigation followed, and the Clinchfield, in order to hold its rights, placed a force of men at work on the tunnel approach. It seems that the case was postponed from time to time, and the Clinchfield's construction gang had been reduced to one aged negro with a wheelbarrow and a spade. The negro remained on his job for about three years, and finally the Southern decided not to construct the line. The point in litigation was not utilized by the Clinchfield, for today it passes along the opposite side of the river.

After leaving the Gorge of the Nolachucky River at Poplar, where the name of the river is changed to the Toe, the road extends up an easy grade of 0.8 per cent, through Spruce Pine to Altapass, approximately the summit of the line where it crosses the Blue Ridge. The summit itself is crossed just south of Altapass in the 1,865-foot Blue Ridge tunnel. From this point to the vicinity of the Catawba River, at the foot of the mountains, there is a difference of about 1,200 feet in elevation. To overcome this, a loop development was built, which is "more

Bridge over Toe River Near Poplar, North Carolina

CONSTRUCTION OF THE CLINCHFIELD

magnificent in engineering detail than any railroad construction east of the Rocky Mountains." This development consists of a series of seven stages, winding around the various smaller valleys that are offshoots from the Blue Ridge.[14]

As an example of the steepness of the slopes upon which the low grade is maintained, after passing through the Blue Ridge tunnel, the road makes a seven-mile loop, to descend an elevation of about 300 feet, returning to within 400 yards of the south end of the tunnel. At another point, the direct distance to a corresponding point on the lower grade is about 100 yards, while the distance by the track between them is two miles. There are nine tunnels in this seven-mile loop; and within fourteen miles, there are eighteen tunnels aggregating 16,391 feet in length. Standing at the mouth of the Blue Ridge tunnel, one can see fourteen different views of a train as it winds its way around the mountain sides.

From Linville Falls station, near the foot of the Blue Ridge, the road follows the North Fork of the Catawba River. This section entailed much lighter construction work than on any of the previous portions. The Catawba River is crossed two miles north of Marion by a steel viaduct about 100 feet high and over 800 feet long.[15] The road does not enter the corporate limits of Marion, but passes about two miles east of it at a junction with the Southern Railway.

"Through one of the wildest and grandest mountain regions on the continent," says an editorial in the *Charlotte Daily Observer*, "a corporation with practically unlimited financial resources has built a railroad which for solid construction and freedom from heavy grades can bear comparison with almost any. . . . But for the problem presented by North Carolina's great mountain walls on the northwest side, such a road, often projected, would have been built long ago. The Carolina, Clinchfield, and Ohio's section between Marion and Johnson City represents the successful solution, at enormous expense, of that problem."[16]

At the south end of the Marion yards, the road passes through the final tunnel of the line, 1,073 feet in length, follows the

---

[14] *Manufacturers' Record*, Vol. LV (Feb. 11, 1909).
[15] *Engineering News*, Vol. LXI (Jan. 21, 1909).
[16] *Charlotte Daily Observer*, Aug. 31, 1908.

valley of the Second Broad River to Bostic, and thence to Spartanburg. For several miles the line of the old "Three C's," now operated by the Southern, is paralleled by the Clinchfield. The country in this section is of a very rolling nature, so that construction work, while not as heavy as that necessary to cross the Blue Ridge, was quite extensive. Terminal facilities have been established at Bostic, where connection is made with the Seaboard Air Line Railway, formerly the Carolina Central Railroad. Numerous streams are crossed south of Bostic, the more important of which are the Second Broad River, Pacolet River, Lawson's Fork, and Broad River. The valley of the latter is traversed by a viaduct 160 feet high and about 1,360 feet long. "Among the special features that impress one traveling the length of the new road is the fact that few stretches exist of what would be called ordinary railroad construction."[17]

The numerous fills on the road were built partly by end-dumping, and partly from temporary trestles. In the case of the high fills, as those along the Clinch River, the work was handled in three lifts, using temporary trestles for each lift. For the 125-foot fill crossing the ravine of Doe Branch, at Starnes Bend, a switch-back railway system was used to bring rock from the adjacent cliffs to form the embankment.

A large percentage of the tunnel work was in hard rock of a granite character. The strata in the Clinch Mountain tunnel were almost vertical, and as a result many different qualities of rock were encountered. The hardest resembled a flinty sandstone. In this material, it took 72 hours to drill a round of six-foot holes, using hard tool steel and chrome steel. The tunnel is 18 feet wide in the clear, and 22 feet high from the base of the rails to the roof. In each side of the floor, there is a ditch 8 inches deep and 14 inches wide at the bottom. An important factor in all of the Clinchfield's tunnels is that they permit sufficient clearance for a man to stand upright on the roof of a box car, and also the use of relatively wide locomotive equipment, as shown in the preceding chapter. The tunnels were originally lined with timbers, or else left bare. Reinforced concrete is now being used for this purpose, and when completed in 1931, it is estimated that there will be an

---

[17] *Manufacturers' Record,* Vol. LV (Feb. 11, 1909).

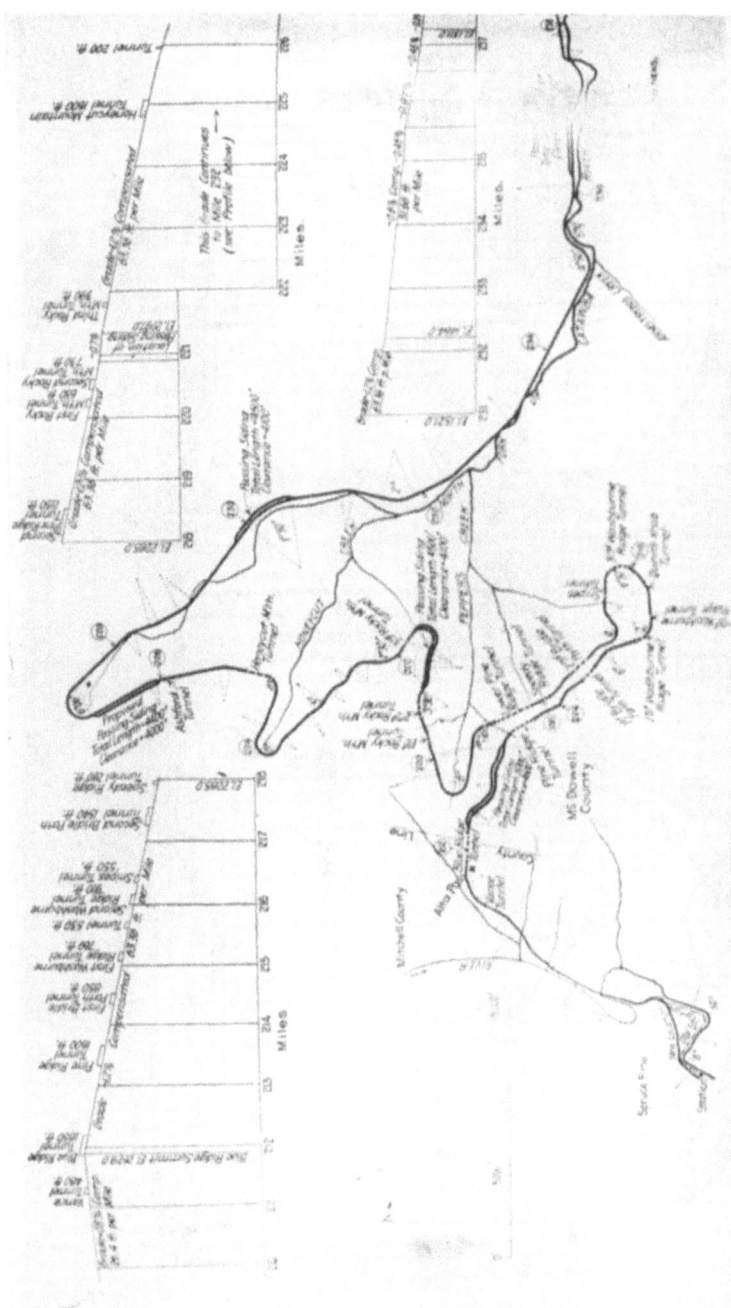

PROFILE OF THE SOUTH SLOPE OF THE BLUE RIDGE
From *Engineering News, January 21, 1909.*

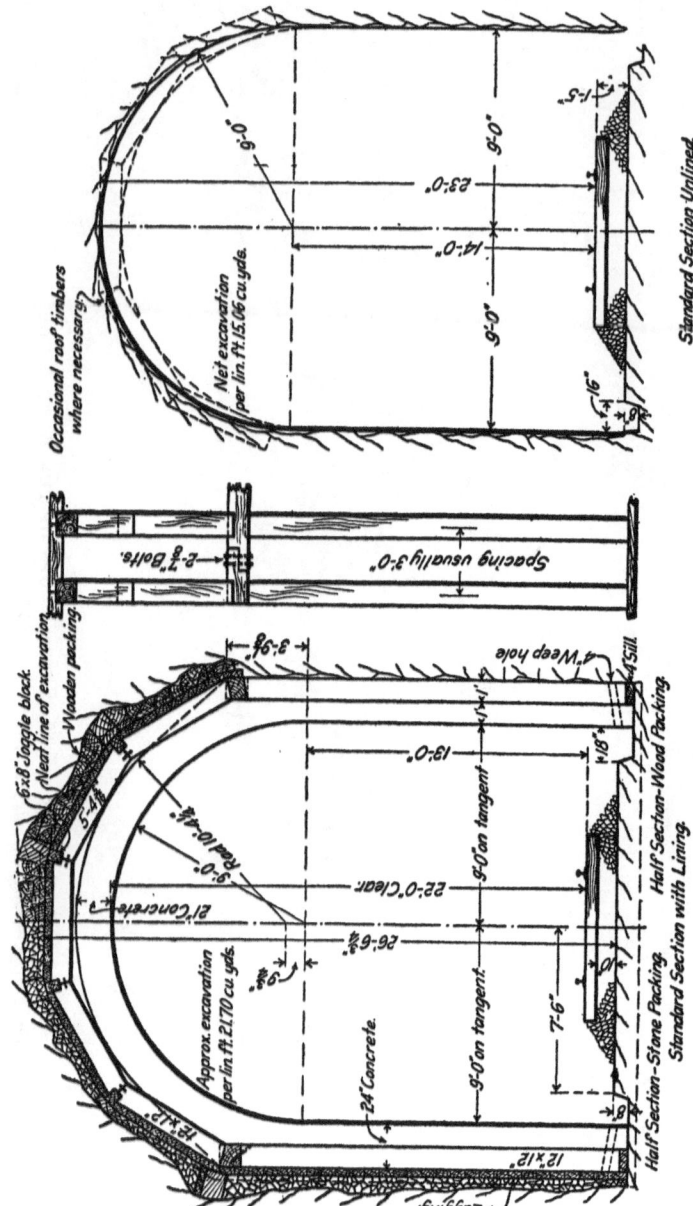

Standard C. C. & O. Tunnel Sections

From Engineering News, October 16, 1913.

THE CLINCHFIELD RAILROAD

aggregate of 50,923 lineal feet of concrete in the tunnels of the road, which will have cost $1,153,383. The following table shows the name and length of each tunnel, and its distance from Elkhorn City:

TABLE XXVIII

Mile Post	Name	State	Length (feet)
2.31	Pool Point	Kentucky	642
3.29	State Line	Virginia	1523
4.76	Towers	Virginia	921
7.11	Skaggs	Virginia	494
9.05	Hill's Mill	Virginia	1073
11.52	Russell	Virginia	448
11.77	McClure	Virginia	331
13.59	Hewitt	Virginia	596
15.59	Goff	Virginia	784
15.99	Red Ridge	Virginia	1359
16.78	Sykes' Mill	Virginia	752
17.96	Perkins	Virginia	496
18.21	Rinehart	Virginia	617
18.58	Short Branch	Virginia	896
19.66	Squirrel	Virginia	650
20.18	Pettit	Virginia	379
23.26	Caney	Virginia	412
26.00	Buffalo	Virginia	352
29.87	Martin	Virginia	387
32.49	Sandy Ridge	Virginia	7854
47.66	Shannon	Virginia	820
54.02	Townes	Virginia	1098
70.31	Starnes	Virginia	517
71.26	North Twin	Virginia	308
71.34	South Twin	Virginia	236
77.59	Clinchport	Virginia	637
78.02	Bald	Virginia	453
79.40	Speer's Ferry	Virginia	1116
80.29	Clinch Mountain	Virginia	4135
88.22	Click	Tennessee	608
88.84	Sensabaugh	Tennessee	348
96.51	Holston	Tennessee	175
98.93	Kendricks	Tennessee	502
108.82	Free Hill (2)	Tennessee	472
113.09	Indian Ridge	Tennessee	1023
163.11	Brush Creek	North Carolina	304
186.65	Vance	North Carolina	527
187.28	Blue Ridge	North Carolina	1865
188.79	Upper Pine Ridge	North Carolina	1600
189.77	Upper Bridle Path	North Carolina	927
190.46	First Washburn	North Carolina	795

CONSTRUCTION OF THE CLINCHFIELD

TABLE XXVIII—Continued

MILE POST	NAME	STATE	LENGTH (feet)
190.72	Second Washburn	North Carolina	370
191.06	Quinns Knob	North Carolina	545
191.41	Third Washburn	North Carolina	915
191.76	Snipes	North Carolina	637
192.63	Lower Bridle Path	North Carolina	1618
193.29	Speedy	North Carolina	288
193.47	Lower Pine Ridge	North Carolina	2211
194.00	Byrd	North Carolina	341
195.52	First Rocky	North Carolina	716
195.84	Second Rocky	North Carolina	757
197.13	Third Rocky	North Carolina	420
197.84	Fourth Rocky	North Carolina	179
200.13	Honeycutt	North Carolina	1688
219.08	Marion	North Carolina	1073
	Total		51,030

Bridges and viaducts are of substantial construction, and were designed for an unusually heavy rolling load. Steel spans or reinforced concrete arches were mainly used, and concrete was used almost exclusively for piers, wing walls, and pedestals. This was prepared with broken stone and a very small amount of gravel. Open hearth steel was used, the specifications for which were based upon those recommended by the American Railway Engineering and Maintenance of Way Association. Spans of 25 to 100 feet were constructed with deck and through-plate girders. Plate girders of 120-foot spans were utilized in the building of the bridge across the Nolachucky River. An interesting feature of the girder bridges is that a solid ballasted floor is placed upon all spans located on curves. Bridges of the riveted type were used for all spans over 120 feet, some of which are as long as 350 feet. The standard bridge floor has ties 8 by 10 inches in thickness and 10 feet long, placed 6 inches apart, and guard timbers 8 feet 2 inches apart. Foot walks have been constructed on all bridges over 200 feet in length. For bridges of a 10 to 24 foot clear span, flat floor reinforced concrete arches were used. The floor, 20 feet wide, is covered with 15 inches of stone ballast. Timber trestles were used to a limited extent only, and at the present time, these are being replaced by either steel or concrete structures.

162 THE CLINCHFIELD RAILROAD

Inside guard rails, 8 inches clear from the track rails, are used on all bridges and in all tunnels. These extend 100 feet beyond the structures and are brought to a point within the last 30 feet. Guard rails are also used on curves, about 3 inches clear of the track rail, between St. Paul and Shannon tunnel, and between Green Mountain and Altapass. In these two districts, there are many curves of ten to fourteen degrees.

The width of the roadbed at subgrade on the main line is 18 feet for fills, and 20 and 22 feet for rock and earth cuts, respectively. All structures were designed for a roadbed width of 20 feet. The side ditches in rock cuts are 12 inches wide at the bottom and 6 inches deep; in earth cuts, 15 inches wide and 8 to 20 inches deep.[18] Standard (A. R. A.) one hundred pound rails are used exclusively on the main line at the present time. The outside rails on all curves are oiled daily, which has resulted in a great saving of rails, fewer derailments on curves, and has lengthened from three to four times the life of locomotive tires. The outside rail on a curve, of course, wears out rapidly; but since this policy was inaugurated in 1926, there had been no renewals up to 1929. The rails ordered for renewal purposes in 1927 were still stored away at this time, and hence there have been no further orders. A unique method is used; the oil is sprayed on the rail by a nozzle attached to the rear wheel of passenger locomotive tenders, and the flow is controlled by a valve.

Crushed stone ballast, 17 inches deep, is used along the entire line, except in some places where crushed slag is obtained from neighboring blast furnaces. The railway company operates its own crushery at St. Paul, at a cost of about one dollar a ton. Approximately 3,000 tons of ballast are used on each mile of the main line.

Hardwood ties only are used on the main line, with white oak on curves. These ties are 8½ feet long and 7 inches thick, and are obtained locally. Steel tie-plates are placed under the rails on all curves exceeding three degrees, and on all bridges. There are about 2,880 ties per mile on the main line. On the entire line, including branches and sidings, about 180,000 new ties are used each year for renewal purposes. The average price

---

[18] *Engineering News*, Vol. LXI (Jan. 21, 1909).

Cut Near Mile-Post 284 in North Carolina

CONSTRUCTION OF THE CLINCHFIELD

is $1.04 per tie. In 1928, the company began treating ties at its plant in Erwin with a preservative, manufactured by the Eastman corporation of Kingsport, called "No-D-K."

In July, 1916, a storm of "unprecedented violence," occurred in western North Carolina which inflicted enormous damages to the road. At Altapass, 22.22 inches of rain fell in twenty-four hours, which, at that time, was reported to be the greatest fall on record in the United States. Through traffic on the Clinchfield was interrupted from July 15 to August 22, a period of five weeks, at a loss of revenue estimated to have been approximately $350,000. The cost of restoring the roadbed and track to the condition before the flood amounted to over $325,000.[19]

THE ELKHORN EXTENSION

Having accomplished the extremely difficult task of building a good line across the ranges southeast of the coal fields, it was decided to secure for the new line of the Clinchfield a share of the through passenger and freight business, from northern and western states, by building an extension northward from Dante to Elkhorn City, the southern terminus of the Big Sandy branch of the Chesapeake & Ohio Railway. A traffic arrangement was forthwith entered into with the Chesapeake & Ohio for the operation of through trains.

A line to connect these two points must cross the Sandy Ridge of the Cumberland mountains. So great were the difficulties in constructing a satisfactory road across this range that several previous attempts had been unsuccessful and the projects abandoned. A line had been located between Dante and Elkhorn in 1881; and in 1900, the South & Western Railway ran a number of lines on high and low locations, and along various standards of curvature and grade. A sixteen degree line could have been fitted to this country quite easily, but in view of the high standards adopted on the remainder of the line, and the heavy traffic which was expected to develop, ten degree curves were adopted as a maximum in the final location. This resulted in increasing the cost of construction by about $1,500,000.[20]

---

[19] *Seventh Annual Report,* Carolina, Clinchfield & Ohio Railway Company, for the year ended December 31, 1917.

[20] *Railway Age Gazette,* Vol. LV (Nov. 7, 1913).

164   THE CLINCHFIELD RAILROAD

Contracts were let for the thirty-five mile extension in June, 1912, and the completed road was opened to traffic on July 1, 1915.[21]

O. K. Morgan, at that time office engineer of the Clinchfield, wrote a description of the construction work for *Engineering News* in 1913. With slight variations and omissions Mr. Morgan's story of the building of the Elkhorn extension concludes this chapter.

"THE ELKHORN RAILWAY EXTENSION"[22]
BY O. K. MORGAN

The original conception of the Carolina, Clinchfield & Ohio Railway embodied a line extending from Elkhorn City, Kentucky, the terminus of the Big Sandy Division of the Chesapeake & Ohio Railway, southward to Spartanburg, South Carolina, which is a railway center, with lines to Atlantic coast ports. For various reasons, however, the construction of the line between Elkhorn City and a point about thirty-five miles south (known as Dante, Virginia) was not undertaken at the same time that the remainder of the line was constructed in 1906, 1907 and 1908.

In May, 1912, it was decided to construct the Elkhorn Extension, or the northern portion of the line, about thirty-five miles long, to its connection with the Chesapeake & Ohio Railway. Its completion will give a short rail route from the Ohio valley to the Carolinas and the South Atlantic seaboard, and will effect considerable saving in distance and time between many of the prominent commercial points in each of these territories. This extension, also, will open up a large undeveloped territory rich in timber, coal, and other minerals for practically its entire length.

The town of Dante, Virginia, lies at an elevation of 1,760 feet above sea level. It is on the south slope and in one of the deep hollows of the so-called Sandy Ridge, a range of the Cumberland Mountains, which has a general northeast and southwest trend for a distance of about a hundred miles, and which connects on the south end with the main range of the Cumber-

---
[21] *Commercial and Financial Chronicle*, Vol. CI (July 3, 1915).
[22] *Engineering News*, Vol. LXX (Oct. 16, 1913).

CONSTRUCTION OF THE CLINCHFIELD 165

land Mountains. The average height of the range in this vicinity is about twenty-seven hundred feet above sea level. Elkhorn City has an elevation of 795 feet at the C. & O. railway station, and lies in a loop of Russell Fork, surrounded by high mountains.

The problem of passing Sandy Ridge by a satisfactory line was the most serious one encountered in building this connecting link and engaged the attention of the engineers from time to time for a period of seven years. This study resulted in the final adoption of the present plan, calling for a tunnel 7,804 feet long.

After passing Sandy Ridge going north, the line follows the valley of McClure Fork (a tortuous mountain stream) for a distance of twenty-one miles. Thence it follows the valley of Russell Fork for eleven miles to Elkhorn City. Russell Fork is a tributary of the Big Sandy River, which breaks through the pine range of the Cumberland Mountains by a deep, tortuous, rocky gorge known as "The Breaks." This region is notable in Kentucky, Virginia, and West Virginia for its general inaccessibility from the outside world.

The difficulties of construction of this line are those usually attendant upon building a 10-degree line in a 20-degree country, which means either many tunnels or many stream crossings. On account of the difficulty of getting in supplies, as well as considerations of future maintenance and satisfactory grades, it was decided to make a free use of tunnels and eliminate as much bridging of streams as possible. For this reason, while there are only eight bridges (with an aggregate length of 2,125 feet) there are 20 tunnels with a total length of 20,531 feet.

The line in general lies on the steep mountain slopes, well above the stream bed. The work is heavy, about 70 per cent of the grading being in solid bed rock. About 3,000,000 cubic yards of grading and 26,000 cubic yards of masonry are required. The work has no unusual features, except those due to the rough topography and generally inaccessible nature of the country. These conditions increase the difficulties of getting in supplies and keeping labor, and required the building of new roads. The labor trouble seems perennial with all jobs remote from the big centres of population.

There are eight steam shovels on this outside work (exclusive of those in the tunnels). Several of the cuts exceed 50,000 yards. One fill has 180,000 yards and is 90 feet high; another has 154,000 yards and is 95 feet high. Viaducts were originally contemplated for these, but fills were decided upon later.

Construction was started in June, 1912, and it is expected that the line will be completed early in 1914. The Sandy Ridge tunnel is the controlling point which determines the time required for completing the line.

The maximum curve is 10 degrees, and 10-degree curves are rather numerous, due to the configuration of the country. The average curvature is 6 degrees 26 minutes and the total curvature 6,339 degrees. The percentage of tangent in the line is 45.7 per cent, which is high for this sort of country. All curves of 3 degrees and over have transition curves (Talbot's System), and all curves on grades are compensated at the rate of 0.035 per cent per degree of curve.

The grades are all ascending southward from Elkhorn City to the southern end of the Sandy Ridge tunnel, beyond which there is a descent for a short distance to the connection with the present line at Dante. The grades are approximately as follows, starting at the Elkhorn end, and all are compensated for curvature: 7 miles with a maximum of 1.5 per cent; 19 miles with a maximum of 0.8 per cent; 6 miles of 1 per cent; 1½ miles of 0.5 per cent through the Sandy Ridge tunnel; and finally 1.3 miles of 1.8 per cent descending grade into Dante.

It is probable the heavier traffic will be southbound, and the 1.5 per cent grade near Elkhorn and the 1 per cent grade up to the Sandy Ridge tunnel will be operated by pushers. The total ascents are 1,046 feet and total descents 76 feet. Much attention was given to the matter of gradient and it is believed these grades give the best operating conditions obtainable for a line of this cost, which will be approximately $5,000,000. The train loads will approximate 2,700 tons, hauled by a single Mallet locomotive of 72,300 pound tractive power, assisted on the pusher grades by a 2-8-0 locomotive of 40,000 pound tractive power.

The standard tunnel section of the C., C. & O. Railway is 18 feet wide and 22 feet high in the clear, after lining is in

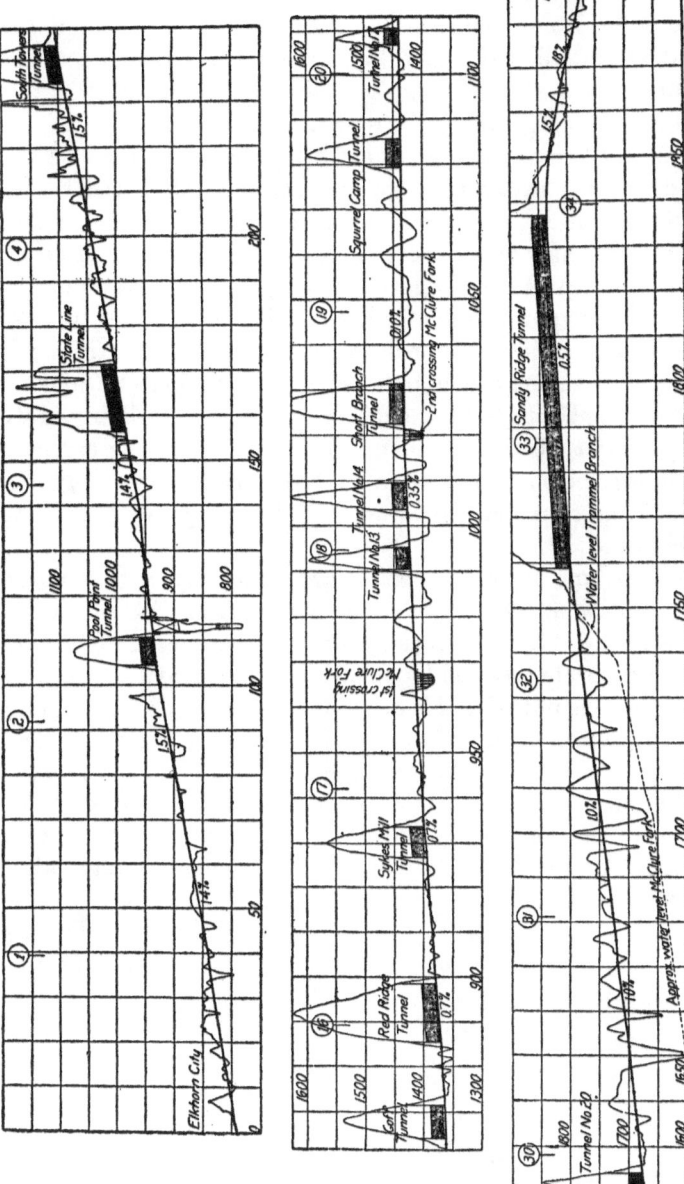

Three Sections of the Profile Showing Some of the Heavy Grading and Tunnel Work

From Engineering News, October 16, 1913.

place, and gives ample space overhead for smoke and ventilation, as well as ample side clearance. Immediately at the south end of the Pool Point tunnel the abutments of the bridge are located which will carry the line across the river. The same condition exists at the Skagg's Hole tunnel, except that this tunnel is not so high above the water.

All except two of the tunnels are being driven by the common method of first excavating the heading and then the bench. The two exceptions are where the material is such as to require immediate placing of a timber lining, in which case the bench is kept close up. A steam shovel is being used to take out the bench of those known as the Goff, Red Ridge and Sykes tunnels. For the lined section of tunnel, the approximate quantities per linear foot of tunnel are as follows: net excavation (to 3 inches outside of timbering), 21.7 cubic yards; concrete lining, 4.61 cubic yards; timbering, 600 feet. In wet tunnels the engineer may require the bottom to be excavated 1 foot below sub-grade, for which the contractor is allowed 0.66 cubic yards per linear foot of tunnel.

While nothing has been done toward lining any of the tunnels of this extension, the methods used will probably be similar to those used for the past three years on the present operated line. The concrete is mixed by a machine at a plant conveniently placed near one portal and is deposited by gravity in a specially equipped scaffold-car. This car is hauled by a cable attached to the drum of a hoisting engine, being moved in and out of the tunnel to and from a temporary siding. From the various decks of this car the concrete is shoveled into place. Wooden forms are used. The method has proved very economical and satisfactory.

The width of tunnel on curves is shown in the following table, which gives also the superelevation and speed allowed. The total width in any case is 18 feet.

TABLE XXIX

Width of Tunnel on Curves

Curve Degree	Inside Curve Feet	Outside Curve Feet	Superelevation Inches	Speed M. P. H.
1	9.14	8.86	1	45
2	9.26	8.74	1¾	36
3	9.35	8.65	2½	35
4	9.42	8.58	3	34
5	9.49	8.51	3½	33
6	9.56	8.44	4	32
7	9.63	8.37	4½	31
8	9.63	8.37	4½	29
9	9.63	8.37	4½	27
10	9.63	8.37	4½	26

The construction of the Sandy Ridge tunnel governs the time required for the completion of the line, as explained above. Consequently, every effort was made to get this under way first. The contractors immediately put two large steam shovels at work on the south approach cut, which contained 70,000 yards; and as soon as a shovel could be got across the mountain, work was begun on the north approach cut, containing 55,000 yards. The south heading was started in the middle of October and the north heading the middle of November, 1912. The present rate of progress is about 100 feet per week for both ends, heading and bench being driven close together.

The tunnel is being driven from each end, no shafts being used. The method of driving is as follows: the heading is driven about 12 feet in advance of a sub-bench, which is in turn about 10 feet in advance of the bottom bench, and all are shot together. Drilling is done by 3¾-inch Ingersoll-Rand drills operated by compressed air. Mucking is done by Marion shovels, also operated by compressed air, the machines being equipped with air receivers instead of boilers. These shovels are fitted with 1½ yard special rock buckets.

Compressed air is furnished from two plants, one near each end of the tunnel, and each equipped with an Ingersoll-Rand compressor with a capacity of 1,800 cubic feet of free air per minute. The compressor is belt-connected to a 300-horsepower electric motor receiving current from a private power plant. The current is 6,600 volts and passes to a transformer at the compressor plant, which delivers it to the motor at 2,300 volts. From the compressor the air goes to a receiver 54 inches in diameter and 12 feet long, thence by an 8-inch pipe to the tunnel portal. At this point it reduces at a 6-inch line for a distance of 1,000 feet, then it is further reduced to a 5-inch line, and carried to the drills and to the air receiver on the power shovel.

Haulage of the muck is done by two electric locomotives at each end of the tunnel, handling 4-yard dump cars. The locomotives at the north end are each of 5 tons weight; at the south end there is one of 5 tons and one of 6 tons. They all receive 250-volt current from a No. 00 wire, current being generated by a 125-horsepower motor at each compressor station.

To expedite ventilation, which during certain weather conditions is poor, there has been installed at the south end a fan, driven by a 20-horsepower, 2,300-volt motor. The displacement of the fan is 2,500 cubic feet of air per minute, which is drawn from the tunnel through an air line of galvanized sheet iron 14 inches diameter. A ventilating plant will soon be installed at the north end of the tunnel. The tunnel is lighted by electricity on a 220-volt circuit, from a small transformer located at the compressor plant.

At present the force is being worked in two 10-hour shifts, except Sundays. At the south end, the material is gray slate with sandstone roof. At the north end, it is gray sandstone with seams and some slate on the bottom. It is probable that a portion of the tunnel will need lining.

Seven of the eight bridges have deck plate-girder spans, and there is only one truss span. The substructure work is of concrete. The Open Fork bridge at Nora has three girder spans of 70 feet, with a height of 40 feet from low-water level to the rails. All the bridges are designed for the E-60 loading of Cooper's specifications. When a bridge occurs as a curve, the span is tilted by varying the height of the shoes, thus securing the proper superelevation of the track without placing corbels under the ties.

The truss span is in the bridge crossing Russell Fork at Pool Point, two miles from Elkhorn City. The bridge crosses the river over a pool 50 feet deep, and is 115 feet above the

CONSTRUCTION OF THE CLINCHFIELD

water. During freshets this pool becomes a veritable whirlpool, and unusual precautions in the erection of this bridge are necessary, as floods are liable to occur at any season of the year. It was finally decided by the bridge company having the contract, to erect the truss span by means of a temporary steel falsework of A-frame construction.

The bridge has a deck span of 270 feet, with a girder span of 50 feet at one end and 70 feet at the other. It is on a grade of 1 per cent, and at its lower end is the spiral or transition curve of a 7 degree curve. It will be seen that the masonry consists merely of four small pedestals for the truss seats and two small abutments. The pedestals are 8 by 8 feet on top, with sides battering 3-12. They are reinforced near the top by two layers of $\frac{3}{4}$-inch bars, the bars being wired together and having the ends bent down vertically about 9 inches. The concrete is a 1:2:5 mixture for the abutments and 1:2:3 for the pedestals and the bridge seats on the abutments. The north abutment is only 50 feet from the tunnel portal.

The roadbed is being constructed 22 feet wide in earth, 20 feet in rock, and 18 feet on embankments. The ditches are made exceptionally wide to accommodate the steam ditcher, which this road uses in maintaining its ditches. The track will be laid with 85-pound openhearth steel rails of the American Society of Civil Engineers section, in 33-foot lengths, with Bonzano joints; $\frac{7}{8}$-inch Harvey grip bolts are used and there are 2,880 ties per mile. Passing sidings with a clear length of 4,000 feet are provided at intervals of about 7 miles.

All location and construction work is under the direction of Ward Crosby, chief engineer of the Carolina, Clinchfield & Ohio Railway. The writer, O. K. Morgan, is office engineer, and the construction work is divided between six resident engineers. The Rinehart & Dennis Company has the general contract for grading and masonry, and the American Bridge Company has the contract for the bridge work.

CHAPTER XI

CROSSING THE BLUE RIDGE MOUNTAINS

COLONEL FRED A. OLDS, of the North Carolina Historical Commission, was probably the first person not connected with the Clinchfield to travel over its line across the Blue Ridge mountains. Colonel Olds wrote a fascinating account of his trip for the *Charlotte Daily Observer*. Permission has been granted to use this story,[1] and it appears below as published in the *Charlotte Daily Observer* of August 30 and September 2, 1908.

"A JOURNEY OVER THE C., C. & O."

BY COL. FRED A. OLDS

"I put down yesterday as a day of days in my life experience, for it is marked by the fact that, barring seven of the officials of the Carolina, Clinchfield & Ohio Railway, I was the first to make the trip over its mountain division, of which the world knows so little, and about which the first newspaper story is now to be told. It is more than worth the telling, for this railway in cloudland is one of the most remarkable in this country, both in point of engineering and construction.

"I had prepared for the trip. *The Observer* had been asked to make interest for me with the officials of the railway; my friends, Mr. C. B. Ryan, of the Seaboard Air Line, Judge Jeter C. Pritchard, and Locke Craig, Esq., had most kindly given me special endorsements. The railway officials, high and low, were more than obliging and so it came about that I never felt for a moment like a stranger in a strange land. . . .

"And now for the story of a most remarkable day's journey. My friend, Mr. James Moore, of Raleigh, farmer, naturalist, and all-around good fellow, who made the notable journey with ·me through the inland waterway in April, was again my companion.

"We left Asheville in the early morning, in a faint drizzle of rain, climbed the high grade of the Blue Ridge to the Swannanoa tunnel and then went down the mountain to Marion, a

---
[1] By a personal letter, July 10, 1929.

really picturesque foothill town, so that travelers see nothing of it. The rain there descended and the floods came. First of all there was a kind welcome by Mr. Hudgens, the local counsel of the Carolina, Clinchfield & Ohio Railway, and another by Mr. Powell, the secretary to Division Engineer Reed. There was a talk over the private telephone with the head officials of the railway at Johnson City, and a special train, the construction train, was put at my disposal. These details arranged, I looked about between showers and saw standing at the top of the court house steps Dr. Stevens, the professor of agriculture at the Agricultural and Mechanical College.[2] He was ringing a handbell with a vigor and grace worthy of any artist in that line at a wayside hotel. This was the outward and visible sign that a farmers institute was being conducted within, and I had the pleasure of hearing clever talks by Dr. Stevens and Mr. Hudson, of the United States Agricultural Department. There were others by Mr. Meacham, of the State farm at Statesville, and more experts.

"The special train was at the crossing two miles from town and we were driven there over roads whose muddiness is inexpressible; mud aggressively red and sticky, with streamlets making cuttings down and across the roadway. It was a real pleasure to board the train, which consisted of an engine and a couple of flats, in charge of Conductor Lewis Scruggs, who was a friend in a minute and with fine courtesy made us feel that both he and the train were ours to command. And so, seated on the end of a flat-car, on a case of Coca-Cola bottles, 'dead men' all, the journey up the mountains began. The rain drizzled amiably, as it does so much in the mountains, and Captain Scruggs said one day was pretty much like another; that he had been three months on the work and it rained every day and he had been told it had been raining three months before he came.

"Naturally the first thing to do was to talk about the road and most opportunely Mr. J. V. Hughes joined us at Camp 10, this being one of the 14 construction camps strung along this division. He is a veteran constructor.

"The first survey of this road was made by James W. Walker, of Shenandoah, Va., who gave two and one-half years' time to

---
[2] North Carolina State College, Raleigh.

this mountain division, and it was made for the railway, then known as the 'Three C's,' which collapsed when the great banking house of Baring Brothers failed at London. This survey made by Mr. Walker was daring in its conception. It was for a crossing of the Blue Ridge at the best 'gap' in that vast mountain wall. In a general way it embraced a line running up the north fork of the Catawba River after crossing the main stream of the latter; then following in a general way Honeycutt's Creek, then striking boldly out and by means of tunnel after tunnel and leap after leap climbing the southern slope of the mountain, on three terraces, so to speak. If you will open your hand, palm downward, and bend the fingers slightly downward and hold them wide apart you will get an idea both of the mountain wall and mode of scaling it. The fingers will represent tunnels, the spaces between them the 'fills,' the latter being the largest I have ever seen, a number being over 100 feet high on the lower side, the ravines on which the bottom stones lie being in some cases 600 feet below the track level. The survey made by Mr. Walker was in later years revived by Mr. W. A. Hankins, but Mr. Walker's locations are practically those today. The first railway construction began in 1891, but not on this mountain division. The original design was for a coal road and when the failure came in the panic of 1895 what was built was used for a log road. Time passed and Thomas F. Ryan and other people who had secured vast areas of coal lands in Kentucky and Virginia, and Col. George L. Carter, of Virginia, took in hand a great project, that of a railway between Elkhorn, Kentucky, and tidewater. In 1905 work began. Thousands of men were put on, no fewer than 4,000 on this mountain division alone. The road was already in operation between Johnson City, Tenn., and Spruce Pine, four miles from Alta Pass, which is the highest station. The name South & Western was given the road and orders were made that a grade of not over one per cent should be secured as shown by the Walker survey, for coal cars bound southeast. This plan was carried out to the letter. The usual grade is only ½ of 1 per cent; that on the mountain division ¾ of 1 per cent, at one point on the southern face of the mountain the grade being for a few miles 12-10 per cent. It is the lowest in the country except the Tidewater road; these two holding

CROSSING THE BLUE RIDGE 175

the highest record for low grades. It is the second road crossing the Blue Ridge at the top, the other being the Southern at Swannanoa.

"The South & Western last year became the Carolina, Clinchfield & Ohio. The work of pushing the road through from Marion to Bostic, 28 miles, was actively begun and by the end of the current year will be completed. There the road will connect with the Seaboard Air Line, and there will be an extensive 'yard' for cars. The division from Alta Pass to Bostic is known as the Marion division. The distance from Marion to Alta Pass is 30 miles, and to Johnson City from Marion 99 miles.

"At the office of the division engineer it was stated that the railway would be in operation by January 1st from St. Paul's, which is in the Clinchfield coal region, 25 miles from Elkhorn, to Bostic, and that it would be ready for service for the public between Johnson City and Marion by September 1st. The link between St. Paul's and Elkhorn will be quickly built and at Elkhorn the road will connect with a branch of the Chesapeake & Ohio Railway down the Big Sandy River and so to Chicago.

"So much by way of introduction. We sat on one end of the flat car, with the engine backing us up the mountain, and it was not long before the wonders of the new line began to unfold themselves and the daring nature of the construction became apparent. The solidity of the line was the first thing remarked; 85-pound rail all the way and 18 cross ties to the rail, against the usual 16 and even 14. We were climbing up almost from the start of our journey, which began at 2:30 P.M., yet so low is the grade that the eye was deceived and we seemed to be going down hill. Mr. Hughes said the grade was 'five-tenths per cent, compensated.' Engineers and railway people generally will know that is a simply wonderful mountain performance. The grade of 12-10 per cent is on the northern slope, so that the loaded cars go down it; the empties against it. As already said, this is the only heavy grade on the entire line.

"The line is literally wrapped in the arms of the mightiest mountains east of the Rockies. From the point where the C., C. & O. crosses the Southern, two miles east of Marion, there is on clear days a noble view of Grandfather Mountain, which stands sentinel over Watauga County, and from the lofty bridge across the Catawba River, Mount Mitchell can be seen to the best advantage. The bridge is of steel, 107 feet high and the fill is 109 feet. This fill required 300,000 cubic yards of earth. Mr. Hughes did a daring piece of work here, by swinging high in the air a track on which the little dumping cars were taken by their engines and discharged their material into the gorge. So the work was done in eight and one-half months. Looking at the massive construction, the wide roadbed, etc., I said to Mr. Hughes and Mr. Scruggs, 'It's the best new road I ever saw. Its construction, not to speak of the scenic effects along the line, is going to surprise the traveling public when it is opened. Take this view up the Catawba Valley, and you will find it will be greatly admired. Then see your engineering and construction difficulties, so wonderfully well mastered, and you will find these will astonish the people.'

"The culverts are of 48-inch iron pipe with concrete heads, where the streams are small and where they are large concrete arches or steel ones are used. No expense is spared. I was told that the cost of 18 miles of this mountain division up which we were climbing, climbing, was $150,000 per mile. There was cost of human life, too, for by premature blasts of dynamite, land slides, etc., over 200 men were killed or died in the well arranged hospital at Alta Pass.

"Not many miles out from Marion we began to see the ballasting and presently the first stone crusher was seen. The material used is what Mr. Hughes speaks of as 'bastard granite,' not excessively hard. There is also stone known as 'bastard limestone,' which looks very much like marble. One of the odd sights along the line, not far from the Catawba River, was a pair of holly trees, so large and handsomely proportioned that they would be considered creditable in eastern North Carolina, that home of holly. They are out of place in these mountains.

"Our wet day, with the ceaseless dripping of the 'Scotch mist,' was uncomfortable in a way, and yet had its charms. I would rather have gone over this wild route in such rough fashion and on so gray a day than to have travelled in a Pullman amidst the most sparkling sunshine, and declared as much to my friends old and new, who said I was right. They added, with congratulations, that I was the very first 'outsider' to make the trip. At this I shook hands with myself, in Chinese fashion.

The charm of doing something new is all-pervading. I rather ranked myself with Columbus, the Conquistadores, Daniel Boone, or any of the great 'path-finders.' I was seeing North Carolina at its grandest. Twelve miles out of Marion a noble view to the northwest unfolded itself. There, set far up on the mountainside, was an engine, its steam and smoke mingling with the cloud masses which now hid and now exposed the vast mountain wall. This engine was near the highest point, the Blue Ridge tunnel, and was on the very border line between McDowell and Mitchell counties. Another engine was then discovered a mile or two away. These three terraces along the south wall were made doubly clear by these engines, one being on the topmost one, and another on the middle one, while the scars of the 'cuts' showed plainly the lowest part of the line. The cloud forms were grand. They bend down sometimes like curtains, or they cover in masses the tops of the ridge, which at the topmost tunnel is 2,628 feet above sea level. From the point where we saw this mighty railway construction to the pass is a good eighteen miles by the road; perhaps not over three and one-half in an air line. Conductor Scruggs remarked with a smile, 'We turn all sorts of ways in getting to Alta Pass. As the sailormen say, we box the compass.' He told the plain truth. We wriggled and toiled around and up that mountain in a way to deceive most compasses. How Walker did the work is a mystery. Mr. Hughes says his 'bump of location' was admirably developed.

"There is a lot of mica in this mountain soil and it gives trouble. It is treacherous. It causes slides in the fills and it will be four or five years before they get down to their bearings, so to speak. As we went along we passed scores of steam shovels. I never saw so many. There are thirty on this mountain work. Most of them are being packed for shipment, but at least three will be kept at work for the next two years, and really there is work enough for half a dozen. The three rock crushers are turning out ballast at the rate of 300 cubic yards a day, and by the end of the month all the line will be ballasted except the nine miles from the first crusher to Marion. Conductor Scruggs called attention to a point where it was clear there had been two thrusts or great mounds of the earth, and where the remains of an ancient stream-bed showed high up on the side of a cutting. Mr. Hughes showed on the mountainside places where great landslips have occurred in past years. These are to be reckoned with, but the engineers know how to master the situation.

"We were now to enter the first tunnel. Like all of them it is through rock, with very little leakage if any. Some are so dry as to be dusty. All are through the 'bastard granite' already referred to. The mica formation is only on top; the granite is below always. There are seventeen tunnels between Marion and Alta Pass, and west of the latter is another, the Vance, while twenty miles further is the last; so there are nineteen tunnels on the route from Bostic to Johnson City. There is one 1,050 feet long between Marion and Bostic. It might be almost termed an underground railway. The first tunnel is Honeycutt's, and its length is 1,650 feet. At the southern portal, or entrance, is a beautiful waterfall, which splashed us as we rolled by it. The longest tunnel is Lower Pine, 2,300 feet. The length of the highest, Blue Ridge, is 1,950 feet. The engineers changed the bed of the North Fork of the Catawba River so as to turn it west instead of east of the railway. This and other streams rush and roar, their noise being heard whenever the train stops.

"At Linville Falls station, fifteen miles out from Marion, a valley is pointed out, up which the route to those beautiful falls lies, the distance being six miles. There is a view of the peak in half a mile of the falls. From this point on the road Mount Mitchell is visible, eighteen miles away, at least. We enter into the great horseshoe form of the railway line, already alluded to.

"At one point Sectionmaster J. R. Cawble and his crew of ten men were taken on and they were needed. Slickers, waterproof coats, were put on, as the mists grew denser. Trackwalkers gave warning of stones which had fallen and these were removed in a minute by the gang of negroes. Blacks are remarkably scarce in these mountains. There were 200 at work on this division, but they were not allowed to work in the Rock Creek section in this (Mitchell) county, where no negro has ever been permitted to stay, so they were used elsewhere. Notices were posted in towns warning against the presence of any negroes.

"Here and there were tiny sawmills, with slides scoring the mountainsides, where oxen pulled down the logs. Mr. Hughes told me that a great deal of the mountain timber was defective, made so by pinholes, made by worms, besides 'windshakes,' etc., and he declared it does not compare with timber of lower altitudes. He said that at one point there was a good quarry of limerock, which burns a good lime.

"All the tunnels except a few are timbered at the ends. All will be lined with cement. At some of them a man was put out with a lantern to see if everything was all right. We had no trouble with falling stones except at the entrance of one. The glare from the fire-box on the engine made the interior clear and showed that the work is thoroughly done. Part of the time I rode on the engine, and found Engineer Samuel T. Duncan and Fireman Ollie Harvey were clever indeed. The fireman was making his first trip over this high part of the mountain division, and to say he was delighted but faintly expresses it. Once or twice we sent a hand-car ahead as a pilot. The lowest tunnel (Honeycutt's) was finished only two and a half months ago. It is the only one which will give trouble until it is cemented, owing to the character of the rock, which scales from air-slack but only in a small way. The tunnels are said to be the best anywhere.

"The view of what I named 'The Horseshoe,' showed up nobly from Camp 5, there being in view on the southern slope twelve cuts and five fills. The line here lay along Honeycutt's Creek and it was only three miles to Alta Pass if one walked across the mountain (a heart-breaking climb, by the way); while it was at least fifteen miles by rail. There was splendid looking timber in the mountain coves and plenty of chestnuts, while the valley looked fertile. Just after crossing Honeycutt's Creek we struck the only grade, 12-10 per cent, which lasted to the Blue Ridge tunnel, 2,628 feet high as the road runs, the real mountain altitude there being 2,800 feet, it being at McKinney's Gap, the best in all the Blue Ridge.

"Here and there are seen the remains of the daring line, twenty-five miles long, used by the tiny dummy engines, which are so great a factor in railway construction. At turns the uncanny steam shovels seem to be lurking as if about to leap out at us, while the tiny dummy engines and their lines of equally babyish cars are the gnomes of modern days; 'the little brown men' of fancy who do such wonderful things. Teams carried supplies down the mountainsides. It took half a day for a mule team to go eight miles, carrying dynamite and all sorts of things. Mr. Hughes spoke of engineering difficulties. The rainfalls, sometimes spoken of as cloudbursts, in this mountain region surpass belief. He said he had seen one of these roll logs three feet in diameter down the mountainside, and on uniform land, not in gorges. The logs were sometimes forced into the drain pipes and had to be blown out with dynamite. These floods roll rocks the same way. Waterfalls have at some points cut deep channels in the rocks.

"Tunnel after tunnel was passed and near one was one of the compress stations, where air was compressed and then sent through pipes, thus operating the drills which cut these tunnels. At one point there are three tunnels in a line, one 420, another 2,300, the third 250, and as we left the last we could see through all. Here our troubles began. A big steam shovel was being installed and was on a gigantic fill at Rocky Point, which the rains and the tricky mica were causing to slip. It was at least 600 feet to the bottom. It will be either filled in with stone or arched. Dusk was coming on. The mist thickened. It blanketed the view of the vast horseshoe gorge most of the time. I ventured to name this the 'Majestic' gorge. It is well worthy of the name. It is threaded by two creeks, Honeycutt's and Pepper's. It will give the tourists a thrill. There is another view of it higher up and from this upper level Mount Mitchell can be seen.

"We had climbed above most of the clouds. Rain was pattering down below. The mists grew thinner, but their moisture was pervading. There was as much water as air as far as one's feeling went. The trees seemed to be bigger, and one pair were linked together, like the Siamese twins. There was a signal to stop. Two engines were ahead of us. On the front one was a working crew, dumping earth into a fill which had given way like that at Rocky Point—a side-track that sunk at least six feet. The place was near the portal of a tunnel. The lead engine went on, but the next one was the heaviest on this division and the track sagged visibly. More work had to be done. Then we left our engine and its cozy cab and walked across the fill to the portal of another tunnel. There we were picked up, mounted on a box car and made our way up the mountain, on the home-

CROSSING THE BLUE RIDGE 181

stretch. We were looping the loop, but ascending instead of descending. We were near the crest of the Blue Ridge. We had won the heights. Ahead loomed the portal of the supreme tunnel, outlined by a lantern. We roared through it, the puffing of the engine reverberating, and the smoke from the preceding engines pouring like a stream, all illuminated by the glare of our engine. We had passed from McDowell into Mitchell. The little train rattled into Alta Pass. There were heavy hand shakes upon our ride, our adventures and on my being the first newspaper man to make the journey. '*The Charlotte Observer* is the first to do this big stunt,' said some one. It was even so.

"Up a rugged slope to the big modern hotel we went and sat down to a typically good supper at 8 o'clock, served by Mrs. Campbell. After that, rest, with dreams of endless tunnels, of railways which wriggled clear up into the sky and stayed there; or crystal streams tumbling in waterfalls.

"Napoleon said, 'Beyond the Alps lies Italy.' It was enough for his troops. They climbed these Alps. All this they did, and far more the Carolina, Clinchfield & Ohio Railway has done. It has made the most wonderful crossing of these North Carolina Alps of ours. In the coming years the tourists will see here new revelations of the Land of the Sky, and new opportunities will be opened to all the world. Roaring trains of coal will be whirled to the lower levels. A plan which has lurked in some great minds a score of years, perhaps, is almost complete. All through the panic the work has gone on on this great road, which is indeed monumental in conception and execution.

"This afternoon I make the journey down the northern side of the mighty Blue Ridge and so on to Johnson City, thence to Asheville. The sun at morn comes out gloomily.

"On the stroke of noon on Saturday, the 22nd of August, the clouds rolled by and the sun came out eagerly and brightened the hamlet of Alta Pass, which is solely the creation of the railway, and a little later I was to begin the journey down the northern side of the mountain. From the station one could look to the southward and see the portal of the Blue Ridge tunnel, altitude 2,828 feet above sea level, and look above it to McKinney's Gap, the right-of-way line cut clear and true through the timber, and looking to the northward there was in plain view the portal of Vance tunnel. Alta Pass is, therefore, between two tunnels. I thought at first Vance tunnel might be named in honor of North Carolina's greatest commoner, but was compelled to ask about this and learned that a man of that name had owned the right-of-way and lived there, so his name was given. I saw this Mr. Vance at the station, a rather shy little man with but little to say. On the platform were perhaps half a score of mountain men. They were to all appearance nearly voiceless. In the east there would have been talk aplenty, but these mountains of ours must cast a spell over the lips.

"I asked a railway man what would be the effect on these mountain folks when a little later on the big trains with their electric headlights, Pullman cars, and tourists came roaring through these mountain wilds, and he replied that a lot of them would 'move further back'—go into the deep recesses of the mountain coves.

"The journey to Johnson City began in perfect weather and after Vance tunnel had been passed the Toe River appeared. It was to be our companion for full fifty miles and a very agreeable companion, too, though this stream is always muddy, thanks to the mica in the soil. The river gave us a surprise. We were running down it, when suddenly at a curve it disappeared, then popped out again and lo and behold it was running exactly the other way! It had made a loop, gone four miles and simply crossed that loop. I never saw anything quite so curious about a stream as this. The trip all the way to Johnson City was made on the rear platform, where folding chairs were specially provided so that *The Observer* could best observe. Four miles from Alta Pass is Spruce Pine, 42 miles from Marion by rail and 22 by rural free delivery route. The road was completed from Johnson City to Spruce Pine in 1902.

"The run was densely bordered with rhododendron. We had traveled all the way from Marion along a route fringed with this noblest of all the mountain flowers and hence the title of the 'Rhododendron Route' is peculiarly fitting. In late May and early June the place must be like a flower garden. The scenery on the north side of the ridge is grand, like that on the south side though tamer, except at the point lower down known as the 'Gorge,' which is simply overwhelming in its grandeur.

Flood Scene in the "Gorge"

CROSSING THE BLUE RIDGE 183

It was observed that the rock formations were quite different in many cases from those on the south side of the ridge. The hemlocks were thick and stately in the extreme; the Toe River, full of rocks, swift and turbulent and bordered by cliffs in most places. Along the line the train, which was running rapidly on 85-pound rails and along a ballasted roadbed, almost brushed the sides of cosy little cottages set in this narrow valley. At one point a mill was grinding kaolin out of which china is made and near it one was cutting mica into forms. Bridges and telegraph wires spanned the river. All these bridges are picturesque and really quite foreign in their aspect. Log cabins of cosy construction are by no means uncommon, as the panorama, which is easily the most picturesque I have seen in the mountains, was unfolded before us. We passed Boone's Ford, where the immortal Daniel, that prince of pioneers, crossed on his way to Kentucky, perhaps. Here the South Toe River joined forces with its larger sister and at right angles. Great numbers of graceful, dark green Carolina poplars marked the junction point and so regularly placed that they appeared to be set out. At Galax, between the road and river, some prominent man had heeded the scriptural injunction and had built his house upon a rock. Here there was much black basaltic rock with considerable silica in it. There was on view some marvelously steep hillside farming, which brought out the remark that it was 'high agriculture' when the big farm on the lofty summit of Pumpkin Patch mountain was seen.

"At the hamlet of Toecave there is the most picturesque little hotel that I have ever seen in this country. One story is set high on a hillock near the road and fringed with graceful trees so plentiful as to seem a part of the structure. It is three miles from Toecave to Bakersville, the county seat of Mitchell. Toecave is so named because Cave Creek there flows into the Toe River. Here is also the last tunnel between Alta Pass and Johnson City, 23 miles from the former. Fruit trees loaded with apples, grapes in full bearing, tobacco, grass and corn, the latter growing alow and aloft, as the sailors say, and in the most impossible places, picturesque cottages galore; these were sights we saw continuously. Green Mountain was especially picturesque. It is six miles from Burnsville, the county seat of

Yancey. A native said people over 100 years old were plentiful there and ventured the assertion that 'mighty few die in these parts.'

"We crossed the Big Rock Creek, whereby hangs a tale, for it is in the valley of this stream that no negro is permitted to live. The true blue Republican of that part of Mitchell will have none of the 'brother in black.' He can't work there or live there though he does both at Bakersville quite near, but such is the unwritten law along Rock Creek. There is a crib bridge here across the Toe and Cave rivers, where it joins the latter stream which has grown larger, swifter and deeper. And now we have reached the spot where in 1905-06 so bitter a fight was waged between the Southern Railway and the C., C. & O. (then the South & Western); when the Southern claimed the right of way and had put a number of men at work sometimes on one side of the river and sometimes on the other and when the S. & W. put its force on both sides too, then there were plenty of fights between these opposing forces and where the Southern located some line, but lost out in the Supreme Court. It is said the Southern spent $100,000 there. The gorge was regarded as the keynote to the whole situation. Later the C., C. & O. will use eight or nine miles of line graded by the Southern, this being higher and giving a really better grade. I saw where on the opposite bank the two sets of men had worked. In one cut the Southern had dug while in the next the S. & W. worked and at one place each had started a tunnel not ten yards apart. The war is all over now. The C., C. & O. has recently done some work on the west side of the Toe. It will have a tunnel there and will cross and recross the river instead of sticking to the east side nearly all the time.

"We entered the grand gorge of the Toe, now, if you please, become the Nolachucky, a little stream marking the boundary between North Carolina and Tennessee. Pile upon pile of rock the cliffs rose, now sloping sharply, now almost perpendicular, all stone with stunted trees. There are eight miles of this canyon. Part of it is like the Palisades. This Toe or Nolachucky River is treacherous in the extreme and seven years ago rose 52 feet in this gorge. It took away 16 miles of the railroad and it required some months to replace it.

"At one point at a curve where the road immediately borders the river the latter is 30 feet deep. The track is being raised at great cost. At other points it is also being raised and straightened. Everything is being made to handle 'King Coal' properly and make his journey easy. It is really at Unaka Springs, the last crossing of the Toe, that it became the Nolachucky. Unaka in the Cherokee tongue means 'Bear.' Here I observed quantities of exceedingly dark mistletoe and sycamore trees on the riverside and high upon the sharp slopes of the mountains, sometimes like a knife edge, I saw long and lone lines of pines all killed or blasted, whether by insects or lightning I could not say.

"At Unaka the landscape changes: softens exceedingly. There are spreading fields. The land flattens. It is fertile and good to look at. At Erwin the shops of the C., C. & O. will probably be located. There is a grand view of the valley toward North Carolina. Here the United States Fish Commission has a very attractive place for trout, etc. Here I saw the first limestone— one of North Carolina's greatest needs. We gave away Tennessee and with it went all our limestone and all the best grain lands. We passed the great farms of A. D. Reynolds, a brother of R. J. Reynolds, of Winston-Salem, and were told that he was the largest land holder in the State of Tennessee.

"The porter gravely announced Johnson City and as we cross a narrow-gauge railway it is pointed out as the line to the Cranberry iron mines in the corner of Mitchell County. General Robert F. Hoke being largely interested, a great deal of this high class ore is brought to Johnson City, where during the panic they have never stopped work. This little railway, 34 miles long, is the East Tennessee & Western North Carolina. At Johnson City station was an alfalfa field and a plant of the leather trust and the neatest, cutest, and tiniest Y. M. C. A. I ever saw, in a box car, painted bright yellow with a little portico and flowers and fairly shedding forth an air of welcome. It was labelled 'Railway Y. M. C. A.' I saw a field sown in cow peas, the first since leaving McDowell County.

"I had the pleasure of meeting most of the officers of the C., C. & O. at the handsome general offices. They were like all the under officials, courteous to the last degree, and very obliging. I told them of my trip over and they were warm in their congratulations and they asked many questions. I did not have the pleasure of seeing President George L. Carter, but Assistant Chief Engineer A. W. Jones and Mr. W. J. Steppins, engineer of bridges, were most kind and furnished admirable photographs which are used to illustrate their story of the 'Rhododendron Route.'

"There is a curiosity on the road four miles north of Johnson City, this being the largest fill in the world. It is at Knob Creek and is 1,500 feet long and 100 feet high. There is not to be a single trestle on this road. Everything is to be steel, concrete, stone or earth. This concluding story of an eventful journey is written for those who are to follow after. They will see much, perhaps far more than it was given these eyes of mine to see, but they will never cherish anything more dear than this maiden voyage over the C., C. & O.

"I found in passing through the high mountain region that the people are chary of speech, use a drawl and broaden their words while the use of obsolete words and indeed phrases is common. In this they are the counterparts of people along the banks in eastern North Carolina. Both are of singularly pure English strain. Both have lived a life apart for generations. Both have won their way. I should like to see fifty men from the 'Banks' along the coast taken to the high mountains, say in Mitchell or Yancey, and watch them affiliate with the mountaineers. The likeness is so singular that I have set it down here.

"Johnson City is an ancient east Tennessee town. The State of Tennessee, like Gaul, is divided into three parts, west, middle, and east, with different soil, climate and people in each. Perhaps in no other State is this so marked. We speak of eastern North Carolina and western, but it is a mere phrase. In Tennessee it means far more. Johnson City has perhaps 5,000 people; a post-bellum place with a magnificent home for United States soldiers. Most of these are of the civil war period. They get a home and pension too. In North Carolina the gentleman who chooses life at the Home surrenders his pension. There are 1,700 in the Johnson City home. The group of buildings set in 1,400 acres of admirably located grounds is very pretty indeed. At the railway station a Confederate and a Federal veteran were talking. The latter had served in the Fifty-first Ohio, the Virginian in the Twenty-eighth Virginia. Both paid a willing and offhand tribute to the North Carolina Confederates. One had fought against them directly and the other beside them. The Federal veteran said he summed up the cause of the war in mighty few words. They were these: 'It was caused by a few fools on each side.' The Confederate said: 'I agree with you.' That ended the conversation."

CHAPTER XII

THE CLINCHFIELD LEASE

THE ATLANTIC COAST LINE RAILROAD COMPANY and the Louisville & Nashville Railroad Company, under an indenture dated October 16, 1924, leased the properties of the Carolina, Clinchfield & Ohio Railway Company for a period of 999 years. The lease was dated May 11, 1923.[1] On December 1, 1924, the Clinchfield Railroad Company was organized as a consolidation of the Carolina, Clinchfield & Ohio Railway, the Carolina, Clinchfield & Ohio Railway of South Carolina, and the Clinchfield Northern Railway of Kentucky. The new company began operations on January 1, 1925.[2] Professor William Z. Ripley, of Harvard University, in his "Report to the Interstate Commerce Commission on Consolidation of Railways" in 1921, recommended the inclusion of the Clinchfield into the Atlantic Coast Line—Louisville & Nashville system.[3]

The stockholders of the Clinchfield approved the proposed lease at a special meeting on June 18, 1923. As required by law, application was then made to the Interstate Commerce Commission for authority to consummate the lease.[4] On July 20, the lessees filed their joint application with the Commission for an order approving and authorizing the lease. A hearing was held in Washington from September 24 to September 29, at which time testimony was heard both favorable and unfavorable to the granting of the lease. Copies of the application and lease had been sent the governors of all the states through which the lines of the Atlantic Coast Line and the Louisville & Nashville passed. South Carolina was the only one which finally expressed disapproval. The public authorities of the other states served by the lessees either favored the granting of the lease,

---

[1] *Fourteenth Annual Report*, Carolina, Clinchfield & Ohio Railway Company, for the year ended Dec. 31, 1924, p. 9.

[2] *First Annual Report*, Clinchfield Railroad Company, for the year ended December 31, 1925, p. 3.

[3] "In the Matter of Consolidation of the Railway Properties of the United States into a Limited Number of Systems," Aug. 3, 1921, 63 I. C. C., p. 460.

[4] *Thirteenth Annual Report*, Carolina, Clinchfield & Ohio Railway Company, for the year ended December 31, 1923, p. 10.

THE CLINCHFIELD LEASE

or offered no objections to it.[5] The greatest opposition came from the Seaboard Air Line Railway, "with certain assistance, apparent on its face to be for the benefit of that company, rendered by some of the southern communities and two southern railroads," the Piedmont & Northern and the Receiver of the Georgia & Florida.[6] "The hearing developed an interesting exposition of railroad strategy as affecting the territory involved," says *Railway Age*, "and also a lively opposition to the application on the part of the Seaboard Air Line ... taking the position that if the lease is to be allowed it should be allowed to participate."[7]

The Atlantic Coast Line controls the Louisville & Nashville by the ownership of a majority of its capital stock, acquired in 1902.[8] The lines of the two systems roughly resemble the letter "V" with the apex in Florida, the right arm extending northeasterly along the Atlantic coast, and the left arm westward to the Ohio River. The main line of the Atlantic Coast Line extends from Richmond, Virginia, to Tampa, Florida; the Louisville & Nashville's, from Cincinnati and Louisville to New Orleans. The only connections between the two companies are at River Junction, Florida; Montgomery, Alabama; and at Atlanta, Georgia, via the Georgia Railroad, a subsidiary. The Atlantic Coast Line, through its affiliated company, the Charleston & Western Carolina Railway, connects with the Clinchfield at Spartanburg. At the present time, there is no direct physical connection between the Clinchfield and the Louisville & Nashville. Branches of the latter company extend to McRoberts, Kentucky, and into Harlan County, Virginia, both of which are relatively near the Clinchfield—the former about 25 miles, the latter about 12 miles. The Atlantic Coast Line-Louisville & Nashville system operates in the following states: Virginia, North Carolina, South Carolina, Georgia, Florida, Alabama,

---

[5] Finance Docket No. 3131, "In the Matter of the Application of the Atlantic Coast Line Railroad Company and the Louisville and Nashville Railroad Company for Approval of a Lease for 999 Years by the Applicants of the Railroad Properties of the Carolina, Clinchfield & Ohio Railway and Its Subsidiaries, and for Authority to Assume the Financial Obligations Involved in Such a Lease," before the Interstate Commerce Commission, 1924, pp. 2-4.

[6] "Brief for the Applicants," Finance Docket No. 3131, I. C. C., p. 5.

[7] *Railway Age*, Vol. LXXV, Sept. 29, 1923.

[8] Mundy: *Earning Power of Railroads*, p. 375.

Mississippi, Louisiana, Tennessee, Kentucky, Ohio, Indiana, Illinois, and Missouri.[9]

It appears that the primary motive of the Louisville & Nashville in acquiring control of the Clinchfield was to relieve an intolerable car supply which was said to exist in the coal area which it serves. In marketing the coal in territory north of the Ohio River, the road is compelled to send its cars over the lines of its connections. These cars were not returned promptly, and serious shortages frequently resulted. Since the termination of Federal control, the Louisville & Nashville has expended a large amount for additional equipment and in double-tracking for the sole purpose of improving its coal transporting facilities. While these improvements have lessened, to some extent, the restrictions under which the mines had been operating, as well as operating conditions on the road, the Louisville & Nashville claimed that permanent relief could be obtained only by securing another outlet from the coal fields. To accomplish this, the railroad company proposed to construct extensions to connections with the Clinchfield. Upon the completion of these links it was expected that cars going to the south would be returned more promptly than those going north and west, because it would be to the interests of the Clinchfield and the Atlantic Coast Line to expedite the return of empties. It was also expected that at least one of these links would open up a new merchandise route.[10] W. L. Mapother, President of the Louisville & Nashville, testified at the hearing before the Interstate Commerce Commission that if his road were to build the links without a lease, it would still be at the mercy of its connections for the return of cars. When asked why the objects to be accomplished could not be served if some road other than the Atlantic Coast Line were allowed to participate in the lease, Mr. Mapother said he would have no assurance that such a plan would prove successful and that he would not be interested in the proposition under such circumstances.[11]

The main desire of the Atlantic Coast Line to acquire the Clinchfield was, in addition to the anticipated profits and additional mileage, that it would have direct connections with the

---

[9] From maps of the two companies.
[10] Finance Docket No. 3131, I. C. C., pp. 7-10.
[11] *Railway Age*, Vol. LXXV (Sept. 29, 1923).

coal fields. There are no coal mines located on the Atlantic Coast Line, and it was believed that the lease would insure it for all time an ample supply of "exceptionally high grade coal," both for its own use and for the use of the industries which it serves.[12]

At the hearing prior to the authorization of the lease, the Atlantic Coast Line pointed out several advantages which the public interests would realize from the lease, as follows:[13] (1) a new and better coal supply for the Carolinas; (2) export coal for the South Atlantic ports; and (3) a new merchandise route between the Ohio River and the South Atlantic states. "The lease will be a distinct benefit to the owners of the Clinchfield in that the unprofitable investment which they have carried all of these years will now assume a stable and fixed status, represented by the annual rental to be distributed as dividends upon the twenty-five million dollars of stock," says the "Brief" of the Coast Line. "During the fourteen years of its operation it has paid to its stockholders dividends aggregating only 9 per cent on $10,000,000 of preferred stock, and nothing on its common stock. It has now succeeded in interesting two strong lines at each end to take it over on terms which are entirely satisfactory to its owners. Not only would it be a great advantage to them to have the whole matter disposed of, but it would be a grievous hardship if they should be prevented from doing this."[14]

E. C. Bailly, secretary of the Clinchfield Railway, testified that the proposed lease had been approved by the stockholders of the company.

C. E. Backus, president of the Clinchfield Coal Corporation, said that the increased facilities which would come to the Clinchfield "would be of tremendous advantage to everybody served." When asked if there had been an agreement between the coal company and the railway regarding an extension of the road to Charleston and the erection of coal terminals there, Mr. Backus testified that he knew of no such agreement.

R. C. Tway, president of the Harlan County Coal Operators' Association, said that his association had passed resolutions supporting the position of the Louisville & Nashville after he

---

[12] "Brief for the Applicants," Finance Docket No. 3131, I. C. C., p. 58.
[13] *Ibid.*, pp. 20-40.   [14] *Ibid.*, pp. 59-60.

had heard a rumor that the Southern and Seaboard were planning to "scout the bushes and stir up agitation in the South." He spoke of the anxiety of his association to secure a direct outlet to the south, and he believed the proposed system would relieve the existing car shortages.[15] The Southern Railway, however, did not oppose the lease.

The Seaboard Air Line vigorously opposed the lease, and advocated joint control of the Clinchfield by the southern railroads, such as in the case of the Richmond, Fredericksburg, & Potomac.[16] Numerous charges and objections were made by the Seaboard.

The applicants claimed that this opposition was without merit. "If there be eliminated the mere partisan opinion of certain witnesses who declared that this lease would constitute a monopoly and would stifle competition, but stated no *facts* in support of such a charge, there is no ground in this record for the contention that the proposed lease will work any public injury. And if it be claimed that any possible loss of revenue will be sustained by the Seaboard (which we strongly believe will not be the case), it would be that kind of loss which would not constitute a public injury; but if it did, it would be simply negligible in comparison with the great public benefits to be derived from the consummation of this lease. It would not even be . . . a legal injury to the Seaboard itself, which must take its chances of just such losses when it enters a business where there is competition."[17]

The arguments between Charles R. Capps, Vice-President of the Seaboard, and George B. Elliott and Edward S. Jouett for the applicants, as represented in their respective "Briefs," are indeed interesting. Mr. Capps said "the position of the Seaboard as to this matter is exactly what it has been for many years; the Seaboard considers that it would be a public calamity of the first magnitude to restrict the functions of the Clinchfield road as is necessarily involved in this proposed lease. An *open Clinchfield road*,[18] by reason of its coal reserves and its

---

[15] *Railway Age*, Vol. LXXV (Sept. 29, 1923).
[16] "Reply Brief on Behalf of Seaboard Air Line Railway Company, an Intervener and Protestant," Finance Docket No. 3131, I. C. C., p. 61.
[17] "Brief for the Applicants," Finance Docket No. 3131, I. C. C., p. 93.
[18] Our italics.

THE CLINCHFIELD LEASE

strategic location through the Appalachian range is of primary public concern."[19] In reply to this, Mr. Elliott stated that "every line of this record shows that up until this time it has been to a material extent *a closed road*, due to the adverse interest of the Seaboard . . . " which, it was claimed, for many years had refused to give the Clinchfield outbound competitive traffic. Again, the Seaboard held that the owners of the Clinchfield should be protected, replying to which Mr. Elliott said: "Certainly Mr. Capps would not be regarded up to this time as a proper guardian of the interests of the Clinchfield road. He it is who has persistently refused to do business with it, and thus has hampered it all these years."[20]

It will be remembered that in 1911 negotiations were made for a joint lease of the Clinchfield by the Seaboard Air Line and the Chesapeake & Ohio railways.[21] It was brought out during the hearing before the Interstate Commerce Commission in 1923 that this lease "was broken up by three directors of the Seaboard itself."[22] In discussing this, Professor Ripley says that the Seaboard "seems not to have been fully alive to the possibilities of the Clinchfield, and the general attitude respecting a lease indicates an anticipation that it might be subsequently acquired more cheaply after its downfall financially."[23] Mr. Campion, Vice-President of the Clinchfield, testified that the Clinchfield had received no support whatsoever from the Seaboard.[24]

The City of Charleston opposed the lease, mainly, it would seem, because the lessee was the Atlantic Coast Line. It apparently would have preferred the Seaboard's taking over the road, for, after considerable discussion in its "Brief" on the early history of the Seaboard's relations with the Clinchfield, it says that the Seaboard was built into Charleston "for the very purpose of handling Clinchfield coal."[25] Another objection,

---
[19] *Railway Age*, Vol. LXXV (Sept. 29, 1923).
[20] "Brief for the Applicants," Finance Docket No. 3131, I. C. C., pp. 94-98.
[21] *The Commercial and Financial Chronicle*, Vol. XCIII (Aug. 19, 1911).
[22] "Brief for the Applicants," Finance Docket No. 3131, I. C. C., p. 102.
[23] 63 I. C. C., p. 553.
[24] "Brief for the Applicants," Finance Docket No. 3131, I. C. C., p. 104.
[25] "Brief in Behalf of the City of Charleston, S. C., and Chamber of Commerce of Charleston, S. C., Interveners and Protestants," Finance Docket No. 3131, I. C. C., p. 21.

THE CLINCHFIELD RAILROAD

it would seem, was that the Atlantic Coast Line refused to promise to make Charleston its chief and only coal port, apparently disregarding the fact that the road also served the larger cities of Savannah, Jacksonville, and Tampa. "We have not at present any intention to make any port, of the ports which we serve, our special port," Mr. H. Walters, Chairman of the boards of the Atlantic Coast Line and of the Louisville & Nashville, respectively, was reported to have said. "We expect to leave that for the ports themselves and the people who live in the ports to inaugurate whatever things are necessary to develop the ports. We do not expect to make any special arrangements with any one port."[26]

If the Atlantic Coast Line had planned to make Charleston its chief coal port, that city undoubtedly would have supported the lease. According to *Railway Age*, in its discussion of the hearing before the Interstate Commerce Commission, "John P. Grace, Mayor of Charleston, said that the proposed lease would be injurious to Charleston and the whole Southeast unless the Commission should attach conditions . . . requiring the carrying out of the original plans of the C. C. & O. to enter the city of Charleston and develop a coal terminal there."[27] After all, one might think that Mercantilism is not entirely a thing of the past!

It is indeed unfortunate that the City of Charleston has manifested, during the last several years, a hostile attitude towards the Atlantic Coast Line. This antipathy has been expressed on more than one occasion, while it would seem that a city, which has undergone and is still experiencing a period entirely different from one of great prosperity, would encourage the major railroad system by which it is served.

On June 3, 1924, the Interstate Commerce Commission authorized the proposed lease.[28] The report of the Commission says, in part: "The applicants and the carriers [the Clinchfield] have entered into a tentative agreement providing for the proposed acquisition of control and assumption of obligation, if approved by us, by the execution of a lease, a copy of which was filed with the application. Under the lease all the property,

---
[26] *Ibid.*, p. 16.
[27] *Railway Age*, Vol. LXXV (Oct. 6, 1923).
[28] *The Commercial and Financial Chronicle*, Vol. CXVIII (June 21, 1924).

rights, and franchises (except the franchise to be a corporation) of the carriers are demised to the applicants, jointly, for a period of 999 years from May 11, 1923, upon substantially the following terms:

"Prior to the execution of the lease, the capitalization of the Clinchfield is to be reduced by proper legal action to $52,292,000, consisting of first mortgage 5 per cent 30-year gold bonds, due June 1, 1938, in the amount of $13,950,000; first and consolidated mortgage 30-year 6 per cent gold bonds, series A, due December 15, 1952, in the amount of $8,000,000; Lick Creek & Lake Erie Railroad first mortgage 5 per cent gold bonds due January 1, 1933, in the amount of $195,000; equipment trust notes and obligations in the amount of $6,147,000; and common capital stock of the par value of $25,000,000. As rental for the leased properties the lessees are to pay $750,000 per annum for 3 years beginning January 1, 1925, $1,000,000 for 10 years beginning January 1, 1928, and $1,250,000 per annum for the remainder of the term, being 3, 4, and 5 per cent, respectively, on the $25,000,000 of common stock. In addition, the lessees are to pay the interest on the bonds and equipment trust obligations, including such obligations as shall be issued by the Clinchfield in connection with the payment for certain locomotives now under construction, and on such other securities as may hereafter be issued under the terms of the lease; the lessees are also to pay the interest on $1,500,000 of Holston Corporation 5 per cent realty and collateral trust convertible notes, due April 1, 1926, guaranteed as to payment of principal and interest by the Clinchfield, if, and to the extent that, the latter is required to pay such interest. They are also to pay all taxes, assessments, and other governmental charges upon the leased properties, and certain other customary charges; money in possession of the lessors on May 11, 1923, and net income from the leased properties are to be applied by the lessors or the lessees in making additions and betterments or otherwise as provided in the lease; the lessees may make additions and betterments, extensions and improvements, to the leased properties and for expenditures made therefor shall be entitled to be reimbursed by the Clinchfield with its stock or bonds or both as the lessees shall specify, such securities to be taken by the latter at fair and reasonable market prices in view of market conditions and other circumstances existing at the time; and in like manner the lessees are to be reimbursed for all payments, costs, and expenditures incurred in taking up maturing obligations of the Clinchfield."[29]

Continuing, the report of the Commission says: "Because of its isolation and the policy of its connections in preferring the longer hauls by more circuitous routes, the Clinchfield is not rendering the service for which it was designed and of which it is capable. The testimony is that its influence on the rate structure of the Carolinas, where its maximum influence should be felt, is practically nothing and that so long as it continues as an independent property its usefulness to the public will be circumscribed. Control of the Clinchfield by the applicants, when the proposed connections are made between the L. & N. and the Clinchfield, especially the connections with the Harlan County branch, should result in added competition among the coal operators serving the Carolina markets; should give the Carolina territory an additional source of fuel in times of emergency; and should result in added competition with the Southern [Southern Railway] for traffic between the Carolina territory and the Northwest, at least between the western portion of the Carolinas on the one hand, and Kentucky and points beyond the Ohio River, west of the Cincinnati-Benton Harbor line on the other.... One of the purposes of the Transportation Act, under the provisions of which the applicants are seeking to acquire control of the Clinchfield, is to foster the weaker carriers. The Seaboard is the weakest of the four great systems serving the Southeast.[30] Its independence and the support of its competitive position constitute an important factor in the public interest in transporation in that territory.

"Those opposing the lease urge that the interest of each of the interveners and of the public in general will be best served if the Clinchfield is maintained as an independent line supported by its connections at each end. They request that any approval of the proposed acquisition be under condition that the Clinchfield be maintained as an open route, neutral or impartial, and

---

[29] Finance Docket No. 3131, I. C. C., pp. 6-7.

[30] These systems are: The Atlantic Coast Line-Louisville & Nashville, Southern Railway, Illinois Central-Central of Georgia, and Seaboard Air Line.

THE CLINCHFIELD LEASE 197

equally available to all connections. They generally urge that unconditional approval of the application be refused. The position of the Seaboard is that the public interest will be best served by placing the Clinchfield in a position similar to that of the Richmond, Fredericksburg & Potomac Railroad, that is, in control of its immediate existing and potential connections at each end in a way that will fairly protect the interests of each. The Seaboard proposes, in the event the application is denied, to submit a plan for such joint control of the Clinchfield. It argues that the question before us is the broadest interest in transportation, not for today, but over an unlimited future; and that disposition of the Clinchfield which does not best serve the public interest is contrary to the public interest. Under the provisions of paragraph (2) of section 5 we are not in a position to consider whether acquisition of control in some other manner than proposed, or by some other carrier than the applicant, would better serve the public interest. The question which we must determine in that regard is whether the acquisition of control proposed is in the public interest.

"On February 9, 1924, before arriving at any conclusion, we sent a memorandum to persons who had intervened or filed appearances in the proceedings requesting that expressions be made regarding the arrangement to be sanctioned and required in case the decision of the Commission should be favorable to the applicants' proposal, and asking for specific consideration of the effect of an order of approval made subject to certain conditions, set forth in the memorandum. The applicants and a number of others to whom the memorandum was addressed have filed representations in regard to the conditions suggested. On consideration of these conditions in connection with the representations filed, we have reached the conclusion that approval and authorization of the acquisition proposed will be in the public interest only upon the following conditions:

1. The applicants shall establish and maintain a separate organization for the combined properties of the Carolina, Clinchfield & Ohio Railway and its subsidiaries, so that the three companies shall constitute a separate operating unit, having a responsible management directly in charge of the operations of such properties.

2. The Louisville & Nashville Railroad Company shall, within twelve months after the effective date hereof, file with the Commis-

sion its application under paragraph (18) of Section 1 of the Interstate Commerce Act for a certificate of public convenience and necessity to construct the proposed connections between its McRoberts line and its Harlan County branch on the one hand, and the Clinchfield on the other, and, in the event it proposes to acquire existing lines for use as part of such connections, under such other provisions of the Act as are pertinent; and shall, if in such proceeding it is found that the present or future public convenience and necessity require or will require the construction of either or both such connections, proceed with such construction in accordance with the terms of the certificate issued in such proceeding.

3. So far as lies within the power of the applicants, existing routes and channels of trade and commerce heretofore established by other carriers in connection with the Clinchfield shall be preserved, existing gateways for the interchange of traffic with such other carriers shall be maintained, and the present neutrality of handling traffic inbound and outbound by the Carolina, Clinchfield & Ohio Railway and its subsidiary, the Carolina, Clinchfield & Ohio Railway of South Carolina, shall be continued so as to permit equal opportunity for service and routing or movement of traffic which is competitive with traffic of the applicants, or either of them, to and from all connecting lines reached by the line of the Clinchfield Companies, without discrimination in service against such competitive traffic.

4. The applicants shall permit the line of the Clinchfield and its subsidiaries to be used as a link for through traffic, via existing gateways or interchange, or via such gateways as may hereafter be established under authority of the Commission by means of the connecting lines which the Louisville & Nashville Railroad Company proposes to build, equally available to such other carriers, now connecting, or which may hereafter connect, with the line of the Clinchfield and its subsidiaries, as may desire to participate in through routes and joint rates between points in territory north and west of the line of the Clinchfield and points at and beyond the Ohio River on the one hand and points in the southeastern and Carolina territory on the other, under divisions to be agreed upon by the applicants, or either of them, and/or the Clinchfield organization, on the one hand, and by the other participating carrier or carriers on the other, and shall not discriminate as to rates, fares and charges against such participating carrier or carriers as compared with the applicants, or either of them; the intention of this provision being that the line of the Clinchfield and its subsidiaries shall be maintained as an open route equally available to all carriers connecting with the Clinchfield for traffic between the points designated.

THE CLINCHFIELD LEASE

5. It shall be expressly provided by the lease, as executed, that no securities shall be issued by the lessors, or any of them, except with our approval where such approval is required under the provisions of Section 20a of the Interstate Commerce Act; and that the par value of stock and/or the principal amount of bonds or other securities issued to refund maturing obligations or to reimburse the lessees for expenditures made as provided in the lease, shall not on the one hand exceed the principal amount of the securities refunded, and on the other, the amount of actual expenditures for additions, betterments, extensions, or improvements properly chargeable under our accounting classifications to capital accounts."[31]

The text of the lease, as ordered by the Interstate Commerce Commission, is as follows:[32]

At a General Session of the INTERSTATE COMMERCE COMMISSION, held at its office in Washington, D. C., on the 3rd day of June, A. D. 1924.

CLINCHFIELD RAILWAY LEASE

A hearing in this proceeding and investigation of the matters and things involved herein having been had, and the Commission having, on the date hereof, made and filed a report containing its findings of fact and conclusions thereon, which said report is hereby referred to and made a part hereof:

It is ordered, That the acquisition by the Atlantic Coast Line Railroad Company and the Louisville & Nashville Railroad Company of the properties, rights, and franchises (except the right to be a corporation) of the Carolina, Clinchfield & Ohio Railway, and its subsidiaries, the Carolina, Clinchfield & Ohio Railway of South Carolina, and the Clinchfield Northern Railway of Kentucky, by lease, as set forth in said report, be, and the same is hereby, authorized and approved: *Provided, however,* That the right of the lessees to require the lessors to issue securities in reimbursement of expenditures made by the former for additions, betterments, extensions, and improvements, and to refund securities of the lessor companies or to reimburse the lessees for refunding such securities, shall be subject to our approval where required by the provisions of Section 20a of the Interstate Commerce Act; *And provided further,* That the making of said lease and exercise of any of the rights conferred by this order shall in all future proceedings, judicial as well as ad-

---

[31] Finance Docket No. 3131, I. C. C., pp. 26-29.
[32] "Clinchfield Railway Lease," Finance Docket No. 3131, I. C. C., pp. 1-3.

ministrative, to which the carriers above named, or any of them be parties, be deemed and taken as conclusive evidence of their acceptance of, and agreement to abide by, the conditions enumerated in said report, and numbered from 1 to 5, inclusive; *And provided further,* That within six months after the date hereof, and within 10 days after the execution of said lease, the applicants shall file with this Commission a certified copy of said lease in the form in which it shall have been executed.

And it is further ordered, That the Atlantic Coast Line Railroad Company and the Louisville and Nashville Railroad Company be, and they are hereby, authorized to assume, as joint lessees, of the property, rights, and franchises of the Carolina, Clinchfield & Ohio Railway, and its subsidiaries as aforesaid, obligation and liability of paying (1) as rental therefor in equal quarterly installments, $750,000 per annum for 3 years beginning January 1, 1925, $1,000,000 per annum for 10 years beginning January 1, 1928, and $1,250,000 per annum from January 1, 1933, until the expiration of said lease, said rental being equivalent to dividends of 3, 4, and 5 per cent, respectively, on $25,000,000, par value, of common capital stock of the Carolina, Clinchfield & Ohio Railway to be outstanding at the time the lease is executed; (2) interest on the following obligations of the Carolina, Clinchfield & Ohio Railway, now outstanding namely, in the amount of $13,950,000; first and consolidated mortgage 30-year 6 per cent gold bonds, series A, due December 15, 1952, in the amount of $8,000,000; Lick Creek & Lake Erie Railroad first mortgage 5 per cent gold bonds, due January 1, 1923, in the amount of $195,000; and equipment-trust notes and obligations in the amount of $6,147,000; and (3) interest on $1,500,000, face amount, of Holston Corporation 5 per cent realty and collateral trust convertible notes, due April 1, 1926, guaranteed as to payment of principal and interest by the Carolina, Clinchfield & Ohio Railway, if, and to the extent that, the latter is required to pay such interest.

It is further ordered, That, except as herein authorized, no obligation or liability in respect of said bonds, or interest thereon, shall be assumed by the applicants, or either of them, unless and until so ordered by this Commission.

It is further ordered, that the applicants, or either of them, shall report concerning the pertinent matters herein involved, in conformity with the Commission's order of May 25, 1922, respecting applications filed under Section 20a of the Interstate Commerce Act.

THE CLINCHFIELD LEASE 201

It is further ordered, That this order shall take effect and be in force from and after 30 days from the date hereof.

And it is further ordered, That nothing herein shall be construed to imply any guaranty or obligation as to any of said securities herein enumerated, or dividends or interest thereon, on by part of the United States.

By the Commission.

(SEAL) GEORGE B. MCGINTY,
Secretary.

The directors of the Atlantic Coast Line and of the Louisville & Nashville railroad companies, respectively, formally accepted the terms of the lease on August 21;[33] and the directors of the Carolina, Clinchfield & Ohio Railway approved it on September 11, 1924.[34]

---

[33] *The Commercial and Financial Chronicle,* Vol. CXIX (Aug. 23, 1924).
[34] *Ibid.,* Vol. CXIX (Sept. 13, 1924).

CHAPTER XIII

THE CLINCHFIELD RAILROAD OF TODAY AND TOMORROW

THIS STORY of railroad development, culminating in the formation of the Clinchfield Railroad, would hardly be complete without mentioning some of the events which have transpired since the Carolina, Clinchfield & Ohio passed into the hands of the Atlantic Coast Line and the Louisville & Nashville railroads. Since only five years have elapsed since the lease became effective, it would be difficult to point out the advantages, and possibly the disadvantages, which have resulted to both the lessor and the lessees. Time alone will tell. We believe, however, that the advantages will overshadow whatever disadvantages may occur in the future. At least, for the first time since the organization of the old Charleston, Cincinnati & Chicago Railroad in 1887, this railway through the Appalachian mountains will realize a profit for its owners, the stockholders. In accordance with the order set forth by the Interstate Commerce Commission in authorizing the lease, the Clinchfield still maintains its own organization, and it is operated independently of the lessee companies.

The only item of importance in the corporate history of the road which has transpired during the period 1925-1930, was the maturity on April 1, 1926, of the $1,500,000 five per cent realty and collateral trust convertible notes of the Holston Corporation, guaranteed by the Clinchfield and assumed by the lessees. To take these up, the Carolina, Clinchfield & Ohio Railway secured authority from the Interstate Commerce Commission to issue $1,500,000 of its first and consolidated mortgage five per cent gold notes, series "B," dated April 1, 1926, and due April 1, 1956. The payment of interest was assumed by the lessees in accordance with the terms of the lease. Authorization for the bond issue and for the payment of interest by the lessees was filed with the Commission in finance dockets 6101 and 6105, respectively. The bonds are redeemable as a whole at 103 and accrued interest.[1]

[1] *Third Annual Report,* Clinchfield Railroad Company, for the year ended Dec. 31, 1927, p. 6.

TODAY AND TOMORROW 203

Group insurance was taken out by the employes of the Clinchfield in 1925. The policy, which became effective on October 1 of that year, was placed with the Prudential Insurance Company of America. Approximately ninety-five per cent of the eligible employes subscribed to the plan. A portion of the premium is borne by the railroad company.[2]

The only equipment which has been added since the date of the lease is two buffet-observation cars, purchased from The Pullman Company in 1926.[3] In the forward end of these cars are twelve standard revolving parlor car chairs; in the center, there is a small kitchen from which meals are served; at the rear, there are club car facilities, with tables, movable chairs, etc., and an observation platform. They are operated on trains 37 and 38 between Spartanburg and Elkhorn City.[4]

RESULTS OF OPERATION

The years 1929-1930 were abnormal for all industries, and this, of course, has had its effect upon the railroads. Earnings have been low, and a period of general depression has prevailed throughout the country. Many roads did not earn operating expenses during this period. While the Clinchfield managed to show a profit, its earnings in 1929 were less than for any year since the date of the lease.

During this period of economic transition, newer forms of competition have arisen to take traffic away from the railroads. The public highways are bearing considerably more traffic than heretofore. Until some form of adequate governmental regulation is inaugurated governing motor truck and bus operations, the inroads on the railways' traffic will continue. Highway carriers present a problem of probably the most unfair form of competition with which any great industrial organization has had to contend. Public sentiment, for a time in harmony with the buses, is becoming more and more favorable towards the railroads, and it should not be difficult for the railroads to convince Congress that regulation of highway transportation is

[2] *First Annual Report*, Clinchfield Railroad Company, for the year ended Dec. 31, 1925, p. 7.
[3] *Second Annual Report*, Clinchfield Railroad Company, for the year ended Dec. 31, 1926, p. 33.
[4] "Time Tables," Clinchfield Railroad Company, Jan., 1928.

THE CLINCHFIELD RAILROAD

an issue of great national significance. The private automobile has also affected passenger earnings in no small degree.

It is interesting to note that since 1925 the ratio of merchandise freight handled by the Clinchfield in respect to total operation has exceeded coal. The tables in the Appendix indicate that the revenues from other classes of traffic have declined, while the returns from merchandise have increased steadily each year. The Clinchfield, therefore, can no longer be called merely a coal road. The increase in income derived from merchandise freight has been due, to a large extent, to the selling policies of the traffic department in securing additional through business. Once secured, the railroad, through its local agencies, advises the shipper when the shipment was received by the Clinchfield from its connections; and then, by quick handling, the shipper and consignee are continuously informed as to the progress the goods are making as the cars pass the various junctions on the road. Large quantities of automobile shipments have been secured, and in 1927, 8,776 car loads were handled on the through freight trains.[5]

The following table shows the service which is maintained by the double-daily time-freight trains:[6]

TABLE XXX

	BETWEEN			AND
CHI-CA-GO	CIN-CIN-NATI	CO-LUM-BUS	TO-LE-DO	
(Hrs.)	(Hrs.)	(Hrs.)	(Hrs.)	
48	29	33	48	Johnson City, Tenn.
58	39	44	58	Marion, N. C.
59	40	45	59	Bostic, N. C.
61	42	47	61	Spartanburg, S. C.
67	48	53	67	Charlotte, N. C. (SAL)
63	44	49	63	Shelby, N. C. (SAL)
65	46	51	65	Lincolnton, N. C. (SAL)
70	51	56	70	Monroe, N. C. (SAL)
76	57	62	76	Gastonia, N. C. (P&N)
95	76	81	95	Wadesboro, N. C. (SAL)
95	76	81	95	Rockingham, N. C. (SAL)

[5] Information received from the office of the General Freight Agent, Clinchfield Railroad Company, Erwin, Tenn., Nov., 1928.

[6] "Time Tables," Clinchfield Railroad Company, Jan., 1928.

TABLE XXX—Continued

BETWEEN				AND
CHI-CA-GO	CIN-CIN-NATI	CO-LUM-BUS	TO-LE-DO	
(Hrs.)	(Hrs.)	(Hrs.)	(Hrs.)	
95	76	81	95	Hamlet, N. C. (SAL)
66	48	52	66	Hickory, N. C. (Sou)
70	52	56	70	Statesville, N. C. (Sou)
94	75	80	94	High Point, N. C. (Sou)
94	75	80	94	Lexington, N. C. (Sou)
71	52	57	71	Columbia, S. C. (C&WC-CN&L or Sou)
73	54	59	73	Augusta, Ga. (C&WC)
85	66	71	85	Charleston, S. C. (C&WC-ACL)
83	64	69	83	Savannah, Ga. (C&WC-ACL)
96	77	82	96	Jacksonville, Fla. (C&WC-ACL)

Additional service has been inaugurated with the establishment of "package cars" operating daily from Chicago, Cincinnati, Columbus, Louisville, and Norfolk. The schedules of these cars are as follows:[7]

TABLE XXXI

FROM	TO	DAYS IN TRAN-SIT	ROUTE
Chicago, Ill.	Charlotte, N. C.	4	C&O-Clinchfield-SAL
Chicago	Charlotte, N. C.	4	Big Four-C&O-Clinchfield-SAL
Chicago	Hamlet, N. C.	5	Big Four-C&O-Clinchfield-SAL
Chicago	Columbia, S. C.	4	C&O-Clinchfield-C&WC-CN&L
Chicago	Spartanburg, S. C.	3	Big Four-C&O-Clinchfield
Chicago	Johnson City, Tenn.	3	C&O-Clinchfield
Chicago	Kingsport, Tenn.	3	C&O-Clinchfield
Cincinnati, O.	Charlotte, N. C.	3	C&O-Clinchfield-SAL
Cincinnati	Johnson City, Tenn.	2	C&O-Clinchfield
Cincinnati	Kingsport, Tenn.	2	C&O-Clinchfield
Cincinnati	Charlotte, N. C.	3	Big Four-C&O-Clinchfield-SAL
Columbus, O.	Johnson City, Tenn.	2	C&O-Clinchfield
Norfolk, Va.	Kingsport, Tenn.	3	N&W-Clinchfield
Norfolk	Johnson City, Tenn.	3	N&W-Clinchfield
Louisville, Ky.	Johnson City, Tenn.	2	L&N-Interstate-Clinchfield

[7] *Ibid.*

THE CLINCHFIELD RAILROAD

The decline in the volume of coal traffic during recent years has caused considerable anxiety on the part of both the coal operatives and the railroads. The coal industry is experiencing a period of great technical transition for its consumers. While the industrial development of the United States has been great, our coal consumption has not materially increased. Marked progress has been made in the efficient use of coal. The transfer of industry to electrically driven machinery, brought about through the development of hydro-electric power, has curtailed the consumption of coal in no small degree. The use of oil as a prime fuel, both for industrial and domestic purposes, has likewise created another competitor for coal. The result is that the development of coal traffic has been considerably retarded. This is true not only for the Clinchfield territory, but for the entire country.[8]

---

[8] The system of "free competition" undoubtedly has failed in the coal industry, although any industry which is tied to a natural resource finds it difficult to follow the lines of real competition. The coal operatives attribute the cause of the bad situation to labor; the public, to no restriction on the operatives. There is a Bill before Congress which calls for a Bituminous Coal Commission which would have wide powers somewhat analogous to the Interstate Commerce Commission regarding railroads. This would give governmental administrative control instead of the long court procedures necessary under the Sherman Anti-Trust Law.

The coal industry may be compared with agriculture, and particularly in the South. Just as there are a large number of small farms scattered over the country, so are there many small coal mines trying to compete with each other. It would seem that combinations within the industry, under governmental administration, is about the only solution to the problem.

The World War brought about over-production and over-expansion. The following table illustrates this over-expansion, as stated on page 264 of Hamilton and Wright: *The Case of Bituminous Coal:*

Year	Production	Capacity	Excess Capacity	
			Tons	Per Cent of Production
1890	111,302,000	153,030,000	41,728,000	37
1900	212,316,000	279,317,000	67,001,000	32
1910	417,111,000	590,965,000	173,854,000	42
1915	442,624,000	674,447,000	231,823,000	52
1920	568,667,000	796,494,000	227,827,000	40
1921	514,922,000	836,535,000	420,613,000	101
1922	422,268,000	915,900,000	493,632,000	117

TODAY AND TOMORROW   207

There seems to have been a general idea that the construction of the Louisville & Nashville's extension would be of no material value to the Clinchfield in so far as its shipments of coal were concerned. Justification for this belief, of course, remains to be seen. However, new markets for Clinchfield coal recently have been created in the West, and the first coal shipments of any consequence to this territory were made in 1928. Favorable freight rates, similar to those for the mines on the Big Sandy Division of the Chesapeake & Ohio Railway, have been put into effect.

The development of local industries along the line of the Clinchfield has been great. Kingsport, Johnson City, Erwin, and Spruce Pine are excellent illustrations, the growth of Kingsport having been almost phenomenal. In 1915, "herds of cattle pastured on the meadows where this model young industrial city now stands ... and an old box car sufficed as a railroad station."[9] The Clinchfield is the only railroad which serves this community. Today, the population is about 18,000, and there are fifteen large industries in operation. These industries, and the products thereof, are as follows:[10]

    Borden Mills, Inc.: Unbleached cotton cloth.
    Kingsport Hosiery Mills: Seamless and full-fashioned hosiery.
    Kingtan Extract Company: Factory sole leather, welting leather, bark extract, liquid chestnut extract, powdered chestnut extract, decolorized chestnut extract, special blend extracts.
    Meade Fibre Company: Bleached soda pulp, book and magazine paper.
    Kingsport Silk Mills: Broad silks.
    Rextex Hosiery Mills: Fancy hosiery.
    General Shale Products Corporation: Brick.
    Pennsylvania-Dixie Cement Corporation: Portland cement.
    Blue Ridge Glass Corporation: Glass and wire glass.
    Tennessee Eastman Corporation: Lumber, charcoal, acetate of lime, methanol, methyl acetone, "No-D-K," and miscellaneous chemicals.
    Kingsport Utilities, Inc.: Electric power.
    Kingsport Foundry & Manufacturing Corporation: Gray iron, brass, and semi-steel castings.

[9] Long, *Kingsport, A Romance of Industry*, p. 82.
[10] *Ibid.*, p. 107.

Slip-Not Belting Corporation: Leather transmission belting.
Holliston Mills of Tennessee, Inc.: Book cloth.
The Kingsport Press: Book manufacturers and publishers.

Johnson City has developed from a town of 5,000 inhabitants in 1910 to a city with a population of over 30,000. It is the site of one of the National soldiers' homes, the grounds of which comprise an area of approximately five hundred acres; it is said to be the most beautiful "Home" in the country.[11] Remarkable industrial development has taken place since the establishment of the Clinchfield.

The principal industries of Johnson City include a blast furnace, two iron foundries, two furniture factories, a hosiery mill, a knitting mill, four machine shops, a mattress factory, seven wood-working plants, a tannery, a cement plant, and a brick and tile manufacturing company.[12]

Erwin is not only the operating headquarters of the Clinchfield Railroad, with its shops, terminal facilities, etc., but it is also the home of the first pottery plant to be established south of the Mason-Dixon line. Three feldspar grinding factories, a porcelain manufacturing plant, a silk mill, a furniture factory, and several lumber mills have appeared since the organization of the Clinchfield.[13]

At Spruce Pine, there are several lumber companies, six feldspar mills, three mica plants, two kaolin companies, and a flour mill.[14]

North Carolina produces almost one-half of the crude feldspar mined in the United States, with an annual production of 100,000 tons valued at $600,000.[15] Maine is second with 30,000 tons. The total production for the United States in 1928 was 210,811 tons valued at $1,418,975.[16] The principal feldspar mines are in Avery, Mitchell, and Yancey counties. Spruce Pine is in Mitchell, and Avery and Yancey border Mitchell on

---

[11] From a letter from Mr. Harry Faw, Secretary, Chamber of Commerce, Johnson City, Tenn., Aug. 5, 1929.
[12] "Industrial Guide and Directory of Industries along the Clinchfield Railroad," Clinchfield Railroad Company, 1928.
[13] *Ibid.*
[14] *Ibid.*
[15] Feldspar is used mainly in the manufacture of ceramic products, and to a less extent as an abrasive, as poultry grit, and as roofing material.
[16] *News Letter*, Aug. 7, 1929.

the east and west, respectively.[17] This section of North Carolina is also rich in forestry products. In McDowell and Mitchell, the two counties through which the Clinchfield passes, there are respectively 220,189 acres in forests, or 77 per cent of the total land area, and 84,306 acres, or 62 per cent of the land area.[18]

The following tables show a summary of freight traffic since the formation of the Clinchfield Railroad Company in 1925. The figures represent revenue car loads, and are not on a tonnage basis.[19]

TABLE XXXII

	1925	1926	1927	1928	1929
Coal loaded on line	50,802	52,165	43,889	33,881	37,129
Coal received from connections	32,262	21,922	21,103	17,096	17,264
Merchandise loaded on line	46,822	50,473	50,870	48,966	42,650
Merchandise received from connections	65,197	93,992	68,650	69,053	64,719
Delivered connections	144,943	141,877	......	120,941	116,040
Total freight handled	195,083	188,552*	185,512*	169,896*	161,762†

* Decrease caused mainly by decline on volume of coal traffic.

† Decrease caused primarily by decline in volume of business throughout the nation.

TABLE XXXIII

Miscellaneous Shipments:	1925	1926	1927	1928	1929
Apples	15	24	5	...	...
Fertilizer	120	315	374	365	420
Lumber	5,783	3,769	5,285	4,495	4,275
Bark	373	275	399	480	49
Wood	2,915	2,333	3,856	2,401	2,093
Logs	1,651	891	1,296	2,100	2,055
Poles	520	964	1,189	844	1,148
Ties	657	689	575	488	777
Cement	6,670	6,726	6,040	5,364	1,680
Brick	3,465	3,186	2,467	2,589	2,317
Flour and mills products	630	880	1,297	1,355	74
Pig iron	61	151	68	90	290
Mica	148	161	148	201	3,884
Feldspar	3,468	3,929	3,871	4,259	514

[17] *North Carolina, The Land of Opportunity*, p. 69.

[18] *News Letter*, Aug. 7, 1929.

[19] Information from the office of the General Freight Agent, Clinchfield Railroad, Erwin, Tenn.

TABLE XXXIII—Continued

Miscellaneous Shipments:	1925	1926	1927	1928	1929
Kaolin	347	483	509	512	174
Stone	1,176	1,351	1,523	1,197	110
Live Stock	263	171	89	93	646
Cotton and cotton products	77	63	297	427	646
Tannery products	69	91	192	195	102
Sand	1,296	1,731	1,214	1,255	824
Tanic acid extract	77	46	65	24	21
Charcoal	907	1,691	1,558	1,810	2,064
Pulp and paper	1,638	1,700	1,847	1,886	1,945
"Package Freight"	12,874	13,049	13,372	12,907	12,270
Miscellaneous	3,421	3,621	3,852	3,264	3,469

Conclusion

Although the Southern Railway is a competitor of the Clinchfield for through merchandise business, very friendly relations exist between the two roads. The Clinchfield's interchange with the Southern is larger than that of any other road with which it connects.[20] This relationship, together with the natural interests of the lessees in the road, should result in an increase in traffic over the Clinchfield, and thereby create larger returns to the lessee companies.

It was pointed out in the preceding chapter that there were several definite purposes for the acquisition of the Clinchfield by the Atlantic Coast Line and the Louisville & Nashville. The development of a through route under unified control for the transportation of passengers and merchandise undoubtedly has great significance; but more important is a direct southern outlet for coal located on the Louisville & Nashville.

There are two main coal fields served by the Louisville & Nashville: the Hazard field on the Eastern Kentucky Division, and the Harlan and Benham fields on the Harlan Branch of the Cumberland Valley Division, both of which are in Kentucky. The former has a daily capacity of approximately 1,000 cars; the latter, 1,200. Contiguous fields are served by the Chesapeake & Ohio, Norfolk & Western, Interstate, and Southern railroads. None has severed the barrier of the Cumberland mountains to connect the two fields.

[20] See Appendix E.

The entire output of the Hazard field, amounting to 210,000 cars per annum, moves to the north and northwest, sixty to sixty-five per cent of which interchanges at Cincinnati. The Harlan and Benham fields, with an annual output of 350,000 cars, likewise send their products in the same direction. Although it was not desired to relinquish any of these movements, the Louisville & Nashville was, and still is, anxious to open new markets in the south and southeast. As has been pointed out, the Louisville & Nashville has no physical connection with the Clinchfield nor with the Atlantic Coast Line whereby this traffic can be moved. The long back haul via Atlanta would not be practical. Hence, the only solution was the construction of a new line.

The route decided upon for the proposed extension involved three stages. The first would branch out from the Eastern Kentucky Division at Ulbah, in the Hazard area, and connect with the Cumberland Division at Chad, a distance of 18 miles. The existing 26 miles of line to Chevrolet, near Harlan, would be utilized. The second stage would traverse Cumberland Mountain to connect Chevrolet with Hagan, 13.6 miles. Hagan is located on the Norton line of the Cumberland Valley Division. The third leg would extend from Hagan, through the valleys of the Powell and Clinch rivers, to Speers Ferry, Virginia, 39.5 miles, where connection would be made with the Clinchfield Railroad. The estimated cost of construction amounted to $22,700,000.[21]

These three projects were approved and ordered constructed by the Interstate Commerce Commission upon ratification of the Clinchfield lease. However, the Commission has subsequently suspended its requirement for construction of the first stage described above, and accepted in lieu of the third an arrangement with the Interstate Railroad to handle Louisville & Nashville traffic from Norton to Miller Yard, on the Clinchfield, a distance of about 18 miles. Construction of the second stage, from Chevrolet to Hagan, was commenced in 1928,[22] and the work was completed and the road opened to traffic on December 1, 1930.[23]

---
[21] *Railway Age*, Vol. LXXXVIII (Feb. 15, 1930).
[22] *Ibid.*
[23] *The Louisville & Nashville Employes' Magazine*, Jan., 1931.

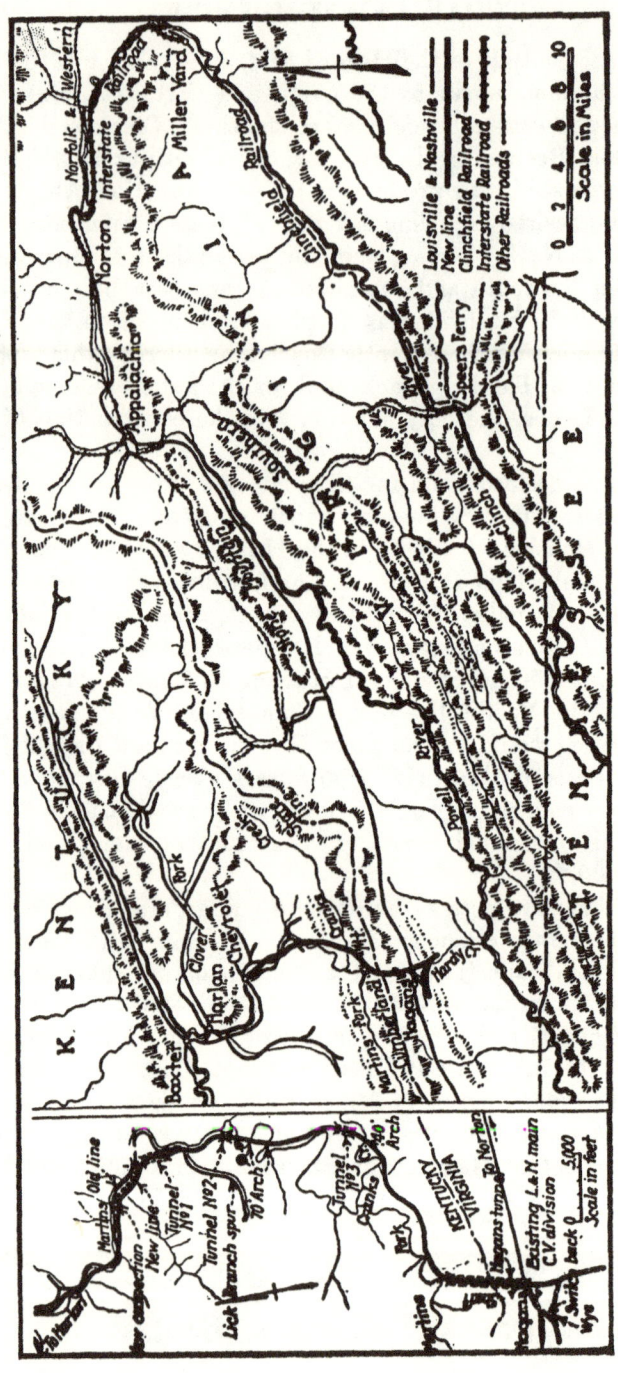

Detailed and General Map of the Chevrolet-Hagan Line. The Small Scale Map Shows the Connection with the Clinchfield via the Interstate Railroad.—From *Railway Age*, February 15, 1930.

TODAY AND TOMORROW 213

The agreement with the Interstate Railroad gives the Louisville & Nashville trackage rights between Norton and Miller Yard, and trains are operated over this line by crews and equipment of the latter company. At the present time, the tonnage of these trains consists almost entirely of coal. The cars are picked up by the Clinchfield's regular trains at Miller Yard. No close figure is available at this time of the number of loads per day which will move over this route, but it is estimated that from forty to one hundred cars will be handled daily. The coal must necessarily find a market in south Atlantic territory, competing with coal now being used, and the volume and rate of increase depends upon the ability of the producers to dispose of it.[24] Utilization of this route for through merchandise business has not been established as yet, pending removal of certain rate restrictions and the inauguration of a dependable schedule. These difficulties are expected to be worked out in the near future, and there should be a considerable movement of freight other than coal via the new line.[25]

Meanwhile, definite steps have been under way to include the Charleston & Western Carolina Railway in the Atlantic Coast Line system proper. It will be recalled that the former company is controlled by the Atlantic Coast Line Company, a holding company of Connecticut which controls the Atlantic Coast Line Railroad Company, through ownership of the entire capital stock of the Charleston & Western Carolina.[26] The directors of the Charleston & Western Carolina authorized the lease of their line for 99 years to the Atlantic Coast Line, to become effective immediately upon ratification by the Interstate Commerce Commission, at a meeting held in Columbia, South Carolina, on January 7, 1930.[27] The Atlantic Coast Line Company has agreed to sell to the Atlantic Coast Line Railroad Company the 12,000 shares of capital stock of the Charleston & Western Carolina Railway Company issued and outstanding.[28] The stock-

---

[24] From a personal letter from Mr. L. H. Phetteplace, General Manager, Clinchfield Railroad Company, Nov. 26, 1930.

[25] From a personal letter from Mr. C. A. Smith, General Freight and Passenger Agent, Clinchfield Railroad Company, Dec. 23, 1930.

[26] Mundy, *Earning Power of Railroads*, p. 381.

[27] *The Augusta Chronicle*, Jan. 8, 1930.

[28] *Ninety-Sixth Annual Report*, Atlantic Coast Line Railroad Company, for the year ended Dec. 31, 1929, p. 22.

holders of the Charleston & Western Carolina approved and authorized the proposed lease at a special meeting held subsequent to the directors' meeting.[29] Under the lease arrangement, the Atlantic Coast Line will acquire control of the Charleston & Western Carolina, thereby furthering the interests of the former company in the development of the latter in connection with the Clinchfield.[30] It is probable that the Charleston & Western Carolina will become a district in the Second Division of the Atlantic Coast Line.

The leasing of the Charleston & Western Carolina is a logical step on the part of the Atlantic Coast Line, especially in relation to the use of the Clinchfield and the Louisville & Nashville's extension as a transmontane link between the Ohio and the south Atlantic, and in the movement of coal. It is evident that the Atlantic Coast Line anticipates the movement of heavy traffic over this route, for the virtual rebuilding of the Charleston & Western Carolina between Spartanburg and Yemassee seems probable.[31] Grades will be reduced between Spartanburg and Augusta, heavier rail will be laid, and a new steel bridge will be constructed over the Savannah River near Augusta, the latter to cost in excess of half a million dollars.[32] Hearings on the proposed lease were held in Washington in July, 1930, and a favorable report was submitted to the Interstate Commerce Commission by Examiner W. T. Wilkinson, upon the condition that the Charleston & Western Carolina be "an open route equally available to all carriers connecting therewith."[33]

Vigorous exception was taken by the Atlantic Coast Line to Examiner Wilkinson's recommendation, which would require the Charleston & Western Carolina to waive that portion of the Interstate Commerce Act entitling every carrier to its long haul. It would seem that this opposition was brought about primarily by the Georgia & Florida Railway, this company having recently completed a new line from Augusta to Green-

---

[29] *Annual Report*, Charleston & Western Carolina Railway Company, for the year ended Dec. 31, 1929, p. 8.

[30] *The Augusta Herald*, Jan. 9, 1930.

[31] Yemassee is the point of connection between the Charleston & Western Carolina and the main line of the Atlantic Coast Line, 60 miles south of Charleston and 52 miles north of Savannah.

[32] *The Augusta Chronicle*, Jan. 15, 1930.

[33] *The Savannah Morning News*, July 29, 1930.

wood, South Carolina, in connection with the Piedmont & Northern, the latter operating southward from Spartanburg. The condition to the proposed consolidation means that the Charleston & Western Carolina would be short hauled by any connecting carrier whenever such a line so desired. This license would be made available not only to the Georgia & Florida, but also to the Southern, Seaboard Air Line, and Central of Georgia, no one of which has intervened or suggested that any such advantage be given.[34]

Still another project in the development of the Clinchfield looms in the foreground. It has been shown in these pages that there is no direct physical connection between the Clinchfield and the Charleston & Western Carolina at Spartanburg, but that the interchange is handled by the Southern Railway. It is proposed to eliminate this undesirable necessity by means of a tunnel, two miles in length, beneath the city to connect the two lines. The expense will be enormous.[35] The Clinchfield originally purchased sufficient lands to permit the construction of a physical connection between all the roads which enter Spartanburg.[36] Authority for this work has been granted,[37] but plans have not yet been definitely decided upon. When completed, the project should result in the consolidation of the Clinchfield and Charleston & Western Carolina yards. Whether such consolidation be on the Clinchfield or the Charleston & Western Carolina side is not known, and until it is decided, it will be impossible to state what, if any, change will be made in the points of interchange. However, topographic conditions are such that a consolidation would seem more practical on the Clinchfield side. The purpose of the tunnel is not only to provide direct connection, thereby facilitating the movement of business, but also to eliminate the transfer charge now being paid the Southern Railway.

Of what significance are these projects to the Clinchfield? Vast sums have been expended in the construction of the Louisville & Nashville extension. At the time this volume goes to press, additional expenditures are proposed for the virtual re-

---

[34] *Ibid.*, Sept. 3, 1930.   [35] *The News & Courier*, Nov. 15, 1930.
[36] From a personal letter from Mr. J. E. Willoughby, Chief Engineer, Atlantic Coast Line Railroad, Dec. 7, 1930.
[37] *Railway Age*, Nov. 29, 1930, p. 1203.

building of the Charleston & Western Carolina, as well as the proposed tunnel at Spartanburg. In operating the Charleston & Western Carolina as a district of the parent company, the Atlantic Coast Line will be making a direct connection with the Clinchfield at Spartanburg, facilitating its exchange of traffic with the Louisville & Nashville on the other side of the mountains. The Atlantic Coast Line and the Louisville & Nashville have a definite purpose in spending money on the Clinchfield's connections. The immediate effect would be to use the Clinchfield as a means to connect the middle west and the coal fields with the Atlantic seaboard. The Clinchfield was not leased for the purpose of leaving it to rust, but to develop a greater volume of traffic for the lessees.

Some port on the south Atlantic must benefit. Where will the connected lines deliver tonnage at deep water? Will Charleston be the principal beneficiary? Savannah? Wilmington? The management of the Atlantic Coast Line has never intimated just where and how it would develop the tonnage movement to and from the Louisville & Nashville. It will be remembered that Mr. Henry Walters, chairman of the boards of the two companies, stated that the matter would be left to the ports to work out, and it would depend upon "the people who live in the ports to inaugurate whatever things are necessary to develop the ports."[38] It has been rumored that the Columbia, Newberry & Laurens, another subsidiary of the Atlantic Coast Line, would be used in this enterprise of operating the Clinchfield as a connecting link.[39] By this route, trains would move between Spartanburg and Charleston via Laurens, Columbia, and Sumter. However, it would appear that Yemassee is destined to be the principal junction for the diversion of tonnage from the Charleston & Western Carolina, either to Charleston or to Savannah and Florida points.

For years, Charleston clamored for a through connection to the Ohio. Millions of dollars were expended by that city on many projects to reach that end. Each project in which that city was vitally interested—the South Carolina Railroad, the Louisville, Cincinnati & Charleston, and the Blue Ridge Railroad—ended in a dismal failure in so far as Charleston's

---

[38] See Chapter XII, above.
[39] *The News & Courier*, Nov. 15, 1930.

"dream" was concerned. Charleston was attempting to cope with the ports of the East. It fought Savannah for supremacy of the South Atlantic. Even before the actual failure of the Louisville, Cincinnati & Charleston Railroad, Savannah and the State of Georgia quietly went about the construction of their own road, and the present Central of Georgia and the Nashville, Chattanooga & St. Louis railways were completed years before Charleston ever had a direct outlet to the middle west.

The South Carolina Railroad and the Louisville, Cincinnati & Charleston are now important links in the Southern Railway's line from the Atlantic seaboard to the Ohio. The Clinchfield, and its connections under unified control, likewise form a line between Charleston and the Ohio. From a physical standpoint, then, Charleston's great desire of former years has been realized. That city has received some benefit therefrom, but certainly not to the extent anticipated. The currents of traffic have been too well established through trunk line territory[40] for the Clinchfield or the Southern to make any great inroad on foreign trade traffic. If the Louisville, Cincinnati & Charleston had been completed by 1850, the story might have been different, and both Charleston and Savannah would doubtless be ports of greater national importance.

We do not mean that the volume of traffic is lacking between the South Atlantic and the middle west. We mean that the possibilities are slim for Charleston, Savannah, or any other south Atlantic port being a serious competitor with the great eastern ports in foreign trade. The Clinchfield is a new road which must compete with such lines as the Southern and the Central of Georgia-Illinois Central combination on the west, and the Norfolk & Western and the Chesapeake & Ohio on the east.

Economic conditions have radically changed since the formation of the Charleston, Cincinnati & Chicago. Local traffic is rapidly passing by the board. The "Three C's" was originally built to handle coal, and coal will continue to comprise a large proportion of the traffic handled by the Clinchfield in the future. Undoubtedly, the Louisville & Nashville's extension will bring about an increase in tonnage for the Clinchfield, but whether or not coal coming from this source will move to Charleston for export is problematical. The future of that city depends

---

[40] As the Baltimore & Ohio, New York Central, and Pennsylvania systems.

upon its ability to attract business. The backers of the "Three C's" gave but little thought to the possibilities of the movement of through merchandise. Today, the Clinchfield secures over one-half of its revenue from that source.

We believe the future of the Clinchfield is bright. We are optimistic of the traffic which will come to it as a result of the several projects mentioned above. Even now, a fast through schedule has been inaugurated in conjunction with the Atlantic Coast Line, Charleston & Western Carolina, and Chesapeake & Ohio for the handling of perishable traffic from Florida and south Georgia, via Yemassee.[41] A nice business of this highly desirable traffic is being moved over the Clinchfield, particularly to points in central and eastern Ohio, Detroit, and other midwestern cities.[42] In 1930, this business had increased approximately one hundred per cent as compared with 1929, and it is likely that the year 1931 will show even a greater increase.

It is not improbable that within a few years the public will be enabled to travel over the "Clinchfield Route" in the solid Pullman trains predicted by Colonel Olds in 1908, and by General Wilder in 1888. Perhaps the "Carolina Special" of the Southern Railway, operating between Chicago, Cincinnati, and Charleston, may some day have a rival in a similar train which will pass over the scenic railway of the Clinchfield. Perhaps the luxurious trains of the Louisville & Nashville and the Atlantic Coast Line between the northwest and Florida, now operating

---

[41] A car of oranges, for example, leaving Jacksonville Monday afternoon is in Cincinnati Wednesday evening. The daily perishable freight schedule for carload traffic from Florida to western territory, via the Clinchfield Route, is as follows:

Leave	Jacksonville	(ACL)	2:00 P.M. (Mon.)
Leave	Yemassee	(C&WC)	12:01 A.M. (Tues.)
Leave	Spartanburg	(Clinchfield)	1:55 P.M. (Tues.)
Arrive	Elkhorn City	(Clinchfield)	3:00 A.M. (Wed.)
Arrive	Cincinnati	(C&O)	10:30 P.M. (Wed.)
Arrive	Columbus	(C&O)	3:00 P.M. (Wed.)
Arrive	Toledo	(C&O)	9:00 P.M. (Wed.)
Arrive	Detroit	(PM)	4:00 A.M. (Thurs.)
Arrive	Cleveland	(NKP)	3:00 P.M. (Thurs.)
Arrive	Buffalo	(NKP)	10:00 P.M. (Thurs.)
Arrive	Indianapolis	(Big Four)	3:15 P.M. (Thurs.)
Arrive	Chicago	(C&O)	2:00 A.M. (Fri.)

[42] From a personal letter from Mr. C. A. Smith, General Freight and Passenger Agent, Clinchfield Railroad Company, Dec. 23, 1930.

Bridge over South Fork of Holston River and Holston Tunnel

via Atlanta, will utilize the improved facilities offered by the Clinchfield.

The Clinchfield was built for permanence. Its rails will not be taken up nor its properties abandoned. It can handle an enormous tonnage across the mountains at a relatively small operating cost. In its organization are men who are capable of coping with the transportation problem with which all railroads must contend. When general conditions become more stable and the business cycle swings into an upward trend, a greater volume of traffic will come to the Clinchfield. Its future as an important transmontane link between the south Atlantic and the middle west is certain.

APPENDIX A

GENERAL BALANCE SHEET
(As of December 31, 1929)[1]

Assets

Investments

Improvements on leased railway property	$ 9,228.77
Deposits in lieu of mortgaged property sold	18,643.38
Miscellaneous physical property	9,581.06
Investments in affiliated companies:	
Stocks	3,484,155.11
Bonds	300,000.00
Advances	402,422.55
Other investments:	
U. S. Treasury Certificates	1,000,000.00
Total investments	$ 5,224,030.87

Current Assets

Cash	$ 1,027,321.63
Time drafts and deposits	2,500,000.00
Special deposits	11,802.00
Traffic and car-service balances receivable	379,829.83
Net balance receivable from agents and conductors	18,879.22
Miscellaneous accounts receivable	114,800.67
Material and supplies	677,726.69
Interest receivable	82,414.36
Total current assets	$ 4,812,774.40

Deferred Assets

Working fund advances	$ 2,018.50
Other deferred assets	1,216,480.66
Total deferred assets	$ 1,218,499.16

Unadjusted Debits

Rents and insurance premiums paid in advance	$ 15,585.07
Other unadjusted debits	159,306.30
Total unadjusted debits	$ 174,891.37
Total assets	$11,430,195.80

[1] *Fifth Annual Report,* Clinchfield Railroad Company, for the year ended December 31, 1929, pp. 12, 13.

APPENDIX

LIABILITIES

Long Term Debt

Non-negotiable debt to affiliated companies:

Open accounts.......................................$ 13,510.64

Current Liabilities

Traffic and car-service balances payable...................$	106,129.41
Audited accounts and wages payable.....................	441,203.90
Miscellaneous accounts payable.........................	294,423.50
Unmatured rents accrued................................	182,542.29
Other current liabilities................................	19,435.39

Total current liabilities...........................$ 1,043,734.49

Deferred Liabilities

Other deferred liabilities..............................$ 5,751,899.96

Unadjusted Credits

Tax liability..$ 257,555.11

Other unadjusted credits..............................$ 2,290,596.63

Total unadjusted credits..........................$ 2,548,151.74

Corporate Surplus

Additions to property through income and surplus........$ 9,228.77

Profit and loss—Balance..............................$ 2,063,670.20

Total surplus....................................$ 2,072,898.97

Total liabilities............................$11,430,195.80

APPENDIX B

OPERATING STATISTICS[a]

Year	Merchandise			Coal		
	Tonnage	Ton-Miles	Av. Haul	Tonnage	Ton-Miles	Av. Haul
1925	2,481,091	299,583,847	120.75	4,118,197	744,687,645	180.83
1926	2,546,276	293,034,134	115.08	3,756,211	636,832,007	169.54
1927	2,549,176	286,927,750	112.56	3,335,994	611,679,158	183.36
1928	2,443,576	291,195,011	119.17	2,668,119	434,651,946	162.91
1929	1,917,219	267,949,039	139.76	2,738,890	453,341,726	165.52

Year	Passenger			
	Number of passengers	Average Haul	Passenger Train Mileage	Av. paid by ea. passenger
1925	389,980	26.20	328,238	92.15c
1926	341,864	26.55	319,174	91.20
1927	326,166	25.03	329,579	86.05
1928	221,568	25.52	309,723	87.42
1929	201,086	24.67	302,016	82.88

[a] Annual Reports, Clinchfield Railroad Company, 1925-1929.

SUMMARY OF OPERATING REVENUES

Yr. end Dec. 31	Coal	Merchandise	Passenger	Mail and Express	Miscl.[3]	Total
1925	$4,386,148.98	$3,848,537.59	$359,384.74	$91,372.67	$74,409.33	$8,759,853.31
1926	3,859,675.13	3,954,607.19	311,765.55	79,402.89	76,748.43	8,282,199.19
1927	3,521,146.88	3,965,629.49	280,669.46	77,147.07	75,451.49	7,920,044.39
1928	2,655,027.35	3,868,276.53	193,689.35	75,991.16	67,136.47	6,870,120.86
1929	2,873,951.74	3,601,297.29	166,655.73	76,549.26	64,780.27	6,783,240.29

Ratio of Each Class of Operating Revenues to Total Operating Revenues

	1925	1926	1927	1928	1929
Coal	50.07	46.60	44.46	38.79	42.37
Merchandise	43.93	47.75	50.07	56.31	53.09
Passenger	4.10	3.76	3.54	2.82	2.46
Mail and Express	1.04	0.96	0.97	1.11	1.13
Miscellaneous	0.86	0.93	0.96	0.97	0.95

[3] Miscellaneous revenue consists of revenue derived from chartered trains, other passenger trains, switching, station and train privileges, storage on freight and baggage, demurrage, telegraph service, rents of building and property, etc.

SUMMARY OF OPERATING EXPENSES [4]

Yr. ended Dec. 31	Maintenance of Way and Structures	Maintenance of Equipment	Traffic	Transportation	General	Total
1925	$1,040,465.88	$2,429,081.33	$281,827.98	$1,741,881.17	$249,547.32	$5,727,048.55
1926	870,192.28	2,134,088.19	271,899.77	1,608,734.86	240,018.63	5,115,595.22
1927	964,466.60	1,965,021.41	275,564.20	1,632,676.26	234,409.62	5,064,727.64
1928	692,479.42	1,587,517.03	264,164.93	1,452,015.04	212,427.16	4,201,065.89
1929	724,252.12	1,722,031.87	263,827.39	1,403,077.05	226,135.74	4,333,573.93

Ratio of Each Class of Operating Expenses to Total Operating Expenses

	1925	1926	1927	1928	1929
Maintenance of Way and Structures	11.88	10.51	12.18	10.08	10.68
Maintenance of Equipment	27.73	25.77	24.81	23.11	25.39
Traffic	3.22	3.28	3.48	3.84	3.89
Transportation	19.88	19.42	20.61	21.14	20.69
General	2.85	2.90	2.96	3.09	3.33

[4] See Appendix C for details of operating expenses.

APPENDIX C

DETAILS OF OPERATING EXPENSES (1925-1929) [a]

I. Maintenance of Way and Structures:	1925	1926	1927	1928	1929
Superintendence	$ 29,453.32	$ 31,983.94	$ 32,542.48	$ 29,382.92	$ 25,745.10
Roadway maintenance	103,260.59	107,151.87	104,366.82	99,616.94	90,380.24
Tunnels and subways	10,996.45	4,602.26	1,898.60	4,324.13	2,698.59
Bridges, trestles and culverts	82,456.05	55,162.19	39,719.88	14,063.53	22,392.01
Ties	192,649.16	146,386.67	181,342.37	175,738.52	203,974.17
Rails	126,164.88	113,940.57	151,178.84	53,757.73	34,150.12
Other track material	58,676.60	24,485.42	49,079.87	31,197.65	27,939.24
Ballast	24,410.90	23,506.63	29,942.62	18,054.62	15,963.66
Track laying and surfacing	292,713.60	245,662.20	231,811.47	186,046.97	196,369.22
Right-of-way fences	917.88	4,149.00	1,559.76	337.01	933.31
Crossings and signs	8,385.72	16,613.25	2,030.69	1,881.38	5,163.26
Station and office buildings	14,060.70	16,123.56	19,397.04	12,088.67	11,746.91
Roadway buildings	334.41	1,562.83	365.61	324.78	335.06
Water stations	11,206.33	8,187.34	4,608.98	6,653.55	5,044.14
Fuel stations	7,192.47	7,362.48	12,507.42	12,726.32	4,663.73
Shops and enginehouses	8,813.67	9,399.98	37,309.99	11,544.42	11,341.08
Gas producing plants	.71				
Telephone and telegraph lines	22,437.07	17,037.27	27,500.07	9,577.87	29,139.88
Signals and interlockers	3,553.54	1,342.09	1,655.64	2,050.67	2,505.43
Power plant buildings		102.58	87.33	54.62	127.68
Power line poles and fixtures	131.58				240.56
Power distribution systems					389.18

APPENDIX

Roadway machines	$ 5,331.38	$ 5,157.65	$ 4,617.49	$ 4,274.86	$ 5,166.86
Small tools and supplies	9,261.21	18,332.68	18,756.76	15,944.15	14,470.49
Removing snow, ice, and sand	161.44	1,001.05	516.65	455.45	954.53
Assessments for public improvements	52.18	....	....	....	....
Injuries to persons	18,074.44	2,356.08	7,726.58	2,835.55	7,197.58
Insurance	1,826.69	2,096.05	2,572.30	2,811.31	2,436.56
Stationery and printing	675.20	574.97	1,007.09	624.00	587.91
Other expenses	19.40	....	297.00	107.25	....
Maintaining joint tracks, etc., Dr.	13,554.76	11,893.94	12,494.79	8,682.58	7,845.04
Maintaining joint tracks, etc., Cr.	6,306.45	5,982.17	12,427.54	12,668.03	5,649.42
Total	$1,040,465.88	$ 870,192.28	$ 964,466.60	$ 692,479.42	$ 724,252.12

[5] Annual Reports, Clinchfield Railroad Company, 1925-1929.

APPENDIX

II. Maintenance of Equipment:	1925	1926	1927	1928	1929
Superintendence	$ 36,830.50	$ 36,574.97	$ 35,849.39	$ 25,730.09	$ 30,327.36
Shop machinery	22,949.20	24,643.01	28,493.37	15,377.77	22,671.13
Power plant machinery	....	1,291.20	1,457.46	1,755.00	2,337.31
Locomotives—Repairs	418,873.90	404,724.76	414,281.15	295,616.41	409,181.10
Locomotives—Depreciation	104,935.00	92,008.20	92,008.20	92,160.75	91,988.52
Locomotives—Retirements	241,354.44	Cr. 2,618.23	....	3,684.96	....
Freight cars—Repairs	1,173,098.13	1,128,936.20	946,157.63	725,648.82	737,956.61
Freight cars—Depreciation	342,995.83	349,578.96	348,107.82	346,903.12	346,792.80
Freight cars—Retirements	6,613.37	3,757.11	3,995.57	6,631.57	7,811.84
Passenger cars—Repairs	29,876.47	38,464.39	50,859.64	39,312.67	39,996.63
Passenger cars—Depreciation	6,446.56	6,613.18	8,012.96	8,249.45	7,970.64
Passenger cars—Retirements	....	....	925.10	....	....
Motor cars—Repairs	64.35	407.10	206.12	....	....
Motor cars—Depreciation	123.20	123.24	123.24	123.24	123.24
Work equipment—Repairs	20,169.98	17,563.04	12,863.33	8,849.43	6,851.19
Work equipment—Depreciation	8,228.85	8,650.80	8,424.56	5,292.68	8,388.46
Work equipment—Retirements	707.42	....	3,476.42	72.00	942.42
Injuries to persons	6,834.63	17,240.08	4,404.59	6,636.56	3,433.34
Insurance	6,593.24	4,283.02	3,677.50	3,882.84	3,559.77
Stationery and printing	2,386.26	1,847.16	1,757.36	1,589.68	1,449.51
Other expenses	....	....	....	....	250.00
Total	$2,429,081.33	$2,134,088.19	$1,965,021.41	$1,587,517.03	$1,722,031.87

III. *Traffic:*

	1925	1926	1927	1928	1929
Superintendence	$ 59,751.14	$ 46,561.82	$ 45,548.36	$ 43,236.33	$ 44,088.99
Outside agencies	197,411.87	197,754.03	202,295.58	195,860.35	194,633.19
Advertising	540.98	1,942.16	1,566.72	908.91	1,842.41
Traffic associations	4,721.58	5,292.50	7,161.79	5,373.68	3,954.80
Industrial and immigration bureaus	362.51	124.21	272.43	187.67	282.58
Insurance	....	....	....	....	....
Stationery and printing	19,039.90	20,225.05	18,719.32	18,597.99	19,025.42
Total	$ 281,827.98	$ 271,899.77	$ 275,564.20	$ 264,164.93	$ 263,827.39

APPENDIX

IV. *Transportation:*	1925	1926	1927	1928	1929
Superintendence	$ 77,034.97	$ 75,969.58	$ 74,948.14	$ 69,366.28	$ 67,741.64
Dispatching trains	39,820.24	35,662.93	37,064.66	21,001.52	23,822.14
Station employees	153,509.45	154,586.24	159,487.88	149,970.97	142,803.59
Weighing, inspection, and demurrage bureaus	957.39	1,137.79	1,038.59	943.92	1,111.99
Station supplies and expenses	7,840.19	6,427.64	7,594.38	7,759.75	7,038.17
Yard masters and yard clerks	33,252.53	29,484.61	28,238.43	29,070.96	29,532.69
Yard conductors and brakemen	66,011.81	68,183.02	66,450.43	63,120.39	61,701.09
Yard switch and signal tenders	2,622.58	1,195.38	1,273.58	1,244.99	1,217.83
Yard enginemen	43,557.54	38,187.60	40,696.86	42,366.90	41,405.59
Fuel for yard locomotives	32,424.42	22,846.73	18,947.89	18,557.02	17,023.03
Water for yard locomotives	1,824.64	1,568.81	1,615.29	1,126.73	1,152.48
Lubricants for yard locomotives	1,266.09	1,124.76	873.16	786.88	775.74
Other supplies for yard locomotives	1,200.73	923.69	900.36	906.33	597.16
Yard enginehouse expenses	15,051.18	13,059.99	10,065.56	9,212.55	8,986.20
Yard supplies and expenses	533.68	1,709.58	1,846.96	1,444.70	1,986.62
Operating joint yards and terminals, Dr.	22,453.75	22,394.79	22,332.22	21,778.98	22,310.01
Operating joint yards and terminals, Cr.	11,660.49	11,800.31	12,040.04	11,724.07	10,310.86
Train enginemen	314,862.12	281,542.47	272,623.34	257,689.61	255,908.34
Train motormen	1,112.11	584.76	1,274.54	6.56	14.50
Fuel for train locomotives	318,413.05	301,987.96	317,169.50	256,991.08	243,173.30
Water for train locomotives	17,600.63	22,533.53	24,596.25	18,020.48	15,722.72
Lubricants for train locomotives	13,227.56	11,853.94	9,422.20	9,025.30	9,410.02
Other supplies for train locomotives	10,816.03	9,538.44	9,628.39	8,535.55	5,689.37
Train enginehouse expenses	93,692.25	86,569.46	80,188.36	69,337.39	65,540.45
Trainmen	312,336.92	282,382.14	287,297.03	259,016.13	254,429.92
Train supplies and expenses	54,172.03	48,075.03	48,056.11	38,926.19	39,336.44

APPENDIX

Crossing protection	$ 3,091.77	$ 5,165.19	$ 4,231.46	$ 2,558.54	$ 2,418.42
Telegraph and telephone operation	1,327.43	676.74	219.09	254.37	82.29
Stationery and printing	15,712.94	14,493.92	14,849.28	12,459.02	12,587.21
Other expenses	2,005.89	4,516.31	3,036.58	5,558.86	3,488.24
Operating joint tracks and facilities, Dr.	30,497.98	26,699.50	25,274.33	23,615.28	20,805.38
Operating joint tracks and facilities, Cr.	4,220.14	4,296.50	4,528.20	3,758.40	3,548.30
Insurance	641.49	2,270.21	2,036.58	2,834.30	2,177.92
Clearing wrecks	11,251.61	8,133.39	5,560.98	7,430.90	6,374.31
Damage to property	2,925.76	9,301.42	17,167.58	919.40	1,982.47
Damage to live stock on right-of-way	7,190.96	6,427.15	6,503.80	7,244.14	6,882.33
Loss and damage—Freight	23,264.58	21,837.06	22,643.45	23,605.61	25,046.99
Loss and damage—Baggage	4.56	19.66	11.62	16.62	134.79
Injuries to persons	24,253.05	15,940.25	24,179.64	24,793.31	16,724.83
Total	$1,741,881.17	$1,608,734.86	$1,632,676.26	$1,452,015.04	$1,403,277.05

V. General Expense:	1925	1926	1927	1928	1929
Dining and club car service	....	$ 873.24	$ 5,658.20	$ 5,649.71	$ 4,991.74
Salaries and expenses of general officers	$ 38,225.80	39,936.78	44,511.60	44,302.15	44,894.77
Salaries and expenses of clerks and attendants	125,069.85	128,108.32	127,019.26	119,568.61	119,272.47
General office supplies and expenses	10,719.22	12,128.18	6,518.23	3,118.22	3,424.41
Law expenses	39,090.80	32,027.38	27,418.07	18,516.29	23,027.26
Insurance	372.79	523.30	275.34	250.14	179.02
Pensions	2,148.38	692.37	3,020.17	3,132.49	6,492.66
Stationery and printing	11,132.26	7,355.28	8,352.21	7,136.03	6,560.85
Valuation expenses	12,938.51	12,609.36	6,660.64	5,715.82	11,965.38
Other expenses	9,849.71	5,764.42	4,975.80	5,037.70	5,327.18
Total	$ 249,547.32	$ 240,018.63	$ 234,409.52	$ 212,427.16	$ 221,144.00

APPENDIX D

EQUIPMENT PERFORMANCE [6]

Locomotives:		1925	1926	1927	1928	1929
Cost Per Mile Run:						
Enginemen	(Cents)	19.92	19.40	19.68	20.28	19.45
Enginehouse expenses	(Cents)	6.04	6.05	5.67	5.31	4.88
Fuel	(Cents)	19.50	19.71	21.11	18.50	17.03
Water	(Cents)	1.08	1.46	1.65	1.29	1.10
Lubricants	(Cents)	0.81	0.79	0.65	0.66	0.67
Other supplies	(Cents)	0.67	0.67	0.66	0.64	0.41
Repairs	(Cents)	23.28	24.56	26.03	19.98	26.77
Depreciation and retirements	(Cents)	19.24	5.43	5.78	6.48	6.02
Total cost per locomotive mile	(Cents)	90.54	78.07	81.23	73.14	76.33
Pounds coal consumed per locomotive mile	(Pounds)	245.95	236.02	239.76	230.07	221.63
per freight locomotive mile	(Pounds)	279.71	285.79	308.66	297.83	277.64
per passenger locomotive mile	(Pounds)	130.09	95.96	73.99	65.03	71.54
per mixed locomotive mile	(Pounds)	308.43	163.18	119.44	121.39	......
per special locomotive mile	(Pounds)	165.14	158.84	102.74	122.45	231.58
per switching locomotive mile	(Pounds)	219.26	171.21	127.51	130.45	141.90
per non-revenue locomotive mile	(Pounds)	149.67	127.50	100.47	171.48	147.19
Locomotive miles per ton of coal	(Miles)	8.13	8.47	8.34	8.69	9.02
Freight locomotive miles per ton of coal	(Miles)	7.15	7.00	6.48	6.72	7.20
Passenger locomotive miles per ton of coal	(Miles)	15.37	20.84	27.03	30.75	27.96
Mixed locomotive miles per ton of coal	(Miles)	6.48	12.26	16.75	16.48	......
Special locomotive miles per ton of coal	(Miles)	12.11	12.59	19.47	16.33	8.64

[6] Annual Reports, Clinchfield Railroad Company, 1925-1929.

	1925	1926	1927	1928	1929
Locomotives:					
Switching locomotive miles per ton of coal ....(Miles)	9.12	11.68	15.69	15.33	14.09
Non-revenue locomotive miles per ton of coal ....(Miles)	13.36	15.69	19.91	11.66	13.59
Locomotive miles run per pint of oil ....(Miles)	10.80	10.08	10.01	10.97	10.92
Average number locomotives in service per month	84.00	85.00	86.00	86.00	86.00
Average mileage per locomotive per month ......(Miles)	1,785.00	1,615.00	1,542.00	1,434.00	1,481.00
Total tons of coal consumed ....(Tons)	221,290.00	194,449.00	190,810.00	170,180.00	169,342.00
Average cost per ton of coal	$1.60	$1.66	$1.78	$1.62	$1.55
Passenger Cars:					
Coal consumed per car mile ....(Pounds)	31.16	23.33	17.72	16.03	17.77
Cars handled one mile per ton of coal ....(Cars)	64.19	85.74	112.88	124.74	112.53
Freight Cars:					
Coal consumed per car mile (excluding caboose) (Pounds)	7.17	7.13	7.26	7.45	7.42
Cars handled one mile per ton of coal ....(Cars)	278.76	280.48	275.61	268.39	269.37

APPENDIX

EQUIPMENT

The following tables show the classification of locomotives as of November 1, 1928 ᵀ

Class	Type	No. Units
G	Ten-Wheel (4-6-0)	5
H	Consolidation (2-8-0)	17
K	Mikado (2-8-2)	21
L	Mallet (2-8-8-2)	27
M	Mallet (2-6-6-2)	11
P	Pacific (4-6-2)	5

Class	Number of Engines	Diameter of Cylinder (Inches)	Stroke (Inches)	Steam Pressure (Pounds)	Diameter of Driver (Inches)	Weight on Drivers (Pounds)	Total Weight (Pounds)	Tractive Force (Pounds)	Length—Engine and Tender	Engine Numbers
G-1	1	19	26	200	63	98,000	137,700	25,400	49'2"	99
G-2	4	20	26	200	63	125,300	163,600	28,000	59'5"	100–103
H-3	2	21	28	200	51	175,000	175,000	41,160	42'1"	51– 52
H-4	15	22	32	190	57	178,650	199,150	43,882	59'8"	300–314
K-1	9	27	30	190	63	230,000	311,400	56,000	67'0"	400–408
K-2	1	23	30	200	58	197,900	262,100	46,500	66'10"	499
K-3	1	22	28	190	51	175,000	228,000	43,000	62'8"	498
K-4	10	27	30	190	63	235,000	317,500	56,000	75'4"	410–419
L-1	7	28–42	32	200	57	467,000	523,600	103,560	88'6"	700–706
L-2	10	25–39	32	240	57	478,000	531,000	101,560	94'6"	725–734

ᵀ Information from the Mechanical Engineer, Clinchfield Railroad Company, Erwin, Tennessee, November, 1928.

EQUIPMENT—(Continued)

Class	Number of Engines	Diameter of Cylinder (Inches)	Stroke (Inches)	Steam Pressure (Pounds)	Diameter of Driver (Inches)	Weight on Drivers (Pounds)	Total Weight (Pounds)	Tractive Force (Pounds)	Length—Engine and Tender	Engine Numbers
L-3	10	25-39	32	240	57	486,500	541,000	101,560	94'6"	735-744
M-1	1	23-35	32	200	57	299,250	342,650	70,640	73'8"	500
M-2	20	24-37	32	200	57	323,800	377,000	77,400	75'1"	510-529
P-1	3	23	30	190	69	153,900	235,000	37,140	66'5"	150-152
P-2	2	25	30	200	69	176,900	280,300	46,200	66'10"	153-154

APPENDIX E

MISCELLANEOUS STATISTICS

Quantity and Cost of Fuel:[3]	1925	1926	1927	1928	1929
Tons of coal consumed by locomotives (excluding work trains)	218,900	192,400	189,088	168,516	167,746
Cost of coal consumed by locomotives (excluding work trains)	$350,837.47	$324,834.69	$336,017.39	$273,655.77	$260,196.33
Average cost of coal per net ton	$1.60	$1.66	$1.78	$1.62	$1.55
Tons of coal consumed in freight service	177,113	163,438	166,678	147,831	146,180
Pounds of coal per freight locomotive-mile	150	148	153	162	161

[3] Annual Reports, Clinchfield Railroad Company, 1925-1929.

APPENDIX F
FREIGHT CAR INTERCHANGE (Loads)*
CHESAPEAKE & OHIO RAILWAY
Elkhorn Yard, Ky.

Month	Merchandise Delivered 1927	Delivered 1928	1929	Received 1927	Received 1928	1929	Coal Delivered 1927	Delivered 1928	1929	Received 1927	Received 1928	1929
January	1,176	1,015	1,312	1,850	2,226	2,270	79	191	468	56	26	155
February	1,070	1,161	1,260	2,038	2,196	2,306	79	198	580	4	19	277
March	1,203	1,309	1,525	2,153	2,367	2,507	66	212	423	20	26	199
April	1,317	1,257	1,743	2,120	2,256	2,527	197	98	376	1	6	88
May	1,328	1,382	1,696	2,284	2,114	2,316	242	300	449	. .	10	96
June	1,230	1,392	1,953	1,865	2,060	2,009	305	424	329	8	. .	145
July	1,273	1,512	1,277	1,968	2,079	2,116	205	513	341	10	14	106
August	1,050	1,114	1,248	2,336	2,315	2,203	327	440	420	9	17	164
September	1,042	1,084	1,177	2,262	2,377	2,262	457	610	438	19	50	212
October	1,004	1,234	1,057	2,565	2,588	2,153	247	746	659	18	113	308
November	1,043	1,246	947	2,220	2,083	1,899	151	630	730	14	108	282
December	926	1,069	855	2,013	1,999	1,555	155	338	533	22	61	360
Totals	13,561	14,775	16,050	25,674	26,660	26,123	2,510	4,700	5,746	181	450	2,392

Grand Totals (Merchandise): 1927, 39,235; 1928, 41,435; 1929, 42,173

Grand Totals (Coal): 1927, 2,691; 1928, 5,150; 1929, 9,138

Total Loads Delivered: 1927, 16,071; 1928, 19,475; 1929, 21,796

Total Loads Received: 1927, 25,855; 1928, 27,110; 1929, 28,515

* Information furnished by the General Freight Agent, Clinchfield Railroad.

CHARLESTON & WESTERN CAROLINA RAILWAY
Spartanburg, S. C.

Month	Merchandise Delivered 1927	1928	1929	Merchandise Received 1927	1928	1929	Coal Delivered 1927	1928	1929	Coal Received 1927	1928	1929
January	1,047	1,003	1,047	820	756	930	1,961	1,486	1,098	...	...	...
February	1,145	1,129	884	770	840	842	2,003	1,420	1,137	...	...	...
March	1,129	1,109	1,117	891	1,043	1,073	2,080	1,397	1,254	...	...	...
April	1,044	1,055	1,086	1,135	1,000	1,186	1,588	1,171	1,074	...	...	...
May	1,015	1,099	1,054	1,060	1,119	1,184	1,540	1,145	1,051	...	...	...
June	1,015	934	965	1,043	1,219	1,489	1,294	878	994	...	...	...
July	1,064	940	943	1,021	1,106	840	1,096	853	914	...	...	...
August	1,080	1,028	976	770	970	744	1,118	947	1,019	...	...	...
September	1,052	1,049	922	792	786	597	1,245	969	959	...	...	...
October	1,202	1,245	847	924	930	629	1,354	1,039	980	...	...	...
November	1,059	1,009	782	891	999	659	1,321	1,035	1,120	...	...	...
December	899	871	671	781	819	529	1,353	1,008	1,166	...	...	...
Totals	12,751	12,471	11,294	10,898	11,584	10,702	16,953	13,348	12,766	000	000	000

Grand Totals (Merchandise): 1927, 23,649
1928, 24,055
1929, 21,996

Grand Totals (Coal): 1927, 16,953
1928, 13,348
1929, 12,766

Total Loads Delivered: 1927, 29,704
1928, 25,819
1929, 24,060

Total Loads Received: 1927, 10,898
1928, 11,584
1929, 10,702

SOUTHERN RAILWAY
Spartanburg, S. C.

Month	Merchandise						Coal				
	Delivered			Received			Delivered			Received	
	1927	1928	1929	1927	1928	1929	1927	1928	1929	1927	1928	1929
January	228	308	299	93	134	159	1,871	1,027	800	...	...	...
February	270	296	246	109	134	119	1,574	978	768	...	...	...
March	223	332	297	167	265	235	1,192	813	790	...	...	...
April	263	295	318	257	231	208	1,024	573	690	...	...	...
May	250	308	309	179	189	162	950	452	544	...	...	...
June	248	266	287	139	174	164	746	440	449	...	...	...
July	257	287	261	169	156	174	689	456	563	...	...	...
August	321	325	359	187	208	194	723	532	663	...	...	...
September	339	359	341	172	207	234	907	647	761	...	...	...
October	352	390	275	189	209	180	1,048	600	658	...	...	...
November	364	358	227	189	143	162	1,041	827	615	...	...	...
December	276	287	204	154	154	116	853	740	656	...	...	...
Totals	3,391	3,811	3,423	2,004	2,204	2,107	12,618	8,085	7,957	000	000	000

Grand Totals (Merchandise):
1927, 5,395
1928, 6,015
1929, 5,520

Grand Totals (Coal):
1927, 12,618
1928, 8,085
1929, 7,957

Total Loads Delivered:
1927 16,009
1928, 11,896
1929, 11,380

Total Loads Received:
1927, 2,004
1928, 2,204
1929, 2,107

SOUTHERN RAILWAY
Marion, N. C.

Month	MERCHANDISE						COAL					
	Delivered			Received			Delivered			Received		
	1927	1928	1929	1927	1928	1929	1927	1928	1929	1927	1928	1929
January	982	1,054	810	100	132	161	329	320	313	...	...	...
February	1,059	966	738	119	259	137	278	342	305	...	...	...
March	1,263	1,040	813	174	295	149	333	348	251	...	...	...
April	1,432	1,061	923	159	262	168	346	387	210	...	...	...
May	1,193	1,036	698	144	265	160	331	341	209	...	...	...
June	1,227	1,006	698	123	154	146	243	250	226	...	...	...
July	1,314	918	672	172	171	137	233	280	196	...	...	...
August	1,310	878	735	177	186	254	222	348	228	...	...	...
September	1,276	771	727	133	180	196	231	267	209	...	...	...
October	1,210	864	702	116	124	153	213	275	293	...	...	...
November	1,197	833	745	120	135	133	217	270	306	...	...	...
December	1,046	812	568	104	103	96	216	277	359	...	...	...
Totals	14,509	11,239	8,829	2,541	2,266	1,890	3,092	3,705	3,104	000	000	000

Grand Totals (Merchandise): 1927, 17,050
1928, 13,499
1929, 10,719

Grand Totals (Coal): 1927, 3,092
1928, 3,705
1929, 3,104

Total Loads Delivered: 1927, 17,601
1928, 14,944
1929, 11,933

Total Loads Received: 1927, 2,541
1928, 2,266
1929, 1,890

SOUTHERN RAILWAY
Johnson City, Tenn.

Month	Merchandise							Coal					
	Delivered			Received			Delivered			Received		
	1927	1928	1929	1927	1928	1929	1927	1928	1929	1927	1928	1929
January	280	288	428	485	422	455	290	193	268	1	7	6
February	294	349	384	497	446	478	237	195	295	10	6	11
March	288	377	413	560	665	541	265	214	111	6	3	8
April	321	355	430	554	636	651	179	175	84	18	5	7
May	315	364	475	580	599	590	329	190	121	6	9	4
June	255	367	439	680	542	544	226	234	128	8	9	1
July	316	326	402	664	635	630	201	262	63	4	10	2
August	384	388	473	565	718	746	183	235	66	8	2	5
September	384	447	435	598	720	669	188	263	74	5	3	11
October	425	462	428	684	742	622	186	281	72	6	11	9
November	319	368	346	613	672	491	191	228	57	9	8	3
December	264	314	231	442	508	357	151	226	77	6	3	6
Totals	3,845	4,405	4,884	6,922	7,305	6,774	2,626	2,696	3,206	87	76	73

Grand Totals (Merchandise): 1927, 10,767
                             1928, 11,710
                             1929, 11,658

Grand Totals (Coal): 1927, 2,713
                      1928, 2,772
                      1929, 3,279

Total Loads Delivered: 1927, 6,479
                        1928, 7,101
                        1929, 8,090

Total Loads Received: 1927, 7,009
                       1928, 7,381
                       1929, 6,847

APPENDIX

SOUTHERN RAILWAY
Frisco, Tenn.

Month	Merchandise						Coal					
	Delivered			Received			Delivered			Received		
	1927	1928	1929	1927	1928	1929	1927	1928	1929	1927	1928	1929
January	74	64	68	130	156	152	430	147	147	222	237	205
February	97	47	52	100	157	134	705	120	155	168	231	201
March	142	76	87	77	183	180	705	141	316	171	277	175
April	173	80	52	211	174	199	347	122	206	215	182	147
May	111	98	115	330	282	256	299	161	254	187	250	240
June	102	95	50	337	343	323	341	129	244	215	203	132
July	97	112	61	481	292	342	145	176	224	258	206	107
August	106	129	49	661	486	601	160	232	346	232	216	129
September	86	147	30	517	353	311	144	168	346	195	237	204
October	115	155	25	260	309	355	138	157	354	213	256	216
November	71	99	32	200	203	238	156	152	273	186	203	99
December	49	90	24	209	151	179	133	156	333	193	208	85
Totals	1,223	1,192	645	3,513	3,089	3,270	3,705	1,861	3,198	2,053	2,706	1,940

Grand Totals (Merchandise): 1927, 4,736
1928, 4,281
1929, 3,915

Grand Totals (Coal): 1927, 5,758
1928, 4,567
1929, 5,138

Total Loads Delivered: 1927, 4,928
1928, 3,053
1929, 3,843

Total Loads Received: 1927, 5,566
1928, 5,795
1929, 5,210

SOUTHERN RAILWAY
Speer's Ferry, Va.

Month	Merchandise						Coal					
	Delivered			Received			Delivered			Received		
	1927	1928	1929	1927	1928	1929	1927	1928	1929	1927	1928	1929
January	2	25	21	...	1	1	...	...	...	...	...	...
February	3	31	19	...	...	6	...	...	...	...	...	...
March	2	34	22	9	8	17	...	...	...	...	...	...
April	15	28	27	4	3	5	...	...	...	...	...	...
May	4	24	15	1	2	15	...	...	...	...	...	...
June	6	35	22	4	29	2	...	...	...	...	...	...
July	5	25	22	9	24	7	...	...	...	...	...	...
August	3	27	38	...	42	33	...	...	...	...	...	...
September	6	31	25	4	35	17	...	...	...	...	...	...
October	10	28	36	10	30	9	...	...	...	...	...	...
November	13	22	19	18	18	10	...	...	...	...	...	...
December	19	18	26	1	3	7	4	...	...	...	...	...
Totals	88	328	292	60	195	129	4	000	000	000	000	000

Grand Totals (Merchandise):
1927, 148
1928, 423
1929, 421

Grand Totals (Coal):
1927, 000
1928, 000
1929, 000

Total Loads Delivered:
1927, 92
1928, 328
1929, 292

Total Loads Received:
1927, 60
1928, 195
1929, 129

SUMMARY OF INTERCHANGE WITH SOUTHERN RAILWAY

	Merchandise						Coal					
	Delivered			Received			Delivered			Received		
	1927	1928	1929	1927	1928	1929	1927	1928	1929	1927	1928	1929
Spartanburg	3,391	3,811	3,423	2,004	2,204	2,107	12,618	8,085	7,957	...	...	...
Marion	14,509	11,239	8,829	2,541	2,266	1,890	3,092	3,705	3,104	...	...	...
Johnson City	3,845	4,405	4,884	6,922	7,305	6,774	2,626	2,696	3,206	87	76	73
Frisco	1,223	1,192	645	3,513	3,089	3,271	2,703	1,861	3,198	2,053	2,706	1,940
Speer's Ferry	88	328	292	60	195	129	4	...	...	...	...	...
Totals	23,056	19,977	18,073	15,040	15,069	14,170	22,131	16,347	17,465	2,140	2,782	2,013

Grand Totals (Merchandise): 1927, 38,096
1928, 35,046
1929, 33,243

Grand Totals (Coal): 1927, 24,271
1928, 19,129
1929, 19,478

Total Loads Delivered: 1927, 45,187
1928, 36,324
1929, 35,538

Total Loads Received: 1927, 17,180
1928, 17,851
1929, 16,283

SEABOARD AIR LINE RAILWAY
Bostic, N. C.

Month	Merchandise						Coal					
	Delivered			Received			Delivered			Received		
	1927	1928	1929	1927	1928	1929	1927	1928	1929	1927	1928	1929
January	661	770	820	220	198	166	607	504	597	...	...	...
February	660	972	823	209	258	154	628	431	651	...	...	...
March	742	1,083	891	240	275	220	632	579	562	...	...	...
April	857	1,055	879	229	251	252	447	403	504	...	...	...
May	913	990	856	276	217	241	442	413	406	...	...	...
June	616	880	808	247	224	243	419	396	409	...	...	...
July	780	853	718	258	238	240	418	409	410	...	...	...
August	848	916	919	228	233	228	299	480	450	...	...	...
September	837	948	860	203	201	218	514	598	472	...	...	...
October	906	967	812	225	248	177	527	896	632	...	...	...
November	760	772	727	242	252	129	503	850	554	...	...	...
December	678	662	516	207	197	149	558	628	656	...	...	...
Totals	9,258	10,868	9,629	2,784	2,792	2,417	5,994	6,587	6,303	000	000	000

Grand Totals (Merchandise): 1927, 12,032 ; 1928, 13,660 ; 1929, 12,046

Total Loads Delivered: 1927, 15,252 ; 1928, 17,455 ; 1929, 15,932

Total Loads Received: 1927, 2,784 ; 1928, 6,587 ; 1929, 6,303

Grand Totals (Coal): 1927, 5,994 ; 1928, 2,792 ; 1929, 2,417

APPENDIX

NORFOLK & WESTERN RAILWAY
St. Paul (Carbo), Va.

Month	Merchandise Delivered 1927	Delivered 1928	1929	Received 1927	Received 1928	1929	Coal Delivered 1927	Delivered 1928	1929	Received 1927	Received 1928	1929
January	774	804	791	609	677	524	62	6	15	871	560	594
February	747	728	749	673	703	583	6	16	76	961	605	551
March	917	907	911	793	719	648	5	4	29	894	599	493
April	1,043	966	1,074	721	759	624	4	7	17	601	400	479
May	1,046	1,107	967	662	697	682	25	...	12	491	411	408
June	1,075	1,046	944	629	520	540	3	5	29	419	360	422
July	1,050	943	947	773	558	626	9	7	52	358	325	396
August	1,083	1,041	903	681	560	646	29	2	60	385	303	422
September	1,010	960	974	631	582	575	6	8	107	436	344	371
October	1,130	1,049	1,028	755	597	667	15	17	136	576	446	369
November	705	931	847	554	469	567	19	8	82	556	400	375
December	851	913	693	572	471	479	4	10	99	575	401	408
Totals	11,431	11,395	10,828	8,053	7,312	7,161	187	90	714	2,173	5,154	5,288

Grand Totals (Merchandise): 1927, 19,484; 1928, 18,707; 1929, 17,989

Grand Totals (Coal): 1927, 2,360; 1928, 5,244; 1929, 6,002

Total Loads Delivered: 1927, 11,618; 1928, 11,485; 1929, 11,542

Total Loads Received: 1927, 10,226; 1928, 12,466; 1929, 12,449

248 APPENDIX

INTERSTATE RAILROAD
Miller Yard, Va.

Month	Merchandise						Coal					
	Delivered			Received			Delivered			Received		
	1927	1928	1929	1927	1928	1929	1927	1928	1929	1927	1928	1929
January	68	58	58	44	50	80	...	...	...	1,340	913	619
February	63	54	64	51	70	45	...	...	...	1,191	818	574
March	128	64	63	55	116	53	...	...	...	1,244	868	446
April	86	57	78	56	94	50	...	...	...	1,142	700	562
May	57	71	71	52	49	51	...	...	...	1,142	709	486
June	56	39	48	56	44	47	...	...	...	947	693	630
July	56	56	60	60	42	71	...	...	...	911	506	653
August	62	55	73	46	56	45	...	...	...	811	528	680
September	76	79	69	60	43	65	...	...	...	1,002	668	712
October	78	95	70	80	80	54	...	...	...	969	923	825
November	49	94	79	62	59	48	...	...	...	799	815	791
December	46	108	60	58	56	39	...	...	...	892	559	673
Totals	825	830	796	680	759	648	000	000	000	12,390	8,700	7,651

Grand Totals (Merchandise): 1927, 1,505
1928, 1,589
1929, 1,444

Grand Totals (Coal): 1927, 12,390
1928, 9,459
1929, 7,651

Total Loads Delivered: 1927, 825
1928, 830
1929, 796

Total Loads Received: 1927, 13,070
1928, 9,459
1929, 8,299

APPENDIX

PIEDMONT & NORTHERN RAILWAY
Spartanburg, S. C.

Month	Merchandise						Coal					
	Delivered			Received			Delivered			Received		
	1927	1928	1929	1927	1928	1929	1927	1928	1929	1927	1928	1929
January	178	206	168	59	101	97	309	201	450	...	...	...
February	193	202	181	60	78	96	267	301	495	...	...	...
March	319	246	203	79	99	113	250	307	349	...	...	...
April	224	226	233	191	141	144	303	239	212	...	...	...
May	219	168	228	105	89	115	197	190	177	...	...	...
June	184	175	196	102	83	167	208	170	185	...	...	...
July	179	159	233	109	109	158	271	190	185	...	...	...
August	272	219	223	93	114	180	278	167	246	...	...	...
September	249	202	232	86	93	160	428	174	371	...	...	...
October	288	213	239	89	117	125	450	165	311	...	...	...
November	253	202	230	127	136	167	264	185	241	...	...	...
December	188	185	218	115	100	190	184	233	182	...	...	...
Totals	2,747	2,403	2,584	2,522	1,260	1,712	3,399	2,522	3,404	000	000	000

Grand Totals (Merchandise): 1927, 5,269
1928, 3,663
1929, 4,296

Grand Totals (Coal): 1927, 3,399
1928, 2,522
1929, 5,988

Total Loads Delivered: 1927, 6,146
1928, 4,925
1929, 5,988

Total Loads Received: 1927, 2,522
1928, 1,260
1929, 1,712

EAST TENNESSEE & WESTERN NORTH CAROLINA RAILROAD
Johnson City, Tenn.

Month	Merchandise						Coal					
	Delivered			Received			Delivered			Received		
	1927	1928	1929	1927	1928	1929	1927	1928	1929	1927	1928	1929
January	78	169	61	266	134	57	24	25	60	1	...	2
February	82	168	55	334	74	57	35	35	72	...	1	2
March	96	277	109	328	82	85	29	34	71	...	3	3
April	89	253	96	183	96	102	44	71	73	...	...	2
May	119	231	112	260	106	73	62	51	53	...	...	...
June	97	166	171	198	103	63	71	60	77	1	2	6
July	104	170	242	241	107	55	40	71	101	...	...	...
August	116	159	189	243	90	99	29	32	101	...	1	1
September	132	152	93	239	73	99	30	34	88	...	...	...
October	134	146	101	323	75	75	31	76	107	...	1	1
November	169	149	101	154	57	77	33	82	85	2	2	1
December	78	95	79	167	79	60	23	75	186	...	...	1
Totals	1,294	2,135	1,409	2,845	1,076	902	451	646	1,074	5	10	18

Grand Totals (Merchandise): 1927, 4,139
1928, 3,211
1929, 2,311

Grand Totals (Coal): 1927, 456
1928, 656
1929, 1,092

Total Loads Delivered: 1927, 1,745
1928, 2,781
1929, 2,483

Total Loads Received: 1927, 2,850
1928, 1,086
1929, 920

APPENDIX

BLACK MOUNTAIN RAILWAY
Kona, N. C.

Month	Merchandise Delivered 1927	Delivered 1928	1929	Received 1927	Received 1928	1929	Coal Delivered 1927	Delivered 1928	1929	Received 1927	Received 1928	1929
January	41	47	22	151	136	98	13	...	7	...	...	...
February	56	46	39	199	140	135	10	...	6	...	...	...
March	56	98	43	315	197	104	10	...	5	...	...	...
April	57	61	59	277	172	100	10	10	1	...	...	...
May	44	50	50	275	168	101	8	6	7	...	...	...
June	66	38	28	275	192	131	21	5	7	...	...	...
July	51	37	37	275	150	100	11	11	2	...	...	...
August	56	59	101	241	113	138	5	4	...	...	...	...
September	56	73	52	294	104	103	...	6	2	...	...	...
October	73	52	45	273	117	109	...	8	...	...	...	...
November	72	47	31	229	103	89	...	7	...	...	...	...
December	45	41	30	235	95	102	...	...	...	...	...	...
Totals	673	649	537	3,039	1,687	1,310	88	47	37	000	000	000

Grand Totals (Merchandise):
1928, 2,336
1929, 1,847

Grand Totals (Coal):
1927, 88
1928, 47
1929, 37

Total Loads Delivered:
1927, 761
1928, 696
1929, 574

Total Loads Received:
1927, 3,039
1928, 1,687
1929, 1,310

APPENDIX

SUMMARY OF INTERCHANGES

	Delivered			Received			Total		
	1927	1928	1929	1927	1928	1929	1927	1928	1929
Southern Railway	45,187	36,324	35,538	17,180	17,851	16,283	62,367	54,175	51,821
Marion	17,601	14,944	11,933	2,541	2,266	1,890	20,141	17,210	13,823
Spartanburg	16,099	11,896	11,380	2,004	2,204	2,107	18,013	14,100	13,487
Johnson City	6,471	7,101	8,090	7,009	7,381	6,847	13,480	14,482	14,937
Frisco	4,926	3,053	3,843	5,566	5,795	5,210	10,492	8,848	9,053
Speer's Ferry	92	328	292	60	195	129	152	523	421
C. & O.	16,071	19,475	21,796	25,855	27,110	28,515	41,926	46,585	50,311
C. & W. C.	29,704	25,819	24,060	10,898	11,584	10,702	40,602	37,403	34,762
N. & W.	11,618	11,485	11,542	10,226	12,466	12,449	21,844	23,951	23,991
S. A. L.	15,252	17,455	15,932	2,784	2,792	2,417	18,038	20,247	18,349
I. RR.	825	830	796	13,070	9,459	8,299	13,895	10,287	9,095
E. T. & W. N. C.	1,745	2,781	2,483	2,850	1,086	920	4,595	3,867	3,403
P. & N.	6,146	4,925	5,988	1,215	1,260	1,712	7,361	6,185	7,700
B. M. Ry.	761	696	574	3,039	1,687	1,310	3,790	2,383	1,884
Totals	127,311	120,788	118,709	87,117	85,285	82,507	214,428	206,073	201,316

APPENDIX G

METHODS OF OPERATION [1]

The Gill Selector Telephone System was recently installed for the dispatching of trains, supplanting the telegraph. The average daily movement on the main line consists of fifty-two trains. All crews, except on passenger trains 37 and 38, and all locomotives are changed at Erwin.

PASSENGER TRAINS (FIRST CLASS)

Four passenger trains are operated daily on the main line. Trains number 37, northbound, and number 38, southbound, run between Spartanburg and Elkhorn City. Number 37 leaves Spartanburg at 10:25 A.M., and arrives at Elkhorn City at 9:05 P.M.; number 38 leaves Elkhorn City at 6:00 A.M., and reaches Spartanburg at 5:00 P.M. In addition to the usual coaches, and the baggage, mail, and express cars, these trains also handle the buffet-observation cars purchased from the Pullman Company in 1926. Trains 36 and 39 operate between Erwin and Elkhorn City. Number 39 leaves Erwin at 8:10 A.M., and arrives at Elkhorn City at 2:45 P.M. Number 36 leaves Elkhorn City at 2:00 P.M., and reaches Erwin at 8:00 P.M.

At Elkhorn City, numbers 36 and 39 connect with trains of the Chesapeake & Ohio Railway operating to and from Cincinnati, via Ashland. Numbers 37 and 38 connect at Spartanburg with the "Skyland Special" of the Southern Railway for Columbia, Charleston, Savannah, and Florida points. In addition, connections are maintained to and from Charlotte, via the Southern; and with Greenville, Anderson, and Greenwood, South Carolina, via the Piedmont & Northern Railway.

Important connections are made at intermediate points. At Bostic, number 38 connects with the Seaboard Air Line Railway to Charlotte, Monroe, and Hamlet, North Carolina. At Marion, number 37 connects with the Southern Railway from Norfolk, Richmond, Greensboro, and Winston-Salem to Asheville; and number 38, from Asheville to Winston-Salem, Greensboro, Rich-

[1] Time Table No. 9, Clinchfield Railroad Company, October 1, 1930, and information furnished by the Trainmaster at Erwin, Nov., 1928.

APPENDIX

mond, and Norfolk. At Johnson City, the following connections are maintained with the Southern Railway: Clinchfield train number 36 connects with a train to Bristol; number 37, with trains to and from New York City, via Lynchburg and Roanoke, and with a train to Knoxville; number 38 connects with trains to and from New York, and from Knoxville; number 39 connects with trains to and from Bristol. At Speer's Ferry, numbers 36 and 37 connect with the Southern Railway between Bristol, and Louisville and Cincinnati, via the Louisville & Nashville Railroad west of Appalachia, Virginia. At St. Paul, number 36 connects with the Norfolk & Western Railway for Cincinnati and Columbus, and for Roanoke and Norfolk; number 38, for Bluefield, West Virginia, and Roanoke; and number 39, from Norfolk and Roanoke.

The G-2, "Ten-wheel" type, locomotives are used on passenger trains between Erwin and Spartanburg; and the Pacific type, north of Erwin. Four crews are assigned to these trains, which work out of Erwin as follows: number 39 the first day, 38 the second day, 37 the third day, and 36 the fourth day.

Two mixed trains are operated daily on the "Dumps Creek" Branch, numbers 46 and 47.

TIME-FREIGHT TRAINS (SECOND CLASS)

These are the fast, through merchandise freight trains which are, of course, operated on regular schedules. Numbers 95 and 97, northbound, leave Spartanburg daily at 12:05 A.M. and 1:55 P.M., and arrive at Elkhorn Yard at 4:30 P.M. and 3:00 A.M., respectively; southward, numbers 92 and 94 leave Elkhorn Yard at 3:30 P.M. and 7:00 A.M., and reach Spartanburg at 9:30 A.M. and 11:00 P.M., respectively. Number 97 is named "The Florida Perishable."

They are handled by the Hocking Valley Railroad from the Toledo and Detroit territories, and then by the Chesapeake & Ohio Railway to Elkhorn Yard. At Spartanburg, the Charleston & Western Carolina, and later the Atlantic Coast Line, handle them en route to Florida. Direct connections are likewise made with the Norfolk & Western Railway at St. Paul, and with the Seaboard Air Line Railway at Bostic. Schedules on all the different roads are arranged so that there is no loss of time

APPENDIX 255

at interchange points, and it is understood that these trains render forty-eight hours' quicker service to the Carolinas than by any other existing route.

Four regular crews are assigned to work between Elkhorn Yard and Erwin, 136 miles, using the large L-3 Mallet locomotives, one engine to the train. Southbound from Elkhorn Yard, these trains move all time-freight and empty box cars delivered by the Chesapeake & Ohio Railway, and pick up such loads and empties at St. Paul as are delivered by the Norfolk & Western; the train is filled out with time-freight loads and empties at Kingsport and Johnson City. Northbound, they move from Erwin all time-freight and empty box cars received from the south, and then pick up such cars at Johnson City and Kingsport. Loads for Johnson City and Kingsport, Speer's Ferry, in connection with the Southern Railway, and St. Paul, connecting with the Norfolk & Western, are carried on these trains. Cars for other intermediate stations are handled by the local freight trains.

Four crews are assigned to work between Erwin and Spartanburg, 141 miles, using K-4 Mikado locomotives, one engine to the train except that southbound trains use two of these engines from Erwin to Altapass, 51 miles. These trains likewise handle only time-freight loads and empty box cars, and stop only at Marion and Bostic to set off and pick up such cars in connection with the Southern Railway and the Seaboard Air Line Railway, respectively.

The car limit for time-freight trains is 85 cars; thereafter, additional sections or extra trains are operated.

SLOW FREIGHT TRAINS (THIRD CLASS)

The slow freight trains are, for the most part, composed of coal cars. They are made up at Dante, southbound, and are operated as through freights to Erwin, where another train is made up, usually by number only, to handle the cars to Spartanburg. Numbers 16 and 18 leave Dante at 12:55 P.M. and 8:00 P.M., and arrive in Erwin at 8:30 P.M. and 4:00 A.M., respectively; numbers 24 and 26 leave Erwin at 7:00 A.M. and 10:00 A.M., and reach Spartanburg at 5:00 P.M. and 8:00 P.M., respectively. Northbound, these trains are operated as extras.

APPENDIX

Four regular crews are assigned to work between Erwin and Dante, 101 miles, to handle empty coal cars to the mines and coal loads from the mines. Northbound, these crews pick up coal empties at Johnson City and at Kingsport, and set off empty coal cars at Miller Yard for the Interstate Railroad, and at Castle for the "Dumps Creek" branch. These trains also handle any loads which may be in the Erwin Yard for Johnson City, Kingsport, or Miller Yard. Southbound, they pick up coal loads at Castle and Miller Yard, and set off coal loads at Kingsport and Johnson City.

Either one L-2 or an L-3 Mallet locomotive is used on each of these trains between Erwin and Dante, except on southbound trains an L-1 Mallet engine is used on the rear from Kingsport to Unicoi, 6 miles north of Erwin. The maximum load is 100 cars.

Four regular crews are assigned to work between Erwin and Spartanburg, 141 miles. Southbound, they handle all coal loads from Erwin to Marion, Bostic Yard, and Spartanburg, for the respective connections at those points. Northbound, these trains handle coal empties from the stations mentioned above, and the loads assembled at Spruce Pine by local freight trains. If neither the tonnage nor the car limit is exceeded, these trains also pick up the empty foreign box cars at the three intermediate connections which the time-freight could not handle; however, if these limits are exceeded, such cars are handled by extra sections of either the time or slow freight trains.

One L-2 or an L-3 Mallet locomotive is used on each train between Erwin and Spartanburg, with an L-1 Mallet pusher engine on the rear from Erwin to Altapass. The car limit for these trains is 82 loaded coal cars; thereafter, "extras" are operated to handle the surplus.

LOCAL FREIGHT TRAINS (FOURTH CLASS)

Thrice a week local freight service, in each direction, is maintained over the entire line. The local freight districts are as follows:

Between Elkhorn Yard and Dante, 35 miles. This train uses the M-1 Mallet locomotive, and works the coal mines at Splash Dam, Honey Branch, and Virginia Banner. The Sunday terminal is Elkhorn Yard.

APPENDIX 257

Between Dante and Erwin, 101 miles. This crew uses the K-3 Mikado locomotive, and handles the usual local business between the two points. The Sunday terminal is Erwin.

Between Erwin and Altapass, 51 miles. An H-4 Consolidation locomotive is used on this train, which handles the local traffic between the two points and assembles loads and empties at Altapass for the through freight trains. The Sunday terminal is Erwin.

Between Altapass and Spartanburg, 90 miles. This train uses a K-1 Mikado locomotive, and switches the yards at Marion and Bostic. The Sunday terminal is Spartanburg.

MINE RUNS

One crew, with an M-2 Mallet locomotive, is assigned to work the coal mines between Elkhorn Yard and Dante, daily except Sunday. This train is always heavy, and about half the time two Mallets are used. The sidings leading into the mines have sharp curves and heavy grades, and as a result the two engines can handle only about 40 coal loads each. A part of this mine work is done by the local freight in the district, as noted above.

One crew is assigned to work the mines at Dante, using an M-2 Mallet, daily except Sunday. This crew also handles the necessary switching in the yard at Dante.

One crew, with an H-4 Consolidation locomotive, is assigned to work between Dante and Wilder, daily. In addition to working all the mines and the necessary switching on the "Dumps Creek" branch, this crew does the yard switching at Boody, the Norfolk & Western connection just north of St. Paul, and at St. Paul. It likewise handles the passenger schedule on the branch.

One crew, with the K-2 Mikado locomotive, is assigned to work between Kingsport and Marcem, Tennessee, daily except Sunday, primarily to handle the empty hopper cars to and the loads of stone from the Marcem Quarry to the Penn-Dixie Cement Mill in Kingsport. Marcem is reached via Frisco and the Southern Railway, 9 miles from Frisco. Frisco is the connection point with the Appalachia Division of the Southern, four miles north of Kingsport. The Marcem Quarry averages about 22 cars of stone per working day for the cement plant in Kingsport. A Southern Railway crew is assigned to this run from

APPENDIX

February 17 to August 4 each year, and a Clinchfield crew the remainder of the time, the time being divided on a mileage basis. A special agreement between the two lines covers charges for handling the stone and operation of the train. The through freight trains set off their loads and empties for Frisco at Kingsport, and they are handled by this crew. It also makes the interchange with the Southern at Frisco, most of which is destined to Kingsport.

SHIFTERS

Yard crews are assigned as follows:

At Kingsport:
First crew	6:30 A.M. to	2:30 P.M.	H-4 Consolidation Engine
Second crew	8:00 A.M. to	4:00 P.M.	H-4 Consolidation Engine

At Johnson City:
First crew	7:15 A.M. to	3:15 P.M.	H-3 Consolidation Engine
Second crew	9:00 A.M. to	5:00 P.M.	H-3 Consolidation Engine

At Erwin:
First crew	6:45 A.M. to	2:45 P.M.	K-1 Mikado Engine
Second crew	3:00 P.M. to	11:00 P.M.	H-4 Consolidation Engine
Third crew	11:00 P.M. to	7:00 A.M.	H-4 Consolidation Engine

The switching at Spartanburg is handled by the Southern Railway.

WORK TRAINS

Two work trains are operated from about April 1 to November 1 each year. One crew is assigned to work between Erwin and Elkhorn City with the G-1 "Ten-Wheel" locomotive, and one crew is assigned to work between Erwin and Spartanburg with an H-4 Consolidation locomotive. In addition to the usual functions of such trains in hauling ballast, ties, etc., for maintenance, they also handle the ditching along the right-of-way. North of Erwin, an American Ditching Machine is used, which loads into dump cars. The Mahoney Ditcher is used south of Erwin, dumping into flat cars.

The regular meeting and passing points for all scheduled trains are as follows:

APPENDIX

Miles from Elkhorn City	Length of Siding (Ft.)	Station	Trains
1.4	Yard	Elkhorn Yard, Ky.	92–95
5.6	4404	Towers, Va.	36–39
14.3	4063	Delano, Va.	36–95
35.1	Yard	Dante, Va.	16–39, 18–37
41.8	Yard	Boody, Va.	16–95
52.5	4161	Miller Yard, Va.	37–92
77.4	4580	Boulder, Va.	18–97, 39–94
80.1	2246	Speer's Ferry, Va.	36–37
87.1	3962	Waycross, Tenn.	94–95
93.9	Yard	Kingsport, Tenn.	16–37, 38–39
111.6	3736	Boone, Tenn.	92–97
119.0	Yard	Barrett, Tenn.	16–36
136.3	Yard	Erwin, Tenn.	16–97, 24–95, 37–94
172.6	4690	Lunday, N. C.	94–97
178.8	4183	Caxton, N. C.	92–95
183.1	4615	Spruce Pine, N. C.	26–37, 26–38, 37–38
205.2	4670	Avery, N. C.	26–97
211.9	4228	Catawba, N. C.	24–37
227.1	4056	Fero, N. C.	38–97
245.1	Yard	Bostic, N. C.	24–97

APPENDIX H

GENERAL OPERATING INSTRUCTIONS [1]

General Rules, regulating the movement of trains, are contained in the Book of Rules for the government of the Operating Department. A book of these rules must be in the possession of each employee in train service while on duty.

STANDARD TIME

1. Clocks showing standard time are located at Elkhorn City, Elkhorn Yard, Dante Yard, Kingsport Passenger Station, Johnson City Telephone Office, Erwin Telephone Office, Bostic Yard, and Spartanburg Yard.

Watch inspections will be held three times each year: January 1st to 15th, May 1st to 15th, and September 1st to 15th. Employees who are required to have standard watches will report to watch inspectors between these dates and have their watches inspected. Inspector will make one trip over the road between the dates mentioned to inspect watches of those who cannot conveniently report to him.

REGISTERING

2. All trains will register at Elkhorn City, Elkhorn Yard, Dante Shop, Carbo, Erwin, Bostic Yard, and Spartanburg.

Dispatcher will register first class trains and trains running on train order schedules at Elkhorn Yard, Bostic Yard, and Spartanburg Yard.

Trains 36 and 38 will get a 31 order, or clearance card, at Elkhorn Yard. All trains will get a 31 order, or clearance card, at Kingsport, Erwin, and Bostic Yard. Nos. 39 and 36 will get a 31 order, or clearance card, at Dante.

BULLETIN BOARDS

3. Bulletin Boards and Bulletin Books are located at Elkhorn Yard, Clinchfield, Dante Yard, Kingsport, Johnson City, Erwin, Bostic Yard, and Spartanburg Yard. See Rule 102.

---

[1] Time Table, No. 6, Clinchfield Railroad Company, June 3, 1928.

APPENDIX

MAXIMUM SPEED

4. First class trains and passenger extras, forty (40) miles per hour, except between Dante and Shannon Tunnel, and Toecane and Berry Gap, and on Dumps Creek Line, twenty-five (25) miles per hour.

Mixed trains, twenty-five miles (25) miles per hour.

Time Freight Trains handling derrick cars only, and northbound slow freight trains hauling no coal, thirty (30) miles per hour, except between Dante and Shannon Tunnel and Toecane and Berry Gap, twenty (20) miles per hour. When Time Freight Trains consist partly of coal loads, maximum speed for southbound slow freight trains will govern.

Southbound slow freight trains, twenty-five (25) miles per hour, except between Dante and Shannon Tunnel, between Toecane and Berry Gap, and on Dumps Creek Line, twenty (20) miles per hour.

Trains or engines backing or with cars ahead of engine, twenty (20) miles per hour.

STATIONS FOR WHICH NO TIME IS SHOWN

5. Nos. 36, 37, 38 and 39 will stop at Domus, Bartlick, Splashdam, Steinman, McClure, Nora, Long Branch, Wakenva, Bonnycrest, Hamlin, Burton's Ford, Carfax, Bangor, Hardwood, Hill, Rye Cove, Rotherwood, Roller, Edgewood, Pactolus, Indian Ridge, and Fishery on signal.

Nos. 36 and 39 will stop at Quarry on signal.

No. 38 will stop at Frisco on signal to pick up passengers.

Nos. 38 and 39 will stop at Normal to let off passengers only.

Nos. 37 and 38 will stop at Unaka Springs, Lost Cove, Roses Branch, Bandana, Cass, Wing, Switzerland, Loop, North Cove, Sevier, Hankins, Glenwood, Tate, Enola, and Lawson on signal.

Relief and Forbes are regular stops for Nos. 37 and 38.

YARD LIMITS

6. Yard limit signs are placed and should be observed as follows, viz.:

South of Elkhorn Yard protects trains in both directions north of this sign to Elkhorn City Station.

APPENDIX

On main track north of Clinchco protects southbound trains to Mill Creek Coal Operation track switch south of Clinchco Station.

On Elkhorn main track north of Dante, protects southbound trains to yard limit sign south of Dante Yard. On main track south of Dante Yard, protects northbound trains to yard limit sign north of Dante on Elkhorn line and to mines.

On main track north of Boody, protects southbound trains to yard limit sign north of Nash. Just north of Nash, protects northbound trains to yard limit sign north of Boody.

On main track north of Frisco connection track, protects southbound trains to yard limit sign south of Frisco connection track. On main track south of Frisco connection track, protects northbound trains to yard limit sign north of Frisco connection track.

On main track north of Kingsport, protects southbound trains to yard limit sign south of Kingsport. On main track south of Kingsport, protects northbound trains to yard limit sign north of Kingsport.

North of Barrett passing siding, protects southbound trains to yard limit sign south of E. T. & W. N. C. Junction. On main track south of East Tennessee and Western North Carolina Junction, protects northbound trains to yard limit sign north of Barrett passing siding and trains on Carnegie Branch.

On main track north of Unicoi, protects southbound trains to Unicoi Station.

On main track north of Erwin, protects southbound trains to yard limit sign south of Erwin. On main track south of Erwin, protects northbound trains to yard limit sign north of Erwin.

On main track north of Kona, protects southbound trains to yard limit sign south of Kona. On main track south of Kona, protects northbound trains to yard limit sign north of Kona.

On main track north of Altapass, protects southbound trains to yard limit sign south of Altapass. On main track south of Altapass, protects northbound trains to yard limit sign north of Altapass.

On main track north of Marion, protects southbound trains to yard limit sign south of Marion. On main track south of

APPENDIX

Marion, protects northbound trains to yard limit sign north of Marion.

On main track north of Bostic Yard, protects southbound trains to yard limit sign south of Bostic Yard. On Spartanburg main track south of Bostic Yard, protects northbound trains to yard limit sign north of Bostic Yard.

On main track north of Wye at Spartanburg, protects trains in both directions to connection with Southern Railway at Spartanburg.

North of Clinchfield Yard protects trains in both directions between this sign and south switch at Clinchfield Yard.

Switching and other engines and trains may work within these limits, with engine under full control, and able to stop within half distance of range of vision, without regard to second class and inferior trains, but must clear the main track immediately upon their approach. Second class and inferior trains must approach and run through these limits under full control, expecting to find main track occupied.

YARDS

Elkhorn City

7. Track between Elkhorn Yard office and bridge just north of Elkhorn City Station will be used by trains of Chesapeake and Ohio and Clinchfield Railroads and all trains including first class trains, will be handled under the control of the engineman and prepared to stop within half range of vision. No train must occupy this track within five (5) minutes of the time of a first-class train without full protection. Chesapeake and Ohio passenger trains will have the same rights and privileges in that territory as Clinchfield passenger trains. Derailing Switch has been placed in main track between north Switch of interchange track and Elkhorn City Station. This Switch must be kept set to derail, except when thrown to clear for trains to pass.

Dante

8. Switches to Dante "Y" must be kept set to run cars from either fork around "Y" and prevent their reaching main track.

A derailer has been placed on south end of track 5, about five car lengths from south end of that track to protect caboose cars.

Boody and St. Paul

9. Northbound trains setting off loads billed to St. Paul Junction and beyond will back them through crossover at south end Boody and into track one on N. & W. yard. Trains delivering empty coal cars will place them on track two. Loads billed to St. Paul proper will be left at Boody. All bills with switch list must be left at St. Paul Station.

Southbound crews picking up at Boody, leaving rear on main track, must not depend on air holding cars left on main track, but protect such cars with hand brakes sufficient to hold cars while pick-up work is being done.

Crews switching St. Paul house track must have one man protect the crossing directly behind station and crossing just east of station while work is being done.

The same train order and block signal at St. Paul Tower is used for Clinchfield and N. & W. trains.

Miller Yard

Deliver empties on track 1 or 2 and loads to house track.

Frisco

10. Check Southern Railway train register at telegraph office before occupying main track to know that first class trains have passed. Frisco yard is protected by yard boards on Southern Railway, located about 1200 feet from outer switches.

Conductors must be careful to know that switch list is left with Frisco operator for each car delivered; that car numbers are absolutely correct and that time delivered is shown on switch list as our interchange reports are made from these lists.

Deliver to Southern Railway on tracks 1 and 2.

Southern will deliver to us on track 3.

Time freight trains will set off perishable loads routed via Frisco at Frisco and other Frisco loads at Kingsport.

Kingsport

11. Northbound trains set off on south yard or dye plant track. Southbound trains set off on south yard opposite tank.

In placing loaded cars of stone on stone dump track at Kingsport, air must be coupled through all cars being handled.

APPENDIX 265

Not more than 5 cars stone shall be handled at one time for placing on stone tipple at Cement Plant.

Pusher engines will go to north end of yard to get on train.

Johnson City

12. Northbound time freight trains set off on E. T. & W. N. C. transfer track or horn track at Barrett, and pick up from transfer tracks and from front Veneer plant track just south of Barrett tank.

Southbound trains set off on scale track and long track at Barrett and pick up on tank track. When setting off shove up to clear on scale track and up to point opposite north switch to scale track when setting off on long track.

Leave turntable track and chemical lead track clear.

On Carnegie branch all trains must come to full stop before crossing E. T. & W. N. C. Railway and Southern Railway tracks. Interlocking derailers have been placed on the main track at Carnegie Branch on each side of Southern Railway crossing at Carnegie. Levers operating these signals are located at Southern Railway crossing and are equipped with switch locks and must be thrown to danger position against Southern Railway trains before derailers on our track can be thrown.

When switching over crossings in Johnson City, not protected by signals, a member of train crew must be stationed at crossing to protect it. Signals at Watauga Street do not operate for trains using front track. Signals at Tennessee Road Crossing, Barrett, do not operate for trains using tank track.

All trains will approach and pass over track between Buffalo St., Johnson City, and south switch Barrett passing track and where third rail is laid near Harris' factory under full control and be able to stop within half range of vision. Trains of the Southern Ry. and E. T. & W. N. C. Ry. use our main track in this territory without protection.

Erwin

13. Engineers arriving Erwin on pusher engines from the south will call dispatcher from south end of Erwin Yard and report their arrival.

Maximum time allowance for passenger engineers at Erwin will be, in reporting, fifteen (15) minutes before leaving time, and in being relieved, ten (10) minutes after arrival of train.

Southbound coal trains will stop on Erwin Yard tracks with engine 15 car lengths north of south switches.

All freight trains coming into Erwin yard will stretch slack in train, after stopping on Yard track, and will set brakes sufficient to hold the slack out.

Trains pulling into Erwin yard with 50 cars or less will set up five hand brakes and trains with more than 50 cars will set up ten hand brakes on south end to prevent train rolling out.

Cars to be re-iced at Erwin must be brought into Erwin on head end or next to caboose so that they can be switched on without delay.

Marion

14. In setting off on interchange tracks, shove up as far as possible. Southbound time freight trains deliver to Southern on track 2. Southbound slow freight trains deliver to Southern on track 3. Do not place bad order or no-bill cars on interchange tracks but leave such cars on station siding or shop track. Leave weigh cars on scale or station track.

Bostic Yard

15. Seaboard Air Line Railway engines have the same rights and privileges on Bostic Yard as Clinchfield engines.

Southbound trains moving into Bostic Yard against northbound trains will go to the north yard switch to head in, instead of taking siding on track known as passing track.

Spartanburg

16. Tracks between Lawson's Fork bridge and Spartanburg station will be used by Southern Railway yard engines. All trains will be handled between these points under control of the enginemen and be prepared to stop within half range of vision.

A derailer is located on cross-over from south end of interchange yard to Southern main line at Spartanburg and is located to clear Southern main track.

Loads handled into Spartanburg must be switched as follows:
All loads for delivery to C. & W. C. to be together.
All loads for delivery to P. & N. to be together.
All loads for delivery to Southern to be together.

APPENDIX

HANDLING OF TRAINS, AIR AND RETAINERS

17. All freight trains must have not less than eighty-five (85) per cent. of all cars in train equipped with air and in working order.

Air brakes must be tested on all trains before leaving terminals. Air hose must be coupled and brakes working on all cars handled to mines and retainers turned up, and brakes tested on cars handled from mines at Dante and Dumps Creek.

Air brakes must not be released after an undesired emergency application until train comes to a stop.

18. All retainers must be turned up on all southbound tonnage freight trains Trammel to Dante Yard, and on all northbound tonnage freight trains Towers to Elkhorn Yard.

All retainers, except 10 on rear, must be turned up on all southbound tonnage freight trains Ridge to Avery, and half as many retainers as there are cars in train from Avery to Bostic Yard.

Half as many retainers as there are cars in train must be turned up on all southbound tonnage trains Dante to Boody, and Unicoi to Erwin.

Do not turn up retainer on tank cars.

19. In turning up retainers be sure to turn them all the way up regardless of the type of retainer.

20. Time freight trains north will make running test of air brakes at Towers.

Time freight trains south will make running air-brake test at south end Sandy Ridge tunnel.

Time freight trains south will stop at Altapass and test air and with 40 cars or more turn up half as many retainers as there are cars in train at Altapass or Ridge. Retainers must not be turned up on empty cars.

Southbound time freight and tonnage trains will stop at Rocky and at Avery and make careful inspection of train for overheated wheels and fallen brake beams and will turn down retainer on any car on which wheels are too hot.

21. All tonnage freight trains north must come to a stop at Towers and all tonnage freight trains south must come to a stop at Trammel, Soldier, Unicoi and Altapass and test brakes by applying and releasing air from leading engine in train and

will not proceed without signal from member of crew who will be stationed at rear car to see that brakes are working properly.

21-a. Conductors of southbound tonnage trains will see that careful inspection is made of their train at Wood, Boulder, Fordtown, Poplar, Ridge, Rocky and Avery, except that trains from Dante or Boody need not stop at Boulder or Fordtown to make this inspection. Trains from Miller Yard or trains filling out at that point must make inspection at Boulder. If not necessary to take water at Boulder, trains may make inspection at Kermit instead of Boulder.

21-b. When weather conditions make it impossible for time freight crews to see over their entire train at least once in each twenty-miles run, head brakeman will drop off, let train pull by him to make inspection for overheated journals, etc., and walk back to engine.

22. Air must be coupled through pusher engines northbound Bostic Yard to Ridge, and southbound Elkhorn Yard to Trammel, Kingsport to Soldier, Johnson City to Unicoi, Erwin to Altapass, and Catawba to Marion. Also at all other points where the number of cars behind pusher engines make it necessary in order to have eighty-five (85) per cent. of the number of cars in the train equipped with air and in working order, controlled by the leading engine.

Feed valves on all pusher engines must be adjusted to conform to the pressure carried on rear of train, care being exercised in adjusting the feed valve to insure the pressure of the pusher engine and that portion of train behind the pusher engine not being higher than the pressure in the rear of the train to be coupled to.

In no case shall pusher engine move rear of train without definite knowledge that the air is working through entire train.

23. In handling cars to and from coal tipples, air must be first coupled on all cars and tested, engines or cars with defective brake equipment must not be used on tipples. Train crew will ride on engine and train must be handled entirely by air brakes. When cars are in position on tipple, air brakes must be released and hand brakes applied to each car. In no case shall a run be taken at incline.

Engines which can be used on coal tipples are 99 to 103, 150 to 152, 300 to 314, 498-499, 500, except that any of our

APPENDIX

engines can be used on tipples at Avery and Bostic Yard.

24. "Slack action" in long trains must be handled as follows:

In starting with two engines on head end, leading engine will start as much of the train as possible, then second engine will be given steam gradually until train is started. If unable to start train leading engine will then blow pusher on rear ahead and this will be signal for pusher to take slack from rear, and brakemen must station themselves on train to transfer this signal. In stopping, the second engine on head end must in all cases shut off steam first, giving the leading engine an opportunity to bunch slack before making application of brakes. In no case should brakes be applied before slack is bunched when pusher is used on rear. On ascending grade where stop is made with independent brake, automatic brake should also be applied and released and sufficient hand brakes set up to prevent rear from running back.

BLOCK AND BLOCK SIGNALS

25. Absolute block for southbound trains applies between Dante and St. Paul Tower. In case of wire trouble, operator or yard master at Dante may issue permissive block card and trains receiving such card will be governed by Rule 707, Book of Rules.

26. Southbound freight trains following passenger train from Barrett will not leave Barrett until such passenger train has left Johnson City Station.

27. Southbound freight train at Hannum following southbound passenger train will not leave Hannum until such passenger train has cleared at Erwin.

28. Following instructions will govern the operation of block signals at Sandy Ridge Tunnel, Clinch Mountain Tunnel and between Altapass and Byrd Tunnel:

Arm horizontal—indicated at night by red light. Stop before entering block.

Arm vertical—indicated at night by white light. Proceed.

Normal position of signals at Sandy Ridge and Clinch Mountain Tunnel—At Danger.

Normal position of signals between Altapass and south end of Byrd Tunnel—At clear.

APPENDIX

Telephones have been installed at automatic signals at Trammel Tank, at south end of Sandy Ridge Tunnel, at Speers Ferry, at Kermit, at south end of Byrd Tunnel; on lower and upper grade at Switzerland, south and north ends of Ridge passing siding and Altapass.

Trains receiving orders to meet within block signals will not be given orders to disregard signals until they find signal against them, when they will call up for order. Trains making meeting points within block signal limits by rule will call up dispatcher upon arrival at meeting point if they do not clear main track so that opposing trains may be given order to disregard signals. Trains following each other will not be given order to disregard signals except in cases of accident or failure of signals, when information that train is ahead will be given. Where view is obstructed, either by curve or smoke in tunnels, following trains will flag ahead through such tunnel and will be handled under control of engineman.

When signal indicates STOP, train must come to stop before reaching signal, communicate with Dispatcher's office and receive order to disregard signal or send flagman in advance, wait five minutes and proceed under control, following flagman at a safe distance until obstruction is reached or a block signal indicating PROCEED.

Conductors and enginemen must report to Train Dispatcher from first telephone office any signal not working properly. Signal should change from PROCEED to STOP when train enters block and its failure to do so should be reported, giving number of signal.

Automatic block signals do not relieve employees of the duty of properly protecting trains by flag in accordance with Rule 99.

The block signal circuit extends to the clearance point on sidings and train and engine crews must see that circuits are cleared, otherwise block signals will not clear for approaching trains.

General

29. Freight extras may run ahead of third class trains.

30. When overtaken at stations slow freight trains will allow time freight trains and locals will allow time freight or slow freight trains to pass promptly.

APPENDIX 271

31. Rear of trains handling derrick cars must be protected at all points.

32. Mill Creek operation track, just south of Clinchco station, will be considered passing track for trains holding meet orders at Clinchco.

33. At points where pusher engine is cut off to take water, at night, green light must be placed on rear of train to assist pusher engine in finding rear to make coupling.

Pusher engine must not attempt to couple to train while train is in motion.

34. In turning engines or trains on wye tracks maintain slow speed and exercise care due to sharp curvature on these tracks.

35. Wooden flat cars must be hauled not more than 10 cars from rear of trains.

36. Engines of this Company weighing seventy-five (75) tons or over will not use the bridge of Black Mountain Railway at Kona.

37. Except to prevent accident, engine whistle must not be sounded within the corporate limits of Erwin, Johnson City or Kingsport. Crossing signals are to prevent accident.

38. To prevent accident at crossing, a train having to cut a crossing at a station where it is to meet or be passed by another train, will have a man stationed at the crossing to protect it on the approach of the other train.

39. Switches on switchback at Dante and at all operation tracks must be so adjusted as to prevent cars from operation tracks reaching main track in case of a runaway.

40. Derails have been placed in a number of our passing sidings.

41. Two derailers are located on Mill Creek operation track at Clinchco, one at clearance point and one two thousand (2,000) feet from clearance point.

Two derailers are located on track serving B. & C. Lime Co., at Ashford; one at clearance point and one beyond nursery warehouse.

42. Enginemen will sound whistle at abrupt curves between Unaka Springs and Poplar between 7:00 A.M. and 4:30 P.M., as warning to section men.

43. Clearance cards issued by operators to trains for which they have no orders while the train order signal is displayed must show for what train or trains the signal is displayed.

44. Trains holding meet orders at points where no operator is located will call dispatcher promptly on arrival if the train to be met has not arrived.

45. Between 6:00 p.m. and 8:00 a.m. all southbound freight trains will call dispatcher at Barrett and all northbound slow freights and pushers will call dispatcher at Toecane unless otherwise directed.

46. Conductors will examine carefully for defects all cars to be picked up at Kona and wire report to Train Master of any cars found to be in defective condition, giving car number and nature of defects.

47. Work train conductors will show on time slips the nature of work in which engaged in order that chargings may be properly distributed. It is very important that Conductors and Engineers show on their time tickets class of services performed and actual miles made as well as miles allowed.

48. Telegraphic report must be made of train accidents and personal injuries as promptly as possible.

49. Conductors of freight trains will give dispatcher consist of their train before leaving terminal or from first station or call-up point after leaving terminal.

50. Loads must not be moved without way-bills. Way-bills which show a change in initial or number of car without notation showing authority for such change must not be accepted.

51. Empty tank cars must have dome cap in place before being moved.

52. Switch lists must be left for cars taken into Elkhorn Yard, Dante Yard, Erwin, Bostic Yard, and Spartanburg, and for all cars set off at Boody, St. Paul, Miller Yard, Speers Ferry, Frisco, Kingsport, Johnson City, Kona, and Marion.

Conductors will show time of arrival on all switch lists.

53. Booth telephones are equipped with either hand or foot switches for the purpose of cutting 'phones off the line when not in use. This is of benefit to the telephones and the line. Watch to see that these switches are properly handled and be careful to see that the doors to telephone booths are locked after using them.

APPENDIX 273

54. When cars are set off on loading sidings, other cars on such sidings being loaded or unloaded must not be displaced.

55. Trains of this Company will be handled over the tracks and will be subject to the rules, order and special instructions of the Norfolk and Western Railway between Carbo and St. Paul. All Clinchfield Railroad crews using this track must be supplied with copies of current book of rules and time table of the Norfolk and Western Railway.

56. When time freight and coal trains are leaving terminals and points where cars have been set off or picked up, conductor or brakeman will let train pull by them slow enough to catch any hand or air brake that may be holding.

57. Weak wooden underframe cars built prior to 1906 must be handled by locals or other short trains.

58. Crews must not jerk nor kick cars over road crossings in switching.

59. Southbound time freight trains having loads for Bristol, routed via Speers Ferry will set off such loads at Speers Ferry.

60. "Water one mile" boards have been removed at Raccoon tank. Rule 99-b will not apply at that point and trains stopping there for water will protect as per rule 99.

INTERLOCKING

61. At interlocking plants engineers must bring their trains to full stop if "Stop" signal is displayed and communicate with leverman at telephone office for instructions. They should not pass any derailing switch under stop signal unless they personally assure themselves that switch has been properly spiked up.

SIGNALS GOVERNING MOVEMENTS THROUGH ST. PAUL INTERLOCKING PLANT

Groups of yellow lights on discs located on poles near crossover give indications to govern all movements.

All indications given by three lights.

Three lights displayed horizontally, or straight across the disc, is a STOP signal.

Three lights displayed at an angle of forty-five degrees is a PROCEED WITH CAUTION signal.

One light displayed under any group of three lights indicates block ahead occupied by another train.

SOUTHBOUND movements governed by one disc of lights.

NORTHBOUND movements governed by lights in three discs on a two bracket pole.

The top disc lights on high, east or right hand bracket indicate movement to be made over Clinchfield main track.

The bottom disc of lights on the same bracket indicate movement to be made from Clinchfield main track to N. & W. main track.

The disc lights on the left hand or lower bracket indicate movement to be made from the interchange track at St. Paul to the N. & W. main track.

Laws and Ordinances

62. The laws of all the states through which our line passes require that whistles be sounded for all grade crossings; that either the bell or whistle be sounded at intervals until the crossing has been passed and that either the engineer or fireman be on the lookout ahead at all times.

Tennessee laws require whistle be sounded at a point one mile from corporate limits of all incorporated towns.

Engineers will be held responsible to see that these laws are complied with and be able to so state, in case of accident at a crossing.

The bell must be rung continuously while passing through incorporated towns and whistle must be sounded for each street crossing in such towns, except at Spartanburg, where the use of whistle is prohibited by ordinance.

Enginemen must be careful to adhere to speed restrictions given in ordinances of incorporated towns.

City Ordinance of the City of Johnson City

63. It shall be unlawful for any Engineer, Conductor, Agent or other person to cause or permit any locomotive engine, car or train of cars to stand upon any street crossing within the city for a longer time than four minutes at one time, which crossing shall not again be obstructed until all travelers awaiting upon the highway over said crossing shall have passed.

APPENDIX

Any person violating any of the provisions of this chapter shall be subject to a fine of not less than $5.00 and not more than $50.00 for each offense, unless otherwise provided.

No railroad, person, or other company shall move or cause to be moved, on its tracks, any steam or other engine, car, or train of cars, at a greater rate of speed than twelve miles per hour in the corporate limits of Johnson City.

The head end of all trains will pass over Maple Street crossing not to exceed four miles per hour.

CITY ORDINANCE OF THE CITY OF SPARTANBURG

64. Sec. 4. That from and after this date it will be unlawful for any person or corporation to unload from a car or cars horses, mules, cattle, hogs or other live stock for the purposes of resting, watering, or feeding, within the corporate limits of the city; and any violation of this ordinance will be punished by fines, not exceeding one hundred dollars, or by imprisonment, not exceeding thirty days. January 8, 1907.

Sec. 6. That on and after the first day of December, 1897, it shall be unlawful for any engineer, fireman, conductor or other officer in charge of any locomotive engine to blow the whistle of the same within the corporate limits of the city of Spartanburg. That any person violating this ordinance shall be guilty of a misdemeanor and upon conviction of the same shall pay a fine of $20.00, or be required to work at hard labor upon the public works of the City of Spartanburg for thirty days.

Sec. 14. (a) That on and after the first day of December, 1907, it shall not be lawful for any corporation or officer, agent or employee thereof, to switch to make freight trains across Magnolia or Main streets.

(b) That on and after this date, it shall not be lawful for any railroad engine to be run at a greater rate of speed than ten (10) miles an hour at any point within the city limits.

(c) That no engine, or car, or train of cars, shall obstruct any of the streets of the city by remaining thereon for a longer period than five minutes.

(d) That all violation of this ordinance shall be punishable by a fine not exceeding one hundred dollars, or by imprisonment not exceeding thirty days.

APPENDIX

First Aid to Injured

65. A. In accidents to persons, the ranking employee of the road present will take command and direct proceedings for the relief of the injured.

B. When there is danger from fire, remove all persons promptly from the train, looking first to those who may be helpless from injury or jammed in the wreck.

C. As soon as practicable, summon the nearest surgeon of the Company, and notify the Superintendent by telegraph. State the number of persons injured and the nature and extent of the injuries as clearly as time will allow, in order that the surgeon may come with what is needed.

D. In urgent cases, if no surgeon of the Company can be had promptly, summon the nearest physician to take charge of the case until the Company's surgeon arrives.

E. If injured is badly hurt or weak, keep him lying flat while treating and transporting him.

F. Don't move injured person until bleeding is controlled or fracture is set, if possible.

G. Keep injured person warm, especially while transporting him.

H. Wounds: If "First Aid Dressings" are at hand, use one of suitable size and follow instructions contained on package. Iodine may be used in and around the wound if it is available. Otherwise put pad of clean gauze or linen over the wound and clean bandage over this. Don't wash or touch the wound with the hands, or put anything in it. Don't touch the part of the clean pad that is to be put next to the wound.

I. Bleeding: If from a limb (1) elevate as high as possible, (2) place clean pad over wound and if bleeding freely make firm pressure on pad with the hand until dangerous bleeding is controlled; then (3) cover with cotton and bandage firmly, but not too tight; (4) if necessary to use tourniquet, put it on above knee or elbow, and draw it tight enough to stop all bleeding. Loosen tourniquet every ten (10) minutes, and remove it as soon as there is no dangerous bleeding when it is loosened.

J. Fractures: If you suspect a broken bone, straighten the limb by pulling firmly on the end of the limb, and do not relax your hold until splints are put on. For splints you may use piece of board, shingle, wire netting, telegraph wires, tin gutter, twigs, etc. Place pad of cotton or other soft material between splint and limb. Don't bandage over the point of fracture, but either side of it. Do not use much force in efforts to straighten limb, and if unsuccessful, place it on pillow in most comfortable position. In case of broken ribs, relief will be afforded by broad adhesive plaster strips, tightly applied over injured side.

K. When there is much weakness from an injury, one teaspoonful of aromatic spirits of ammonia may be given with water, at intervals.

L. In severe shock, or when an internal injury is suspected, NO medicine, water or food is to be given.

M. Take hold of the injured gently but firmly, and without fear. Lay the injured one down on cushions, blankets, clothing or straw where he will have perfect ventilation and not in a draft or strong current of air. Loosen the clothes about the neck and body, to permit easy breathing. Do not permit strangers to approach and talk to or ask injured one questions. Place him, if possible, in charge of one or two friends.

N. In moving an injured person, place a board, door, shutter or mattress with one end at the patient's head, and lift or slide him gently on it. If patient can sit up he may be carried in a chair or upon the locked hands of two persons, around whose necks he throws his arms to steady himself.

O. When forwarding a patient who has been seen by a surgeon, obtain from the surgeon a written statement as to his opinion of the nature and extent of the injuries, and attach this statement, together with the name of the injured one (if it can be obtained), securely to his clothing.

P. When the injured person is able to be moved, take or send him to the nearest surgeon of the Company in the direction in which the first train is moving. It can then be decided whether the patient will be treated there or taken to some other point.

Q. When injured is not able to be moved, place him in charge of station agent, section master, or some official of the road, and summon the surgeon of the Company most easily obtained.

R. In a General Emergency, summon the surgeons of the Company in both directions and wire the Superintendent if more surgeons are needed.

66. WATCH INSPECTORS

Ewald & Co., Erwin, Tenn., General Inspectors.
I. N. Beckner, Johnson City, Tenn.
Dunn & Son, Kingsport, Tenn.

BIBLIOGRAPHY

I. BOOKS

Beard, Charles A., and Beard, Mary B. *The Rise of American Civilization,* The Macmillan Company, New York, 1928.

Bogart, Ernest L. *Economic History of the United States,* Longmans, Green, and Company, New York, 1920.

Brown, Cecil K. *A State Movement in Railroad Development,* The University of North Carolina Press, Chapel Hill, N. C., 1928.

Brown, Henry G. *Transportation Rates and Their Regulation,* The Macmillan Company, New York, 1916.

The Bureau of Railway Economics, Washington, D. C. *Catalogue of Books on Railway Economics,* The University of Chicago Press, Chicago, 1912.

Cunningham, William J. *American Railroads: Government Control and Reconstruction Policies,* A. W. Shaw Company, New York, 1922.

Dozier, Howard D. *A History of the Atlantic Coast Line Railroad,* Houghton Mifflin Company, New York, 1920.

Haines, Henry S. *Efficient Railway Operation,* The Macmillan Company, New York, 1919.

Hamilton, Walton H., and Wright, Helen R. *The Case of Bituminous Coal,* The Macmillan Company, New York, 1925.

Haney, Lewis H. *The Business of Railway Transportation,* The Ronald Press, New York, 1924.

Hines, Walker D. *War History of American Railroads,* Yale University Press, New Haven, Conn., 1928.

Huebner, Grover G., and Johnson, Emory R. *The Railroad Freight Service,* D. Appleton and Company, New York, 1926.

Hunt, Gaillard. *John C. Calhoun,* G. W. Jacobs and Company, Philadelphia, 1908.

Interstate Commerce Commission Reports, Vol. 90, May-October, 1924, Government Printing Office, Washington, D. C., 1925.

Jennings, Walter W. *History of Economic Progress in the United States,* Thomas Y. Crowell Company, New York, 1926.

Jervey, Theodore D. *Robert Y. Hayne and His Times,* The Macmillan Company, New York, 1909.

Johnson, Emory R., and Huebner, Grover G. *Railroad Traffic and Rates,* D. Appleton and Company, New York, 1911.

Jones, Eliot, and Vanderblue, Homer B. *Railroads: Cases and Selections,* The Macmillan Company, New York, 1925.

Long, Howard. *Kingsport, A Romance of Industry*, The Sevier Press, Kingsport, Tenn., 1928.
Loree, Leonor F. *Railroad Freight Transportation*, D. Appleton and Company, New York, 1922.
McGrane, Reginald C. *The Panic of 1837*, The University of Chicago Press, Chicago, 1924.
McPherson, Logan G. *The Working of the Railroads*, Henry Holt and Company, New York, 1907.
Meigs, William M. *The Life of John Caldwell Calhoun*, The Neal Publishing Company, New York, 1917.
Miller, Sidney L. *Railway Transportation: Principles and Point of View*, A. W. Shaw Company, New York, 1924.
Moody, John. *The Railroad Builders*, Yale University Press, New Haven, Conn., 1921.
Mundy, Floyd W. *Earning Power of Railroads*, J. H. Oliphant and Company, New York, 1928.
North Carolina, The Land of Opportunity, North Carolina State Board of Agriculture, Raleigh, N. C., 1923.
Phillips, Ulrich B. *History of Transportation in the Eastern Cotton Belt to 1860*, Columbia University Press, New York, 1908.
Poor's Manual of Railroads, New York.
Raper, Charles L. *Railway Transportation*, The Knickerbocker Press, G. P. Putnam's Sons, New York, 1912.
Ripley, William Z. *Main Street and Wall Street*, Little, Brown, and Company, Boston, 1927.
Ripley, William Z. *Railroads: Finance and Organization*, Longmans, Green, and Company, New York, 1915.
Smith, Alice R. Huger, and Smith, D. E. Huger. *The Dwelling Houses of Charleston, South Carolina*, J. B. Lippincott Company, Philadelphia, 1917.
Splawn, Walter M. W. *Government Ownership and Operation of Railroads*, The Macmillan Company, New York, 1928.
Wolf, Harry D. *The Railroad Labor Board*, The University of Chicago Press, Chicago, 1927.

II. NEWSPAPERS AND PERIODICALS

The Augusta Chronicle, Augusta, Georgia.
The Augusta Herald, Augusta, Georgia.
The Charleston Courier, Charleston, S. C.
The Charleston Mercury, Charleston, S. C.
The Charlotte Daily Observer, Charlotte, N. C.
The Commercial and Financial Chronicle, New York, N. Y.

BIBLIOGRAPHY

DeBow's Review, New Orleans, La.
Engineering News, New York, N. Y.
The Harvard Business Review, Cambridge, Mass.
Hunt's Merchants' Magazine, New York, N. Y.
Louisville & Nashville Employees' Magazine, Louisville, Ky.
Manufacturers' Record, Baltimore, Md.
The News and Courier, Charleston, S. C.
Niles' Register, Baltimore, Md.
Niles' National Register, Baltimore, Md.
Niles' Weekly Register, Baltimore, Md.
Quarterly Journal of Economics, Harvard University, Cambridge, Mass.
Railroad Man's Magazine, The Frank A. Munsey Company, New York, N. Y.
Railway Age, New York, N. Y.
Railway Age Gazette, Chicago, Ill.
Railway Review, Chicago, Ill.
The Savannah Morning News, Savannah, Georgia.
Scientific American, New York, N. Y.
The Sumter Item, Sumter, S. C.
The Sumter News, Sumter, S. C.
The Sunday News, Charleston, S. C.
The University of North Carolina News Letter, The University of North Carolina Press, Chapel Hill, N. C.

III. ARTICLES, MANUSCRIPTS, REPORTS, ETC.

"Address of Colonel A. Blanding to the Citizens of Charleston on the Louisville, Cincinnati, and Charleston Railroad," 37 pp., Columbia, S. C., 1836.

"An Address Respecting the Charleston and Hamburgh Rail-Road and on the Rail-Road System as Regards a Large Portion of the Southern and Western States of the North American Union, by Elias Horry, President of the South-Carolina Canal and Railroad Company, Delivered in Charleston at the Medical College of the State of South Carolina on Wednesday, the 2nd of October, 1833, upon the Completion of the Road," 38 pp., A. E. Miller, Charleston, S. C., 1833.

Annual Reports, Atlantic Coast Line Railroad Company.
Annual Reports, Carolina, Clinchfield & Ohio Railway Company.
Annual Reports, Charleston & Western Carolina Railway Company.
Annual Reports, Clinchfield Railroad Company.
DeBow, J. B. D. "Will Charleston Command the Trade of the West," *DeBow's Review*, Vol. 22, April, 1857.

BIBLIOGRAPHY

Dixon, Frank H. "Federal Operation of Railroads During the War," *Quarterly Journal of Economics*, Vol. 33, August, 1919.

"Here Is an Opportunity," *The News and Courier*, Charleston, S. C., October 1, 1894.

"Industrial Guide and Directory of Industries along the Clinchfield Railroad," 32 pp., issued by the Industrial Department of the Clinchfield Railroad, Erwin, Tenn., October, 1928.

Interstate Commerce Commission Reports, Vol. 90, May-October, 1924, Government Printing Office, Washington, D. C., 1925.

Interstate Commerce Commission, 63, "In the Matter of Consolidation of the Railway Properties of the United States into a Limited Number of Systems," Government Printing Office, Washington, D. C., August 3, 1921.

Interstate Commerce Commission, Finance Docket No. 1102, "In the Matter of Application of Carolina, Clinchfield and Ohio Railway for Authority to issue $5,000,000, Principal Amount, of Its Fifteen Year Six Per Cent Cumulative Income Debentures," Government Printing Office, Washington, D. C., 1920.

Interstate Commerce Commission, Finance Docket No. 2684, "In the Matter of the Application of the Carolina, Clinchfield & Ohio Railway for Authority to Issue Bonds," Government Printing Office, Washington, D. C., 1923.

Interstate Commerce Commission, Finance Docket No. 2849, "In the Matter of the Application of the Carolina, Clinchfield & Ohio Railway for Authority to Assume Obligation and Liability in Respect of Certain Equipment Trust Certificates," Government Printing Office, Washington, D. C., 1923.

Interstate Commerce Commission, Finance Docket No. 3131, "In the Matter of the Application of the Atlantic Coast Line Railroad Company and the Louisville and Nashville Railroad Company for Approval of a Lease for 999 Years by the Applicants of the Railroad Properties of the Carolina, Clinchfield and Ohio Railway Company and its Subsidiaries, and for Authority to Assume the Financial Obligations Involved in Such a Lease," Government Printing Office, Washington, D. C., March 25, 1924.

Interstate Commerce Commission, Finance Docket No. 3131, "Brief for the Applicants," Westerfield-Bonte Company, Incorporated, Louisville, Ky., 1923.

Interstate Commerce Commission, Finance Docket No. 3131, "Brief in Behalf of the City of Charleston, S. C., and Chamber of Commerce of Charleston, S. C.," Byron S. Adams, Washington, D. C., October 26, 1923.

BIBLIOGRAPHY

Interstate Commerce Commission, Finance Docket No. 3131, "Reply Brief on Behalf of Seaboard Air Line Railway Company, an Intervener and Protestant," November 10, 1923.

Interstate Commerce Commission, Finance Docket No. 3131, "Clinchfield Railway Lease," Government Printing Office, Washington, D. C., June 3, 1924.

Interstate Commerce Commission, Finance Docket No. 4097, "Carolina, Clinchfield & Ohio Equipment Trust Series I," Government Printing Office, Washington, D. C., 1924.

Interstate Commerce Commission, Finance Docket No. 6101, "Bonds of Carolina, Clinchfield & Ohio Ry.," Government Printing Office, Washington, D. C., 1927.

Interstate Commerce Commission, Valuation Docket No. 364, "Tentative Valuation Report of the Properties of the Carolina, Clinchfield and Ohio Railway, as of June 30, 1917," Government Printing Office, Washington, D. C., 1917.

Lewis, J. O. "The Costliest Railroad in America," *Scientific American*, "Supplement," Vol. 61, July 31, 1909.

"The Mineral Resources of the Clinchfield Territory," 24 pp., issued by the Industrial Department of the Clinchfield Railroad, Erwin, Tenn., 1928.

Morgan, O. K. "The Elkhorn Railway Extension," *Engineering News*, Vol. 70, October 16, 1913.

Morgan, O. K. "The Story of the Clinchfield," an unpublished manuscript, 9 pp., Johnson City, Tenn., October, 1928.

Oldham, John E. "The Problem of Railroad Consolidations," *The Harvard Business Review*, January, 1923.

Olds, Fred A. "A Journey over the C. C. & O.," *Charlotte Daily Observer*, August 30, and September 2, 1908.

"Operating Time Table, No. 6," Clinchfield Railroad Company, Erwin, Tenn., June 3, 1928.

"Outline of History of the Carolina, Clinchfield, and Ohio Railway," 4 pp., an anonymous, unpublished manuscript, Erwin, Tenn.

"Report of the Chief Engineer of the Blue Ridge Railroad," 36 pp., Carolina Printing Company, Columbia, S. C., July 24, 1871.

"Report of Col. Long to the Estillville Convention," 40 pp., Alexander, Abington, Va., 1831.

"Report of the Several Committees of the City Council of Charleston, the Blue Ridge Railroad of South Carolina, the Chamber of Commerce, and the Board of Trade of Charleston, South Carolina, on the Subject of the Blue Ridge Railroad," Charleston, S. C., 1866.

BIBLIOGRAPHY

"Report of the South Carolina Commissioners to the Knoxville Convention on the Subject of the Proposed Railroad from Charleston to Cincinnati and Louisville," 35 pp., Knoxville, Tenn., 1836.

Ripley, William Z. "Report to the Interstate Commerce Commission on Consolidation of Railways," 63 I. C. C., Government Printing Office, Washington, D. C., 1921.

"South Carolina," 14 pp., United States Railroad Commission.

"Time Tables," Clinchfield Railroad Company, Erwin, Tenn., January, 1928.

IV. MISCELLANEOUS SOURCES OF INFORMATION

Blue Prints furnished by the Chief Engineer, Clinchfield Railroad Company, Erwin, Tenn., November, 1928.

Blue Prints furnished by the Mechanical Engineer, Clinchfield Railroad Company, Erwin, Tenn., November, 1928.

Letters received from the following:

Mr. E. C. Bailly, Secretary, Clinchfield Railroad Company, New York, October 25, 1928.

Mr. Joseph C. Barbot, Clerk of Court, The City of Charleston, S. C., November 7, 1928.

The Hon. Luther M. Carlton, Sr., Roxboro, N. C., September 28, October 4, 1928; July 1, 1929.

Mr. Harry Faw, Secretary, Chamber of Commerce, Johnson City, Tenn., August 3, 1929.

The Hon. Theodore D. Jervey, Charleston, S. C., July 19, 1929.

Mr. G. A. Kent, Mining Engineer, Bristol, Va., April 26, 1929.

Mr. Alfred B. Lindsay, Assistant Librarian, Bureau of Railway Economics, Washington, D. C., October 12, 1928.

Mr. O. K. Morgan, Consulting Engineer, Johnson City, Tenn.

Mr. C. D. Moss, Train Master, Clinchfield Railroad Company, Erwin, Tenn., December 3, 1928.

Colonel Fred A. Olds, North Carolina Historical Commission, Raleigh, N. C., July 10, 1929.

Mr. L. H. Phetteplace, General Manager, Clinchfield Railroad Company, Erwin, Tenn., November 26, December 22, 1930.

The Hon. J. A. Raffield, Mayor of the City of Sumter, S. C., July 20, 1929.

Mr. C. A. Smith, General Freight Agent, Clinchfield Railroad Company, Erwin, Tenn., August 22, 1929; December 23, 1930.

Mr. J. P. Walker, General Superintendent, Atlantic Coast Line Railroad Company, Savannah, Georgia, October 8, 1928.

BIBLIOGRAPHY

Mr. O. T. Waring, Superintendent, Atlantic Coast Line Railroad Company, Charleston, S. C., October 2, 1928; August 13, 1929.
The Rev. William Way, D.D., Charleston, S. C.
Mr. J. E. Willoughby, Chief Engineer, Atlantic Coast Line Railroad Company, Wilmington, N. C., December 7, 1930.
Mr. John Wilson, President, The Northwestern Railroad of South Carolina, Sumter, S. C., July 17, 1929.
Map, Atlantic Coast Line-Louisville and Nashville Railroad System, Dozier, *A History of the Atlantic Coast Line Railroad*.
Map, Carolina, Clinchfield, and Ohio Railway, Annual Reports of the Company.
Map, Charleston, Cincinnati, and Chicago Railroad, *Commercial and Financial Chronicle,* Vol. 50.
Map, Clinchfield Railroad, Annual Reports of the Company.

Personal interviews with the following:
Mr. P. C. Alford, Traffic Department, Clinchfield Railroad Company, Erwin, Tenn.
Dr. C. K. Brown, Professor of Economics, Davidson College, Davidson, N. C.
The Hon. L. M. Carlton, Sr., Roxboro, N. C.
Mr. J. L. Cox, Assistant General Freight Agent, Southern Railway Company, Charleston, S. C.
Mr. L. B. Davidson, office of Commercial Freight Agent, Atlantic Coast Line Railroad Company, Charleston, S. C.
The late Mr. W. C. Hattan, Chief Engineer, Clinchfield Railroad Company, Erwin, Tenn.
Dr. M. S. Heath, Associate Professor of Economics, University of North Carolina, Chapel Hill, N. C.
Mr. Charles Hewett, General Auditor, Clinchfield Railroad Company, Erwin, Tenn.
The Hon. Theodore D. Jervey, Charleston, S. C.
Mr. L. L. McIntyre, Superintendent, Clinchfield Railroad Company, Erwin, Tenn.
Mr. J. C. Mixon, Chief Clerk to General Superintendent, Atlantic Coast Line Railroad Company, Savannah, Georgia.
Mr. O. K. Morgan, Consulting Engineer, Johnson City, Tenn.
Mr. W. S. Moseley, Mechanical Engineer, Clinchfield Railroad Company, Erwin, Tenn.
Mr. C. D. Moss, Train Master, Clinchfield Railroad Company, Erwin, Tenn.
Dr. C. T. Murchison, Professor of Applied Economics, University of North Carolina, Chapel Hill, N. C.

Mr. C. A. Smith, General Freight and Passenger Agent, Clinchfield Railroad Company, Erwin, Tenn.
Mr. J. P. Walker, General Superintendent, Atlantic Coast Line Railroad Company, Savannah, Georgia.
Mr. O. T. Waring, Superintendent, Atlantic Coast Line Railroad, Charleston, S. C.
Dr. H. D. Wolf, Associate Professor of Economics, University of North Carolina, Chapel Hill, N. C.
Dr. J. B. Woosley, Associate Professor of Economics, University of North Carolina, Chapel Hill, N. C.
Dr. E. W. Zimmermann, Professor of Commerce and Resources, University of North Carolina, Chapel Hill, N. C.
Personal observation.

INDEX

Abbeville, S. C., 38.
Abbot's Hill, 5.
Adams, E. D., 112.
Aiken, S. C., 38, 44.
Albert Yard, Va., 130, 133.
Alexandria, Va., 2.
Allaire, Charles M., 97.
Alleghanies, 8.
Alleghany Mountains, 4, 11, 152.
Allport, James H., 113.
Alpine Region, 15.
Altapass, N. C., 98, 99, 101, 105, 118, 151, 156, 162, 163, 174, 175, 176, 177, 178, 179, 181, 182, 183, 255, 256, 257, 262, 267, 268, 270.
Altapass Tunnel, 269.
American Bridge Company, 171.
American Railway Engineering and Maintenance of Way Association, 161.
American Railway Express Company, 126.
American Society of Civil Engineers, 171.
Anderson, S. C., 38, 39, 45, 51, 52, 253.
Anderson County, S. C., 43.
Appalachia, Va., 254.
Appalachian Mountains, 1, 193, 202.
Asheville, N. C., 7, 13, 17, 25, 31, 39, 42, 44, 69, 95, 172, 181, 253.
Ashford, N. C., 271.
Ashland, Ky., 56, 59, 60, 66, 69, 80, 82, 85, 253.
Atchison, Topeka & Santa Fe Railroad, 123.
Athens, Ga., 16, 33.
Atlanta, Ga., 2, 33, 34, 35, 43, 46, 63, 94, 133, 136, 189, 211, 219.
Atlanta and West Point Railroad, 124.
Atlantic Coast Line Railroad, 3, 19, 43, 56, 62, 69, 85, 92, 123, 131, 133, 188, 189, 190, 191, 193, 194, 196, 199, 200, 201, 202, 205, 210, 211, 213, 214, 216, 218, 254.
Augusta, Ga., 2, 10, 14, 15, 16, 17, 26, 30, 33, 56, 64, 65, 66, 205, 214.
Averill, Col. J. H., 71, 75.
Avery, N. C., 259, 267, 268, 269.
Avery County, N. C., 208.

Backus, C. E., 115, 191.
Baffals Mountain, 11.
Bailly, E. C., 127, 191.
Baker, Henry K., 68.
Bakersville, N. C., 183, 184.
Bald Tunnel, Va., 160.
Baldwin Locomotive Works, 86, 111, 145, 174.
Baltimore, Md., 2, 20, 81, 103.
Baltimore and Ohio Railroad, 1, 23, 31, 80, 123, 217.
Bandana, N. C., 261.
Bangor, Va., 261.
Bangs, Anson and Co., 39.
Bankers Trust Co., 110, 113.
Baring Bros., 69, 86, 174.
Barker Bros., 81, 82, 83.
Barker, Wharton, 81.
Barkley, R. C., 70.
Barr, J. M., 97.
Barrett, Tenn., 259, 262, 265, 269, 272.
Bartlick, Va., 261.
Battery, The High, 35.
Bay Line, 81.
Bayer, Henry, 70.
Beans Creek, 9.
Beaufort, S. C., 47, 48.
Beckner, I. N., 278.
Bell, George, 70.
Belton, S. C., 45, 51.
Benham Coal Fields, 210, 211.
Berry Gap, 261.
Bessemer Steel, 60.
Big Four Railroad, 123, 205, 218.
Big Moccasin Gap, 6, 8, 12.
Big Rock Creek, 184.
Big Sandy River, 5, 6, 10, 11, 69, 92, 102, 103, 165, 175.
Big Stone Gap, Va., 79.
Birch Creek Gap, 12.
Bird, Wm. M., 53.
Birdsall & Co., 39.
Birmingham, Ala., 52.
Bishopville, S. C., 61.
Bituminous Coal Commission, 206.
Black Mountain, 11.
Black Mountain Railroad, 27, 118, 120, 143, 251, 252, 271.
Blacks, 65.

288 INDEX

Blacksburg, S. C., 55, 56, 61, 64, 65, 66, 77, 82, 93.
Blair, C. L., 26, 112, 126, 127.
Blair, J. A., 97, 109, 114.
Blair & Co., 95, 96, 97, 103, 106, 107, 108, 109, 110, 113, 117, 119, 120, 122, 130.
Blanding, Col. A., 21, 22, 28.
Blanding, James D., 68, 90.
Blanes Creek, 5.
B. & C. Lime Co., 271.
Block signals, 269.
Blountville, Tenn., 7.
Bluefield, W. Va., 254.
Blue Ridge Glass Corporation, 207.
Blue Ridge Mountains, 1, 7, 8, 9, 11, 12, 13, 15, 24, 51, 56, 69, 78, 86, 149, 152, 153, 156, 158, 172, 174, 179, 181.
Blue Ridge Railroad, 24, 38, 40, 41, 42, 43, 44, 45, 46, 50, 51, 52, 92, 154, 175, 216.
Blue Ridge Tunnel, 156, 157, 160, 177, 178, 179, 181.
Boat Yard, 10.
Bock, Joseph, 70.
Bonnycrest, Va., 261.
Boody, Va., 257, 259, 262, 264, 267, 268, 272.
Boone, Daniel, 177, 183.
Boone, Tenn., 259.
Boone's Ford, N. C., 183.
Borden Mills, 207.
Bostic, N. C., 97, 110, 133, 134, 152, 158, 175, 178, 204, 246, 253, 254, 255, 257, 259, 266, 267, 272.
Bostic Yard, N. C., 133, 256, 260, 263, 268, 269.
Boston, Mass., 46, 47, 59, 84, 86.
Boston & Maine Railroad, 123.
Boston Safe and Deposit Co., 67, 68, 81, 89.
Boston Safe Deposit and Trust Co., 82, 94.
Boulder, Va., 259, 268.
Bradley, Capt. W. A., 71.
Branchville, S. C., 16, 18, 19, 25, 28, 52, 71.
"Breaks" of the Big Sandy River, 69, 92, 102, 103, 105, 131, 153.
Bremer, H. F., 70.
Brewer, E. S., 68.
Brisbane, Col. A. H., 23, 24.
Bristol, Tenn., 39, 96, 109, 131, 254, 273.
Broad River, 65, 158.
Brownlow, W. P., 152.
Brush Creek Tunnel, N. C., 160.
Bryan, Hon. George D., 70.

Buchanan County, Va., 97, 104, 105.
Buck Creek Gap, 7, 12.
Buckner, M. N., 126.
Buffalo, N. Y., 136, 218.
Buffalo Creek, 9.
Buffalo Mountain, 9, 11.
Buffalo Tunnel, Va., 160.
Bullock's Creek, S. C., 65.
Burnsville, N. C., 118, 183.
Burrows, Major E. F., 90.
Burton's Ford, 261.
Butler, M. C., 59, 60, 68.
Byrd Tunnel, N. C., 161, 269, 270.

Calendar, Wm. F., 68.
Calhoun, Andrew Pickens, 29.
Calhoun, John C., 13, 26, 27, 28, 29, 30, 31, 35, 87.
Camden, S. C., 5, 9, 10, 59, 60, 61, 62, 65, 67, 68, 69, 71, 74, 75, 77, 80, 87, 90, 91, 92, 93.
Campion, J. J., 127, 136, 193.
Caney, N. C., 95.
Caney Tunnel, Va., 160.
Cape Fear & Yadkin Valley Railroad, 3.
Caples, M. J., 149.
Capps, Charles R., 192, 193.
Carbo, Va., 127, 133, 260, 273.
Carfax, Va., 261.
Carnegie, Tenn., 262, 265.
Carolina Central Railroad, 57, 78, 79, 159.
Carolina, Clinchfield & Ohio Railroad, Chaps. VIII, IX; 96, 99, 102, 103, 104, 105, 107, 108, 112, 123, 126, 131, 133, 143, 149, 151, 157, 164, 166, 171, 172, 173, 175, 181, 184, 185, 186, 188, 194, 197, 198, 199, 200, 201, 202.
Carolina, Clinchfield & Ohio Railroad of S. C., 109, 127, 129, 132, 133, 143, 188, 198, 199.
Carolina Construction Company, 98.
Carolina Gap, 27.
Carolina Midland Railroad, 64, 66.
"Carolina Special," 218.
Carrington, W. P., 53.
Carter, Col. George L., 95, 96, 99, 102, 106, 112, 119, 151, 174, 186.
Caryville, Tenn., 44.
Cashiers, N. C., 27.
Cass, N. C., 261.
Catawba, N. C., 259, 268.
Catawba Junction, S. C., 81.
Catawba River, 7, 8, 12, 72, 107, 156, 158, 174, 176, 178.
Cave Creek, 183.

INDEX 289

Cave River, 184.
Caxton, N. C., 259.
Cement, 135, 207, 209.
Central of Georgia Railway, 31, 34, 43, 196, 215, 217.
Central Railroad, 62.
Central Railroad of New Jersey, 123.
Chad, Ky., 211.
Chamberlain, D. H., 83, 84, 85, 87.
Charleston, S. C., 2, 4, 9, 10, 13, 14, 16, 17, 18, 19, 20, 21, 33, 34, 35, 37, 39, 40, 41, 42, 45, 46, 47, 48, 50, 51, 52, 53, 54, 55, 56, 58, 59, 60, 61, 62, 64, 65, 66, 67, 69, 70, 71, 72, 73, 74, 75, 77, 78, 79, 80, 81, 82, 83, 85, 86, 87, 93, 96, 112, 113, 115, 116, 118, 144, 152, 191, 193, 194, 205, 216, 217, 218, 253.
Charleston & Augusta Railroad, 26.
Charleston, Cincinnati & Chicago Railroad, Chaps. V, VI; 10, 51, 55, 70, 79, 81, 89, 90, 91, 92, 95, 103, 105, 153, 158, 174, 202, 217, 218.
Charleston-Hamburg Railroad, 15, 16, 18, 38.
Charleston National Bank, 130.
Charleston & Savannah Railroad, 46, 56.
Charleston Steamboat Company, 71.
Charleston, Sumter & Northern Railroad, 92.
Charleston & Western Carolina Railroad, 18, 189, 205, 213, 214, 215, 216, 218, 239, 252, 254, 266.
Charlotte, N. C., 56, 65, 73, 93, 204, 205, 253.
Charlotte, Columbia & Augusta Railroad, 56.
Charlotte and South Carolina Railroad, 46, 56.
Chase National Bank, 130.
Chatigua River, 18.
Chattanooga, Tenn., 2, 33, 34, 35, 38, 55, 68.
Cheraw & Chester Railroad, 56, 72.
Cheraw & Darlington Railroad, 46.
Cherokee Nation, 80, 81.
Chesapeake & Ohio Railroad, 42, 69, 80, 85, 112, 113, 123, 136, 163, 164, 175, 193, 205, 207, 210, 217, 218, 238, 252, 253, 254, 255, 263.
Chester, S. C., 46, 47, 56, 72, 73.
Chester, Tenn., 81, 105.
Chestoa, Tenn., 87, 105.
Chevrolet, Ky., 211.
Chicago, 1, 36, 44, 56, 58, 60, 112, 136, 175, 204, 205, 218.

Chicago, Burlington & Quincy Railroad, 123.
Chicago, Milwaukee & St. Paul Railroad, 123.
Chicago & Northwestern Railroad, 123.
Chicago & Rock Island Railroad, 123.
Cincinnati, 2, 10, 16, 17, 19, 20, 21, 22, 24, 25, 26, 35, 38, 40, 41, 42, 44, 56, 78, 89, 92, 95, 189, 204, 205, 218, 253, 254.
Cincinnati, New Orleans & Texas Pacific Railroad, 95.
Civil War, 1, 31, 32, 40, 41, 47, 55, 63, 78.
Clarendon County, S. C., 55, 92.
Clark, Jas., 97.
Clayton, Ga., 38, 41.
Cleveland, Ohio, 56, 218.
Click Tunnel, Tenn., 160.
Clinch Mountain, 6, 11, 12, 154, 158.
Clinch River, 8, 79, 107, 153, 154, 158, 211.
Clinch Tunnel, Va., 160, 269.
Clinchco, Va., 262, 271.
Clinchfield, Va., 260.
Clinchfield Coal Corporation, 96, 97, 102, 103, 113, 114, 115, 116, 191.
Clinchfield Navigating Company, 116.
Clinchfield Northern Railway of Kentucky, 104, 105, 107, 112, 119, 129, 131, 132, 133, 143, 144, 188, 199.
Clinchfield Railway Lease, 199, 211.
Clinchfield Syndicate, 114.
Clinchport, Va., 95, 153, 154, 160.
Coal, 26, 58, 59, 60, 61, 77, 92, 94, 97, 103, 104, 112, 115, 116, 134, 135, 136, 137, 145, 149, 150, 174, 181, 185, 191, 193, 194, 204, 206, 209, 210, 213, 214, 217, 255, 256, 257, 258.
Coapman, E. H., 121.
Coast Region, 14.
Coats, D. N., 68.
Collier, John J., 90, 91.
Columbia, S. C., 2, 5, 9, 13, 15, 16, 17, 18, 19, 25, 28, 30, 43, 45, 46, 65, 66, 75, 95, 152, 205, 213, 216, 253.
Columbia, Newberry & Laurens Railroad, 19, 205, 216.
Columbus, Ga., 2, 204, 205, 218, 254.
Commerce of S. C. prior to Civil War, 46.
Commercial Trust Co., 119.
Congaree River, 71.

INDEX

Connellsville, Pa., coal, 58, 135.
Coolidge, T. J., 97.
Copper Creek, 8, 154.
Copper Mountain, 11.
Corporations, 32.
Cotton, 13, 21, 23, 29, 32, 33, 49, 72, 73, 92.
Cotton Panic, 29.
Courtenay, W. A., 70.
Coxe, Frank, 68.
Crabtree Creek, 9.
Craig, Locke, 172.
Cramer, A. F. C., 70.
Cranberry Creek, 8, 58.
Cranberry Iron Mines, 185.
Cranes Nest Coal Co., 103.
Cres, 135.
Crosby, Ward, 171.
Cumberland Corporation, 96, 99, 101, 102, 103, 107, 108, 109, 111, 113, 114, 117, 118.
Cumberland Gap, 7.
Cumberland Mountains, 1, 6, 8, 11, 12, 15, 21, 56, 69, 163, 164, 165, 210, 211.
Cunningham, Prof. Wm. J., 123.

Dalton, Ga., 33, 34.
Dante, Va., 88, 104, 105, 107, 110, 112, 113, 115, 119, 129, 132, 134, 151, 152, 153, 163, 164, 166, 255, 256, 257, 259, 260, 261, 262, 263, 267, 268, 269, 271, 272.
Davis, Jefferson, 63.
DeBow, J. D. B., 32, 39, 40, 41.
DeKalb, S. C., 71.
Delano, Va., 259.
Dennis, J. B., 97, 106, 112, 119, 126.
Detroit, Mich., 218, 254.
Detroit-Southern Railroad, 103.
Devault Ford, Tenn., 87, 88.
Dickinson, P. P., 68.
Dickinson County, Va., 97, 104, 105.
Doe Branch, 158.
Doe River, 8, 9.
Domus, Va., 261.
Donham, W. B., 112, 114.
Dozier, Richard, 68.
Drake, B., 22.
Drake, C. M., 70.
Drayton, Charles H., 53.
Dumps Creek, 104, 105, 110, 128, 151, 254, 256, 257, 267.
Dumps Creek Line, 261.
Duncan, Samuel T., 179.
Dunn and Son, 278.

East Tennessee and Western North Carolina Railroad, 152, 185, 250, 252, 262, 265.
East Tennessee and Georgia Railroad, 34, 38.
East Tennessee and Virginia Railroad, 38, 39.
East Tennessee, Virginia, and Georgia Railroad, 44, 56.
Eastman Corporation, 163.
Eatonton, Ga., 16.
Economic provinces prior to Civil War, 1.
Edgefield, S. C., 18, 38, 68.
Edgewood, Tenn., 261.
Egan, George, 70.
Elizabethton, Tenn., 7, 8.
Elkhorn City, Ky., 69, 103, 107, 113, 131, 132, 133, 134, 136, 151, 152, 153, 160, 163, 164, 165, 166, 170, 174, 175, 203, 218, 253, 258, 260, 261, 262, 263, 264, 267, 268, 272.
Elkhorn Creek, 8.
Elkhorn Extension, 112, 113, 115, 119, 122, 132, 151, 163.
Elkhorn Southern Railway, 104, 105, 107, 112, 131.
Elkhorn Yard, Ky., 238, 254, 255, 256, 257, 259, 261, 267, 268, 272.
Elliott, George B., 192, 193.
Embreeville, Tenn., 156.
Enola, 261.
Enslow, J. A., 70.
Equipment, 66, 77, 84, 109, 110, 111, 114, 115, 116, 118, 119, 122, 125, 126, 128, 129, 130, 145, 158, 200, 203, 233.
Equitable Trust Co., 111, 127, 129.
Erwin, Tenn., 100, 118, 136, 154, 156, 163, 185, 207, 208, 253, 254, 255, 256, 257, 258, 259, 260, 262, 265, 266, 267, 268, 269, 271, 272, 278.
Eskota, N. C., 118.
Estillville Convention, Chapter II; 4.
Estillville, Va., 4, 7, 8, 10, 56, 95.
Eutawville Railroad, 71.
Ewald & Co., 278.

Farmers Loan and Trust Co., 109, 129.
Fayetteville, N. C., 2, 10.
Federal Control, 120, 121, 126, 190.
Feldspar, 135, 208, 209.
Fero, N. C., 259.
Ficken, John, 51, 52, 53.
Finance Co. of Pennsylvania, 90, 93.

INDEX

Financing prior to Civil War, 3.
Fink, Va., 88, 104, 105, 129, 151, 154.
Finley, W. M., 152.
First Aid to Injured, 276.
First Rocky Tunnel, N. C., 161.
First Washburn Tunnel, N. C., 160.
Fisher, Elwood, 46, 47.
Fishery, Tenn., 261.
Flat Lick, Va., 8.
Flat Rock, N. C., 27.
Florence, S. C., 16, 43, 46, 61.
Forbes, N. C., 261.
Fordtown, Tenn., 268.
Fort Motte, S. C., 75.
Fourth Rocky Tunnel, N. C., 161.
Franklin, N. C., 41.
Fredericksburg, 2.
Free Hill Tunnel, Tenn., 160.
French Broad River, 10, 12, 13, 17, 18, 24, 25, 26, 27, 28, 31, 39, 42.
Frisco Line, 123.
Frisco, Tenn., 130, 133, 243, 245, 252, 257, 258, 261, 262, 264, 272.
Frost, President, 39.

Gadsden, Col. James, 23.
Gaffney, S. C., 93.
Gaillard's Cross Roads, S. C., 90.
Galax, N. C., 183.
Garland, N. C., 9.
Gastonia, N. C., 204.
Gate City, Va., 4, 95.
Gate Creek, 154.
General Shale Products, 207.
Georgetown, S. C., 68.
Georgia Railroad, 16, 30, 33, 34, 46, 189.
Georgia, Carolina & Northern Railway, 73.
Georgia & Florida Railroad, 189, 214, 215.
Gill Selector Telephone System, 253.
Glasgow, 59.
Glenwood, N. C., 261.
Goff Tunnel, Va., 160, 168.
Goldthwait, John, 84.
Gonzales, A. E., 74.
"Gorge," the, 8, 156, 182, 184.
Gourdin, 87.
Grace, John P., 194.
Grandfather Mountain, 11, 175.
Grassy Creek, 9.
Green Mountain, N. C., 9, 11, 162. 183.
Green River, 11, 25.
Greensboro, N. C., 253.
Greenville, S. C., 9, 18, 45, 84, 253.

Greenville, Tenn., 10.
Greenville & Columbia Railroad, 39, 43, 46.
"Greenville Express," 71.
Greenwood, S. C., 52, 214, 253.
Guarantee Period, 124, 126.
Guaranty Trust Co., 122, 126.
Guests Mountain, 11.
Gulf of Mexico, 20.
Gwynn, Col., 41.

Hagan, Va., 211.
Haile Gold Mines, 72.
Hamburg, S. C., 15, 18, 28, 30.
Hamkins, N. C., 261.
Hamlet, N. C., 14, 205, 253.
Hamlin, Va., 261.
Hankins, W. A., 174.
Hannum, 269.
Hardwood, Va., 261.
Harlan Coal Fields, 210, 211.
Harlan County, Va., 96, 189, 196, 198.
Harlan County Coal Operatives Association, 191.
Harriman Junction, Tenn., 95.
Harris, A. B., 83, 84.
Hartford, Conn., 68.
Harvard University, 188.
Harvey, Louis, 63.
Harvey, Ollie, 179.
Hastie, William S., 70, 75.
Hayne, Robert Y., 15, 23, 24, 27, 28, 29, 30, 32, 87.
Haysi, Va., 134.
Hazard Coal Fields, 210, 211.
Heath Springs, S. C., 71.
Hellier, C. E., 86, 89.
Hewitt Tunnel, Va., 160.
Hiawassie Railroad, 33.
Hickory, N. C., 205.
Hickory Nut Gap, 17.
High Point, N. C., 205.
Hill, Va., 261.
Hills Mill Tunnel, Va., 160.
Hines, W. D., 122, 126.
Hocking Valley Railroad, 254.
Hoke, Robert F., 185.
Holliston Mills of Tenn., 208.
Holmes, James B., 10, 11, 12, 23, 24.
Holston Corporation, 113, 118, 125, 128, 129, 143, 144, 145, 195, 200, 202.
Holston River, 7, 8, 10, 42, 154.
Holston Tunnel, Tenn., 160.
Honey Branch, Va., 256.
Honeycutt Creek, 174, 179, 180.

INDEX

Honeycutt Tunnel, N. C., 161, 178, 179.
Hornblower and Weeks, 126.
Horry, Elias, address delivered by, 4 n., 5, 16, 17, 18, 19.
Horse Creek, 10.
Howe, F. P., 152.
Hudgens, 173.
Hughes, J. V., 173, 175, 176, 177, 178.
Hunt, N. A., 70, 90, 91.
Hunt, Samuel, 84, 89, 93, 94.
Huntsdale, N. C., 95, 98, 105, 153.
Hurricane, Va., 110, 133.
Hutchins, Stilson, 104.

Illinois Central Railroad, 123, 196, 217.
Indian Creek, 8, 9.
Indian Creek Gap, 8.
Indian Ridge, Tenn., 261.
Indian Ridge Tunnel, Tenn., 160.
Indianapolis, Ind., 21, 218.
Indiantown, S. C., 43.
Indigo, 21.
Interlocking, 273.
Interstate Coal and Iron Co., 97.
Interstate Commerce Act, 198, 199, 200.
Interstate Commerce Commission, 124, 125, 126, 129, 136, 188, 190, 193, 194, 197, 198, 199, 200, 202, 206, 211, 213, 214, 252.
Interstate Railroad, 130, 205, 210, 211, 213, 248, 256.
Investment Company of Pennsylvania, 90.
Iron Mountain, 9, 11.
Ironton, Ohio, 103.
Israel, M., 53, 70.

Jackson County, N. C., 27.
Jacksonville, Fla., 194, 205, 218.
Johnson, O. E., 70.
Johnson, Col. R. A., 59, 61, 62, 69.
Johnson, William, 70.
Johnson City, Tenn., 57, 69, 82, 84, 87, 95, 100, 101, 105, 107, 110, 118, 127, 136, 151, 152, 154, 157, 173, 174, 175, 178, 181, 182, 183, 185, 186, 204, 205, 207, 208, 242, 245, 250, 252, 254, 255, 256, 258, 260, 265, 268, 269, 271, 272, 274, 275, 278.
Johnston, Capt. W. J., 68.
Jones, A. W., 186.
Jonesboro, Tenn., 7, 8, 84.
Jouett, Edw. S., 192.

Kaolin, 135, 183, 208, 210.
Kendricks Creek, 9.
Kendricks Tunnel, Tenn., 160.
Kenefick, William, 84.
Kennedy, W. H., 43.
Kentucky River, 11.
Kermit, Va., 268, 270.
Kershaw, S. C., 55, 68, 71.
King, Mitchell, 17.
Kingsport, Tenn., 7, 10, 118, 135, 154, 205, 207, 255, 256, 257, 258, 259, 260, 262, 264, 268, 271, 272, 278.
Kingsport Foundry and Manufacturing Corp., 207.
Kingsport Hosiery Mills, 207.
Kingsport Press, 208.
Kingsport Silk Mills, 207.
Kingsport Southern Railway, 100, 101.
Kingsport Utilities, 207.
Kingstree, S. C., 43.
Kingtan Extract Co., 207.
Kingville, S. C., 16, 28.
Kiser, Va., 104, 105.
Knauth, Nachod & Kuhne, 116.
Knob Creek, 154, 186.
Knoxville, Tenn., 2, 17, 24, 25, 31, 33, 34, 38, 39, 40, 41, 42, 44, 51, 52, 80, 84, 92, 95, 254.
Knoxville & Ohio Railroad, 44.
Kona, N. C., 118, 251, 262, 271, 272.

Ladenburg, Thalman & Co., 126.
Lafayette, Ind., 21.
Lake Michigan, 21, 44.
Lake Superior, 57.
Lancaster, S. C., 55, 56, 67, 71, 72, 73, 74, 75, 81, 82.
Lanes, S. C., 52.
Laurel Junction, Va., 127.
Laurens, S. C., 18, 19, 216.
Lawson, S. C., 261.
Lawsons Fork, 159, 260.
Lee, H. D., 68.
Lehigh Valley Railroad, 26.
Lenoir, N. C., 56.
Lewis, J. O., 152.
Lexington, Ky., 21, 24.
Lexington, N. C., 205.
Lick Creek, 104.
Lick Creek & Lake Erie Railroad, 88, 104, 105, 107, 128, 143, 144, 145, 195, 200.
Licking River, 11.
Lincolnton, N. C., 204.
Linville Falls, 157, 178.

INDEX

Linville Mountain, N. C., 5, 8, 9, 10, 11.
Linville River, 9.
Little Sandy River, 5.
Little Stone Gap, 8.
Little Tennessee River, 24, 27, 38, 51.
Livingston, Ky., 44.
London, England, 86, 174.
Long, Col. S. H., 5, 8, 9, 10, 11, 12.
Long Branch, Va., 261.
Loop, N. C., 261.
Lord, Samuel, 83.
Lost Cove, N. C., 261.
Louisville, Cincinnati & Charleston Railroad, 10, 20, 25, 28, 29, 30, 31, 32, 33, 34, 45, 95, 216, 217.
Louisville & Great Southern Railway, 43, 44.
Louisville, Ky., 2, 21, 24, 25, 34, 38, 40, 41, 42, 44, 78, 92, 95, 189, 205, 254.
Louisville & Nashville Railroad, 31, 52, 79, 123, 131, 133, 136, 188, 189, 190, 191, 194, 196, 197, 198, 199, 200, 201, 202, 205, 207, 210, 211, 213, 214, 215, 216, 217, 218, 254, 271.
Lower Bridle Path Tunnel, N. C., 161.
Lower Pine Belt, 14.
Lower Pine Tunnel, N. C., 161, 178.
Lowndes, T. P., 70, 75.
Lunday, N. C., 259.
Lynchburg, Va., 254.
Lynch's Creek, 72.

McAdoo, W. G., 120, 122.
McBee, Vardrey, 29.
McClure, Va., 261.
McClure Fork, 165.
McClure Tunnel, Va., 160.
McCobb, A. J., 70.
McCormack, W. J., 70, 74.
McDonald, Shea & Co., 80, 84.
McDowell County, 177, 181, 185, 209.
McGahan, T. R., 53, 70.
McGinty, G. B., 201.
McKinney's Gap, 7, 8, 12, 179, 181.
McQuilkin, I., 127.
McRoberts, Ky., 189, 198.
Macon, Ga., 2, 52.
Madison, James, 18.
Mann, I. T., 112, 114.
Mapother, W. L., 190.
Marcem, Tenn., 257.

Marion, N. C., 55, 56, 68, 69, 82, 87, 93, 95, 98, 110, 126, 134, 151, 157, 172, 175, 176, 177, 178, 182, 204, 241, 245, 252, 253, 255, 256, 257, 262, 266, 272.
Marion Tunnel, N. C., 161.
Marshall, W. Y. L., 90.
Marthaville, Ga., 63.
Martin Tunnel, Va., 160.
Maryville, Tenn., 44, 51, 53.
Mason and Dixon Line, 1.
Massachusetts and Southern Construction Co., 60, 80, 81, 82, 84.
Matthews, C. G., 70.
Mattson, Col. T. E., 69.
Maysville, Tenn., 21, 25, 41.
Mazyck, W. G., 35.
Meade Fibre Co., 207.
Meadows Co., 99, 101, 104, 107, 108.
Meldrum, N. S., 124, 126, 127, 137.
Memphis, Tenn., 2, 26, 34, 35, 37, 82.
Memphis Convention, 35.
Memphis & Charleston Railroad, 35, 38, 46.
Mercantilism, 194.
Meriwether, J. A., 16.
Metropolitan Trust Company of New York City, 130.
Mica, 177, 178, 182, 183, 208, 209.
Michigan Central Railroad, 123.
Michigan City, Mich., 44.
Mill Creek, 271.
Milledgeville, Ga., 2.
Miller, W. W., 126.
Miller Yard, Va., 130, 211, 248, 256, 259, 264, 268, 272.
Minneapolis, Va., 79, 81, 82, 95.
Mississippi River, 20, 22, 27, 34, 35, 38, 39, 94.
Mississippi Valley, 26.
Missouri Pacific Railroad, 123.
Missouri River, 27, 39.
Mitchell County, N. C., 177, 178, 181, 183, 184, 186, 208, 209.
Mobile, Ala., 2, 20.
Moccasin Gap, 9, 11.
Monroe, N. C., 204, 253.
Montgomery, Ala., 2, 189.
Mood, T. P., 70.
Moore, Jas., 172.
Morgan, O. K., 55, 86, 106, 134, 135, 164, 171.
Morganton, N. C., 7, 9.
Morrison, H. C., 127.
Morristown, Tenn., 31, 39, 44.
Mortgage Trustee and Finance Co., 93.
Moss, Va., 134.

INDEX

Mount Mitchell, 176, 178, 180, 181, 183, 184, 208, 209.
Munroe, N. C., 72, 73.
Murphy, J. D., 70.
Muscle Shoals, Ala., 16.

Nantahala, N. C., 41.
Nash, Va., 262.
Nashville, Tenn., 2, 3, 34, 35, 84, 107.
Nashville, Chattanooga & St. Louis Railway, 3, 33, 217.
Natchez, Miss., 2.
National City Bank, 126.
National Soldiers Homes, 208.
Nelson, P. H., 67.
New Bern, N. C., 10.
Newberry, S. C., 18, 56, 66, 82.
New Orleans, La., 2, 18, 21, 23, 47, 189.
New York Central Railroad, 31, 80, 123, 217.
New York City, 18, 20, 39, 46, 47, 55, 68, 80, 81, 84, 95, 96, 97, 107, 109, 110, 116, 126, 254.
New York Stock Exchange, 117, 119, 131.
New York Trust Company, 97, 113, 114, 115, 116, 119, 122, 129.
Nolachucky River, 8, 10, 25, 99, 156, 161, 184, 185.
Nora, Va., 170, 261.
Norfolk, Va., 2, 40, 47, 112, 205, 253, 254.
Norfolk & Western Railroad, 56, 79, 80, 104, 123, 127, 133, 134, 136, 205, 210, 217, 247, 252, 254, 255, 257, 264, 273, 274.
Normal, 261.
North Carolina Historical Commission, 172.
North Carolina Railroad, 3.
North Carolina State College, 173.
North Cove, N. C., 261.
Northeastern Railroad, 43, 46, 61, 92.
North, Edward W., 19.
North Twin Tunnel, Va., 160.
Northwestern Railroad of South Carolina, 92.
Norton, Va., 130, 211, 213.

Oakhurst, S. C., 71.
Ohio River, 4, 5, 8, 11, 16, 17, 19, 20, 21, 23, 24, 26, 27, 30, 31, 33, 35, 39, 41, 55, 56, 70, 94, 103, 150, 189, 190, 191, 193, 198, 216, 217.

Ohio River & Charleston Railway, 87, 89, 92, 93, 94, 95, 98, 100, 101, 105.
Ohio Valley, 2, 61, 106, 113.
Old Dominion Line, 81.
Olds, Col. Fred A., 172, 218.
O'Neill, J. P., 70.
Orangeburg, S. C., 16, 28.
Orangeburg County, S. C., 70, 71.

Pacolet River, 65, 158.
Pactolus, Tenn., 8, 9, 261.
Paint Creek, 5, 10.
Paint Mountain, 16.
Paint Rock River, 10, 17.
Panic, of 1819, 13; of 1837, 29; of 1857, 40.
Panknin, F., 70.
Paris, Ky., 16.
Peach Orchard Mines, 56.
Peachtree Creek, 63.
Pendleton, S. C., 39, 43.
Pennsylvania Railroad, 31, 80, 123, 217.
Pennsylvania-Dixie Cement Co., 207, 257.
Pepper's Creek, 8, 180.
Pere Marquette Railroad, 123, 124, 218.
Perkins Tunnel, Va., 160.
Petersburg, Va., 2.
Pettit Tunnel, Va., 160.
Phetteplace, L. H., 127.
Philadelphia, 20, 47, 68, 81, 86, 90, 93, 119, 126, 152.
Phillips, Prof. U. B., 1.
Pickens, S. C., 70.
Pickens County, S. C., 24, 70.
Piedmont & Northern Railway, 189, 204, 215, 249, 252, 253, 266.
Piedmont Region, 14, 46, 55, 145.
Pigeon Roost Creek, 8.
Pike County, Ky., 131.
Pikeville, Ky., 5, 8, 102, 103.
Pinckney's Ferry, S. C., 65.
Pine-barrens, 1, 55.
Pittsburgh, Pa., 20, 56, 136.
Plantation system, 3.
Pleasant Hill, N. C., 72.
Pless, J. W., 126.
Pocahontas Coal, 134.
Pool Point Tunnel, Ky., 160., 168, 170.
Poplar, N. C., 156, 268, 271.
Portsmouth, Va., 5, 6, 11.
Potter, M. W., 112, 113, 115, 118, 119, 121, 124, 125, 136, 150.
Pound Fork, 8, 11.

INDEX

Powell River, 211.
Powell's Mountain, 11.
Pregnall, S. C., 71.
Pressed Steel Car Co., 110.
Pritchard, Judge J. C., 172.
Providence, S. C., 90.
Prudential Insurance Company of America, 203.
Pullman, 182, 203, 218, 253.
Pumpkin Patch Mountain, 183.

Quarry, Tenn., 261.
"Queen and Crescent," 52.
Quinn's Knobb Tunnel, N. C., 162.

Rabun Gap, 24, 27, 38, 51.
Raccoon, 273.
Raffield, J. A., 61, 92.
Rafting Creek, S. C., 90.
Railroad Labor Board, 126.
Raleigh, N. C., 10, 172.
Rates, 135.
Read, W. M., & Co., 115.
Ream, N. B., 97, 112, 114.
Ream, R. C., 112.
Red Hill Region, 14.
Red Ridge Tunnel, Va., 167.
Reedy Creek, 8.
Relief, N. C., 261.
Rembert, Dr. J. E., 90.
Reynolds, A. D., 185.
Reynolds, R. J., 185.
Rextex Hosiery Mills, 207.
Rhett, R. G., 53.
Richardson, Ky., 69, 85.
Richmond, Va., 2, 40, 47, 58, 63, 124, 189, 253.
Richmond & Danville Railroad, 56, 59, 63, 73, 76, 80.
Richmond, Fredericksburg & Potomac Railroad, 124, 192, 197.
Rice, 13, 22, 49.
Ridge, N. C., 267, 268, 270.
Rinehart Tunnel, Va., 160.
Rinehart & Dennis Co., 171.
Ripley, W. Z., 188, 193.
Ritter, W. M., 112, 126.
River Junction, Fla., 189.
Riverside, 73.
Roan Mountain, Tenn., 11.
Roanoke, Va., 39, 254.
Rock Creek, 178, 184.
Rock Hill, S. C., 55, 56, 69, 70, 71, 72, 73, 74, 75, 77.
Rockingham, N. C., 204.
Rocky Mountains, 151, 157.
Rocky Point, 180.

Rocky, N. C., 267, 268.
Roddey's Hall, 74.
Roller, Tenn., 261.
Rosen, W. T., 112, 114, 126.
Roses Branch, N. C., 261.
Rosser, Gen. T. L., 80.
Rossville, Tenn., 33.
Ross' Landing, Tenn., 33.
Rotherwood, Tenn., 261.
Russell County, Va., 11, 97, 104, 105, 170.
Russell Fork, 166, 170.
Russell Tunnell, Va., 161.
Rutherford County, N. C., 17.
Rutherfordton, N. C., 55, 56, 60, 77, 78, 79, 82, 97.
Ryan, C. B., 172.
Ryan, T. F., 97, 112, 114, 126, 174.
Rye Cove, Va., 261.

St. Louis, Mo., 2, 44, 57.
St. Louis-San Francisco Railroad, 123.
St. Lukes, N. C., 71.
St. Paul, Va., 56, 88, 92, 110, 127, 133, 162, 175, 247, 254, 255, 257, 264, 266, 269, 272, 273, 274.
Salem Church, S. C., 72.
Saluda Gap, 13, 18, 28, 31.
Sanders, J. W., 127.
Sand Hill Region, 14.
Sandy Ridge, Va., 115, 160, 163, 164, 165, 270.
Sandy Ridge Tunnel, Va., 166, 169, 267, 269, 270.
Santee Hills, 71.
Santee River, 55, 92.
Savannah, Ga., 2, 10, 14, 15, 25, 34, 39, 40, 43, 47, 60, 65, 194, 205, 216, 217, 253.
Savannah River, 14, 15, 30, 214.
Saw River, 18.
Scruggs, Lewis, 173, 176, 177.
Seaboard Air Line Railway, 56, 81, 96, 97, 103, 109, 110, 112, 113, 133, 158, 172, 175, 189, 192, 193, 196, 197, 204, 205, 215, 246, 252, 253, 254, 255, 266.
Second Broad River, 158.
Second Rocky Tunnel, N. C., 161.
Second Washburn Tunnel, N. C., 161.
Security Construction Co., 53.
Seignous, J. M., 70.
Sensabaugh Tunnel, Tenn., 160.
Sevier, N. C., 261.
Shaft, Va., 133.
Shannon Tunnel, Va., 160, 162, 261.
Shelby, N. C., 55, 56, 68, 77, 79, 204.

INDEX

Shenandoah, Va., 173.
Sherman Anti-Trust Law, 206.
Short Branch Tunnel, Va., 160.
Shreveport, Miss., 2.
Simonds, J. G., 53.
Simons, H. R., 70.
Simonton, Judge, 93.
Sims, R. M., 70.
Sinclair, P. J., 68.
Sinking Creek, 100.
Skagg's Tunnel, Va., 160, 168.
Slave trade, 13.
Slavery, 3, 78.
Slip-Not Belting Corp., 208.
Smith, A. E., 74.
Smith, H. A. M., 70.
Smythe, J. A., 53.
Snipes Tunnel, N. C., 161.
Soldier, Tenn., 267, 268.
Soldiers' Home, 154.
Sounding Gap, 6, 8, 11, 12.
South Carolina & Georgia Railroad, 93, 94, 95.
South Carolina Canal and Railway Co., 15, 29.
South Carolina Commissioners, 25.
South Carolina Railroad, 17, 24, 26, 28, 29, 34, 44, 55, 56, 59, 61, 64, 67, 69, 70, 71, 75, 77, 80, 85, 93, 94, 216, 217.
South Twin Tunnel, Va., 161.
South & Western Railway, 95, 96, 97, 98, 99, 100, 101, 102, 103, 105, 107, 108, 151, 156, 163, 174, 175, 184.
Southern Railway, 3, 16, 19, 31, 34, 43, 45, 56, 94, 95, 112, 115, 116, 121, 123, 124, 130, 133, 136, 152, 154, 156, 157, 158, 175, 184, 192, 196, 205, 210, 215, 217, 218, 240, 241, 242, 243, 244, 245, 252, 253, 254, 255, 257, 258, 263, 264, 265, 266.
Southport, N. C., 98.
Southport Harbor Co., 98, 143, 144, 145.
Southwestern Railroad Bank, 20, 28, 29.
Spartanburg, S. C., 13, 31, 56, 68, 93, 95, 103, 107, 108, 109, 110, 112, 127, 132, 133, 134, 152, 158, 164, 189, 203, 204, 205, 214, 215, 216, 218, 239, 240, 245, 249, 252, 253, 254, 255, 256, 257, 258, 260, 263, 266, 272, 274, 275.
Spartanburg Land Co., 143, 144, 145.
Speedy Tunnel, N. C., 161.

Speers Ferry, Va., 154, 160, 211, 244, 245, 252, 254, 255, 259, 270, 272, 273.
Splashdam, Va., 256, 261.
Spring Hill, S. C., 90.
Springdell, S. C., 73.
Springfield, Mass., 68.
Spruce Pine, N. C., 98, 99, 102, 136, 156, 174, 182, 207, 208, 256, 259.
Squirrel Tunnel, Va., 160.
Standard Time, 260.
Starnes Bend, Va., 153, 158, 160.
State Line Tunnel, Va., 160.
State Road, 13.
Statesville, N. C., 173, 205.
Steinman, Va., 261.
Steppins, W. J., 186.
Stone Mountain, 11.
Stone, W. H., 151.
Stoney, T. P., 38.
Stump House Mountain, 40.
Stump House Tunnel, 51.
Sullivan, D. A. J., 70.
Sullivan's Island, S. C., 18.
Summerville, S. C., 71.
Sumter, S. C., 55, 56, 60, 61, 62, 67, 68, 69, 71, 85, 90, 91, 92, 216.
Swannanoa, N. C., 172, 175.
Switzerland, N. C., 261, 270.
Sykes Mill Tunnel, Va., 160, 168.

Tampa, Fla., 189, 194.
Taft, A. W., 70.
Tate, Samuel, 82, 83, 261.
Taylor, F. E., 70.
Taylor, H. N., 84.
Tennessee Eastman Corporation, 207.
Tennessee River, 4, 11, 12, 15, 20, 33, 34.
Thicketty River, 25.
Third Rocky Tunnel, N. C., 161.
Third Washburn Tunnel, N. C., 161.
Thomas, E. S., 17.
Timber, 92, 104, 117, 135.
Toecave, N. C., 183, 261, 272.
Toe River, 9, 157, 182, 183, 184, 185.
Toledo, Ohio, 56, 204, 205, 218, 254.
Tom's Creek, 5.
Towers Tunnel, Va., 160, 259, 267.
Townes Tunnel, Va., 160.
Trade centers, 2.
Trammel, Va., 134, 267, 268, 270.
Transportation Act, 123, 125, 126, 196.
Trenholm, G. A., 41, 42, 87.
Tuckasiege River, 27.
Tugaloo River, 18.
Turkey Cove Gap, 7, 9, 12.

INDEX 297

Tway, R. C., 191.
Tygerts Creek, 5.

U

Ulbah, Ky., 211.
Unaka Mountain, 8, 9, 271.
Unaka Springs, Tenn., 87, 153, 185, 261, 271.
Unicoi, Tenn., 256, 262, 267, 268.
Union, S. C., 65, 66.
Union Trust Co., 96, 102, 111.
United States Fish Commission, 185.
United States Railroad Administration, 14, 122, 127.
United States Railroad Labor Board, 124.
United States Topographical Bureau, 5.
United States Topographical Engineers, 10.
Upper Bridle Path Tunnel, N. C., 160.
Upper Pine Belt, 14.
Upper Pine Ridge Tunnel, N. C., 160.

V

Vance Tunnel, N. C., 160, 178, 182.
Vanderlip, F. A., 112.
Vicksburg, Miss., 2.
Vienna, S. C., 18.
Virginia Banner, Va., 256.
Virginia & Southwestern Railway, 130, 154.

W

Wabash Railroad, 123.
Wabash River, 27.
Wadesboro, N. C., 204.
Wagener, F. W., 79.
Wagener, George A., 51, 52, 53.
Wakenva, Va., 261.
Walhalla, S. C., 40, 41, 43, 44, 45, 51, 53.
Walker, Elisha, 126.
Walker, J. W., 173, 174, 177.
Walter, C. L., 70.
Walters, Henry, 194, 216.
Waring, E. I., 70.

Washington, D. C., 10, 94, 126, 188, 199, 214.
Washington County, Tenn., 100.
Watauga County, N. C., 175.
Watauga River, 8, 88, 154.
Wateree Swamps, 71.
Watson, E. T., 112.
Waxhaws, the, 73.
Waycross, Tenn., 259.
Webster, Daniel, and Robert Y. Hayne, 23.
Welch, S. E., 70.
Wentz, D. B., 126.
Westcoat, J. J., 70.
Western & Atlantic Railroad, 3, 25, 31, 33, 34, 43, 46.
Western North Carolina Railroad, 9, 56, 68.
Westville, S. C., 71.
Wheeling, W. Va., 20.
Whigham, W. K., 112.
White House, Ky., 69, 87.
Wilbur, T. A., 70, 75.
Wild Cat Valley, 8.
Wilder, Gen. J. H., 55, 58, 59, 60, 68, 69, 81, 86, 218.
Wilder, Va., 104, 105, 133, 257.
Wilkinson, W. T., 214.
Williams, E. C., Jr., 70.
Wilmington, N. C., 2, 10, 56, 72, 79, 98, 216.
Wilmington, Columbia & Augusta Railroad, 43, 56.
Wilmington & Manchester Railroad, 46.
Wilson, John, 92.
Wilson, Woodrow, 120.
Wing, N. C., 261.
Winston-Salem, N. C., 185, 253.
Wise County, Va., 97, 103, 104, 105.
Wood, Va., 268.
Worth, Wm. E., 98.
Wulbern, Carston, 53, 70.

ancey County, N. C., 184, 186, 208.
Yellow Mountain, 11.
Yemassee, S. C., 52, 214, 216, 218.
York, S. C., 53, 55, 56, 65, 75, 76, 81, 82.

THE UNIVERSITY OF NORTH CAROLINA SOCIAL STUDY SERIES

UNDER THE GENERAL EDITORSHIP OF HOWARD W. ODUM. BOOKS MARKED WITH * PUBLISHED IN COÖPERATION WITH THE INSTITUTE FOR RESEARCH IN SOCIAL SCIENCE.

BECKWITH: *Black Roadways: A Study of Folk Life in Jamaica* $3.00
BRANSON: *Farm Life Abroad* 2.00
*BREARLEY: *Homicide in South Carolina* ..... *In Preparation*
*BROWN: *Public Poor Relief in North Carolina* 2.00
*BROWN: *State Highway System of North Carolina* 2.50
*BROWN: *State Movement in Railroad Development* 5.00
CARTER: *Social Theories of L. T. Hobhouse* 1.50
CROOK: *General Strike, The* 6.00
FLEMING: *Freedmen's Savings Bank, The* 2.00
GEE: (ED.): *Country Life of The Nation, The* 2.50
*GREEN: *Constitutional Development in the South Atlantic States, 1776-1860* 4.00
GREEN: *Negro in Contemporary American Literature, The* 1.00
*GRISSOM: *Negro Sings a New Heaven, The* 3.00
HAR: *Social Laws* 4.00
*HEER: *Income and Wages in the South* 1.00
*HERRING: *History of the Textile Industry in the South* ..... *In Preparation*
*HERRING: *Welfare Work in Mill Villages* 5.00
HOBBS: *North Carolina: Economic and Social* 3.50
*JOHNSON: *Folk Culture on Saint Helena Island* 3.00
*JOHNSON: *John Henry: Tracking Down a Negro Legend* 2.00
*JOHNSON: *Social History of the Sea Islands* 3.00
JORDAN: *Children's Interests in Reading* 1.50
KNIGHT: *Among the Danes* 2.50
LINDQUIST: *Family in the Present Social Order, The* 2.50
LOU: *Juvenile Courts in the United States* 3.00
*METFESSEL: *Phonophotography in Folk Music* 3.00
MILLER: *Town and Country* 2.00
*MITCHELL: *William Gregg: Factory Master of the Old South* 3.00
*MURCHISON: *King Cotton is Sick* 2.00
NORTH: *Social Differentiation* 2.50
ODUM: *Approach to Public Welfare and Social Work, An* 1.50
*ODUM: (ED.): *Southern Pioneers* 2.00
*ODUM and WILLARD: *Systems of Public Welfare* 2.00
*ODUM and JOHNSON: *Negro and His Songs, The* 3.00
*ODUM and JOHNSON: *Negro Workaday Songs* 3.00
POUND: *Law and Morals* 2.00
*PUCKETT: *Folk Beliefs of the Southern Negro* 5.00
*RHYNE: *Some Southern Cotton Mill Workers and Their Villages* 2.50
ROBINSON: *Changing Psychology in Social Case Work* 2.50
ROSS: *Roads to Social Peace* 1.50
SALE: *Tree Named John, The* 2.00
SCHWENNING: (ED.): *Management Problems* 2.00
SHERRILL: *Criminal Procedure in North Carolina* 3.00
*STEINER and BROWN: *North Carolina Chain Gang, The* 2.00
*VANCE: *Human Factors in Cotton Culture* 3.00
*WAGER: *County Government and Administration in North Carolina* 5.00
WALKER: *Social Work and the Training of Social Workers* 2.00
WAY: *Clinchfield Railroad, The* 5.00
WHITE: *Some Cycles of Cathay* 1.50
WILLEY: *Country Newspaper, The* 1.50
WINSTON: *Illiteracy in the United States* 3.50
*WOOFTER: *The Plight of Cigarette Tobacco* 1.00

www.ingramcontent.com/pod-product-compliance
Lightning Source LLC
Chambersburg PA
CBHW021117300426
44113CB00006B/183